NEGOTIATOR OUT OF SEASON

NEGOTIATOR OUT OF SEASON

THE CAREER OF WILHELM EGON VON FÜRSTENBERG 1629 TO 1704

BY
JOHN T. O'CONNOR

ATHENS
THE UNIVERSITY OF GEORGIA
PRESS

Printed in the United States of America
Set in 10 on 12 point Mergenthaler Sabon type

Library of Congress Cataloging in Publication Data

O'Connor, John T
  Negotiator out of season.
  Bibliography.
  Includes index.
    1. Fürstenberg, Wilhelm Egon, Graf von, Cardinal, 1629–1704.   2. Statesmen—Holy
Roman Empire—Biography.   3. Holy Roman Empire—History—Leopold I, 1658–1705.
I. Title.
DD177.F8O26   943'.044'0924 [B]   77–23872
                ISBN 0-8203-0436-0

Grateful acknowledgment is given to the editors of *French Historical Studies*, *Revue d'Histoire Diplomatique*, and *Proceedings of the Western Society for French History* for permission to reprint some material that previously appeared in those journals.

TO MY PARENTS,
JOHN AND MARY E. O'CONNOR

CONTENTS

ACKNOWLEDGMENTS

I AM INDEBTED to the United States Educational Commission for two Fulbright grants which provided the opportunity to do research in Europe and to the Graduate School Research Committee at the University of Wisconsin for a travel grant which facilitated additional research in France.

During my years of graduate study at the University of Minnesota I received advice and encouragement from Professor John B. Wolf who was everything a thesis director ought to be. Since then, his friendship and his critical comments on my work have been a sustaining influence on me.

In France I profited from the advice of Professors Georges Livet, Antoine Prost, and René Rémond as well as from conversations with M. Georges Dethan, Conservateur des Archives, Ministère des Affaires étrangères, and with Prof. Dr. Hermann Weber, then director of the Institut Historique Allemand in Paris and now Professor of History at the University of Mainz. Prof. Dr. Josef Wysocki at the University of Salzburg has helped considerably to clarify my ideas on Rhineland politics in the *ancien régime*. In Germany I was privileged to have an enlightening discussion and an exchange of correspondence with the late Prof. Dr. Max Braubach of the University of Bonn. Professor Braubach's superb book on *Kurköln* originally stimulated my interest in Fürstenberg's career. When I was a graduate student, he very graciously supplied me with information and advice that aided me in pursuing the traces of Fürstenberg's activity scattered in libraries and archives across Paris. I am much indebted to him for his encouragement and his example.

May I here express my gratitude as well to the many archivists and librarians who must go unnamed but whose time and consideration in my behalf will always be remembered. These include the library staffs at the University of Minnesota, the University of Wisconsin, the University of New Orleans, Tulane University, the New York Public Library, the Bibliothèque Nationale in Paris, the Biblioteca Nazionale in Rome, the Nationalbibliothek in Vienna, and the Bibliothèque Municipale in Strasbourg. In addition, there were the many helpful archivists who did so much to smooth the way for me at the Archives des Affaires étrangères, the Archives Nationales, the Archives du Ministère de la Guerre, all in Paris; the Haus,-Hof-und-Staatsarchiv in Vienna; the Fürstlich Fürstenbergisches Archiv in Donaueschingen; the Archivo di Stato in Lucca; and the hospitable staff of the Vatican Archives.

All or part of an earlier draft of this book was read by Professors Ragnhild M. Hatton, Orest Ranum, Herbert H. Rowen, Paul Sonnino, and John B. Wolf.

Their criticisms and suggestions were invaluable and helped to sharpen the focus of the work. Naturally I alone bear responsibility for facts and interpretations presented.

For their assistance in manuscript typing I am indebted to Paulina de la Torre Miller and to the secretarial staff of the History Department at the University of New Orleans, especially to Nita Walsh.

I wish to extend my appreciation to the editors of the University of Georgia Press, notably to Robert Buffington, Karen Orchard, and my skillful and alert copy editor, Hilde L. Robinson.

Finally, I wish to thank my wife, Win, for her unfailing patience, her critical comments and her good humor throughout the completion of this work.

NOTE ON MONEY

DURING THE PERIOD under review, references to French money are to the livre and the écu. An écu was worth three livres. The German thaler was equivalent to one écu. In the Germanies, the guilder and the florin were important in addition to the thaler. "In the latter seventeenth century, the thaler was reckoned as equivalent to 1½ guilders, or 3 French livres, or about 4 English shillings, the pound sterling containing about 5 thalers or 7½ guilders." For a sense of the value of the currency in the period, various yardsticks can be used. Twelve thousand livres was considered a respectable dowry for each of three daughters of a prosperous Paris merchant. In 1683 one could rent a three-storey *hôtel* in the area that is now the rue des Archives in Paris for 1700 livres per year.† This throws into relief the importance which Louis XIV attached to German affairs for (as we shall see in chapter 5) he was willing to give an annual pension of 3600 livres to just one advisor at the court of the Elector of Cologne. Fürstenberg was liberally recompensed for his services but his spending habits usually outpaced his income.

†F. L. Carsten, *Princes and Parliaments in Germany* (Oxford, 1959), p. viii. Janine Fayard, "L'Ascension social d'une famille de bourgeois parisiens au XVIIe Siècle: Les Bidal d'Asfeld," *Bulletin de la Société de l'Histoire de Paris et de l'Ile de France* 90 (1965):91, 103.

NEGOTIATOR OUT OF SEASON

I
THE FÜRSTENBERGS
1629 TO 1661

COUNT WILHELM EGON VON FÜRSTENBERG was nineteen when the Thirty Years' War ended in the Germanies in 1648. The treaties signed at Münster and Osnabrück in Westphalia concluded a war that had killed his father, scattered his family, and devastated the Holy Roman Empire. After a generation of fighting no one side or faction had triumphed; most of the structural and constitutional ambiguities in the Germanies remained unchanged. The Holy Roman Empire appeared to be a federation of sovereign states with central parliamentary and judicial institutions and an elected emperor. In practice, it was a twilight world of laws, traditions, and myths, with changing alliances, multiple allegiances, and no fixed frontiers. Fürstenberg sought to use this confusion to serve his own and his family's ends. He sought power with cool premeditation and estimated the prospects of achieving it as a partisan of Austria or Spain before allying with France in 1658. In that year he secretly pledged to further the interests of Louis XIV in the Empire, all the while remaining in the service of the Elector-Archbishop of Cologne. This association would carry him through a maelstrom of wars and high politics; through accusations of treason, five years in Austrian prisons, and notoriety as the leading German advocate of French interests in a career during which he became a prince of the Holy Roman Empire, the colonel of a French regiment, prime minister of the electorate of Cologne, and a bishop and cardinal of the Church. Among contemporaries who discussed his life and character, one depicted Wilhelm in the following terms: "German by birth and in his heart a Frenchman, half warrior and half prelate, and above all else, Minister of State. Such opposing traits were incompatible in the same person, particularly in a man as lively and as violent as he was. He had to choose if he wanted to preserve himself, and not doing so it was naturally impossible to avoid falling into some great misfortune."[1] Fürstenberg spent the last fifteen years of his life in France, at once debt-ridden and the recipient of as much income as any prelate in the kingdom. There he had ample time to mull over a career that brought benefits and contumely in equal measure, making him the black sheep as well as the best-known member of his illustrious family.

A descendent of the Heiligenberg line of the Fürstenberg family from Swabia, prominent since the thirteenth century, whose distant ancestry has been traced back to the ninth century, Wilhelm was one of the eleven children of Landgraf Egon von Fürstenberg, an artillery general who died in 1635 in the service of the Elector of Bavaria. His mother, a Hohenzollern countess, was an intensely energetic woman according to the testimony of canons in the cathedral chapter of Cologne who once described her as *ferventissima domina*. The qualities of each parent were present in their child. Egon von Fürstenberg was a good example of the German military entrepreneur, numbering among his ancestors one of the most adventuresome and notorious figures of the Reformation era, Count Wilhelm von Fürstenberg. During the Reformation wars, Fürstenberg, a convert to Protestantism, sold his services to the highest bidder, changing sides from the emperor to France and then back again. His ambitions conformed to the following typology of a fifteenth-century Italian *condottiere*: "To sell oneself dearly . . . to fight well for the pay . . . to get hold of a State so as to retire there and to live in the fashion of a duke or a king: that is the rule which governs actions, the unique end of life. . . . Tranquility spells ruin."[2]

A military entrepreneur was often a nobleman educated at a prestigious *Gymnasium* and at a university, after which he traveled widely and sometimes resided at a court. This experience, together with his military education in the field, prepared him for cosmopolitan service with political as well as military functions. After the death of Egon von Fürstenberg, Wilhelm and his elder brother Franz Egon, born in 1625, were sent to Cologne where they attended the *Gymnasium* of the Three Crowns, the Tricoronatum, from 1637 till 1642. Founded in the sixteenth century, this institution was one of the largest and most influential of Jesuit schools in all Europe. Pupils came from the Germanies, from France, and from the Spanish Netherlands.[3] A significant friendship was formed during this period between the brothers and Maximilian Heinrich of Bavaria, future Elector of Cologne. Although Franz and Wilhelm were younger than Max Heinrich, who was born in 1622, they nonetheless dominated him from the very outset of a relationship which would knit them together for life.

Wilhelm's Jesuit training continued in Louvain (1643–1645), after which he pursued classical and theological studies in Rome at the renowned Collegium Germanicum Hungaricum, compiling a distinguished record in the years 1646–1647. We have little information on Fürstenberg's experience in the Rome of Bernini. His interest in architecture, evident in later years, may well have been kindled at this time. He would subsequently confess to a lack of fluency in writing Italian, but he must have been more versed in the language during this earlier period. In times of stress he would sometimes speak of retiring to a monastery in the hills of Italy; undoubtedly he traveled in those hills in his youth and they remained in his memory as an idyllic, dream-like retreat. In Italy he was also exposed to the opulent life style of the Roman aristocracy, to sumptuous decor in churches, private palaces, and the residences of church dignitaries. Here indeed were models worthy of emulation. (How he would have agreed with Talleyrand's determination never to be a poor devil!) At age nineteen he was noticed and presented to the pope, Innocent X. In a funeral oration after Wilhelm's death in 1704, Abbé Le Prevost spoke of "the air of candor and intelligence which informed his manners, which was imprinted on his features, and which charmed the wise pontiff." Enticing prospects of future eminence were spread before his eyes in an attempt to retain him for papal service. But young Wilhelm, the orator continued, "was not dazzled, he remembered his homeland [*patrie*]. To abandon his homeland, something more legitimate, more pressing than ambition would be necessary. This could be nothing less than the pursuit of justice." [4]

Wilhelm would surely have relished this apologia for his career; had he been there and heard the preacher's words echoing through the lovely church, he would probably have been amused as well. As a young man he doubtless thought about his future as he wended his way northward from Rome. His reading of Loyola's *Spiritual Exercises* may even have suggested a vast panoramic scene in which the forces of Ambition confronted a small band of men who rallied round the banner of Justice. That may indeed have passed through his mind, but we cannot be as positive in such matters as was Abbé Le Prevost. Wilhelm arrived in Bonn as the war in the Empire was drawing to a close and quickly joined his brother Franz in seeking fortune and power in the Church and in politics. Here again, their assumptions and tactics so closely paralleled those of their military forebears that they would soon be referred to as *condottieri* of diplomacy.

In his *Simplicissimus*, Grimmelshausen compared society to a tree with the peasantry down below and the nobility in the upper branches where there was "a perpetual climbing and swarming . . . for each would needs sit in those highest and happiest places." The Heiligenberg line of the Fürstenbergs were from birth perched in the high branches, possessing holdings in Heiligenberg, Trochtelfingen, Jungnau and Werewag (all in Swabia) as well as in Weitra (Lower Austria) and in the Wartenberger

Baar.[5] But since their father had spent much of his fortune in supporting the imperial cause, the family did not possess the wealth which its tradition, rank and land might lead one to imagine. This state of affairs was not uncommon within the German nobility in the mid-seventeenth century. Financial insecurity undoubtedly honed the edge of the Fürstenbergs' ambition and contributed to their perpetual quest for cash, benefices, land, and protection. Franz was the more greedy but Wilhelm was not far behind. Their rank and connections facilitated entrance into cathedral chapters, from whose membership bishops were elected in the Germanies. The attainment of bishoprics would ensure immersion in politics as well as financial benefits.

Careers in the Church could begin at an early age with the aid of appropriate dispensations from Rome. Franz entered the cathedral chapter of Cologne when he was nine; at nineteen he was made a subdeacon. He began attending the privy council of the Elector-Archbishop of Cologne in 1644 and undertook his first diplomatic mission in 1647. Wilhelm became a subdeacon at Cologne in 1648 at the age of twenty and first appeared on the privy council in 1649.[6] In the following year, Elector Ferdinand died. His nephew, Maximilian Heinrich, assumed power, having previously been elected coadjutor by the cathedral chapter with the right to succeed the reigning archbishop upon his death. In fact, he succeeded his uncle at Liège and Hildesheim as well as at Cologne. One notable exception, however, was Münster, a bishopric he greatly coveted and would finally attain in 1683. The possession and accumulation of bishoprics had become part of dynastic politics among the more important families in the Empire. Bishoprics provided prestige and income for younger sons and their strategic territories were vital political and military assets for the families that controlled them. Max Heinrich ruled territories of the utmost strategic importance: they bordered on the Spanish Netherlands, the United Provinces, and the territories of Mainz, Trier, and Paderborn. When he invited the Fürstenbergs to stay on in Bonn in his service, they leaped at the opportunity, being only too willing to use the power which the elector possessed.

Max Heinrich was a curious figure. Pious in his personal life, he was responsible for promulgating important ecclesiastical reforms in the archdiocese of Cologne. As the scion of one of Europe's greatest dynasties, the Wittelsbachs, he was a fiercely proud man with a ready tongue and the habit of holding grudges. Like all of his peers in the electoral college, he was exceedingly jealous of his prerogatives, ambitious to acquire more land and titles, and eager to promote the interests of his family. In public he could be haughty and capable of violent repression; in private he was by turns timid and irascible, unduly prone to vacillate and to be influenced by the last person he spoke with. His behavior suggested that of a man who tries to persuade himself and others that he is master. By inclination solitary and hesitant to grant audiences, his favorite pursuit was the science of alchemy.[7] Perhaps he was best fitted to be a monk, far withdrawn from political and military affairs. European statesmen soon perceived the Fürstenbergs to be the real rulers of Cologne.

In 1650 Franz Egon was appointed prime minister and chief negotiator for Cologne. He also insinuated himself into religious bodies administered by the elector, becoming dean of the cathedral chapter of Cologne in 1655 and a member of the chapters in Liège and Hildesheim. Franz also became dean of the most prestigious cathedral chapter in all of Europe, that of Strasbourg. In each chapter he participated in screening applicants and cultivating his own clientele, his "creatures." Under Franz's tutelage Wilhelm began a series of diplomatic missions throughout the Empire, developing the experience and self-assurance which ultimately made him superior to his brother in political savoir-faire. The two almost always worked together—contemporaries dubbed them "the Egonites"—and gradually amassed a fund of information on German politics and the foibles of German princes which was virtually unrivaled. In addition they possessed keen analytical minds and a sure instinct for the diplomatic and political consequences of every maneuver. All these qualities were detected by the principal French minister, Cardinal Mazarin (1643–1661), when he took refuge in the territory of Cologne in the spring of 1651 during the Fronde. While he plotted his return to power, Mazarin became acquainted with the Egonites and saw that their cooperation could influence the course of French relations with the Rhineland and with the Empire at large. Since they mingled on intimate political terms with leaders in the Germanies, they were well situated to glimpse shifts of opinion or confidence and recommend ways of solving emerging problems. Their influence over Max Heinrich, of course, was of primary concern since good relations between France and the sovereign of the territories of Cologne and Liège were of inestimable importance during the continuing war between France and Spain. Mazarin, like Richelieu before him, cultivated German princes whose territories might serve as a buffer zone as well as a salient for the furtherance of French designs, thus transforming foreign states into "strategic frontiers."[8]

Historically, it was in France's interest to diminish the power of the emperor in the Germanies. Her entry into the Thirty Years' War and the provisions which French delegates sought to insert into the peace treaties were all directed to this end. A German historian, Fritz Dickmann, recently argued that the peace treaties "ended only *one* phase of a long-term struggle and . . . by no means provided a definitive solution to the constitutional problems of the Empire." As part of the territorial independence (*Landeshoheit*) officially accorded to German states, the sovereign princes could enter into alliances with foreign powers, make war and peace, carry on diplomatic negotiations and maintain embassies anywhere they pleased. All this underlined the independence of the individual states and the defeat of the principle of central control from Vienna. But alliances with foreign powers, according to Article 8 paragraph 2 of the Treaty of Osnabrück, could not be concluded against the emperor and Empire or the public peace of the Empire. This key clause was not inserted by the House of Austria but by Bavaria, with the special approbation of the smaller German states.[9] Its inclusion reflected the widespread fear of new wars in the Empire after the recent holocaust.

In addition to such a restricting clause, especially important when the emperor had political and military forms of persuasion at his disposal, psychological factors played an important role. Though many princes feared or mistrusted the emperor there was a general reverence for his title. Depending on the political climate within the Germanies and the prospect of aggression from without, the pendulum could swing from outright hostility toward Vienna to a quasi-mystical state of solidarity, usually buttressed by such phrases as *Reichspatriotismus*. The fact that *Reichspatriotismus* usually coincided with Habsburg dynastic interests did not wholly escape the notice even of those who were convinced that the common weal was being served.

The Austrian Habsburgs, repeatedly elected as emperor, had failed in their attempt to win hegemony in the Empire but they remained the most powerful dynasty in the Germanies in the aftermath of the Thirty Years' War. The House of Austria controlled Austria itself, the hereditary lands, the kingdom of Bohemia and a portion of Hungary, together with the sizable patronage at the disposal of the emperor. Mazarin knew that Franz von Fürstenberg received a pension from Austria with the prospect of still more benefits to come. At the same time, Franz and Wilhelm worked hard for the formation of defensive alliances among Rhineland princes, associations clearly inimical to the interests of the emperor.[10] The prospects for maneuvering were apparent to Mazarin, a past master of the game. Ultimately, he wanted a French candidate placed on the imperial throne. One possibility was Bavaria, traditionally a makeweight against the Habsburgs. With the advice of the Fürstenbergs, Max Heinrich might support French wishes and even influence the decision of his fellow Wittelsbach in Munich. For the moment, however, the Egonites were putting out feelers in all directions, to Spain as well as to Austria and France.

In the years following his sojourn in the territory of Cologne, Mazarin persisted in his courtship of the German counts in spite of being stung by their fickleness on several occasions. Spanish penury as much as political considerations eventually led them to intensify their overtures to France. Mazarin gave the abbey of St. Michel en Thiérache to Franz who in turn transferred it to Wilhelm on November 6, 1656. After visiting his abbey, near Soissons, Wilhelm stopped at the French court to express his gratitude in person. To all appearances, Mazarin was finally successful. With Wilhelm, perhaps he was; but Franz soon resumed his contacts with the Habsburgs. When a French envoy learned that Franz was showing his letters to the Spanish and Austrians, he reviled him as "a base creature" who could in no way be trusted. Wilhelm acknowledged that there may have been grounds for this low opinion of his brother but claimed that he himself was eager to forward French interests.[11] Though his assurances were received with more than a few grains of salt, Wilhelm soon had the chance to prove himself: Emperor Ferdinand III died on April 2, 1657, before a successor had been elected. An election campaign which was to be a classic in the era of high politics was about to begin. The Empire pulsated with rumor, intrigue, bribery and "understandings." Amidst all the conniving and calculations, no person or group was more active than the Fürstenbergs. Venal, ambitious, and energetic, they gazed with shark-eyes on the wondrous scene before them and began to move.

Soon after hearing of Ferdinand's death, Mazarin sent his best diplomat in the Germanies, Robert de Gravel, on a reconnaissance mission to Mainz. The Elector of Mainz, Johann Philipp von Schönborn, was archchancellor of the Empire and titular leader of the Electoral College; his opinion on the successor to the throne carried great weight. If the French favorites, the Elector of Bavaria and the Duke of Neuburg, were either unacceptable to their peers or refused to joust, Gravel would discreetly suggest the candidacy of Louis XIV. Mazarin asserted that the king "had no ambition for the Empire, unless it were judged that it was in the best interest of the Catholic religion, the general welfare of Christendom, the peace of Germany and to the advantage of the electors, princes, and estates of the Empire." At the same time he arranged for the distribution of pamphlets detailing the benefits to the Empire should Louis XIV be elected. This was not the first time that a French king schemed to become emperor; in the event, Mazarin was persistent and even sanguine, despite formidable obstacles.[12]

A report from Bonn informed Mazarin that Max Heinrich opposed the deceased Ferdinand's son, Leopold, King of Hungary, and favored Ferdinand's brother, Leopold Wilhelm. The cardinal's comment was pithy: "If I'm not mistaken, there is a lot of Fürstenberg in that." Among his other titles, Leopold Wilhelm was Bishop of Strasbourg; were he elected emperor, the road would be open for Franz to succeed him. Mazarin believed Franz would drop his support of the Austrian archduke if given the bishopric of Metz instead of Strasbourg.[13] That could be handled by the French envoys at Frankfurt.

The French delegation was led by Marshal Antoine de Gramont, a veteran of military and diplomatic campaigns, and by Hugues de Lionne, who in many ways was Mazarin's alter ego. Having earlier carried out missions in Italy for Richelieu, Lionne had worked intimately with Mazarin in Paris on all details of the Westphalia negotiations (Lionne's uncle, Servien, led the French delegation at Münster) and was one of his political confidants during the Fronde. His knowledge of European courts, his facility in most of the major languages and his demonstrated ability as a negotiator made him a natural choice to accompany Gramont. Their instructions were drawn up by Servien, using notes supplied by Mazarin. The overriding concern was the defeat of the Habsburgs. If a Habsburg won, then his hands had to be tied by rigorous conditions in the capitulation agreement and a league formed to see that those conditions were observed. Naturally the French would not speak of a league of German princes until all hope of Louis's election had dissipated. Mazarin assured Gramont that "even if I would have to sell my silver and gold plate, to pledge everything I have, you will not lack the money for this affair, provided that it will be used well." In a postscript he exclaimed: "The money to aid the good success of your negotiation will be furnished even if I have to remain in my night shirt!"[14]

Meanwhile, the Electors of Cologne, Mainz, and Trier commissioned Wilhelm von Fürstenberg together with a minister from Mainz to sound out the Elector of Bavaria on his intentions. The latter proved to be amiable though noncommittal, noting the possible revenge of the Habsburgs, the expenses involved, the irrevocable political commitments, and so forth. Fürstenberg argued that once he accepted the crown, everything would fall into place. Indeed, the Bavarian court was already more sumptuous than the Viennese court; he could adopt a policy of retrenchment and still live in the accustomed imperial style. Though these comments pleased the elector, he continued to fence, to make no positive commitments. Soon after Wilhelm left the court, the elector secretly informed Leopold that he would not be a candidate and put his vote at the disposal of the court of Vienna.[15]

By prearrangement, Wilhelm traveled from Munich to French military headquarters at Sedan where he briefed Mazarin on recent developments. Young Louis XIV was present and apparently made a strong impression on Wilhelm as the latter recounted to friends. In the first of three long conversations with Mazarin, Fürstenberg told him that the ecclesiastical electors opposed Leopold of Hungary and were of the opinion that Louis XIV's candidacy was impossible. If Bavaria refused the crown they would support Leopold Wilhelm. If he declined, they would still oppose Leopold and remain united so as to ensure the election of a suitable candidate. Wilhelm's report clarified the general picture and the cardinal found it far from satisfying. He told Wilhelm that if Leopold were elected, money earmarked for those who opposed Leopold would be used to build an army.[16] His message was clear enough: if the electors did not find a way to avert a Habsburg victory, they would lose subsidies and risk a war in their lands. This was a warning that the French were serious in their anti-Habsburg crusade, but might also have been intended to prepare the electors for the future union of France, and French funds, to the Rhineland alliance then in existence. Wilhelm asked what would happen if the crown had to remain in the hands of the Habsburgs. Which Habsburg did the French prefer? The cardinal avoided any sign of acquiescence in the election of Leopold Wilhelm but told the envoys that he preferred him over Leopold.

The remaining discussions at Sedan concerned the benefits which the Fürstenbergs might expect if they committed themselves to work for French interests; abbeys, bishoprics, and a cardinal's hat were mentioned. Before Wilhelm's departure, Mazarin gave him a ring worth 800 écus and two watches with gold chains, assuring him that all travel and incidental expenses he and Franz incurred during their diplomatic travels would be absorbed by the French treasury. In a letter to Gramont and Lionne he noted that the king would give the Fürstenbergs an additional 18,000 livres if they served French interests: "These are persons of worth and I cannot believe that they would engage themselves to take our money with the intention of tricking us."[17] Nevertheless, the negotiations were still in the exploratory stage. When Wilhelm returned to Frankfurt it was to report on his findings; in no way was he or his brother committed to France. They consulted frequently with the French envoys but their lines of communications with the Austrians as well as the Spanish remained open.

What especially vexed the Fürstenbergs were the implications of a total commitment to France if a Habsburg again became emperor. In conversations with Gramont and Lionne, Wilhelm spoke of sleepless nights, of an inescapable premonition that the Hapsburgs would triumph. And then, what would become of the Fürstenbergs? They would be "the most miserable noblemen in Europe," said Wilhelm. Some or all of this may have been play-acting but his concern was clear enough. What could they expect from France if a Habsburg were elected? When Lionne asked Mazarin what assurances could be made to the Fürstenbergs in the event of a Habsburg victory, the reply was forthright: the king wanted people of such spirit and ability in his service. Mazarin thought France might be able to live in harmony with Leopold as emperor provided that he "did not blindly submit to the will of the Spanish ministers." He suggested further that a suitable approach to Leopold might be devised by Count Wilhelm von Fürstenberg "who is very adroit and in whom one can have complete confidence."[18] Here was an excellent way of ascertaining Wilhelm's reliability since French agents and spies were on the alert for signs of double-dealing in any Fürstenberg approaches to Austria. The importance of their mediation was underlined later that month when Mainz officially supported Leopold. This made his election a certainty and ushered in a new stage in the proceedings, the drafting of a stiff capitulation statement to be approved by Leopold before his elevation.

Franz Egon returned to Cologne in January for consultations with Max Heinrich but Wilhelm stayed behind in Frankfurt. Otto Ottens, the Hanoverian deputy, "could not sufficiently extol the extent to which Wilhelm's particular qualities, especially his knowledge of languages, were daily becoming more apparent." He also remarked Wilhelm's spirited communication with Gramont and Lionne.[19] Soon, however, the envoys learned of a new Austrian attempt to court the Egonites. Their knowledge was certain since the Austrian contact, always referred to as "l'Amy," was also employed by the French. In his first rendezvous with Franz Egon, "the friend" was not rebuffed. Instead he was asked to return with a more specific offer; as Franz jokingly put it, "before you have a baptism you must produce the child." Lionne engaged Wilhelm in a long conversation, probing to find just what it was that he and his brother wanted. Wilhelm noted that with Leopold's election foreordained the position of the Fürstenbergs became more complicated. Franz wanted to succeed the

Elector of Cologne; with Habsburg opposition this would be quite difficult. In any event, they did not intend to make a compact with France
before receiving a promise of full protection and complete details of
the benefits they would receive. Gramont and Lionne advised Mazarin
that "they be deprived of any reasonable pretext for disengaging themselves from us." They recommended a written statement itemizing what
the Fürstenbergs could expect. With such a document, Wilhelm promised
that he and his brother would not fail them. Two days later, Lionne exclaimed: "Count Wilhelm has done marvels here on this occasion and his
very life isn't too secure, for all the rage of the opposite party is descending upon him whom they believe to be the author of all these machinations." Shortly thereafter, Franz told "l'Amy" that "he would listen to
nothing . . . and that by the evil which he would do to the Austrians perhaps they would one day recognize the good which he could have done
for them." [20]

On April 27 Max Heinrich finally arrived in Frankfurt and the Cologne delegation became one of the strongest bastions of opposition to
Habsburg dominance in the Empire. The Fürstenbergs lobbied in official
sessions, in the corridors, and at social events. Franz Egon, portly, gre-
garious and pleasure-loving, had a talent for giving large parties with
copious food and drink and his residence became a popular gathering
place for diplomats and their masters. Gramont described one such affair
at which the guests included the Electors of Cologne, Mainz and Saxony:
"The dinner lasted from noon until nine o'clock in the evening, amidst
the noise of trumpets and kettledrums which was always in one's ears;
there one drank to the health of two or three thousand people; the table
was cleared, all the electors danced on top of it; the marshal, who was
limp, led the dance: all the guests were intoxicated. Since that day the
Elector of Saxony and Marshal Gramont have remained the best of
friends." [21] Wilhelm von Fürstenberg and Lionne began their friendship
in the midst of such gatherings, a friendship which flourished until the
Frenchman's death in 1671. They worked closely on all political matters
at Frankfurt, especially on a strong capitulation statement and the formation of a league of German princes linked to France.

Amidst these larger concerns, further discussions led to a preliminary
draft of a pact between the Fürstenbergs and France. Wilhelm used the
pretext of mediating the Franco-Spanish war to make a lightning visit
to Mazarin, then at Amiens, in the middle of May. Perhaps he calculated
that he could get more from the cardinal in person. In company with a
delegate from Mainz he received an audience but the minister had little
time to spare in private sessions. Once back in Frankfurt, Fürstenberg ex-

pressed his annoyance to Lionne concerning the reception accorded him at Amiens; he and Franz continued to hesitate over the pact with France. On May 28 "l'Amy" reported a Spanish offer of 60,000 écus in cash to Franz as well as the promise of the bishopric of Strasbourg, the abbey of Murbach, and hopes for a succession to the Electorate of Cologne. This intensified the soul-searching of the Germans, especially since the French could not at that time make so positive an offer. On the other hand, how could they be sure that Spanish promises would be honored? Finally Gramont and Lionne presented them with a declaration, signed and sealed, clearly stating what they could expect from France and asking for their response. They accepted on June 4, 1658.[22]

The contract affirmed the king's desire to give Franz Egon and Wilhelm Egon von Fürstenberg "solid proof of his affection and esteem and to recognize the zeal they had shown for his service and for the interests of his crown since the death of the emperor." He wished to be assured that the counts would continue to attach themselves to France, to work as they had up till now "with all their power and industry for all the plans and interests of His Majesty in Germany which are none other than the welfare and peace of the Empire itself and the conservation of the rights and liberties which pertain to the Electors, Princes, and States of the Empire, especially His Highness the Elector of Cologne, their master, and the exact observation of the Treaty of Münster, so as to ensure that the stipulations regarding him and his allies are carried out, to redress any violations which may be committed in this connection and to prevent such violation from occurring."[23]

In return, Franz would receive the bishopric of Metz, from which Mazarin voluntarily resigned, and Wilhelm the abbey of St. Arnoul within the city of Metz. The bishopric had a guaranteed income of 12,000 écus and the abbey 4000 écus. If the current war brought the revenues below normal, the king would supplement their income from salt mines in Lorraine or some other equivalent; if the Egonites thought it prudent at that moment to conceal these church positions, they could leave them in the hands of Mazarin with all the emoluments diverted to them. In addition they were given 40,000 livres in cash and promised all necessary assistance to succeed to positions, including bishoprics and archbishoprics, in churches in the Empire in which they were members of the chapter. Further, they and their brother Hermann Egon, an important figure at the court of the Bavarian elector, would be fully compensated in France for any property or goods lost in territories controlled by the House of Austria. Since such an eventuality would usually occur in time of war, the

French pledged that the German counts would be included in the peace terms and that their lost property and belongings would be restored.

The Fürstenbergs promised "to give His Majesty continued proofs of the true zeal and affection which we have shown to have for his service and for the interest of his Crown since the death of the late emperor, and to attach ourselves with the same affection, and cooperate sincerely with France as we have done until now with all of our power and industry for all the plans and interests of His Majesty in Germany," and so forth exactly as in the royal declaration.

The reasoning of the Fürstenbergs in allying with France is clear enough. France then had a dominant position in Alsace, was winning the war against Spain in the Spanish Netherlands, and gave every indication of being the strongest power in Europe in the next generation. Spain was eclipsed, the Austrian menace had been beaten back in the Thirty Years' War, and the Austrians were still feared and mistrusted by the majority of German princes, especially in the Rhineland. The Elector of Cologne could scarcely be described as a friend of the Habsburgs; Bavaria, the traditional balance against Vienna, was linked by family ties with Cologne. To side with France was to ride the crest of the future. French power threatened the territory of Liège, controlled by Max Heinrich; the French presence in Alsace could be crucial to Fürstenberg ambition in Strasbourg as in Liège. The military threat of France in the event of non-compliance with her wishes was inevitably felt in the Rhineland. Finally, there was the money at the disposal of the French crown.[24]

Wilhelm and Franz more than any other German noblemen came to be associated with the "French party" in the Empire. They did not, however, sign a carte blanche; the precise wording of the agreement must be emphasized. "The plans and interests of His Majesty in Germany" are defined as "none other than the welfare and peace of the Empire itself and the conservation of the rights and liberties which pertain to the Electors, Princes and States of the Empire." Here, to be sure, we become immersed in "interpretations."

One issue is whether the pledges of fidelity made to the emperor and to the Elector of Cologne were contradicted by the contract with France. The behavior of the Fürstenbergs would stretch to the limit the elasticity of what passed for an imperial constitution and the reciprocal rights and obligations of German princes. At each turn, theirs was an exercise in casuistry. They operated always in practice, not in theory, fully aware of the traditions, perhaps myths, which were cherished by German princes, including "German liberties" and the need for leagues and alliances to protect mutual interests. With French backing and French money they could play a much greater role in international affairs than they would as mere ministers of the Elector of Cologne. But they did remain as ministers at Cologne and the ensuing state of affairs was not without its contradictions, especially since, as Wilhelm was fond of saying, they had to protect their "own particular interests."

Mazarin was quite pleased to receive the signed copy of the contract but he glimpsed possible loopholes in the agreement. For example, the Fürstenbergs could demand an exorbitant sum to gain a bishopric and, if refused, claim the contract was broken. The cardinal admitted that this was "a delicate scruple" and consoled himself with the thought that they would not hazard the loss of all they possessed in France by engaging in such chicanery.[25] He had every reason to be satisfied with them during the remainder of the Frankfurt assembly since they worked diligently for the creation of the League of the Rhine as well as for a clause in the capitulation statement denying Leopold the right to send any aid to Spain. Leopold was forced to accept this and the other clauses in the capitulation statement before being elected on July 18, 1658. He was crowned by the Elector of Cologne on July 31.

Shortly after the coronation, Max Heinrich approached the young emperor and declared: "'You have found things very bothersome here and you have waited for a long time; but things might have been much worse if Your Majesty had not signed the capitulation in the same form that we presented it to you, for it is certain that then you would never have become emperor.' This speech was as laconic as it was significant and upon hearing it His Imperial Majesty, not being able to promptly come up with a riposte, merely opened his large mouth and made no response whatever."[26] Max Heinrich's terse statement should be kept in mind for while he would one day regret his alliance with France he cannot be simply viewed as a puppet in the hands of the Fürstenbergs. Their arguments against Habsburg policy often reenforced his own convictions.

In the month following the imperial coronation, most of the activity in Frankfurt centered around the creation of a league of German princes to guarantee that Austrian aid to Spain did not pass through the Rhineland and so risk embroiling that region once more in war. At the eleventh hour, the Austrians said they would forget all the Fürstenbergs had done to oppose them. All previous offers obtained if they would stop the formation of the League with Cologne's participation. This overture was rebuffed.[27] On August 14, 1658 the League of the Rhine came into existence.

In effect, the League fused various alliances contracted by German states one with the other in the wake of the Thirty Years' War. Membership was rather evenly distributed among Catholics and Protestants. Among the latter were the Margrave of Hesse-Cassel, the princes of the House of Brunswick-Lüneburg, and the King of Sweden, who was the Duke of Bremen. The Catholics included the Electors of Mainz and Cologne and the Duke of Neuburg. Later additions in 1660 included the two Catholic rulers, the Elector of Trier, and the Bishop of Münster as well as a Protestant, the Duke of Württemberg. The treaty was renewable every three years and had as its object the protection of "German liberties." France gained entrance as a guarantor of the Treaty of Westphalia. The role of France in the League illustrates the part that Mazarin intended to play in German affairs: the checking of Habsburg power and the cultivation of a sizable clientele of princes. It was not, however, a clear victory for French diplomacy. It was effective—indeed, it was renewed—only when it served the interests and aspirations of the German princes themselves. To achieve such a delicate balance required the tact and agility that Mazarin possessed to such a consummate degree. The cardinal proved to be much more adept at concealing domination under the appearance of "protection" than was his royal pupil.[28]

Mazarin worked closely with the Fürstenbergs on all matters pertaining to the Germanies. Several months after the Frankfurt business had been concluded, he asked Max Heinrich to send Wilhelm to Paris as his representative so that he might review "many important matters with him."[29] Among the topics would be the possibility of having the Franco-Spanish war settled at a peace congress in the Empire under the auspices of the Electors of Mainz and Cologne. This may have been merely a tactical maneuver in the cardinal's general strategic design to end the war, but it flattered Max Heinrich and other German princes that they were involved in the achievement of the peace. At the same time the meeting afforded another opportunity for Mazarin to impress on them the need to stand firm so that Austria would keep her promise not to intervene in the war.

During the next year Wilhelm von Fürstenberg became an increasingly familiar figure at the French court and followed it in its peregrinations to Dijon, Lyon, Toulouse, and St. Jean-de-Luz. In the latter city, at the time of the signing of the Peace of the Pyrenees which ended the war in November 1659, he dealt not only with Lionne and Mazarin but also had a private, two-hour audience with the principal Spanish negotiator, Don Luis de Haro. At thirty years of age, Wilhelm was indisputably one of the most prominent and active diplomats in Europe. Mazarin employed him as his intermediary in explaining French policies and desires to German statesmen, especially to those in the League of the Rhine. In addition to information, he carried French subsidies back home to Max Heinrich and other French allies. The combined pressure of Mazarin and those German princes was in part responsible for the conclusion of the Northern war at the Peace of Oliva in 1660. As France became increasingly involved in imperial affairs, a saying became current in the Germanies that "if Mazarin was more cunning than the sultan, the Fürstenbergs were more dangerous than his pashas." Though the cardinal may well have been pleased to hear of this, he was aware of the differences between Wilhelm and Franz. The elder brother was always suspected of having reserves, of being overly opportunistic and ready to listen to other offers. Of Wilhelm Mazarin remarked that "a Frenchman would not act with more zeal than he does for all the interests and satisfaction of the king." [30] The cardinal died in the following year but his judgment of Wilhelm was shared by the young king who assumed full power in 1661. The Age of Louis XIV was about to begin and the Fürstenbergs would be very much a part of it.

I I
THE CHESSBOARD
SPRING 1661 TO SPRING 1668

MAZARIN'S DEATH in March 1661 left Louis XIV with the harvest of
the cardinal's statecraft and a competent team of ministers to perpetuate
it. Mazarin's aides and protégés included Le Tellier for war, Colbert for
finance and Lionne for foreign affairs. Lionne, the least known of Louis's
important ministers in the first decade of his reign, helped shape and
execute the foreign policy of France in an era which has been cited as one
of continual negotiation.[1] Mercurial, glib, resourceful, and possessing
few scruples that his friends were aware of, Lionne was fifty years old at
the death of Mazarin and worked well with the young monarch. The
affairs of the kingdom to which Louis most applied himself were precisely those with which Lionne dealt. And Lionne set a very fast pace.
The reams of his correspondence preserved at the Quai d'Orsay attest
to the wealth of information at his command, his discernment and sense
of nuance in handling political problems. While pursuing his myriad
negotiations, he nonetheless managed to keep up a very spirited social
life. He alone among the great ministers of Louis XIV's reign retained
the playfulness and high spirits which had distinguished Mazarin even in
the most desperate straits. Lionne proved to be the best friend of Wilhelm
von Fürstenberg at the French court.

Wilhelm had been in Paris a full three months before Mazarin's death
and remained there for months afterwards. He was then serving as an
intermediary in the proposed marriage between Mlle de Montpensier and
the Duke of Lorraine. She evaded the subject of matrimony but she was
delighted by Wilhelm's conversation during their daily strolls through the
gardens of the Luxembourg Palace, her residence in Paris. In her memoirs, she described him as a man of intelligence and wit who spent a great
deal of money and who knew much about the French court as well as
"all the secrets from foreign countries."[2] Such traits were ascribed to him
throughout his lifetime.

His appearance in a later engraving by Larmessin cannot have been
much different from what it was at the age of thirty-two at the outset
of the Sun King's reign. Fürstenberg is shown in the full wig current at

the time. He has a high and wide forehead, an aquiline nose, and widely-spaced eyes which appear observant, skeptical and amused; his mouth, full and mobile, is topped by a thin moustache; the chin is round with the suspicion of a second chin below. Described by contemporaries as being less than average height, he later tended toward plumpness. His portrait reminds us of the young Louis XIV with its reserve, hauteur, sensuousness and more than a hint of good living betrayed on his features. Accustomed to lavish entertainment and prodigal with money, he reveled in the social life offered by Paris. It had already been noted in Rome that he was more at home with cards in his hand than with a breviary, and he was far from indifferent to women. In a word, he was a perfect companion for Lionne. In fact, it was widely believed—and perhaps true—that Mme de Lionne was his mistress. In any event, nothing seemed to spoil their friendship or the esteem each felt for the ability of the other. Even with so talented an ambassador as Robert de Gravel in the field, Lionne clearly treated Count Wilhelm as the expert on German affairs. Pagès aptly described Fürstenberg as an "Undersecretary of State for the Empire."[3] Both he and Lionne were faithful to the spirit of Mazarin's statecraft and shared common assumptions on the role which France should play in European affairs.

In their conversations, one topic kept recurring: the need to keep Franz Egon in line. Circumstances abetted Franz's natural inclination to play both sides against the middle. His official travels often brought him into close contact with the Habsburgs and he used these occasions to engage in "reconciliation politics." Despite his secret pact with France, the elder Fürstenberg did not want to alienate the emperor since he aspired to the highest ecclesiastical positions in the Germanies. Successive dispatches from Lionne's informants throughout the Empire unveiled the game that Franz was playing. In October 1662 Lionne told Wilhelm of an Austrian pledge to support his brother for the coadjutorship at Cologne if Franz detached his master and the Elector of Mainz from the League of the Rhine.[4] Since Franz made the initial overture to Austria, Wilhelm exclaimed to Lionne, "My brother was rather inconstant or fickle and I dare say cowardly to make such a proposition." Lionne told Franz that Leopold had no intention of letting him succeed at Cologne, that he had reserved it for his brother, Archduke Karl Joseph, then thirteen years old. The difficulty in bringing Franz back into the fold seemed to melt away when the Bishop of Strasbourg died on November 21, 1662. According to the papal nuncio at Frankfurt in August 1658, Franz "with great frankness" asked Leopold that he be considered for a prelacy which brought with it the status of a prince of the Empire. The bishopric of Strasbourg was in that category and he meant to achieve it. The French gave Franz 10,000 écus to sweeten the disposition of the Strasbourg chapter, but the spies still circulated.[5]

The battle for the bishopric was a kind of test case for the future of French influence in Alsace. At Westphalia in 1648 the Alsatian question had been so controversial that conflicting clauses were inserted into the final peace treaty. In Article 75, the emperor, speaking for himself, the Empire and the House of Austria (including Spain, which was still at war with France and which had eventually to ratify the provisions) ceded to France all the rights, properties, domains, possessions and jurisdictions in upper and lower Alsace and the Sundgau as well as the town of Brisach, on the right bank of the Rhine, which had hitherto belonged to him, the Empire and the House of Austria. France appeared to be given full sovereignty over this territory, as was recognized by Spain in the Treaty of the Pyrenees (1659). But the German delegates were remorseful at this excision of Alsace from the Empire. They wanted France to be substituted for Austria in the territory without cutting off the bonds with the Empire. In Article 87 they asserted that the territory ceded to France retained its *immédiateté*, its direct judicial links, with the Holy Roman Empire. This was a flat contradiction of the earlier provision. The French attempted to right the balance by forcing through still another clause in Article 87 to the effect that this provision regarding *immédiateté* was not to prejudice "the right of sovereign power which has been conceded above" (i.e., in Article 75). Shortly before the treaty was signed, a French plenipotentiary wrote that each party "must remain with his own claims and each should be content to interpret the treaty as he understands it." The Austrian representative, Isaak Volmar, was more explicit when he exclaimed, "The strongest will carry it off!"[6] Volmar's exclamation could in a sense serve as the topic sentence for the next two generations of European history.

In addition to the controverted territorial cessions made at Westphalia, the French occupation of Lorraine had begun in 1662. To displease France in Alsace was to create endless risks in the future. Certainly that was how the Protestant magistracy of Strasbourg viewed the problem. Although they favored the Habsburg candidate for the bishopric, Archduke Sigismund, they kept prudently to the side; open opposition might inflame the situation. The cathedral chapter was similarly torn, especially when Austria offered 100,000 livres in cash, administrative and economic benefits, and the assurance that Sigismund would be an absentee bishop. The latter point was important since the chapter expected less leeway under Franz. Indeed, Wilhelm allegedly stated that what the chapter needed was a bishop who would file their nails a little closer.[7] Although the preliminaries were not without suspense, the coup de grâce came when it was learned that Sigismund would have to succeed his recently-deceased brother as Archduke of Innsbruck. No other candidate was strong enough to joust with Franz and it became the better part of wisdom for everyone to support him on January 18, 1663.

The background maneuvers over the Strasbourg bishopric further illumine the complexity of ecclesiastical affairs in the Empire. Subject to papal confirmation, bishops in the Germanies were chosen by a majority vote of members in a cathedral chapter. Candidates who were already bishops had to be postulated by two-thirds of the chapter instead of being elected by the majority. It was technically possible to receive a papal dispensation from the two-thirds provision but that was most difficult to obtain. In 1658 Cardinal Mazarin had transferred his bishopric of Metz to Franz Egon. Franz did not receive confirmation from Rome but he nonetheless managed to receive full income from the bishopric. To preclude difficulties over his election and confirmation at Strasbourg, Franz had earlier given over his rights to the bishopric of Metz to his brother with the proviso that Wilhelm allot him a yearly pension of 8000 thalers. Wilhelm agreed after complaining that "the conditions for me are hard enough"; after payment to Franz, the revenue from the bishopric would "at most come to 12–13,000 thalers." Wilhelm was not confirmed at Metz by the pope either but he received revenue from the bishopric down through 1668 when, with Louis XIV's approval, he exchanged it for two abbeys, including Saint-Rémy in Reims. He subsequently transferred Saint-Rémy and an abbey in Metz to the Bishop of Reims for a large sum of money in 1680. Braubach has rightly referred to the Egonites as "brokers in church offices."[8]

Clearly the Fürstenbergs, like so many other noble families throughout Europe, tried to force the outermost limits of the system in their quest for money and future security. It took the effrontery of Franz Egon to discover what those limits were. Scarcely two weeks after his election, he sent a ciphered dispatch to Rome in which he stated that he would accept the bishopric of Strasbourg only if he could be guaranteed in advance of the right to resign from it of his own free will at any time in the future. (This would have freed him to be elected by a majority of the cathedral chapter of Cologne when Max Heinrich died.) The reply from Rome was emphatic. Such a procedure flew in the face of everything the bishop's office represented, there was a sacred relation between a bishop and his diocese which could be broken only for the most serious of reasons and then only with papal approval. Franz did not persist but asked for permission to keep his other benefices. This request was favorably received; after the Cologne nuncio investigated his fitness as a prospective candidate, Franz Egon's election at Strasbourg was confirmed.[9]

Several motives lay behind the pope's benevolence towards Franz Egon on this occasion. As prime minister of a Wittelsbach prince at Cologne, Franz's victory at Strasbourg was viewed as part of an overall balance between the Habsburg and Wittelsbach parties in the acquisition of church offices. Another consideration was the long history of tensions between the Curia and German prelates regarding the freedom of a bishop vis-à-vis Rome and, more immediately, in relation to the nuncio in residence. The capitulation signed by Leopold I in 1658 included his pledge to accede to the wishes of the three ecclesiastical electors if they requested the revocation of the nuncios' jurisdictional claims in the Empire. Max Heinrich and the Fürstenbergs were among the chief proponents of this scheme. In 1662 the elector had Wilhelm propose an extraordinary plan to the French: a union of the churches of France and the Empire which might impose reform upon the papacy. Louis XIV approached the Elector of Mainz who, in turn, discussed the subject with Wilhelm von Fürstenberg. Ultimately, the elector was convinced that the Egonites would cease their activity in favor of unifying the churches if given satisfaction on other matters from Rome. He was further persuaded that Louis's pressure for reform would likewise subside if his partisans, the Fürstenbergs, were accorded such satisfaction.[10] The proposal was accordingly shelved, though the king had not entirely dismissed such a reform project; it was a useful threat in his arsenal of anti-papal weapons.

This flurry of activity transpired just before Franz von Fürstenberg's election as Bishop of Strasbourg. Small wonder that the Cologne nuncio was willing to cultivate him. Franz promised the nuncio that the clause in the capitulation would not be pressed if he were granted the see of Strasbourg and allowed to keep other benefices then in his possession. (His self-assurance in making such a promise left little doubt concerning his influence over the Elector of Cologne.) He further pledged to block any action taken against the nuncios at the Imperial Diet. Pope Alexander VII was quite willing to grant dispensations in exchange for such services. As Fabio Chigi, Alexander had earlier been the papal nuncio who participated in the negotiations prior to the Peace of Westphalia. He had a sure grasp of German affairs and was personally acquainted with many of the leading figures in German politics. He estimated that the Fürstenbergs might mediate future quarrels between Rome and Paris. They might also have leverage in ensuring an imperial resistance to the Turkish threat, always one of the main concerns of any pope; in the very year of his brother's election at Strasbourg, Wilhelm von Fürstenberg officially represented the pope in a mission to Vienna. Still another dividend would be the zeal with which the Fürstenbergs promoted Counter-Reformation policies in the areas they ruled. A noted historian of Alsace has argued that Franz Egon's episcopate was the principal reason for the resumption of religious quarrels in the province.[11]

As zealous as he may have been in religious matters, Franz soon asserted his political independence. He dismissed numerous officers and accorded several important posts to partisans of the House of Austria. The French intendant feared that the bishop had forgotten his obligations to Louis XIV, that he was a trimmer. But the king chose to be patient while Franz rearranged the affairs of his diocese and attempted to walk the tight-wire. Soon after his election, he formally requested investiture from Emperor Leopold.[12] Relations between Franz and the city of Strasbourg as well as with the many vested interests in Alsace were not as strained as might have been the case without an equilibrium between Bourbon and Habsburg interests. In any event, his chief usefulness was not at Strasbourg but in the Electorate of Cologne. Before the year ended, he left his diocese in the hands of a suffragan bishop and returned to Bonn.

While Franz celebrated his victory at Strasbourg, an imperial diet convened at Regensburg on January 20, 1663 to deal with the imminent Turkish invasion. Many German princes, notably the Elector of Mainz, heeded the emperor's plea for support and contributed men and money to the cause. Louis XIV chose to do likewise, for, as Wolf argues, "if the King of France should fail to join against the Moslems, he could be sure that many of his nobly-born subjects would run off to another army as volunteers anxious for fame, excitement, and perhaps fortune; by allying with the emperor or with Venice, this military ardor could be channelized and perhaps made to reflect glory upon the king." Accordingly, a contingent of 10,000 troops was sent by "the Margrave of Alsace." Wilhelm was then at Regensburg, grappling with the politics of the Turkish threat. He wanted the Diet to create a council of war which would screen and approve all actions taken by the emperor so as to prevent his having a free hand over the troops at his disposal as well as over the timing of peace and war. In addition, he urgently requested that the march of French troops through Alsace avoid incidents in the territory

of the Bishop of Strasbourg.[13] The French used the march to flaunt their power before the ten imperial towns of Alsace (the Decapolis), towns which claimed to remain under the emperor's authority. It was a harbinger of events to come.

What could not have been predicted, however, was that at this very moment (May 12, 1664), Leopold saw fit to elevate the Fürstenberg family to princely status. The official document stressed the role played by the family for centuries in the service of the emperor's interests.[14] The title of prince was to be hereditary in the family of Hermann Egon, then chief minister at Munich, and to be a life title for Franz and Wilhelm. Why did the emperor elevate the Egonites to princedom at this time? True, they were active in organizing support for the war effort against the Turks. But they were hardly alone or preeminent in this endeavor and indeed were striving to limit the emperor's prerogatives vis-à-vis the Diet. The fact that Franz was already a prince of the Empire in his capacity as Bishop of Strasbourg and that Fürstenbergs were influential in Bavaria and the Rhineland were obvious considerations. Was it simply to lure them into Habsburg service, to create bonds of indebtedness which would enable them more easily to slip away from France and into the service of the House of Austria? Leopold and his ministers were well aware of the difficulties involved but if this was their motive it was perhaps worth the gamble. Regardless of why the emperor bestowed the title of prince on the Fürstenbergs, it did not affect their relationship with France. Hermann Egon remained well-disposed to France while both Franz and Wilhelm, especially Wilhelm, used their added prestige to forward their own designs as well as the interest of Louis XIV.

At the beginning of May 1664, before they learned of their new title, Franz asked Wilhelm to travel through Alsace to settle administrative affairs and handle litigation connected with abbeys in the province. As he set out Wilhelm informed Lionne that he might just as well go to Paris for five or six days after completing his business. He presumably arrived in Paris in the early summer; at the end of October he was still there. Franz complained to Lionne that his brother had done very little with the abbey litigation. "It seems," he continued, "that he doesn't have a great desire to hasten his return."[15] One can imagine Wilhelm and Lionne laughing as they read this letter aloud. It was not the last time that Wilhelm stretched a week into a sojourn of many months under most agreeable circumstances. Enjoyable as it must have been, it was also filled with working sessions. The king's interest in German affairs was growing, as can be seen in a dispatch to Gravel. "I will tell you, for your own information, that my design is to apply myself more than ever before to the affairs of Germany and, for that, I propose several principal objectives: (1) To make the Alliance [of the Rhine] subsist via all possible means; (2) To prevent the emperor from maintaining considerable [military] forces." [16]

Lionne and Wilhelm also discussed the future of the Spanish Netherlands. Fürstenberg had earlier probed the Elector of Mainz's views regarding a peace between Spain, the Empire and France and what would happen to the Spanish succession in case both the Spanish king and his son should die. [17] Despite many soundings on this subject, Louis was reluctant to bind himself too stringently in any treaty since his intention was to get as much of the territory as possible. The mingling of German affairs in the area of the Netherlands came to a head in June 1665 when the Bishop of Münster, allied with England, invaded the United Provinces. In fulfillment of a treaty obligation, Louis sided with the Dutch and found himself warring against one of his allies in the League of the Rhine (Münster) while obtaining from another (Cologne) a passage through Liège for French troops.

In the midst of this political and military scramble, Philip IV of Spain died in September 1665. When Lionne informed Fürstenberg of Philip's death he expected Charles, the sickly heir to the throne, to die very soon. An arrangement with Vienna over the Spanish succession, particularly in the Lowlands, was imperative. Lionne believed that the emperor leaned toward such a treaty but wanted it kept secret from the Spanish. He instructed Wilhelm to approach the Elector of Mainz, it being an obvious advantage for an independent and influential prince to propose a settlement. Lionne's friendship and respect for Wilhelm were nowhere more evident than in the conclusion of this letter. "I do not perceive that in reciting so many details I am teaching my master. I have only to tell you: the time has come that we must work, and let you carry on from there. The king is as persuaded of your good intentions as His Majesty is of my own. Besides, I know your capability and address in arriving at the ends which you propose. After that, I have nothing to tell you, except to say that we are very much looking forward to receiving your next letter." The dispatch reached Wilhelm at his family territory in Heiligenberg. After expressing satisfaction at the king's belief in his good intentions, he asked Lionne "to prescribe very precisely what it is I am to do in those affairs in which the king will have the goodness to avail himself of my services." But Fürstenberg understood his man well. Appended to this little exercise in rhetoric was the draft of a letter which Lionne could send

It was at Prince Lobkowitz's residence that Wilhelm encountered "Count Serin" (Peter Zrinyi), a representative of the Hungarian dissidents:

He asked me if he could again take the same confidence in me as at Regensburg [in 1664] and told me that the Hungarians were more dissatisfied with this Court than ever before, that he would reveal to me the means which one could use to put them entirely at the service of the king and to make them declare against the emperor as often as His Majesty would like. He has since sent word to my house two or three times asking to speak with me but I have believed I ought to avoid seeing him because I knew that the count and several other Hungarian noblemen had already divulged the above particulars to the Chevalier de Grémonville [the French envoy in Vienna] and because I was afraid the emperor might be able to play a bad trick on me if he came to know that I had listened to such propositions. If nevertheless the king was of a mind to make war, in my humble opinion here is an affair not to be neglected, all the more since I find that one could not make a stronger diversion against the emperor than from that side.[29]

It is difficult to find in all of Fürstenberg's correspondence a better example of tight-rope walking. Of French links with the Hungarian insurgents there can be no doubt. Bérenger has noted Louis XIV's declaration in 1666: "I entered into a secret intelligence with Count Serin in order to bring about some trouble in Hungary if I went to war against the emperor."[30] Obviously Wilhelm approved of such contacts yet there is no compelling reason to believe that he handled the Hungarian overture differently from what he reported in his dispatch. Zrinyi would later be executed by Leopold after an abortive rebellion in 1671.

Once Wilhelm received Max Heinrich's authorization to proceed with his negotiation, the Austrian ministers were perturbed because the partition proposal came from the Elector of Cologne. "They are beginning to enter more and more into suspicions that I do nothing here except through the orders of the king, who would be quite pleased to know the emperor's sentiments without committing himself to anything and then using the information for his own advantage as circumstances permitted." Such suspicions were scarcely allayed by Louis XIV in his *Mémoires*: "I also listened to proposals from the Electors of Mainz and of Cologne for a treaty that they wanted to conclude immediately between the Emperor and myself for the partition of the domains of the King of Spain, for although the thing did not appear very feasible to me, I wanted to let all the difficulties accumulate so that all the blame for the rejection of this plan would be directed against him."[31]

On the evening of February 9 the emperor received Fürstenberg for one and one-half hours. The audience would have lasted longer, according to Wilhelm, had not Leopold been successfully importuned several times by the empress to come to her apartment to see a new comedy. This malicious detail pointing up Leopold's weakness of character was precisely what Louis would wish to hear. Though Wilhelm promised a longer account of his interview there is no trace of it in the archives, if it ever existed. Leopold purportedly rejected a partition for it would affront Spain and "expose him to the mockery of the rest of Europe for having wanted to split up something over which neither the one nor the other had any rights until after the death of the King of Spain who was only five, in strong and robust health, and who was expected to outlive both of them." (That cannot have been taken seriously by either man; while Charles did survive till 1700, news of his death was expected with the arrival of every courier from Madrid for a period of thirty-five years.) The emperor said he would have to reflect further on the subject and would have to see Wilhelm once or twice before he left the city.[32]

For two weeks the issue hung fire while Leopold and his ministers studied the possibilities and pitfalls of each facet of the proposal. Previously the emperor would have accepted the plan "if he believed it could be done without Spain knowing anything of the matter." But how could France be trusted to keep the secret? Confronted with the evidence, the Spanish might conceivably league with France against Austria! If any partition were to be made, the Spanish could not be kept ignorant. For the moment, however, the Austrians did not want to commit themselves to anything so far-reaching until they despaired of their cherished defense of the Low Countries.[33]

In his final audience with the emperor, Wilhelm stated that the electors would find Leopold's dependence on Spain distressing, especially when France was at the peak of its grandeur. "Nevertheless," he continued, "since the emperor is gifted with so high a degree of prudence, he, better than anyone else, is able to judge what [is] good for himself and for his house. I would fail in the respect which I owe him if I were to pursue the above line of thinking further but I cannot conceal from His Imperial Majesty my fears that the electors and princes will be obliged to take such resolutions that the Spanish themselves would eventually regret that their king had not drawn advantage from such a partition treaty." Leopold expressed the hope that "the electors and princes proceed against the first power who gave reason for the other to take up arms. . . ." In conclusion, the emperor made clear that "even though I was obliged to the king for several graces and benefices he was nonetheless persuaded that I would not cease to be a good German and to remember the attachment which my predecessors had always had for the House of Austria, and that I could be sure that not only would he be pleased to see happiness and fortune come my way but that he would willingly contribute to it himself." Did these routine good wishes and the talk of his being a "good German" contain an implied threat? Wilhelm could hardly have thought otherwise. Among other considerations, the process of elevating his family to princedom had not been completed; papers still had to be sent to Regensburg. (The Fürstenbergs were finally introduced into the College of Princes in 1667.) Wilhelm mused about future difficulties "if I were obliged to carry on a negotiation contrary to the intentions of this court." [34] Such language might open Louis XIV's purse still wider in his behalf but it remained a legitimate concern.

After the final audience, despite Lionne's pleas that he return home, Wilhelm remained in Vienna for two more weeks. An amusing episode occurred toward the end of his stay. The Spanish ambassador, the Marqués de Malagón, had made no move to return Wilhelm's earlier visit. Since the reason for Fürstenberg's trip to Vienna was known to him, the ambassador's rage can be imagined. But diplomatic protocol demanded that he return the visit, so just before Fürstenberg's departure he sent word that he would be happy to visit him were it possible. Wilhelm saw this for what it was: a little comedy in which he would write a cordial note regretting that there was no time left to receive visitors, etc. Instead, Wilhelm said he would be delighted to receive him and would even delay his departure for several days to ensure that he had the opportunity of seeing him again. [35] We have no record of this meeting, but it surely served as a good anecdote to divert Lionne upon his return. One glimpses an amused self-assurance tinged with malice in his handling of the ambassador, almost as if he wished to twit the Habsburgs and their representatives just to keep in practice. Fürstenberg left Vienna on March 24, 1667. Seven years later he returned, as the prisoner of Emperor Leopold.

What had he accomplished in Vienna? Apart from family business, he provided a reasoned analysis of the Viennese court and its stand on the partition question. It may be objected that with the French envoy, the Chevalier de Grémonville, on the spot, some of what Wilhelm reported was already known. Further, several Austrian ministers told Grémonville that Wilhelm was much too suspect, that he was the wrong man for the assignment. The papal nuncio confided that Wilhelm was regarded as a smooth-talking charlatan, unfit for concluding such a historic agreement. [36] Even if this be admitted, Louis wanted the representative of a third party for this move on the chessboard of European politics. Certainly Wilhelm was "used" by the king but he was not merely a passive piece in the hands of his benefactor; witness his independence in the face of Lionne's repeated pleas that he return to the Rhineland. Nor can he be faulted for describing his mission as "useful," as "preparatory." The time was not ripe for a negotiation between the two crowns, regardless of the intermediary involved.

Fürstenberg returned to Bonn on the eve of the War of Devolution which gave a new turn to the partition scheme. The Spaniards received no aid from Vienna; Leopold had disbanded his troops after the Turkish war and faced endless difficulties in raising money from his lands, especially since aid to Spain was viewed as the purest expression of dynastic politics. Thus when Lionne again brought up the partition treaty in the fall of 1667, an accord seemed imperative to Leopold. The hope of forming an alliance for the defense of the Spanish Netherlands, the hypersensitivity over Spanish reactions, all that seemed part of the distant past. The pact was concluded on January 19, 1668, the first of several partition treaties in the latter seventeenth century. If the Spanish king died without an heir, France would inherit the Spanish Netherlands, Franche-Comté, Navarre with its dependencies, the Philippines, Naples and Sicily, Rosas, and fortifications on the African (Moroccan) coast. Austria would receive Spain, the West Indies, Sardinia, Milan, the Balearic and Canary Islands, and territory and ports in Tuscany.[37]

The next step, foreordained during Fürstenberg's mission to Vienna, was to ask for Spain's consent. The Marchese di Grana, a member of the Aulic Council, informed the Spanish that if the war continued the emperor could not be counted on to join them. Despite widely varied reactions in Madrid, the French winter campaign against Franche-Comté was enough to convince even the most obdurate opponents of partition that the days of Principle were limited. The Spanish Council of State accepted the partition arrangement as well as the cession to France of fortified places captured in 1667. Bérenger argues that it was not so much the Triple Alliance which temporarily arrested Louis's ambitions as the prospect of long-term political gains based upon a reconciliation with Vienna.[38] These, of course, were not mutually exclusive. Another possibility is that Louis XIV entered into the treaty in bad faith, obviating future litigation over French claims to the Spanish inheritance.

While the partition was negotiated at Vienna in January 1668, Wilhelm engaged in discussions with John de Witt and other leaders of the Dutch government. During the previous summer the Dutch had repeatedly asked for a clarification of French designs in the Spanish Netherlands, a concern shared elsewhere in Europe. When Louis declared a three-month truce so as to allow the Spanish time to consider surrendering territory, he provoked a burst of diplomatic activity. Fürstenberg went to The Hague as Lionne's emissary but he used the occasion to forward the interests of Cologne, especially regarding territorial disputes with the Dutch. Franz Egon joined him in these endeavors at The Hague. The principal business with De Witt concerned France's desire to preserve the Dutch alliance. De Witt shared this desire but cautioned against unlimited expansionism, noting the possibility of a future Anglo-Dutch alliance if French claims became insupportable. (De Witt himself did not possess the power to settle anything; that power lay with the Estates-General and the Dutch provinces, where anti-French sentiment was quite pronounced.) Wilhelm and De Witt had extended conversations ranging from the effect of the revolution in Lisbon in November 1667, to the possible division of the Spanish Netherlands into cantons to be split between the French and the Dutch. De Witt had unrestrained admiration for Wilhelm's qualities of mind and his skill as a negotiator and stated that nobody was better acquainted with the secrets of France's political operations in Europe.[39] They corresponded several times but Wilhelm did not see the Dutch leader again in the five years preceding his murder in the summer of 1672.

De Witt's violent end was directly linked to the invasion of the Spanish Netherlands in the Devolution conflict. The French strike had already produced severe repercussions. In 1667 there appeared the polemical and widely-read *Bouclier d'Etat*, a spirited and trenchant attack against the designs of Louis XIV. Its author, Franz Paul von Lisola, the most accomplished ambassador and publicist in the service of Austria, would soon be Fürstenberg's most determined opponent. In the same year the League of the Rhine elapsed and was not renewed; member states were reluctant to involve themselves in French quarrels with Spain. Nowhere did the Devolution campaigns have a greater impact than in the United Provinces. Men like Coenraad Van Beuningen, a leader in Amsterdam who had formerly hoped for a rapport with France, were now convinced of her imperialistic intentions. Wilhelm had spoken with Van Beuningen and others like him during his sojourn in Holland and witnessed the rising tide of francophobia there. At that very time secret discussions, chiefly due to the initiative of the English government, were leading to the formation of the Triple Alliance. On the surface, the allies (England, the United Provinces and Sweden) offered to mediate the quarrel between France and Spain. But a secret article stipulated that if the French were obstinate in coming to terms or if they wanted more Spanish territory than was considered reasonable, the three powers would then enter the war on the side of Spain. Their intent was to preserve the Spanish Nether-

lands from French control. When the French learned of the secret provisions, Louis XIV developed a virtually unlimited hatred of the Dutch
and reserved special scorn for De Witt. As Rowen points out, the king's
attitude was especially ironic since De Witt fervently wished to preserve
the alliance but was swamped by popular sentiment against the French
and in favor of strong ties with England. This development was totally in
the interest of De Witt's domestic opposition, the Orange party; the
formation of the Triple Alliance contributed to his death.[40]

The war between France and Spain officially ended at Aix-la-Chapelle
in May 1668, with a curious mixture of French and Spanish enclaves
further confusing existing "boundaries."[41] This settlement symbolized
nothing so much as "unfinished business" for the king and his ministers
were still preoccupied with the Spanish Netherlands. Louis viewed the
Dutch as the main obstacle to his ambitions there as in so many other
spheres of political and economic activity. The existence of the Triple
Alliance and Louis's reaction to it now made war with the Dutch appear
ineluctable. For the Fürstenbergs, the war which they initially supported
would drag them through calamity and disgrace.

III
"SUCH A FINE BEGINNING"
SUMMER 1668 TO WINTER 1672–73

FÜRSTENBERG'S NOTORIETY as a German in French service reached new heights (or depths) prior to the Dutch War. He stayed in Paris for much of 1668 and was in close contact with Lionne after the peace of Aix-la-Chapelle. In October he itemized the principal goals to be achieved in the Germanies: the renewal of the League of the Rhine, the blocking of any attempt in the Empire to guarantee the Spanish Netherlands, and the prevention of an imperial war constitution. Soon thereafter he began a reconnaissance mission in the Empire after conferences with his brothers which enabled them to block out Fürstenberg family interests in the development of the intended coalition. Gradually Wilhelm wended his way northward, reporting to Lionne from Wertheim that "there is very little going on in this region worth telling you about. All the same, I could not be busier than I've been in the past fifteen days playing the role of the good German; that is, drinking a lot and eating a lot." He added that as far as the armament of the Empire was concerned, the majority of princes and states considered it "absolutely necessary for [the Empire's] honor and advantage." [1]

In mid-December 1668 he conferred with the Elector of Mainz, who opposed the renewal of the League of the Rhine. He preferred instead the renewal of the electoral union, including the Elector of Bohemia (the emperor), which could be linked with the Triple Alliance and amount to a vast defensive network to curtail French expansion. His fears of the Rhineland again becoming the cockpit of Europe were surely not idle; the recent French assault on the Spanish Netherlands suggested the need for immediate and drastic measures. Wilhelm would use Mainz's hostile position to serve his personal ends, as we shall see. After another flurry of meetings, Wilhelm spent a month supervising the training and outfitting of his regiment at Lille. It was probably in the late 1660's that he became colonel of this regiment which was incorporated into the French army. Military command appealed to his sense of family history and also enabled him to keep some money from the subsidies accorded by the king for troop expenses.[2]

Symbolically, his involvement in French military operations put another weapon in the hands of propagandists hostile to Wilhelm. Already the resentment and mistrust caused by his political and diplomatic activity had begun to weigh heavily on his mind. We have excellent testimony on this point in a letter from Wilhelm's secretary, Breget, one of his most faithful friends and one of the best possible witnesses to his state of mind. He reported that Wilhelm was tormented by the knowledge that many of his earlier friends, especially men in cathedral chapters, were beginning to turn away from him because of his overtly pro-French position: "Unfortunately, one cannot be for God and the devil at the same time and this service for France which our prince is striving to perform is as well known in Germany and elsewhere as at the French court itself."[3] Breget's note offers us the merest glimpse into Wilhelm's state of mind. Regrettably, there are few comparable pieces of evidence throughout his entire career. It is difficult, virtually impossible, to penetrate his secret drives and emotions. Apart from the money and preferment he received from France, the motives for his actions are those of a man convinced that the Habsburgs were bad for the Empire, their policies different from those which Wilhelm conceived to be the best interests of the Germanies and himself.

Upon arrival in Paris Wilhelm presented Louis XIV with an account of his travels and negotiations during the previous six months, mingling fact and exaggeration in a minor masterpiece of duplicity. He noted Max Heinrich's willingness to join France in a war against the Dutch, the remunerations expected at the court of Cologne, and the inherent danger in Mainz proposals for an assembly of electors which could result in a plan to arm the Empire. He mentioned the possibility of a Dutch embassy at such an assembly and expatiated on Dutch schemes which were disclosed during previous conversations with De Witt and Van Beuningen. One involved forbidding Dutch subjects to buy grain or wine from France if electors and princes along the Rhine modified tolls on these products. Another was a reciprocal treaty by which neither the German states nor the United Provinces would sell French goods. Fürstenberg claimed that many German princes would consent to such an agreement.[4] The alarmed reaction among French ministers, especially Colbert, when confronted with the prospect of an economic pact between Holland and the Rhineland was precisely what Wilhelm sought to achieve. On July 15 (from Saint-Germain-en-Laye) he wrote to his brother Hermann Egon, including a copy of the above memorandum:

I hope that the enclosed mémoire will result in my getting the 40,000 écus from the king which will be very useful for us in buying the island of Meinow [situated in the Lake of Constance, Meinow was to be used as a refuge during future wars and would also serve to extend their territory of Heiligenberg]. . . . I will tell you confidentially that I believe it of the utmost importance to agree on this electoral assembly. Moreover, it should be secretly arranged that the United Provinces send somebody to the assembly under the pretext of commerce with the Germans, seeing that it is a topic that touches the French to the quick and will make them see that they need us. . . . Work secretly for the convocation of this assembly and see to it that Mainz suggests to the Estates-General of Holland that they send someone for the establishment of commerce. Make sure the French do not perceive that you are intriguing to bring about this assembly.[5]

"Make them see that they need us!" Here was the mainspring of all Fürstenberg activity since the Thirty Years' War. The more problems, the more work, and the more opportunities for pensions and benefices. Yet Wilhelm cannot simply be labeled an opportunist or a cynic. (Bernard Shaw once defined cynicism as "a word which connotes powers of accurate observation, most often employed by those who do not possess such powers.") His allegiance to France and his opposition to the Habsburgs would be proved at the risk of his life; in no way can he be called a fairweather friend. More than profit was involved, but profit, of course, was never spurned.

While he was successfully inveigling the French, Max Heinrich berated him for spending so much time with his regiment and so little effort in the service of Cologne: "Since you arrived in Paris you have sent your brother . . . nothing but general statements and vague hopes, nothing whatever solid and sure concerning my affairs. I have always believed you to be perfectly sincere, very firm and disinterested, but for some time, I must admit to you frankly, I no longer know what to think. . . . Either you no longer care about my interests, and worry only about your own, or else you see little disposition at the court to satisfy me and do not want to press much more."[6] After Wilhelm passed the letter on to Lionne, they surely exchanged pleasantries on his alleged sincerity and disinterestedness, the more so since Franz Egon probably drafted the letter for Max Heinrich. Wilhelm advised Lionne as to what fraction of Max Heinrich's and Franz's pensions might be accorded at that time and what might be withheld until a later date. His recommendation was accepted by the king.[7]

At the same time, Wilhelm suggested that a Franco-Bavarian alliance be linked to a general coalition dominated by France. He proposed that he meet with his brothers as well as Robert de Gravel to formulate a plan of action. Lionne concurred and the conference took place at Saverne on September 20. The participants discussed the entire spectrum of German problems; since Gravel had not been to Paris for consultations, Wilhelm von Fürstenberg coordinated the debate. The Fürstenbergs also met separately to discuss, among other things, the issue of war with Holland. Gravel and Wilhelm each sent dispatches to Paris. Gravel dealt mainly with the Bavarian alliance and asked whether he might be empowered to enter negotiations. Wilhelm announced that his brothers were disposed to bring Cologne and Bavaria into a war against Holland. He wished to speak to the king in person to discuss winning the electors to his side. Above all, he argued, Brandenburg must be brought into such an alliance; he proposed that he himself go to Berlin after consultations in Paris. As in the case of the Spanish partition negotiation, his trip would be made under the pretext of a commission from Cologne.[8]

The two dispatches reached Lionne in Paris on September 28. Since Louis was at Chambord, Lionne consulted Le Tellier and Colbert before sending his advice to the king. They urged that Brandenburg be brought into an alliance at any price and that offensive pacts be made with several other German princes. But they counseled against Wilhelm's returning to the court; instead, he could go directly to Berlin via Cologne. They recommended that Gravel conclude an alliance with Bavaria. Lionne transmitted these opinions on October 1, adding that perhaps Wilhelm could come to Paris first: "Since he is very fertile in producing new ideas, perhaps something of importance might occur to him which he might want to communicate to us before embarking so as to receive [His Majesty's] final orders."[9]

At Chambord Louvois and Turenne noted that much of what was being proposed was purely the result of conversations between Lionne and Fürstenberg. Turenne opposed negotiations with Bavaria, claiming that it was in part Prince Wilhelm's personal scheme which had not been ratified by the king. This, of course, was a weak objection since it did not touch on the merits of the proposal. Further, he feared that if Brandenburg were consulted at the same time, the negotiations could collapse should news of a Franco-Bavarian pact leak out. Louis accepted these arguments and ordered that Fürstenberg begin negotiations with Brandenburg without returning to the court. Louvois informed Lionne that the king did not judge it apropos to send Gravel the power to conclude a treaty.[10]

Lionne met these arguments head-on, explaining why he thought it imperative that the treaty with Bavaria be concluded. Even if Brandenburg learned of the Bavarian alliance, the need for secrecy was clearly understood and would be observed by all concerned. Besides, while Brandenburg was indeed more important than Bavaria in a war against the Dutch, France had as much need of the one as of the other if she were to undo the schemes of the Elector of Mainz and attain a plurality of votes in the electoral college. As for the alliance itself, how could Gravel hope to learn the sentiments of the elector in Munich if he were not able to speak for the king? As an experienced diplomat, he could always protract negotiations under various pretexts. According him the power to conclude a treaty did not ipso facto signify the immediate conclusion of the treaty. All the same, he continued, the treaty should be concluded. The king had to decide if it were a bad or a good treaty. If bad, it should be dismissed. If good, why wait? "One cannot lose an hour's time. In political affairs, the main point is to act immediately upon the right combination of circumstances." Louis XIV accepted this advice and reversed himself: Gravel could conclude the treaty and offer an annual subsidy of 100,000 livres to the elector.[11]

Though we would like to know more about the discussions in Paris and at Chambord, these exchanges afford a glimpse into the decision-making process as practiced by the king and his ministers. The rapid series of events and the incompleteness of archival material make it the more necessary to attempt a reconstruction of what happened. Before leaving for Saverne, Wilhelm probably told Lionne that he would seek tentative approval for the scheme of an offensive alliance. The idea of his going to Berlin cropped up at Saverne. It did not alter his determination to return to France since he believed he could achieve more in person. Though Lionne preferred that Wilhelm leave directly for Berlin, in his dispatch to the king he was willing to stress the usefulness of his returning briefly. Fürstenberg did return to Paris at the beginning of November and stayed until the 20th of the month. His conferences with Lionne included the final arrangements for the exchange of his bishopric of Metz for two abbeys as well as the principal German matters treated at Saverne.[12]

A crucial point involved the kind of alliance system France would set up prior to the Dutch War. Whether Lionne and Fürstenberg desired the war as much as Louvois or Louis XIV is debatable. But since the king had made his decision, they sought to make the best accommodation possible. Wilhelm wanted Cologne in an offensive alliance system to ensure maximum subsidies and territorial gains for Max Heinrich. He also wanted as many German allies as possible since that would eliminate them from the ranks of future enemy armies marauding through the territory of Cologne and afford a greater chance to contain French expansionism. Moreover, if Fürstenberg served as a go-between in channeling French subsidies and Dutch territory to German princes, his personal prestige in the Empire would increase commensurately. The main opposition came from Louvois who scorned the military prowess of German armies and urged a defensive alliance with the money saved going into French units. These divergent positions are the key to understanding the shifts and changes in French policy before the outbreak of the war.

On returning to the electorate, Wilhelm spent four days with Max Heinrich hammering out the draft of a treaty with France. It stipulated that England and Brandenburg together with Münster or the House of Brunswick be part of the alliance before any offensive took place, an 8000–man Cologne army would be subsidized, and the elector demanded Rheinberg as well as Maastricht and adjacent territories at the end of the war.[13] Though the conditions were rather stiff, the essential thing was that Max Heinrich had committed himself to the offensive alliance. Fürstenberg left for Berlin on Christmas Day; he arrived on January 6, 1670.

The Berlin negotiations were a failure from the outset: though Friedrich Wilhelm claimed territory occupied by the Dutch, he was leery of an enterprise which could lead to French hegemony on the continent and grave injury to the Protestant cause. During his first audience with the elector, Fürstenberg broached the Dutch question by referring to the armament taking place in Holland and France, asking whether a German prince ought to remain neutral or take sides. Both in conversation and in a memorandum he implied that Cologne was still wavering, that it had not yet decided its course of action. The discussion continued after dinner. The German historian Böhmer contends that since there was so much ill will between them, it was highly unlikely that they said much to each other, if anything, as reported by Wilhelm. There is no trace of these private conversations in the court records at Berlin. According to Wilhelm's version, they discussed the question of the next imperial election. Here one is persuaded to accept Wilhelm's account, at least to the extent that some conversation was exchanged. Since Leopold was seriously ill and without heirs, speculation about his successor arose inevitably, however much it may have enraged the Habsburgs and their partisans. (That is precisely the kind of topic that would have been omitted from the court records at Berlin!) Fürstenberg claimed that the elector feared the effect of Louis XIV's candidacy on Protestantism; he preferred the Duke of Neuburg to the Elector of Bavaria as a possible successor to Leopold

but doubted that he could persuade Neuburg to run.[14] We do not know
if such a conversation took place, especially in such fine detail, but evidence of Wilhelm's having discussed his successor would one day bring
Leopold's wrath down upon him after his capture in 1674.

On the following day, Wilhelm began negotiations with two ministers,
Schwerin and Meinders, the former a decided opponent of France.[15]
After preliminary sparring, the elector allowed his officials to discuss
contingency planning relative to a Dutch war, probably to glimpse Cologne's ties with France and her present stand vis-à-vis the Dutch. Wilhelm purportedly raised the question of partitioning the United Provinces,
a prospect which he believed would bring Brandenburg in against the
Dutch. Next he sketched a possible military alliance to ensure their capacity to win back their fortifications. His interlocutors responded that
while their master doubtless agreed with most of this, he would not agree
on the rejection of neutrality in case of a war between France and the
United Provinces. In any event, such talk was premature.

Wilhelm refused to leave without pressing the point. To smoke them
out, he outlined Max Heinrich's position, all the while trying to keep it
as close as possible to what he thought the position of Friedrich Wilhelm really was. Thus, Cologne would strive to prevent a war. If war did
come, Max Heinrich would remain neutral if he received satisfaction in
advance from the Dutch on the question of occupied fortifications, including Rheinberg and Maastricht. If there was difficulty here, he would
ally himself with France on condition that the French alliance network be
so strong that he ran no danger. (This item implied, among other things,
the adherence of England.) Since the likelihood of the Dutch giving back
fortifications was not too great, Wilhelm underlined the opportunity to
win them back with French aid. If they remained neutral, they could
hope for few gains. Siding with the Dutch against France and her allies
would subject their populations to terrible calamities. In any event, a
deputation could be sent to the United Provinces to try to recover the lost
possessions; if they refused, their wrongful occupation of these places
could be publicized. Max Heinrich would soon send Wilhelm to Paris to
inform the king of the proposed deputation to The Hague and to ask that
French representations be made in his behalf there. In addition, he could
try to learn what France wanted from the Dutch and so be able to use
his good offices to maximum effect.

After perusing Wilhelm's memorandum, both Schwerin and Meinders
were unable to say anything except that they would make a faithful report to Friedrich Wilhelm. Fürstenberg seized the occasion to announce

that since he would be leaving the following day, the elector's demeanor at the parting ceremony could be a suitable answer to the memorandum. If he said nothing, then that would be understood as tacit approval.[16]

Friedrich Wilhelm was not silent and he made no commitment. Fürstenberg nonetheless reported that the elector "will not fail to enter into an offensive alliance with the king against the Dutch on the understood conditions if they do not offer him entire satisfaction." Or, he continued, since Friedrich Wilhelm wanted to avoid a war which could hurt his co-religionists, he could refuse to accept any satisfaction from the Dutch unless they first offered some advantages to France. Perhaps he sought to stave off hostile criticism at the court before he arrived there in person. To a degree he may have been camoflaging the truth from himself; the Brandenburg alliance was so central in his overall scheme that it became a kind of mirage which he pursued with determination, even obstinacy. He believed that money and Dutch territory would bring Brandenburg into the alliance, but in this he was mistaken.

Wilhelm delayed his departure from Berlin because of the loss of some baggage which included his personal papers as well as money. On the following day his belongings turned up: the papers were there but 1500 écus were missing as well as several rings worth that much again. On the surface it appeared to be a simple theft and Wilhelm soon departed none the wiser. In fact, his papers had been systematically searched and at least one of them, concerning plans for the succession to the imperial throne upon Leopold's death, was stolen. This document was cited during the interrogation of Fürstenberg after his capture.[17] It is possible that the operation was accomplished by agents working for the emperor. Perhaps they were employed by Friedrich Wilhelm who later transmitted the material to Vienna out of hatred for Fürstenberg. Nothing is clear except that it was deftly done.

On arrival in Bonn, Wilhelm exclaimed "that the opinion of everybody is that the emperor cannot live much longer and that according to the news from Vienna he must even have had a relapse." This information was guaranteed to warm his heart! (Here he inserted the alleged discussion with Friedrich Wilhelm over Leopold's successor.) As for the prospects of his alliance scheme, he remained optimistic, allowing that the one real drawback was that "a bit of time will be necessary in order to adjust everything, but I believe that it is better late than never."[18]

Soon thereafter (February 17, 1670) Gravel signed the Bavarian pact. France pledged to support Bavaria in her disputes with Austria in exchange for Bavarian support of French interests at Regensburg. If the King of Spain died and the emperor refused Bavaria's mediation between

French and Austrian claims, Bavaria would not vote for war against France in the Diet and would close her territory to the passage of imperial troops: in sum, it was a promise of benevolent neutrality. If the emperor died, the French and Bavarians would work for the election of Louis XIV as Holy Roman Emperor. The Elector of Bavaria would become King of the Romans and would administer the Empire in the absence of the French king. The alliance became definitive on November 28, 1670 and proved to be an important one; Bavaria did not oppose France during the Dutch War.[19] The treaty also provided for a marriage between the daughter of the elector and the French dauphin as soon as both children were of age; the match was concluded after the Dutch war.

Despite their success with Bavaria, Brandenburg remained the weak pillar in the grand edifice which Fürstenberg and Lionne had sketched. The Treaty of Dover (June 1, 1670), which assured an English alliance against the Dutch, undoubtedly encouraged Wilhelm in his hopes for future alliances but Friedrich Wilhelm remained impervious. In this same month of June a Cologne mission to Holland was announced. The Dutch wanted Max Heinrich to join the Triple Alliance, while the elector was interested in discussing the return of Rheinberg. Wilhelm intended "to deceive and lull them . . . and remove all suspicions they may have that [the elector] would be capable of entering into an alliance with France against them. . . . The negotiation will be handled in a way to ensure that nothing will be concluded and . . . to furnish the elector with the pretext of breaking with them with even more applause from everyone, above all from his chapters and subjects."[20]

Fürstenberg's sojourns in the electorate included time for divertissements. It was probably in 1670 that he began his liaison with Katharina Charlotte von Wallenrodt, then twenty-two, whose father was a general and a minister at the court of Saxony. This extroverted and beautiful young woman, the wife of Count Anton von Schleiden und Lumain, was best known as the Countess von der Mark. Circumstantial evidence, amplified in contemporary polemical tracts, makes it likely that she became Wilhelm's mistress. He was not her only interest—her flirtations were part of society gossip—but they spent a good deal of time together. The French ambassador to Cologne in 1673 spoke of Fürstenberg's love for her, his passionate attachment to her. Indeed, it was rumored that Wilhelm was the father of one of her sons, born in the year of his arrest, 1674. (The close resemblance of the young man to Wilhelm was widely remarked in later years.) When the countess's husband died (June 1680), Wilhelm became guardian of her three sons. She afterwards married his nephew Emmanuel, probably in 1685, but he died several years later.

Wilhelm and the countess were thus closely associated both before and after his prison term; she accompanied him to France in 1689 and remained with him until his death in 1704. Whether she was his mistress after he became a priest and a bishop in 1683 is open to conjecture. Naturally their friendship was an ever-bubbling source of rumor and scandal. The countess subsequently proved to be a dominating personality, very opinionated, and, according to universal testimony, possessing a decided influence on Fürstenberg. It is impossible to know how strongly she may have influenced him during this early stage of their relationship but it is beyond question that he was much attached to her and often seen in her company.[21]

In October 1670 Fürstenberg's proposals for an alliance of German princes and his suggestions concerning the means of bringing this about were debated in the royal council and approved by the king. If the Elector of Cologne were brought into the alliance, Dutch possessions in the bailiwicks of Daelem, Fauquemont, and Rolduc, all situated beyond the Meuse, would be transferred to the Heiligenberg branch of the Fürstenberg family at the end of the war. Before Wilhelm left Paris, however, the king informed his ambassador in London that since the German alliance system would probably not be ready for the spring campaign, the declaration of war might have to be deferred until 1672.[22]

Wilhelm first presented the alliance scheme to the Duke of Neuburg but he backed off until the adherence of Brandenburg was assured. He next sent memoranda to Brandenburg, Hanover, and Münster, informing those rulers that France and England had concluded an offensive alliance against the Dutch. After inviting them to join and indicating the benefits that would accrue, he stated that he had been empowered to conclude these alliances in the name of France and that he would serve as intermediary in all matters respecting the ensuing network. From the outset Brandenburg's response was crucial; the elector refused to join.[23]

The king commissioned Louis de Verjus, Count of Crécy, to work with Fürstenberg on "la grande affaire," the alliance scheme: "His Majesty desires that M. Verjus go directly to Saverne and meet with this prince, that he receive from him instructions concerning what he is to do, and that he execute them with the same application and punctuality as if they had been given to him by His Majesty himself." After the rendezvous at Saverne, Verjus worked steadily in Westphalia during March and April. Fürstenberg visited the principal courts of the region before an April session at Bielefeld with representatives of the Circles of Westphalia and the Lower Rhine, at which he tried to persuade them to enter the alliance. All his entreaties were in vain, especially before Brandenburg.[24] The master plan had not jelled. Verjus was sent to Berlin while Fürstenberg prepared for a special meeting at Dunkirk with the king and his ministers during which all aspects of French foreign policy would be reviewed.

If preparations for the war seemed out of joint, this was partly due to Wilhelm's overly optimistic predictions in 1669 and also to his having urged German princes to hold out for more money, to refuse to come to terms with the French at the going price. For example, he told the ruler of Hanover that the Bishop of Münster "thinks it best that we conclude with the king on the conditions that he will accord us rather than lose so good an occasion to beat the Dutch. . . . Even though the Elector of Cologne is of the same opinion, I have nevertheless believed it necessary to advise them to show M. de Verjus a little less impatience and to put up more difficulties in the affair so that I may be able to extract from the French court all that can be drawn for the advantage of German princes and, above all, for Your Highness." Verjus presently reported that the Duke of Hanover and the entire House of Brunswick were prospective allies but were asking for a good deal of money.[25] Wilhelm could thus expect to be questioned and chided about delays which he was promoting.

Before going to Dunkirk, Fürstenberg went to Bonn, where he witnessed renewed tension between the elector and the city of Cologne. An imperial commission had been set up to mediate the quarrel, with the Marchese di Grana serving as Leopold's emissary. Though Max Heinrich stalled, Franz Egon seemed receptive to a secure peace between the two parties. Wilhelm immediately tried to undo all traces of cooperation between the electoral court and Grana. He swung the majority of the elector's council over to his position and sought to erect barriers against the proposed imperial commission. Grana soon characterized him as "the well-known *turbator publicae quietis.*"[26] He might have used even stronger language had he seen Wilhelm's next dispatch to Lionne: "[The city of Cologne] seems to have taken such strong engagements with the States-General that if we do not try to break them before they are definitely concluded, or by force, it is to be feared that they will completely upset the measures we will have been able to take for the grand design, seeing that the city is announcing the emperor's permission that they lodge and keep with them a Dutch garrison of up to 5000 infantry and 1000 cavalrymen."[27] The seizure of Cologne would solidify Max Heinrich's position in the upcoming war and afford an important salient to

French troops in the Rhineland. But it would be a decided risk which might catalyze opposition to France in the Germanies. Wilhelm urged this drastic policy since Dutch interest in securing Cologne was coupled with reports that the United Provinces might well take the initiative in stirring up trouble in the Empire. They already had regiments camped along their eastern borders, experienced little difficulty in raising troops in the Germanies, and had hopes of being joined by Spain once hostilities began. Rumors of a faction in the Netherlands disposed to strike first moved Louis XIV to exclaim: "I would gladly give a most beautiful present to the person who brings me the good news that the States have wished to assume the quality of aggressors, a glory I would willingly leave to them." [28] One wonders what the Dutch would have done if the French had seized Cologne in the spring of 1671. Fürstenberg had time to speculate on such matters as he traveled toward Dunkirk on May 4; his route took him through Holland.

The Dunkirk conference promised to be a cockpit for the Louvois and Lionne factions. The gulf between the two can be glimpsed in Lionne's dispatch to Fürstenberg on February 17. Wilhelm had previously written to Louvois concerning his regiment in France and also asked Lionne to speak directly to the king in his behalf. Lionne was alone with Louis when he read Wilhelm's letter dealing with his personal interests. As Lionne tells it, "The king began to respond, 'It is money that he is asking me for . . .' when suddenly M. Le Tellier [Louvois's father] entered, obliging His Majesty and myself to be silent. . . . I have not yet had time to read the copy of your letter to M. de Louvois which you have sent me. When I have seen its contents, I shall conduct myself afterwards with the king according to what I believe to be your best interests and will above all try to discover if he [Louvois] will have read it to His Majesty or if he will have rendered a faithful account of it to him." [29] Here was a remarkable situation: Louis XIV attempting to avert a row among his ministers over the demands of Fürstenberg. It goes to the heart of Wilhelm's relationship with Lionne and (via Mazarin) with the king himself and perfectly illustrates the intense power struggle behind the scenes.

The royal party was already at Dunkirk when he arrived. But no fierce debate took place; the scheme for an offensive alliance had already been scrapped in favor of treaties of neutrality. Fürstenberg's proposed seizure of Cologne was considered and probably approved at the conference, though that decision would later be rescinded. In balance, Louvois's side had won this round. Pomponne was sent to Stockholm to bring Sweden into the alliance; the knowledge that France was negotiating with the Swedes would presumably make German princes more tractable. Finance seemed the paramount issue. Lionne informed Wilhelm that the king could not subsidize the Swedes as well as the German states at the same time.[30]

Though the proposed neutral league of German princes called for the participation of Brandenburg, the news from the north was still unpromising. Since so much of what was presented to Berlin concerned the ideas, proposals and travels of "Prince Wilhelm," it is hardly surprising that Friedrich Wilhelm agreed with those pamphlets circulating in the Germanies which warned of the French menace and the use which the Sun King was making of his acolytes in Cologne. Wilhelm told Lionne that according to information he received from Vienna, "the Elector of Brandenburg is speaking ill of us, especially me, before the emperor." This campaign of denigration soon intensified: "The emperor is strongly animated against me [and says that] I am rendering myself unworthy by my conduct and by the continual negotiations which I am pursuing against the interests of the Empire and of His Imperial Majesty." According to a friend of Wilhelm's (a canon from Strasbourg), Leopold made it clear that anyone who opposed Wilhelm's advancement in Cologne or in any part of the Germanies would be rendering him a great service.[31] These warnings did not in the least diminish his travels and negotiations.

On July 11, 1671 Fürstenberg signed a treaty of neutrality with France in behalf of Max Heinrich. It included rights of passage, permission to buy supplies en route, to set up warehouses in the territory of the elector, to construct a bridge on the Rhine wherever they saw fit and to establish depots in fortified towns along the invasion route. In early modern Europe, a treaty of neutrality allowed one power to make an inoffensive transit (*transitus innoxius*) through another state. The consequences of this right could be "the permission to buy—indeed, to carry off—provisions for the troops and the authorization to occupy strong points in the territory. Besides, the neutral state tolerated the recruitment of volunteers." The territory of Cologne could thus be numbered among France's strategic frontiers. The king agreed to an annual *gratification* of 20,000 écus, a monthly subsidy of 10,000 écus, the restitution of Rheinberg and also Maastricht if it were taken during the war, and full protection for Max Heinrich in case of attack. The Fürstenbergs were assured of territories in the United Provinces as per agreement the previous summer; at the end of July, the Bishop of Münster was also brought into the fold.[32]

Despite these successes, Wilhelm steadfastly opposed neutrality pacts. He urged Lionne to reconsider the new policy: "Even should I pass for opinionated before the king and yourself, [I still say that] if His Majesty does not make an effort to form a party in Germany which will act and break with the States-General at the same time as he does, one of two things will result: either he will have spent money uselessly without drawing the advantage he expected or else he will be constrained to fight the war against the Germans themselves." He claimed that the House of Brunswick might be won over to an offensive alliance which would not cost much more than the projected Swedish alliance; such an alliance would preclude Swedish or Brandenburg opposition to France. Fürstenberg sent still another dispatch on July 23, reiterating all the points he had made previously. After reviewing Wilhelm's arguments with Lionne, the king overturned the decisions taken at Dunkirk. An alert went out to Pomponne to stop his negotiations; a system of offensive alliances was once more the prime objective. But if the House of Brunswick refused to join this new system, Pomponne would reopen the original alliance negotiations with Sweden. Fürstenberg was commissioned to build and offer subsidies to a party of German princes which would act in unison with France in a war against the Dutch.[33]

This dramatic reversal of policy disclosed the doubts and uncertainties in the French camp. It also indicated Fürstenberg's continuing influence at the court in spite of the failure of his earlier predictions and the hostility of the Louvois faction. Nor were all his schemes part of a concerted family operation. On August 7 he informed Lionne that he had not given Franz a copy of either Lionne's or Louvois's cipher "for fear that he may have the wish to open my letters and I would not be happy if he saw everything." For a sample of what Franz may have missed, witness Lionne's dispatch of August 22 informing Wilhelm that the king decided to defer a siege of Cologne until 1672 so as not to alienate German princes being courted as prospective allies.[34] This illumines Wilhelm's attempts to delay the work of the Intermediary Commission and confirms the assumption that the seizure of Cologne was discussed and approved at Dunkirk.

Whatever satisfaction and even euphoria Wilhelm may have experienced was shortlived, for not all members of the House of Brunswick cooperated and no prompt decision was likely. Yet this development, from Wilhelm's point of view, must have been the merest bagatelle compared to the shock of Lionne's death on September 1. On the first news of his friend's illness Wilhelm wrote: "I adjure you to take very good care of a health which is so precious to the State and so dear to your friends."[35] When this letter was sent, the minister had already been dead for six days.

Wilhelm grieved the loss of his best friend in France and his most influential ally at the court. Lionne's death ended a period in Fürstenberg's
career which had begun with his recruitment by Mazarin. Now he was
in a drastically altered situation. Pomponne succeeded Lionne but until
he returned from Stockholm the business of the foreign affairs ministry
was entrusted to Louvois. In short order, the scheme for offensive alliances was thrown into the dustbin: neutrality pacts after the manner of
Dunkirk were soon in vogue. This pirouette confused German princes
and infuriated Fürstenberg. He viewed neutrality as "a pestilence" for
the Germanies since the interested princes would be deprived of money,
troops, and territory, especially if the Swedish alliance were concluded.
In a conversation with the chief minister of Hanover he exclaimed that
if all that remained were treaties of neutrality, his hope was that "all the
French designs come to nothing and that they be roundly beaten." [36] One
can easily imagine him spitting out these words in anger and frustration.

Venting his spleen hardly solved his predicament. He asked the king
to reconsider, arguing that even an alliance restricted to Cologne, Münster, and Hanover was better than neutrality. (This was already under
discussion in Paris.) For the moment, Wilhelm was immersed in war
preparations. The military depots in the electorate, the pontoon bridges,
the stocking of warehouses, all the visible signs of "neutrality" were
portents of doom to the local inhabitants. Their anxiety was shared by
Max Heinrich and Franz Egon who, in turn, blamed Wilhelm: "A thousand times a day they are inspired to see me as the author of all their
trouble. . . . I must confess to you, Sire, that a long time ago I would
have given up everything so as to retire in Italy or elsewhere until this
storm blew over were it not for the gratitude which I owe to Your Majesty." [37] This language may have accurately described the scene at the
electoral court but it was also an implicit warning: for the elector to with-
stand the increasing pressure he would have to be given better terms.

Wilhelm's next letter to Louvois (still substituting for Pomponne)
began with a wonderfully outlandish declaration: "I would as much like
to row in a galley as to always find myself obliged to make new demands
of the king in behalf of the elector [who] asks for many things at once
. . . but I do not believe that there is a single prince in all the world who
would do what the Elector of Cologne is doing." The last phrase may
well have been one which Max Heinrich intoned daily, to himself and to
others. Meanwhile, just when that dispatch was arriving at the French
court, Franz and Wilhelm had an argument which almost led to blows.
In the presence of the Bishop of Münster, Franz, rather drunk, berated

Wilhelm for his willingness to deceive everybody if it were useful to the king and charged that he had misused the negotiating powers entrusted to him. According to Wilhelm's account, Franz would have lunged for his throat had not the Bishop of Münster come between them.[38]

The scene brightened somewhat with word of the emperor's declared neutrality during the coming war. But Leopold pledged not to interfere on condition that French troops did not trespass on Spanish territory; he would enter the war if the Spanish Netherlands were violated. In these circumstances, the lands of Max Heinrich, especially the territory of Liège, would afford the most direct invasion route to the United Provinces. That in turn provided enough leverage for the elector and produced the alliance which Fürstenberg desired. Louvois personally negotiated this pact in a trip which included some comic relief. After cleverly concealing his destination, making numerous detours and assuming several disguises, Louvois arrived at Brühl only to discover that even the pages in Franz Egon's entourage knew he was coming! "All that you can imagine to be most ignorant is less so than M. de Strasbourg; if you add to that a continual irresolution and a sordid avarice, I am sure that you will feel sorry for those who have to deal with him. Nevertheless, it is on this man that everything depends around here, without whom one can achieve nothing."[39]

An offensive alliance with Cologne was concluded on January 2, 1672. The elector would receive 28,000 écus per month for the support of an army of 18,000; if the emperor sided with the Dutch, Max Heinrich could withdraw from the alliance after selling horses and men to the king and renouncing further subsidies. Louis pledged not to attack the emperor, the Empire, or the Spaniards unless they aided the Dutch; 10,000 French troops would be given to the elector and subsidized by the king. In a separate agreement, the king was allowed to fortify the city of Neuss in exchange for a loan of 400,000 livres, a loan which would plague the elector to his deathbed. Other treaties were signed with the Bishops of Münster, Osnabrück and Paderborn.[40]

The alliance was complete but Louvois retained his scorn of German princes. The very signing of the treaty with the Electorate of Cologne was delayed because of an evening of drunkenness and celebration presided over by Franz Egon and the Bishop of Münster. The Bishop of Strasbourg was so incapacitated on the following day that Louvois had to wait for twenty-four hours.[41] His opinion of the lot of them would never improve, but for the moment he resumed his efforts to bring everything into readiness for the spring campaign. In April pacts between Sweden and France, and England and Sweden rounded out the grand design.

England fired the first shot at the end of March and the French offensive began on April 6. A month later, Brandenburg sided with the United Provinces.

The campaign began with one fortification after another falling before the French juggernaut. By June 12 the king and his army had crossed the Rhine but ten days later the Dutch cut the dikes to isolate Amsterdam from attack. The Dutch sued for peace, offering the fortifications already seized on the Rhine, the city of Maastricht, territories in Brabant and Flanders occupied by the Dutch, and an indemnity of 10,000,000 livres. As Wolf observes, "the Dutch would in effect give up their possibility of opposing eventual absorption of the Spanish Netherlands in return for their right to live . . ."[42] Louis XIV refused these terms, preferring to annihilate the enemy economically and militarily. By any criterion one chooses to select, this was one of the major mistakes of his reign. France had already taken Rheinberg and would have received Maastricht, two of the principal prizes promised to Max Heinrich. For him and the other allies to see this peace refused was difficult, especially since the war would increasingly move into their lands.

In June the emperor and Brandenburg pledged to defend the Empire against French incursions. French occupation of the Duchy of Cleves, ruled by Brandenburg, was an infringement of imperial territory and could, if need be, serve as a pretext for Leopold's action. The emperor agreed to furnish 12,000 troops under his most talented general, Montecuccoli, but his objectives included the checking of any rash moves by Brandenburg that would have brought war into the Empire and preventing Friedrich Wilhelm from posing as the sole defense of the Germanies. The emperor's moves could be construed as a form of holding action, made more difficult by the uncertainty as to what Louis XIV's ultimate aims really were. At this point France could, in the words of Sir William Temple, be compared to a "man that leaps into the water in strength and vigour, and with pleasure. [No one can say] how far he will swim; which will be, till he is stopped by currents or accidents, or grows weary, or has a mind to do something else."[43]

On July 25 the emperor allied with the Dutch. In the following month the De Witt brothers were massacred by a frenzied mob. By now the supreme leadership in the United Provinces had passed into the hands of young William III of Orange who would remain the spearhead of European opposition against Louis XIV for the next generation. The menace of a German coalition ineluctably drew the king's armies into position to combat this coalition which, in turn, escalated the struggle militarily and psychologically in the Germanies. The territories of France's allies were invaded and plundered to such an extent that by November Fürstenberg exclaimed: "I am at my wits end and ruined [financially]. . . . Please realize that I have committed myself to this affair, that I have also engaged others in it only to serve the king and that it would assuredly not be for the service or for the reputation of His Majesty to have the elector's nose rubbed into the ground and to have me become the laughing stock of the whole world."[44] Louvois probably sneered when he read of this German allying with France "only to serve the king." He could well dismiss such dispatches as miserable whining, but he could not still the growing resentment in the tributary states. After all, Max Heinrich had entered the alliance on the understanding that he would not be opposing the emperor or the Empire; the mood in the Germanies was worsening with each passing week.

Wilhelm returned to this theme in every dispatch, notably in mid-January 1673: "Since the age of eighteen I have been employed in affairs [of state] and have never been involved in any which I have not brought to term with honor and to the entire satisfaction of those for whom I have worked. It would be all the more annoying if, in those in which I am presently sunk above my head, and which have had such a fine beginning, I should not only ruin my health and my private affairs by continual exertions and by the excessive expenses which I am obliged to make every day but should lose as well the little reputation which I have acquired in the world." He insisted that Max Heinrich would lose "his honor, his reputation, and perhaps his estates" without immediate and massive aid from France or else an alliance with France's enemies. "I could pass for an ingrate if the latter happened and would be made to seem unfaithful if the Elector of Cologne lost everything for both he and my brother are openly proclaiming that they have allowed themselves to follow my counsel, persuasions and assurances; now the opposite of what I predicted is occurring." If the king did not aid Cologne, then Wilhelm wanted to either reside at the court or be employed elsewhere in French service. He pledged even his life if need be "but to serve as a counsel to the Elector of Cologne or to permit him to rely on my conduct without my serving him with integrity and zeal as an honest man is assuredly something which Your Majesty will not ask of me since I would not be able to do it without losing the esteem and the confidence of Your Majesty."[45]

This letter reveals the dilemma into which his double allegiance had led him. He refused to follow Max Heinrich into an alliance with the emperor; in any choice between Leopold and Louis, Fürstenberg's preferences were clear and constant. Wilhelm's most immediate obligation was

not to the emperor or the Empire but to Max Heinrich: discussions relating to betrayal or treason should logically begin with the electoral
court. In the secret contract with France "the interests of His Majesty"
were to coincide with the welfare of the Elector of Cologne. Of course
Fürstenberg was concerned about his honor and his public reputation.
But to judge from his own words, money and military protection were
apparently sufficient to preserve his honor and that of the elector. At
issue was not the fact that a German elector had sided with France but
rather the possibility that this alliance could lead to his ruination through
defeat in war. *That* would have tainted Max Heinrich's honor. Louis
XIV's response was to enmesh the elector still further in the golden
chains of the French alliance: a supplementary pact, good for three years,
gave Max Heinrich 100,000 livres for expenses, 16,000 écus per month
beginning in February, 1673, and a sum of 20,000 écus for damages
incurred in the Liège territory since the elector could not collect contributions there. Wilhelm signed the new treaty on April 5, 1673.[46] Its terms
may have placated Max Heinrich for the moment but a new spring campaign was approaching, one which promised far less than "the fine beginning" of 1672.

I V
CAPTURE & IMPRISONMENT
JANUARY 1673 TO MAY 1679

WHILE EXPLORING the possibility of a general armistice involving the emperor, Brandenburg, and the Dutch, Louis XIV learned that Friedrich Wilhelm was ready to act on his own, leaving his alliance partners in the lurch.[1] The king directed Verjus to negotiate "according to the counsels and orders of . . . Turenne and the participation of Prince Wilhelm von Fürstenberg." Cologne's and Münster's claims for damages to their respective territories could not be allowed to interfere with the conclusion of the treaty with Brandenburg nor with the establishment of a general peace for the Germanies. Their territorial gains and indemnities could come at Dutch expense. The final sentence in these instructions reads: "Above all [Verjus] will receive the opinions and will act as he has been instructed above in close contact [*une exacte participation*] with Prince Wilhelm von Fürstenberg in whom he knows His Majesty reposes a complete confidence." Pomponne reaffirmed Wilhelm's important role: "You will have in your hands, Monsieur, a great opportunity of serving the Empire in giving it peace, and by depriving the Dutch of the support they expect from Germany you will oblige them to accept just and equitable conditions for the king and for his allies."[2] Between these mellifluous lines Wilhelm read the real message: he was to bear the brunt of Max Heinrich's outrage once Brandenburg left the war without paying indemnities to Cologne. The elector's former tirades would be fluff when compared to his certain reaction to Wilhelm's latest "opportunity of serving the Empire."

Fürstenberg's only hope lay in the promised collaboration with Verjus. A French settlement with Berlin, however, was reached with disconcerting speed once Pomponne began negotiating directly with Stratmann, the Brandenburg envoy in Paris. The French terms were quite generous: most of the occupied territories were returned; a few places would be retained until a general peace was established. Friedrich Wilhelm was offered protection if attacked by his former allies. Instead of formally renouncing his alliance with the Dutch, he promised not to give any assistance to the king's enemies. While Louis refused to pay damage claims, he did assent to a subsidy. Stratmann provisionally ratified the treaty on April 11.[3]

The news from Paris produced immediate shock waves in Cologne since Max Heinrich's territory had been overrun by Brandenburg troops and he expected retributions. Wilhelm's standing with the elector was so threatened that he went directly to the king's headquarters before Maastricht at the beginning of June. Louis was "surprised to learn he had arrived without permission."[4] His disregard of protocol betrayed grave anxiety over the drift of French policy. Yet despite his protests, Fürstenberg failed to change that policy. All he got was a present of 45,000 livres; this may have eased his resentment, but no amount of money could have dispelled his anxiety. Cologne had been double-crossed but worse still was Louis XIV's refusal to withdraw his troops from imperial territory after the peace with Brandenburg. That decision, more than any other, provoked a general German resistance against France. "Explanations" by French diplomats in the Empire were looked upon as mere word spinning.

The refusal to withdraw the troops came just when Spain was expected to enter the war. At the end of June, Maastricht was captured under Vauban's direction. Maastricht afforded control over the Meuse, assured communications with the Rhine and covered French positions in the region. In every respect it was the major event of the year and could serve as a springboard to further adventures.[5] Though Maastricht belonged to the Elector of Cologne, French troops would occupy it at least until the end of the war. Fürstenberg saw Louvois behind these developments and believed that disaster could be averted only by a league of German princes joined to France but not totally subservient to her, a league alive to the danger of Viennese ambition and willing to block the emperor's involvement in the Dutch War. This "third party" could include Mainz, Trier, Brandenburg, Bavaria, Neuburg, and Hanover. He promoted and refined this project throughout the summer months but his plans were soon swamped and made meaningless by events.[6]

Ironically, amidst all the plans for war, a peace congress opened in the Imperial Free City of Cologne. Inspired by Sweden and strongly supported by Pomponne and Fürstenberg, the congress began on June 27 with delegates registered from France, England, Holland, Sweden, Münster, Cologne, Spain, and the emperor. Lisola led the imperial delegation. Franz and Wilhelm von Fürstenberg represented the Elector of Cologne —on June 1 he gave them full powers, singly or together, to treat in his behalf.[7] The French delegation included the Duke de Chaulnes, Governor of Brittany; Paul Barrillon d'Amoncourt, a military intendant who had served with Turenne; and Pierre Honoré Courtin, who had extensive experience stretching back to the peace treaties of Münster and the Pyrenees and who was the effective leader of the group. Just the presence of the Fürstenbergs and Lisola in the same assembly assured polemical fireworks and cast doubts on the prospects for a peace being worked out at the congress. In fact, Lisola did not arrive until August 21, Fürstenberg was still at Maastricht when the congress convened, and many of the principals took side trips, whether for business or pleasure, during the course of the sessions. Most of the actual business took place in private conversations, often at the homes of the delegates and at dinners or parties in Cologne or neighboring towns.[8]

As at Frankfurt in 1658, Franz Egon was the premier party-giver. The summer's festivities reached their zenith at a masked ball in his residence on July 20. Diplomats arrived in the garb of sultans, viziers and Venetian gentlemen, and were joined by twenty-four ladies, many of them relatives and friends of the Egonites, including the Countess von der Mark. (According to Courtin, she was then infatuated with one of the Swedish plenipotentiaries.) It did not take long for Franz to earn the sobriquet "Bishop Bacchus." In August he organized a hunt near Brühl during which it was reported that more wine than game was destroyed. Amidst this gaiety and abandon, politics were never far from the surface; at the masked ball, for instance, Wilhelm and Franz discussed the Cologne claim to Rheinberg with the leaders of the Swedish delegation.[9] Yet despite their opportunities for contacts, the Egonites knew that the main action in Europe lay outside Cologne. Several days after the ball, Wilhelm was in Mainz.

The French presence in the Empire, their continuing war against the Dutch, and the expected entry of Spain emboldened Emperor Leopold to assert himself. An imperial army under Montecuccoli grouped in Bohemia and was expected to move toward the Rhine. At this juncture the territory and the politics of the Elector of Mainz were of crucial importance to both sides. The elector, Lothar Friedrich von Metternich (Schönborn died in February 1673), desired a general truce affording time to discuss peace terms. Wilhelm argued that such a scheme would only increase Dutch intransigence. But Lothar Friedrich agreed with William III of Orange that the cause of the Dutch was the cause of the Germanies; he believed Leopold owed it to his dignity and "to all the innocent states who implored his protection and assistance to be delivered from the violence and oppression which they suffered at the hands of His Majesty's troops."[10] He refused to consider a separate pact with

France or to use his offices in promoting a German league. It did not take a man of Fürstenberg's intelligence and experience to see that the political winds were blowing stiffly against France.

At one point, the elector took Wilhelm aside to inform him of rumors that his life was in danger. Fürstenberg dropped plans to travel to Munich and promised Pomponne to take more precautions than he had in the past: "I admit to you that I would be very angry to be shut up in a prison for several years or even to be treated as a traitor, which is what I have the honor of being called in Vienna." [11]

Another incident at Mainz reveals Wilhelm's mood of frustration and combativeness. During one of the diplomatic dinners in the monastery of the Carthusian Fathers he refused to drink a toast to the emperor; instead, he poured water in his glass before raising it. At the time of Wilhelm's seizure by imperial troops in February 1674 this incident of pouring water in his wine was the first thing Franz Egon thought of when trying to give reasons for the capture. There were, of course, many more pressing reasons for the emperor's action but it is significant that Franz should have given it such prominence. Perhaps he heard Wilhelm more than once rue this impetuous gesture. In any case, Franz's account is the only record of the incident in the Paris archives. Other sources tell a different story. The most famous of these was recounted by Petrus Valkenier, a Dutch publicist and diplomat who hated Fürstenberg. According to this account, when the toast to Leopold was proposed, Wilhelm spilled the contents of his glass on the table, provoking an uproar. When the time for toasting Louis XIV arrived, an imperial envoy went up to Wilhelm, snatched the glass from his hand, and threw the wine in his face. [12] This admittedly makes a better anecdote, but Valkenier is the most hostile witness imaginable. We can content ourselves with the account offered by Franz at a time when he could have no motive except to report the very worst that he knew. Even in this milder account, Wilhelm's passionate involvement in the service of France, and his even greater hostility toward Leopold, is sharply underlined.

Meanwhile, Louis XIV had left Maastricht for Alsace; Lorraine and Alsace were transferred from Pomponne's jurisdiction to that of Louvois. In August the king supervised the dismantling of the walls of the ten imperial cities in Alsace despite the pleas from Gravel in Regensburg. When Louvois learned that the Austrians and Spanish planned to seize Trier, thus threatening French gains in the Netherlands, Louis ordered a siege. The city fell on September 7, 1673. The reaction in the Germanies was instant and violent; Gravel reported that "fury against France is the dominant passion and virtually the universal distemper in Germany." It was the perfect propaganda weapon for Lisola just at the time when Leopold concluded a military alliance with Spain, Lorraine, and the United Provinces (August 30, 1673). Grémonville was expelled from Vienna; Montecuccoli's army headed westward towards the Rhine; "a good long war" was at hand. Fürstenberg pleaded for a "third party," this time comprising Sweden, Brandenburg, Neuburg, Bavaria, Hanover, and Württemberg. He wanted to argue his case in person before the king at Nancy. Sensing that his presence was not desired, he sent a memorandum instead.[13] His absence at Nancy perfectly illustrates the changes which had taken place just two years since Lionne's death. By now an ambivalence, even a contradiction, had arisen between military and strategic necessities and political and diplomatic necessities. French diplomats had different responsibilities from those that Louvois was shouldering. What once was "the grand design" was now a shambles. Those who supported France must have viewed the next few months as nothing less than a nightmare.

The first serious setback came when the Bishop of Würzburg allowed Montecuccoli to use his bridge to cross the Main. A feint toward Alsace threw Turenne off the track. Montecuccoli then descended the Rhine to Coblenz; his troops presently crossed the territory of Trier and headed for Bonn, where they would rendezvous with William III of Orange.[14] It was not the most sparkling month in Turenne's career.

By now the pursuit of "peace" at Cologne seemed beside the point; the city and the electorate of that name were focal points of the war. The approach of the allied armies filled Max Heinrich and his entourage with panic. Strong differences of opinion between Wilhelm and his brother were daily more evident. At one point Franz contacted Lisola through Baron Plittersdorf, an imperial diplomat. They plotted to persuade Max Heinrich to abandon the French alliance and to join Leopold with the guarantee of his personal security and several fortified places put at his disposition. Wilhelm got wind of this arrangement and was present with the French negotiators when Plittersdorf showed up for a conference with the Bishop of Strasbourg. The baron was reduced to speaking of other matters while the French envoys predicted that Condé's troops would soon bail them out. This intrigue, at least, came to nothing.[15]

By October 28 Dutch troops reached Cologne en route to Bonn. Though Wilhelm and Franz begged Max Heinrich to seek shelter in Kaiserswerth, a fortification in the electorate garrisoned by French troops, the elector instead retreated to the monastery of St. Pantaleon in the city of Cologne. Wilhelm urged prompt action for there were rumors that the burghers of Cologne would deliver the elector, himself and Franz over to Montecuccoli. Max Heinrich, he said, might well accept "propositions of accommodation which Baron von Lisola has sent to him without my knowledge. . . . For the love of God, send a man to reassure the elector!" [16]

On November 3 the siege of Bonn began; that same day Franz left for Kaiserswerth. Wilhelm determined to stay but he continually beseeched Max Heinrich to escape in time. There is evidence that he arranged to have bombs explode near the elector's residence to frighten Max Heinrich all the way to Kaiserswerth. This ruse might have worked had not Lisola persuaded some Cologne magistrates to visit the elector and guarantee his security. He agreed to stay but was totally unstrung, wanting simply to remain in the monastery and to forget the outside world. When Wilhelm arrived at St. Pantaleon soon thereafter for a conference the elector sent out word that if his leaving Cologne was all he wished to negotiate, then he could walk away; he refused to discuss the matter. Max Heinrich lamented that he had spent six sleepless nights in a row and described Louis XIV as a king "who treats his allies like his subjects." [17] In the midst of this chaos, with everything toppling down upon him, Louvois railed at Wilhelm for his anxiety over the approach of enemy troops. That was all Fürstenberg needed! He riposted with one of the bitterest letters that he ever sent or that Louvois ever received:

You ought to have known that the course of action adopted during the last few months and against which everyone, even the most faithful servants which the king has in Germany, have protested, could produce nothing else but what we see now: the affection of German princes for France is dwindling day by day and the territory and fortifications of the Elector of Cologne ruined by an army which you say is in such bad condition it should be pitied—and all this happened in front of the king's army. It is very well indeed for you to speak so glibly at Versailles and to make the enemy armies as small as you like and to march just as it may suit you. But since these armies don't stop when you would want or expect them to but continue to march toward their target it becomes rather embarrassing. . . . I know I'm not a great military leader and that I have fewer insights in these matters than other men and that I may be mistaken. But unfortunately for the king and for those of us here, the ambassadors and ministers of the king in these parts will bear witness when I say that I've predicted all that has happened. Now, Sir, it's up to you, you who want everything left in your hands and who normally disapprove of everything proposed to the contrary, now it's up to you to suggest the means of righting the state of affairs. [18]

Never had Wilhelm seemed more exasperated. It was some time since the king followed his advice; now he no longer seemed to listen to his protests. Franz had already half-deserted the camp; Wilhelm chose to stick it out. Why? Courtin cited his passionate attachment to the countess and declared that it was one of the best possible aids to the French cause, "for I believe that without this love he would not have remained here with the elector." Courtin advised Louvois to placate Wilhelm by exempting the lands of his mistress from contributions being imposed by the French commandant at Thionville. As a further sweetener, he quoted the countess as having stated that of all the men whom she had ever seen, Louis XIV was the one who had pleased her most.[19] The territories of the countess were exempt from contributions.

The presence of Countess von der Mark may have influenced Wilhelm's decision to stay but it is difficult to believe that this liaison explained everything. Courtin was a friend of Louvois and such a letter, politic and urbane, was calculated to blunt the edge of the dispute, perhaps to muffle Wilhelm's criticisms in the sound of laughter over his amorous escapades. The letter also obscured Fürstenberg's vicious struggle with men who sought to destroy him politically, to erase his influence in Cologne and in the Empire at large. Wilhelm had always been as much an opponent of the Habsburgs, above all in the Rhineland, as he was a partisan of France. He was gambling that some breakthrough could be made, that he and Max Heinrich could recoup their losses. Nobody needed to remind him that time was running out.

On November 12 Bonn was taken by the allied army. Leopold informed Max Heinrich that all would be well if the Fürstenbergs were chased from his service. And if he did not comply with this request? Rumor had it that the imperial forces might install a garrison in Cologne, arrange for a coadjutor to be elected, set him up in Bonn and give over the government of the archbishopric to their creation. The only hope for French interests was *"un coup d'ésclat"* which would drive the emperor's troops back over the Rhine and take Bonn before they had a chance to fortify it. Franz obviously had his doubts for he was in Wesel and contemplated a further retreat to Hildesheim. Courtin characterized him as a clever but weak man who knew how to begin an action but did not have the courage to see it through.[20]

By the end of November Turenne and Louvois were each blaming the other for the fall of Bonn. Hope revived when Montecuccoli resigned his command and William III of Orange left field headquarters with the onset of winter. Their troops became less tractable, more problems arose, and Lisola himself bemoaned the failure to follow up their good fortune. Fürstenberg repeatedly tried to convince the elector that French reenforcement would soon arrive. He was equally zealous among members of the cathedral chapter, urging them not to be duped by Lisola. (Here he was given a great boost by the resignation of Montecuccoli.) This kind of activity, the mingling of friendship, bribery, and political pressure is what Fürstenberg excelled at and his presence in Cologne infuriated the imperial delegation. Lisola presently left the city and traveled to Liège. Some respite seemed possible.[21]

On the second day of the new year, Wilhelm warned that the elector might reach "an accommodation with the emperor if [Louis XIV] only deceives him with hopes [of support] and if one puts difficulties in the way of according him the proper and necessary remedies for the illnesses he is suffering from." In this same dispatch, he referred to the king's having nominated him for a cardinal's hat and having promised sufficient income to support the dignity with honor "so as to shelter me from the hate and persecution of the enemies I have made for the love of him and to console me for the loss of my fortune in Germany."[22] To nominate him for a cardinal's hat in the midst of this Götterdämmerung is proof enough that humor and high politics are not mutually exclusive.

Fürstenberg's letter was part of a master plan, or choice, offered to the king. On the one hand, the elector could treat with the emperor and declare his neutrality; French troops could then withdraw from the electorate while a separate peace was worked out between Cologne and the United Provinces. The alternative was a new treaty entailing a larger subsidy to the elector and increased support for his army, a commitment of 25,000 French troops to drive enemy forces from the Lower Rhine, and the creation of a "third party" in the Empire. Further, Max Heinrich's forces would control the fortifications in his territories now occupied by French troops. These proposals were taken to Paris by one of Wilhelm's creatures, the Liège canon Douffet, on January 15, 1674.[23] Max Heinrich promised to avoid other arrangements until the results of Douffet's mission became known. A week later he asked for money and support to avoid "the necessity of indispensably doing all that the emperor wishes" and hoped for "such an advantageous change in my affairs that there would be no reason to repent for having allowed myself to be drawn into a war which up until now seems to have been as unfortunate and harmful to my states and subjects and to myself as it has been glorious and advantageous to Your Majesty."[24] It would have been refreshing for the elector to have admitted at least once that he had coveted Dutch territory every bit as much as his ministers and allies.

As the days went by with no word from Douffet, Wilhelm's anxiety deepened. His daily activity went on as usual; he went to the balls, dances, and receptions in the city, but inwardly he was torn. He spoke of retreating to a French abbey, of becoming a simple monk, of taking refuge at the court. Cologne was ringed by enemy troops and he received numerous warnings of the danger he was courting.[25] On January 30 Douffet received his audience with the king. We have no record of the council meetings at which the elector's proposals were discussed but on February 20, a full five weeks after Douffet left Cologne, the king decided to give massive aid to Max Heinrich and to the Bishop of Münster. In a most cordial letter to Wilhelm, he told him that his counsel was indispensable and requested that he come to the court as soon as possible. In the meantime, he sent 20,000 écus to Max Heinrich to tide him over during Wilhelm's absence, insisting that he not leave until all precautions had been taken to ensure that "the elector will not change from the sentiments in which you will have left him. Please be assured of my entire satisfaction at the zeal which you have shown for my service. . . . I will have even greater pleasure to give evidence of it to you in person."[26] The letter was sent off but it never reached its destination. On February 14 Fürstenberg was captured in the streets of Cologne. The orders for his arrest had been issued by Emperor Leopold.

On the morning of February 14 Fürstenberg told the French delegates of reports that an attempt might be made to seize him dead or alive. There is no evidence that they took this alert more seriously than others which had circulated in the preceding months.[27] That afternoon Wilhelm spent several hours in the company of the countess. At four o'clock he left her house to keep an appointment with Max Heinrich at the monastery. In his coach were three companions: his secretary Jean Breget, his stablemaster Champillion, and Cortt, a cavalier friend of the countess. In addition to the coachman there were five lackeys and two liveried attendants. This was small protection indeed on the very day that he received a warning! No sooner had they set off than a detachment of twenty men under Major Obizzi surrounded the carriage amidst shots, shouts, and orders to stop. Pandemonium broke loose. Breget was seriously wounded after killing one of the attackers and gravely wounding Obizzi himself. Cortt was shot in the head, Champillion wounded by a bullet, and several in the train shot or knocked down trying to flee. All the while Fürstenberg stayed in the coach. In the midst of the tumult his coachman leaped back onto the driver's seat and drove the horses forward. After a frenzied pursuit the coachman was again knocked to the ground, from where he saw the horses galloping off with the reins loose and flying. When the careening carriage finally came to a halt, Wilhelm jumped out and tried to run for cover but he was caught by the horsemen and at gunpoint forced to climb back into the carriage. What was left of the detachment spirited him and the coach out of the city. His abductors allowed him to write a note to his sister, Countess von Löwenstein, assuring her that he was unhurt. Then he was taken under heavy guard to Bonn.[28]

Fürstenberg was brought before the Marchese di Grana, Obizzi's superior, who had received direct orders to arrange the capture. Ironically, Grana had set up his quarters in Franz Egon's residence in Bonn and it was in these familiar surroundings that Wilhelm began to piece things together. On the fifteenth Grana dictated a letter explaining the situation:

His Imperial Majesty having found it apropos to arrest and bring here Prince Wilhelm von Fürstenberg, apparently to sooner arrive at a good peace, against which and against the union of Germany, he has for so long brought so many obstacles, I should inform you . . . that yesterday the deed has been accomplished in the evening. Although one hoped to reach this end without any violence, all the same several people who were with him having put up a very vigorous defense, there have been men wounded on both sides. . . . There was an order to leave the prince rather than to do him the slightest harm, as a result of which he is now at Bonn in perfect health and he is receiving all good treatment imaginable. For me, I have no other role than that of obedience and I would like with all my heart to render him service in all that which is apart from [my duty to] my master.[29]

An accredited delegate to an international peace congress had been captured in a neutral city of the Empire on orders of Emperor Leopold. Strong representations were made by the French and many other participants and observers, claiming that diplomatic immunity had been flouted, that accepted rights of peoples and nations had been broken. Some sought Wilhelm's return to Cologne, but Grana awaited orders. Vienna alerted its polemicists, Lisola above all, to the need for providing suitable justifications. Wilhelm's brother was aghast and blamed Louvois: "There are the effects of the direction of a certain person who treats everybody so badly." Franz could not know that shortly before his brother's capture Louvois had ordered that Lisola be taken dead or alive.[30]

Louis XIV assessed the recent events in cold political terms: "[I] lost with Prince Wilhelm the strongest means I had of acting with the elector." There remained Franz, "if his feebleness does not give him reason to prefer a shameful accommodation with the emperor to a just vengeance." He ordered his delegates in Cologne to suspend their negotiations and to remain in the city. Three days later the king instructed them to inform the Dutch that France was ready to conclude a separate peace.[31] The reappraisal of government policy was given further impetus with the news that Fürstenberg had been transferred from Bonn and taken under heavy guard to Austria. Louis insisted that the question of Fürstenberg's arrest be linked to the peace congress at Cologne. If Fürstenberg were released, then the sessions could continue; if not, they had no meaning. The removal of the prisoner to Austria and Leopold's admission to the Swedish ambassador in Vienna that he had ordered the action settled the matter.

As for Max Heinrich, he had not exhibited much concern at the news of Wilhelm's arrest. A majority on his council and in the cathedral chapter favored the emperor, indicating a growing German unity against France. The fact that such sentiment was not as pronounced in the previous year is a testament to Wilhelm's influence in the council and in the chapter. In these circumstances, Louis XIV decided to break his ties with the elector "since he is weak and surrounded by men who have influence over him." The king resolved "to put him at liberty to make his accommodation with the emperor," and was willing to give him 5000 écus per month if he would accept a treaty of neutrality. Louis hoped that an accommodation between the elector and Leopold would lead to Wilhelm's freedom and he determined to abandon all fortifications in the electorate by April 20 "as proof of my good will." He instructed his envoys to leave Cologne.[32] (The congress soon thereafter disbanded.)

The only one who seemed genuinely shocked by this withdrawal was the Bishop of Strasbourg: "I don't know what could have been given as the reason for a resolution so unexpected and so contrary to the service and the *gloire* of Your Majesty." Franz was living in a dream-world wholly divorced from reality. He no longer had any influence at the electoral court; indeed, by his flight in November he had abdicated his right to influence well before Wilhelm was captured. By June 11 he was in Paris expressing his gratitude for having received protection in France.[33]

If Franz resembled the survivor of a shipwreck, Max Heinrich was likewise scrambling for something to cling to. In discussions concerning a treaty with the emperor, the cathedral chapter urged him to include a provision for Fürstenberg's release. On May 7 Max Heinrich sent a letter to Leopold in an attempt to intervene in Wilhelm's favor. This was the last gesture that he made. On May 11 he came to terms with the Dutch. One of the provisions in this pact was a full amnesty for participants on both sides, with the express omission of those guilty of high treason. Thus did Max Heinrich dismiss Fürstenberg from his mind! In December 1674 he pledged in a treaty with the Austrians to keep the Fürstenbergs apart from his service forever but he was so frightened of any French reaction that the existence of the treaty did not become known until March 1677. The Austrians continued to occupy Bonn.[34] Intimidated and dejected, Max Heinrich desired little more than the necessary peace to continue his alchemy experiments in the monastery of St. Pantaleon while the war swirled on without. That is where we shall find him in the spring of 1679.

While Fürstenberg remained totally isolated, the controversy over his seizure became a separate branch of the publishing industry. In this special genre no work surpassed that of Lisola, himself one of the first to have interviewed Wilhelm in Bonn. Writing in his accomplished polemical style shortly before his death, the Austrian agent inveighed against the ruses and maneuverings of Prince Wilhelm, depicting him as

a false, cunning minister who played so many roles at the same time in this illustrious Theater of Peace [the Congress of Cologne], who changed into more figures than Proteus himself so as to have all the more opportunity to scoff at the emperor and the Empire. Sometimes he was seen armed, the colonel of a French regiment who recruited and reviewed troops, preparing them for combat and displaying artillery so as to make French presence felt everywhere. Soon after he would appear wearing a miter and the habit of a canon, insolently intruding upon the peaceful deliberations of the cathedral chapter. Next he would arrive wearing the mask of a Prince of Germany, acting as an emissary of France and attempting to entice German princes into the lair of the enemy. Suddenly he would be in the guise of a polemicist, disseminating tracts and libels against the emperor, only to turn around and introduce himself as an ambassador with an olive branch while at the same time weaving new alliances and lining up new enemies for the emperor and the Empire: always changed, always changing, yet always the same in the midst of so many roles and malicious designs, all of them reflections of himself. But why are we lighting candles in broad daylight . . . ?[35]

Despite these verbal pyrotechnics, Lisola was unable to convince many of his readers that Fürstenberg was not an authorized delegate at the congress working in behalf of the Elector of Cologne. Much was made of the fact that Wilhelm had not been formally accepted by Leopold I as a bona fide delegate or officially given a safe-conduct pass. But Fürstenberg and Lisola exchanged visits. Lisola heatedly protested that these visits did not have an official diplomatic character, that they could not be adduced as recognition. But he himself, in a letter to Hocher on October 5, 1673, referred to the Fürstenbergs as delegates. Beyond all of this is the fact that Max Heinrich officially declared Franz and Wilhelm to be his representatives on June 1, 1673. They were so recognized by the other participants at the congress. Perhaps Lisola was so exercised over this issue precisely because he knew he was lying in his teeth. Similarly, there can be no doubt that the city of Cologne was neutral territory; it was declared neutral by Leopold on April 19, 1673.[36] But such items would have seemed mere debating points to Fürstenberg as he was taken to prison in April 1674. He had every reason to believe that his life would soon be forfeit. Indeed, his place of confinement at Wiener-Neustadt was where the Hungarian rebels Zrinyi and Frangepan had been executed in 1671.

Wilhelm's arrest can be viewed from several vantage points. Leopold believed that the Fürstenbergs were bent on a policy to wreck Habsburg influence in the Empire, that they wanted to see Louis XIV as emperor. In a symbolic sense, Wilhelm was the insolence of German princes who dared to defy the emperor and his conception of what the Empire truly was. He incarnated the independence and fickleness of German princes not only since Westphalia but before it as well. Leopold's forebears sought to eradicate this independence, to smash it by military force. They had failed to do so in the Thirty Years' War, yet the peace treaties of Westphalia need not have remained an insuperable obstacle to an emperor's ambition. As with many such documents, it was often a matter of interpretation coupled with sufficient force to back up one's interpretation. Leopold's move against Fürstenberg reflected the mood of aggressive confidence in his authority as exhibited in the recent suppression of the revolt in Hungary and the stern measures taken against Hungarian Protestants. What action would he take against Fürstenberg? The options open to him included summary execution or a political trial. Leopold began with interrogations.

The first of these interrogations took place on April 12 at Vösendorf; the second was on May 19 at Wiener-Neustadt. After considerable resistance Wilhelm agreed to sign the combined minutes when assured that they would not be used as a final document to judge him but instead would record his agreement that this was the substance of his remarks. The interrogator was Johann Paul Hocher, the Austrian Court Chancellor and the most influential minister in the Habsburg government in 1674. Hocher possessed considerable legal experience and had conducted the trials of the Hungarian rebels in 1671. He was not so much out to prove Wilhelm's guilt or innocence as to obtain information from him, especially regarding the French alliance system. Fürstenberg gave sensible, balanced answers, omitting information where he could, often denying knowledge of material in which he was well versed, and lying when convenient.[37]

Although his pact with France was unknown, Wilhelm in no way denied his ties with Louis XIV or his gratitude to him for benefits received and made no excuses for what he had done. Bluntly he said that he received "his piece of bread and support" from the French crown. At that moment he enjoyed a yearly income of 90,000 livres from his French benefices and admitted receiving 45,000 livres during his sojourn before Maastricht. Since 1662 he had relinquished all his holdings in the Empire and for the past ten or eleven years had carried French letters of naturalization. Letters of naturalization meant little at the time; they were juridically necessary in order to own benefices in France.[38] Here Fürstenberg made much of them, though he would minimize their importance in 1688 and finally request the king to revoke them! He insisted that he had no particular obligation toward Spain nor toward the House of Austria: "He was no Austrian servant but rather believed that as a free German he could seek his fortune as best he could before foreign rulers." He claimed he was virtually driven into the employ of a foreign ruler since he was blocked from entering Habsburg service back in 1653 by Prince Auersperg and Castel-Rodrigo.

Concerning agitation for a non-Habsburg successor to the throne, Wilhelm stated that in January 1670 he discussed the question with Friedrich Wilhelm at a time when Leopold was very ill. Again he was blunt, noting that at Berlin he raised the possibility of the King of France's being elected emperor with the Elector of Bavaria slated to succeed him. This arrangement would not, he told Hocher, rule out the possibility of a Habsburg succeeding in the future. But when discussing Bavaria's treaties with France and Cologne, he emphasized the Bavarian troops sent to Cologne and paid for by Max Heinrich. He claimed to know very little concerning other matters, including the terms of the pact between France and Bavaria. This was lying in the grand style since he drafted the pact in the first place and insisted upon the clause dealing with Louis XIV's election as Holy Roman Emperor.

Of equal importance to Hocher were Wilhelm's relations with the recently executed Hungarian rebels, Zrinyi and Frangepan. Wilhelm admitted that he spoke with them at Regensburg in 1664 and said that he relayed their plans and "chimeras" against the emperor to the Elector of Mainz, archchancellor of the Empire. This was a most convenient revelation since Schönborn was dead. In fact, Schönborn knew about Hungarian links with France and supported them. Spiegel refers to Wilhelm's sojourn in Vienna in 1667 and feels certain that he was implicated in the negotiations between the rebels and Grémonville at that time.[39] As we have seen in treating this episode, Wilhelm reported to Paris at the time that he had been approached but refused to engage himself, believing that the negotiations could be handled satisfactorily by Grémonville. But he clearly favored the rapport between France and the rebels and believed nothing more propitious for his own and French interests than to have the Austrians diverted by uprisings in the Hungarian territories. It is understood that the Hungarian business had nothing to do with Wilhelm's relations to Leopold as emperor but as leader of the House of Austria.

The remainder of these hearings was largely devoted to Fürstenberg's activity in forming the French alliance system. Here he supplied a grab-bag of information, some of it accurate, the rest plausible, but always imbued with the tact of omission. Under the circumstances it was a sufficiently artful presentation. He emphasized that the alliance between France and Cologne was aimed at the United Provinces, not at the Empire. As for the passage of French troops through the elector's territories, other princes besides Cologne allowed passage of French troops. He claimed never to have seen the treaty between England and France and to have no knowledge of the secret articles. Here again the contrary could not be proven, as Wilhelm well knew. In a closing remark, he observed that he had been working for the establishment of peace but had been interrupted by his arrest.

If the proceedings up until this point seem strange it is largely because his captors did not know what to do with him. Already Leopold was besieged by requests to let Wilhelm go. Representations were made by Sweden, Bavaria, Charles II of England, even by Friedrich Wilhelm of Brandenburg, who made it clear that he was interested in Wilhelm's release solely as a means of promoting the peace. The emperor refused these requests. He likewise refrained from setting up a political trial. Wilhelm desired a trial and requested a third hearing to plead his case; on July 14 a final interrogation took place in Pottendorf.[40] Wilhelm asked for an opportunity to justify himself before the general public. He admitted that he may have made errors, he may have sinned, but the crime of treason or the charge that he was an irreconcilable enemy of His Imperial Majesty was something which he sought to disprove. Again he stated his inability to find employment with Emperor Ferdinand III, his need to seek his fortune elsewhere. He attempted to bring France and the Germanies together, not to make them enemies. If his ties with France were blamable, then so too were the ties of other German princes, for he was following the same maxims, the same practices as they were. Besides, as a result of his naturalization in France he no longer had any obligation vis-à-vis the emperor or the Empire.

This last declaration was most interesting! To argue that German princes were allowed to contract alliances with foreign powers was one of the best points in his defense and one of the reasons why the emperor would never allow a public trial. Wilhelm was claiming to the limit his rights as a prince of the Empire. But to argue that he had no obligations was most questionable, to say the least. His assertion was certainly bold. Perhaps it was a challenge to them to stage a trial, to force them to produce the gravamen of a charge of treason. Hocher asked him whether as a prince, as the representative of an imperial elector, as the member of cathedral chapters in Cologne and Strasbourg, both linked to the Empire and from both of which he drew benefits, whether this did not entail a relationship to the emperor and the Empire? Wilhelm skirted a direct response to this question. He preferred to expatiate on the claim that his earlier dealings with France were carried on with the apparent foreknowledge and approval of Ferdinand III and that the present emperor also understood his relations to France. (Though he did not say it in so many words, here was a reminder that he had been made a prince as recently as 1664, a title confirmed in 1667.) Whatever he had done in the Empire was done as the representative of the Elector of Cologne, from whom he had taken orders. Wilhelm used this occasion to ask what was happening back in Cologne, had the elector come to terms with the emperor? Upon learning that a treaty would soon be concluded and that Cologne would contribute several regiments, he said that he received this news with pleasure.

The discussion then turned to the stolen baggage in Berlin, which we have discussed in the last chapter. The attention paid by the Austrian ministry to the business of electing a non-Habsburg reveals this to be one of their major grievances against Fürstenberg. One can understand their lack of enthusiasm for the existence of an electoral instead of a hereditary system. But the system as it existed allowed ample room for maneuver. The interrogation ended with Wilhelm's urging that his relations with France not be construed as treasonous, maintaining that his actions had always been honorable and upright. After declaring his gratitude to Hocher and to His Imperial Majesty, he again asked that his case be brought before the pope and the Empire. When Hocher insisted that jurisdiction remained in the hands of the emperor, Wilhelm simply expressed concern that a misunderstanding might arise between the emperor and the pope on his account. After three hours the session had ended.

Hocher commented on the increased self-assurance displayed by the prisoner during the final interview. This behavior seemed explicable when a plot to free Fürstenberg was uncovered late that summer. The conspirators were Wilhelm's sister, Countess von Löwenstein; Dr. Burmann, a Cologne counsellor and friend of Franz Egon; and a brother of Fürstenberg's wounded secretary, Breget. Their plan involved the bribery of guards and the complicity of military figures but it was discovered in time and resulted in the expulsion of Wilhelm's sister from Vienna and jail sentences for Burmann and Breget, among others.[41] Naturally the detection of the plot led to greater restrictions on Wilhelm, resulting in bitter laments on his part.

Fürstenberg constantly pressed for a trial to clear his name. A letter which he wrote to his sister earlier in the summer gives us a good picture of his plans if he had been allowed to present his case in public. He calculated that his clerical status could aid him immensely; a church tribunal would have been safer than any other court. But since a church tribunal was his best hope, it was unlikely that the emperor would turn him over to one. Regardless of what kind of trial he received, Wilhelm thought it best to have three lawyers:

One from Bavaria, for the other [I want] Professor Conring of Helmestat if the Duke of Hanover finds it apropos, and then one well versed in canon law whom the Official of Cologne [his friend Quentel] would be able to propose, even if [all of this] would cost more than 20,000 écus. Nothing should be spared since my honor and my life depend upon it, because in my present state I am consuming myself, perishing within myself at the sight of my honor so unjustly torn apart in the world. On the outside I pretend to be a man fairly unshaken but you who know me can well judge my inner sentiments because I see my honor, which I have always cherished more than my life, so unjustly attacked without my having the opportunity to be able to justify myself before the world.[42]

He begged his sister to pull all possible strings in his behalf: "Try . . . to get the ministers of the emperor to have me absolved or declare me innocent regarding the crime of perduellio [treason] and others which I have not committed and that only to save my honor before the world or to permit me to justify myself . . . before the Holy Father or the Empire." Again and again, Wilhelm returned to the theme of honor. He wanted Max Heinrich to know that he did not blame him for not mentioning him in the treaties, but the elector must realize that it went against his honor to have it said that he could not govern and that he was ruled by Wilhelm. He should intercede for him. If possible, he wanted to make a deal with the emperor whereby he would be released and remain apart from the political scene until the war was over, provided that conditions for the salvation of his honor were met. He asked his sister to write to the English, French, and Swedish ambassadors as well as the nuncios and to keep the pressure constant: "I am causing you a lot of trouble, my very dear sister, but I know that you are working with joy and pleasure to conserve my honor and my life. If I am not able to maintain the former, I would not at all wish to retain the latter and in that case I would rather die today than tomorrow." In light of the code of honor prevailing at the time, Wilhelm's words were not empty rhetoric. For a gentleman, to say nothing of a prince, his honor was indeed worth his life.

At one point in this fairly lengthy letter he suddenly exclaimed: "They need proof of perduellio and they have not produced *any*." Here was the nub of Wilhelm's defense. Since the Austrians doubtless read the letters that he sent from prison, the words were equally directed at his jailers and underscore one of the central issues in any discussion of treason— whether it can exist as a state of mind, a disposition of the spirit, so to speak, as opposed to something that must be laid out and proven in precise legal detail. Historically, the crime of treason has conveniently covered a great number of misdeeds by subjects. As an authority on the law of Ancient Rome has noted, "Treason in early times was the simplest, as it was the most characteristic, conception of Roman criminal law. Originally it embraced almost every conceivable offence that could be thought of as endangering the safety of the State. It is not so much a crime in early law, as a special point of view from which crimes of very different character might be regarded." [43] In Roman law, *perduellio* connoted hostility to the State. The Habsburgs viewed Wilhelm's activity as having amounted to treasonous collusion with the (present) enemy of the emperor and the Empire. Wilhelm, of course, demanded a trial yet despite all his pleadings and the intercession of kings and princes in his behalf, Leopold refused to authorize one. The most likely explanation is that a show trial would have made it all too evident that many prestigious princes of the Empire could have been seized for reasons similar to those which animated him against Fürstenberg. The fact that Hocher did not press Fürstenberg on his assertion that he had no obligations to the emperor indicated that the Austrians were not seriously interested in pursuing the matter judicially. But the arrest itself, the pamphlets, the circumstantial evidence all amounted to what we would call "character assassination," to something quite close to an official verdict of treason handed down against the accused. It is against this that Wilhelm was struggling, for without vindication in court his name would forever be besmirched.

Fürstenberg's case is so absorbing precisely because one is operating in a twilight zone of ambiguous political rights and responsibilities. Wilhelm argued that he was carrying out the orders of Max Heinrich but did not emphasize his role in influencing the content of those orders. Nor did he broach the question of possible conflict between his duty to Cologne and his duty to France. As we have seen, in January 1673 he wanted to retire to France if he risked disservice to the elector. The secret contract stipulated that "the plans and interests of His Majesty in Germany . . . are none other than the welfare and peace of the Empire itself and the conservation of the rights and liberties which belong or pertain to the electors, princes, and states of the Empire, especially His Highness the Elector of Cologne." Here again, technically, he was "covered." In Fürstenberg we have a man who is eely, duplicitous, one who succeeded in getting much more than his "piece of bread." Unquestionably he stretched to the limits the elasticity reserved for princes in the constitution of the Empire. He may have been less than patriotic, but to brand him a traitor pure and simple is to ignore too many obstacles. In Wilhelm's eyes, one of those obstacles was the lack of proof, yet in the circumstances it was a meager consolation. For Leopold it was a point of honor not to release the prisoner, not to give any indication that he was wrong in arresting him or that he harbored any doubts. Wilhelm in effect was a pawn in the game of high politics being played by the Habsburgs and the Bourbons. This part of the game would last for five years. No trial was ever held.

What of Fürstenberg's life in prison? Thanks to the solid work of Käthe Spiegel we are reasonably well-informed on the details of his prison routine. From the outset he was treated with the respect due him as a prince of the Empire. The superintendent's records for his first two weeks at Wiener-Neustadt, for instance, indicate that one evening meal included fourteen different kinds of food, accompanied by good Austrian wine and followed by lemonade. On the next day, the noon-time meal consisted of fourteen varieties of food, the evening repast of ten. It is heartening to learn that at Wilhelm's special request lemonade was again on the menu. Special care was taken to provide fowl, game, fish, fine pastries, and the like and added attention was devoted to their preparation.[44]

Every day Wilhelm heard Mass in his chamber, but he was forbidden to speak to anyone, even the priest, after the service. Spiritual conferences were not permitted. He secured the services of a renowned Viennese physician but could converse with him only in the presence of a guard. Wholly cut off from the outside world, he continually sought chances for diversion. He requested permission to go for walks with officers in the town; he asked for books. To amuse himself, he decided to design a chapel and asked for the necessary pencils, paper and instruments to carry on the hobby. Eventually, books not forbidden to him were brought by Capuchins and Jesuits. Drawing material was likewise provided but a close watch was kept on the use he made of them. Money was sent from Paris to allow him to pay for special dishes and wines of his choosing, for bookbinding costs, for alms to the poor, and for tips, particularly to those who brought his letters to Vienna.[45]

In the early months he spent much time in drafting letters and memoranda to Hocher and other ministers, requesting a public trial. Gradually he became discouraged, even drifting into melancholy. He must have been informed of the death of his brother Hermann Egon in September 1674. Perhaps he heard that before the end of the year the Countess von der Mark gave birth to a boy, Ludwig Peter Engelbert von der Mark, who in later life so closely resembled Wilhelm. In the winter of 1674–75 many believed that Wilhelm would never live to see the end of the war. His health was even discussed in the imperial council and every effort made to ensure that he got proper medical attention. Numerous purges seemed to do little good. In the first two years he estimated that he spent eleven weeks with a strong fever and much of the remaining time in generally poor health. The subsequent years were apparently less miserable. Throughout 1677, for example, he consumed a great variety of fine wines and imported many books on architecture. In addition, his place of confinement was changed several times and sometimes he went for (guarded) walks on the grounds of a chateau. Whenever the emperor visited Wiener-Neustadt the prisoner was transferred elsewhere, it not being considered seemly that the two reside in the same town. In the summer of 1676 he was on the estate of Count Zinzendorf in Brunn am Steinfeld. For all of the next year he stayed at Pottendorf. During the last months he stayed in Baden, close by Vienna, where he was allowed to frequent the baths.[46]

During these years Wilhelm had almost no knowledge of the course of the war or the politics of Europe. A succession of terrible campaigns, provinces overrun by troops of both sides, material and human exhaustion—this was the story of the Dutch War. In France the need for money led to renewed exactions on an already-burdened populace; major revolts in Bordeaux and Brittany were only the best known of scores of uprisings throughout the land. The king desired peace; his occupation of Franche Comté and other territories made it likely that Spain could absorb much of the cost of the war. Nijmegen in the United Provinces was chosen as the location of the future peace conference.

Louis's initial position was that no delegates would be sent to Nijmegen until Fürstenberg was either released or given over to a third party such as the pope. His honor was at stake in the matter. Leopold's honor dictated another course of action: under no circumstances would he release his prisoner before the conclusion of the peace. A way out of this dilemma was found by Franz Egon in collaboration with Charles II of England. Franz proposed that the Fürstenberg question not be allowed to hinder the conclusion of a general peace for Christendom. Wilhelm's friend Dücker went to Vienna in early 1676 in behalf of the English king, requesting that Wilhelm be released or given over to a third power. Leopold denied the request. He also refused Dücker permission to visit Fürstenberg; all contact had to be in writing. Wilhelm cooperated with the scheme presented by Dücker: he wrote letters to both Charles and Louis XIV, beseeching them not to allow his fate to interfere with the opening of the peace talks. There was further haggling with the Austrian ministry until Wilhelm wrote still another letter to Charles stating that he wanted to remain in captivity until the peace congress had ended.[47] This overture cleared the air somewhat, but only after interminable minor delays did the Nijmegen parleys finally begin.

Franz Egon presented the case for the Fürstenbergs in October 1677. Since November 1674 he had been denied a seat and a voice in the Reichstag at Regensburg until a reconciliation with Leopold had been reached. His estates, properties, and offices in the Empire were also affected. The property of the deceased Hermann Egon had been sequestered. Franz demanded that all damages to the honor and the property of the Fürstenberg family be repaired.[48] His request was supported by France, England, the Dutch, and other powers.

The French detached the Dutch from the allied coalition and signed a peace with them in August 1678; in Article 18 both Franz and Wilhelm von Fürstenberg were cited as "interested parties in this past war." In the treaty signed between France and Spain in the following month, the same clause was inserted in Article 29. To soothe Austrian sensitivities, Charles II proposed that the Egonites expressly ask Leopold for clemency and pledge fidelity and obedience in the future. In return for their "due submission" and in deference to the urgent pleas of the King of England and the pope, the emperor would declare clemency and restore them to all their former rights. Article 23 of the peace treaty between France and His Imperial Majesty (February 5, 1679) fully restored to Franz Egon, Wilhelm Egon and Anton Egon (son of Hermann Egon) their reputation, dignities, votes, benefices, offices, and all feudal and allodial rights which appertained to them. Wilhelm would be released from prison as soon as the peace treaty was ratified.[49]

On May 14, 1679 peace was declared in Vienna—Wilhelm was a free man. Franz acclaimed Leopold for his clemency to the Fürstenberg family. For Wilhelm, however, the long-awaited moment was soured by his lingering illness. In the official ceremonies before his departure he went through all the servile motions of a sycophant in rendering his gratitude and homage to the emperor. We can well imagine the thoughts behind his mask for the occasion, as Lisola would surely have called it had he been alive. During the first of two audiences, Leopold spoke harshly and sternly appealed to his conscience as a prince of the Empire. The second audience was more pleasant; the emperor gave Wilhelm a diamond-studded crucifix as a parting present. The Venetian ambassador reported that every care was taken to ensure that Wilhelm was content, the imperial court being especially solicitous that he leave with a favorable impression of the reception he had received.[50] This after five years in prison!

In the midst of the incense waved before Leopold, there was never any prospect of Fürstenberg leaving French service. Among the letters which he sent to Paris shortly before his release, none gives us a better sense of his desire to be back in harness than the one to Louvois. Its tone is far different from those he sent him before his arrest: "All that I have learned of the great advantages and extraordinary success in the affairs of His Majesty have further increased the esteem in which I have always held your merit and your savoir-faire. It will be a great pleasure for me to congratulate you and to listen to you speak of these matters. I am sure that from such conversations and the charm [*douceur*] of your company which I hope to enjoy in those rare moments when you can steal away from the affairs of state, I will soon make up for the despondency into which my illnesses and past chagrins and my long sufferings have cast me."[51] Soon after his audience with Leopold he set out for Cologne.

V

FENCE MENDING

MAY 1679 TO JULY 1681

WILHELM LEFT VIENNA with his health impaired and his future uncertain. As he passed through territories which for five years had been only a memory he received a warm letter from Pomponne: "I hope that the end of your imprisonment will be accompanied by every possible satisfaction and that you will find in the presence of the king the consolation for all the sufferings you have undergone for his service. His Majesty has appeared to be well pleased with the letter you have sent him. The memory of all the services you have rendered is very much appreciated and you know what this can produce in the heart of the noblest and most generous Prince in the world." Though spurred on by this news from France, he was repeatedly stricken by his "indisposition," even after his arrival in Cologne. "I believed that the influences of my evil star had ended with my imprisonment but I have again experienced its malignity with the unfortunate tertian fever which has attacked me." His evil star at least spared him continued residence near Vienna for a terrible plague was then making its way into the city. By August the emperor fled the capital and thousands were cut down as "the city was subjected to the worst scourge in its history." [1] Wilhelm might not have survived a sixth year in prison.

On July 5, 1679 he was greeted by relatives and friends in Cologne. The Belgian historian Huisman wrote that "the Elector of Cologne would not delay in falling once again under his imperious domination." Fürstenberg's achievement is fascinating and reveals his astuteness, but it was a process which took at least three years. "Domination" of the elector was neither easy, nor rapid, nor inevitable. As Franz lamented soon after his return from exile: "My brother and I cannot avoid being accused at every turn of being the sole authors and the unique origin of all his misfortunes." [2]

Max Heinrich was especially infuriated by charges that the Fürstenbergs had subjugated him since 1650. Their enemies, particularly the Neuburg family, wanted them permanently removed from the elector's entourage. Like the Fürstenbergs, the Neuburgs coveted the coadjutorship of Cologne with the right of future succession.[3] During the war, Max Heinrich finally declared in writing that he would dispense with the services of the Fürstenbergs in the future. Afterwards the elector could and did argue that Article 23 of the Nijmegen treaty nullified any agreement concerning their removal. Naturally, the question of the coadjutorship hovered over the scene. Knowing Louis XIV's repugnance toward the Neuburg family, Max Heinrich hoped to use the coadjutorship as political leverage in recovering towns in the Liège area occupied by French troops. More importantly, he sought French aid in subduing his rebellious subjects in Liège. Perhaps Louis XIV would forgive the 400,000-livre debt if a coadjutor suitable to France (i.e., a Fürstenberg) were elected. The Neuburgs would give Max Heinrich more than enough money to liquidate the debt if assured of succession, but that could entail French reprisals. Actually, Max Heinrich shunned the notion of having a coadjutor since he viewed it as the harbinger of his own death. Besides, his strong sense of family loyalty militated against candidates who were not Wittelsbachs. His tactic was thus to procrastinate and get what he could without committing himself irrevocably to any one course of action. Since French and Austrian troops still occupied his territory, procrastination approached statesmanship.

Determined to evade the elector's wrath, Wilhelm soon set off to see the king, confident that "the happiness of being in his presence will entirely dissipate the remains of chagrin which a long spell of suffering has produced in me and I even flatter myself to think that the contentment of my mind will affect my body and contribute not a little to the recovery of my health which is not yet very promising." Franz received the brunt of Max Heinrich's displeasure while Wilhelm received a warm welcome at the court. The royal gratitude hinted at by Pomponne was spelled out: he would be nominated for a cardinal's hat.[4]

Fürstenberg was not long under the care of Paris doctors before being pressed back into diplomatic service at the end of September, 1679. The Elector of Mainz had died and Wilhelm was asked to concert French opposition to the imperial delegation sent to influence the election. At the slightest hint of a bishop's illness dispatches criss-crossed Europe. When the bishop in question happened to be an elector of the Holy Roman Empire the reaction matched that of sharks upon the scent of blood. The attempt to influence elections was an accepted practice in the seventeenth century and the emperor sent a delegation to each important conclave, usually with the express purpose of supporting a given candidate. At Mainz the French candidate beseeched Fürstenberg not to visit him, for it would be equivalent to the kiss of death.[5] Wilhelm retired to

Frankfurt to look after alleged family affairs but not even his absence was enough to offset the victory of Anselm Franz von Ingelheim who leaned toward imperial rather than French interests. Quite apart from the results of the election, it was clear that many political fences had to be mended before Wilhelm's pre-war influence could be restored.

Though tormented by kidney stones, Wilhelm gradually resumed his former work habits, sending off long, detailed reports to France. At the end of November he spoke with imperial minister Stratmann, a temporary resident in Bonn whose unstated purpose was to forward Neuburg interests and drum up support for an imperial standing army. Stratmann told Fürstenberg that his trip to Mainz was most suspect; there were rumors of the sum of money at his disposal to influence the election. Wilhelm denied all such reports and said that his intention on setting out from Paris had been to go to Padua "so as to honor a vow which I had made to visit the tomb of St. Anthony as soon as the peace was made" and also to regulate certain family affairs with his brother and nephews. This delightful piece of obfuscation can hardly have convinced Stratmann but it indicated that Fürstenberg was returning to his old form. On the same day he asked the king what he was to do with the unused letters of exchange for 100,000 écus which he had taken with him to Mainz.[6]

Since Austrian troops had left Bonn on August 9 and the city was already occupied by Max Heinrich's soldiers, the French ended their occupation of the territory of Cologne. Louis XIV instructed his envoy to remind the elector periodically of the 400,000-livre debt and summoned Wilhelm to Paris for consultations. Fürstenberg left Cologne on December 26; he would not return for six months. Shortly after his departure, Dupré des Marets was replaced by La Vauguyon as envoy at Cologne. Louis requested "an exact account, and in detail, of everything which is said to you by the elector and particularly by the Bishop of Strasbourg, because being well informed of all the propositions which will be made to him it is necessary that I know by the reports which you give to me whether or not he reveals them to you. I can then judge what assurance I can take in his good offices [entremise]."[7] This dispatch was certainly drafted after briefings by Wilhelm in Paris. It was known that Franz resented the French refusal to sanction any bargaining with the Neuburgs concerning the coadjutorship. He was also jealous of Wilhelm's preferment at the French court and was suspicious of his activity there.

His suspicion was well founded. For all the fraternal affection Wilhelm may have felt, Franz impeded his career at Cologne. Wilhelm intended to manage his brother in such a way as to neutralize his potentially harmful influence before Max Heinrich and advance his own career and French interests in one stroke. Naturally, things were not so tidy. Wilhelm by no means considered all of Franz's claims and tactics to be "excessive" and gave special support to those which affected their family. Since he expected to succeed to many of the posts that Franz now held, it was to his interest to keep his brother's political and territorial prerogatives intact.

During Wilhelm's residence at court, he was in close contact with the new secretary of state for foreign affairs, Colbert de Croissy, who replaced Pomponne.[8] In March 1680 he submitted a memorandum to Croissy outlining the steps necessary to restore his former position of trust and power at Cologne and to restore French influence there. The principal items included the stipulation that coadjutors at Cologne and Liège be suitable to both France and the House of Bavaria; Max Heinrich would act in concert with the Elector of Bavaria in all affairs concerning the Empire; the 400,000-livre debt would be forgiven and the elector given a cash payment plus a yearly pension of 20,000 écus; Louis XIV would contribute to the rebuilding of the Citadel, the fortification overlooking the city of Liège which had been blown up by retreating French forces during the Dutch War; the French would aid in bringing the city of Liège back under Max Heinrich's control; and finally, to secure French (and Fürstenberg's) interests at the electoral court it would be necessary to gain two key ministers, Quentel and Widman, at respective annual pensions of 1200 and 800 écus a year, payable in advance.[9] At the end of his memorandum, Wilhelm stressed the importance of an atmosphere of calm. Accordingly, he stayed in Paris for a while "to bring order into his affairs." In the second week of June he was still in Paris and preparing for a swing through Alsace. Perhaps this relaxed pace did help establish the requisite "atmosphere of calm." In any case, it was convenient to depict extra weeks in Paris and a lackadaisical progress towards Cologne as elements in a far-reaching political strategy.

When he returned to Cologne on June 24 the scene was in some ways unchanged: Franz had been in bed for eight days due to the gout and was on a diet which "gave him a relief from his ordinary debauches."[10] Wilhelm made a fairly good start in insinuating himself into Max Heinrich's favor, in part because he did not at first broach any points desired by Franz or expected by the elector. According to La Vauguyon, the very word *coadjutor* produced in Max Heinrich "the same shivers as those produced in the Bishop of Strasbourg at the sight of a cat, the one animal in the world which he fears most." Wilhelm told the elector that Louis

XIV wanted a report on the grievances that existed between Franz and Max Heinrich. If necessary, Wilhelm would bring Franz into line. "If this course fails," he said, "I shall inform His Majesty so that he himself might interpose his authority to put him on a better path, which seemed to please the elector no end." However, Wilhelm added, "His Majesty believed it would redound to his *gloire* and his reputation to give full protection to my brother against everyone if he found that basically his conduct was not such as would reasonably draw the discontent and the ill will of the elector upon him." That provoked Max Heinrich into something close to a fit. He recognized in this talk the work of Franz, "who wanted to persuade His Majesty that he was not receiving good treatment because of his devotion to His Majesty and not because his bad conduct gave grounds for such treatment . . . " [11]

This kind of spat had long since become stylized. The elector wanted to make his independence clear (the possible nomination of a Neuburg as coadjutor was mentioned); Wilhelm believed that French money would make him tractable. Threats to name a Neuburg coadjutor were viewed as rhetoric, a means to move the wheels a bit at the French court. Nor was Wilhelm wrong in these assumptions. As much as he might fulminate against Franz, the elector knew that he could not summarily dismiss him without provoking the "displeasure" of the king. During this same interview, Wilhelm proposed that he meet with Quentel and Widman to determine what might reasonably be asked of Louis XIV. Max Heinrich quickly agreed, the more so since French "reunion" gains had already begun to affect his territories.

The reunion policy was still another device to expand the frontiers of France. Clauses in the treaties of Münster and Nijmegen awarded towns and territories to France "along with their dependencies." The obscurity of the term *dependencies* left ample room for interpretation. In practice this amounted to a rigorous search in archives to determine the extent of a given city or territory and thereby to determine just what had been ceded to France. In an age where there were few, if any, sharply defined frontiers, litigation could become very complicated, especially since many of the former boundaries had long since passed out of use. Since the early medieval period, European princes had usually avoided treaties that involved clear limits, preferring to extend control and sovereignty via judicial interpretation and/or military might. The kingdom of France had expanded from the Ile de France partly as a result of what may be called the "reunion mentality," a legalistic attitude of mind which served the aggrandizement of the monarchy. The principle of reunions goes back at least as far as 1633 with the creation of the Parlement of Metz by Richelieu.[12] French judges determined what belonged to France and French troops then occupied the territory.

Reunion decrees soon affected many German princes in the western Empire, including Max Heinrich as sovereign of the territory of Liège. Naturally the possibility of French leniency might be used to good effect by Wilhelm in discussions with his German master. During the summer Fürstenberg steadily consolidated his position. As planned, he held discussions with Widman and Quentel, interviewing each man separately and holding out the prospect of a pension. (Quentel was soon telling Widman that Wilhelm had become more reserved towards him than before!) Since annual *gratifications* seemed to be the "most persuasive arguments" for Max Heinrich and his aides, Wilhelm asked Louis XIV for 80–100,000 livres in letters of exchange to prove that money was available for subsidies. The king immediately sent the letters of exchange and authorized *gratifications* of 1200 écus for Quentel and 800 écus for Widman.[13]

These lures and assurances were in Wilhelm's hands at the beginning of August but only in October could he report a relative success. From the evidence, it appears that Widman tentatively accepted and then drew back after reflection; Quentel seemed well-disposed from the outset. To comprehend Wilhelm's handling of the matter, we must refer to a letter which he sent to Paris when he believed that both men had been landed:

So that there will be no misunderstanding in all this affair I judge it necessary to make it known to Your Majesty that while these two men surmise quite well that I do not advance or do anything without the participation and the express command of Your Majesty, they would never have accepted these pensions if I had not assured them that it was I who furnished this sum to them. And this because on the one hand it obliges them not to leave the service of the elector and on the other hand that they may second and support through their opinions and good offices before the elector all those things which I would be able to insinuate to him by myself or through others concerning affairs dealing with the interests of the Church, or Your Majesty, or my brother, above all with regard to the coadjutorship of Cologne.[14]

That Widman and Quentel surmised that Wilhelm did nothing without the express command of Louis XIV is questionable, but they probably did (or would) balk at direct ties with France, especially to avoid possible Austrian charges. Wilhelm's prison sentence was still a fresh memory for all concerned. What is clear is that Fürstenberg would be in direct control; in his absence the French envoy could not automatically expect cooperation from men receiving money from the French treasury.

Quentel accepted the offer of 1200 écus with the assurance of payment a year in advance. Wilhelm described him as "a man of strong common sense, adroit and bold in taking resolutions, not less prompt than firm and as wicked and dangerous an enemy as he is a good friend to those to whom he is obligated." [15] Quentel told Wilhelm that the surest way for him to retain the confidence of Max Heinrich was to seem to be hostile to Franz and friendly towards the Neuburg faction. But, added Wilhelm, "he would never do anything without my knowledge and my consent which is, in my opinion, all that one can desire of him in availing oneself of his services." Widman finally declared "that he had never accepted a *gratification* from anyone before he had rendered the service for which it was given, but that he would not fail to be obligated to me to the limits of good will." [16] Wilhelm must have taken this flowery language with more than a grain of salt (surely the French ministers did) but he claimed to be satisfied with the results he had obtained. And well he might be, since reaction to the reunions had begun to intensify.

Resentment over the reunion decrees led the deputies at Regensburg to send a list of grievances to Louis XIV on August 5, 1680. At the same time, a campaign to arm the Empire was launched from Vienna. In this atmosphere, and amid rumors that the French had designs on Strasbourg and Cologne, the king pledged to send a delegation to negotiate with the Empire. On October 4 Wilhelm submitted a memorandum dealing with the overall relationship between France and the Germanies.[17] In many respects, it is the best available statement of his political beliefs. He averred that France had more to fear from the Germanies than from the rest of Europe put together. So far, this fear had been checked by fomenting jealousy and defiance of the emperor among the German princes. A more positive approach was needed. Wouldn't this jealousy and defiance be used to better advantage "by ensuring the maintenance of liberty and sovereignty of the princes and states, however imaginary and chimerical they may be, rather than in depriving them of the rights and prerogatives which they have peacefully enjoyed for centuries? For in the latter instance they would be forced in one way or other to blindly throw themselves into the hands of the emperor and all the enemies of France in the hope of thus maintaining what belongs to them." He counselled persuasion, not brute force, noting that the Romans had treated subjugated peoples better than they had been treated before.

These precepts were akin to those of Mazarin and Lionne. Since Wilhelm was clearly on the side of French influence, even sovereignty, the debate hinged less on ends than on means. He urged Louis to conserve those German "liberties" for which his two predecessors "had spent so much money and spilled so much French blood." German princes "should not be more maltreated under the shadow of the blooming lilies of France than under that of a languishing eagle of Austria and to this end His Majesty should allow the princes and states of Germany to enjoy, with regard to the territory which he claims is presently under his sovereignty, the same rights . . . they had hitherto enjoyed with reason and justice under the emperors." He allowed that so long as the local population were in no way molested the king might, at his own expense, build fortresses and set up garrisons for the greater surety of his kingdom. In addition to retaining the right to levy the *taille* on their lands (the German *Collectation*), princes should be permitted to collect two thirds of the extraordinary impositions levied in their lands in time of peace, with one third going to the king. In time of war against Germans the proportion would be reversed, provided that the princes contributed neither directly nor indirectly to the cause of war, in which case they would be treated as felonious vassals. Wilhelm argued, chiefly with reference to Alsace, that the princes and estates of Germany "which are presently interested in the affair, and all others, will prefer to consent that the king remain sovereign in the territory where he is already so established rather than enter into a new war in which the emperor, under pretext of defending them, will maintain on the Rhine frontiers a body of troops which will result in his being in a position to do what he wants." If, because of some change or unforeseen trouble, the Germanies did band together against France, she would have less to fear if neighboring princes who were French vassals were well-treated instead of being entirely oppressed and annihilated. If all of his conditions were well observed, he continued, the princes and estates would have a great consideration for France and a great contempt for the emperor. Whenever they had need of any assistance or protection, they would address themselves to the king rather than to the emperor. Lastly, when the emperor died, it would be most likely that the imperial crown would be placed on the head of the king or on that of his successors without any contradiction, thereby rendering "His Majesty the sole arbiter of Europe, the protector of the oppressed, the true support of orthodox religion and the scourge of infidels which is the crowning point and the highest degree of *gloire* that a great monarch and Christian prince like the king may be able to wish for."

Several of Wilhelm's deep-set convictions were revealed in this memorandum. One was the flat assumption that state borders and legal definitions meant little to princes and estates when compared to the prospect of peace and the assurance of rights and revenues. What was lacking was a clear idea of French objectives. Wilhelm wanted Louis XIV to woo German princes away from as many imperial ties as possible. Perhaps he viewed his own career as the precursor of future developments in the Empire. The use of the word "contempt" with reference to the emperor is hardly surprising. The fear and mistrust of Austria shared especially by princes and estates in the western Empire were intensified in Wilhelm and doubtless spurred his activity in French service. Of special interest was his advocacy of Counter-Reformation policies toward "infidels." Despite his strong bent for political accommodation, he was assuredly not in favor of religious coexistence if it could be avoided.

The course of action suggested by Wilhelm must also be examined from the vantage point of Fürstenberg family interests. Reunion decrees of March 22 and August 9, 1680, brought the territory of the bishopric of Strasbourg under French sovereignty and the armorial bearings of France were affixed to the main door of the episcopal palace at Saverne as a symbol of this formal possession. Although the king accorded Franz Egon a handsome pension of 60,000 livres in April, 1680, partly to indemnify him for his losses in Alsace, it was by no means considered a "closed case" by the Fürstenbergs. Once a bishopric lost its ties to the Empire, its territorial superiority was lost. Franz, fearing "that he would be exposed to the laughter and mockery of his numerous enemies," [18] urged that he be able to retain all the rights which he enjoyed as a vassal of the Empire.

By the autumn of 1680 the French had achieved dominion over all of Alsace except Strasbourg. Wilhelm's memorandum concerned the ways in which this dominion might be made more palatable. In this context, the suggestion which he sent off the next day, October 5, 1680, is of the highest interest: he proposed the assimilation of the Imperial Free City of Strasbourg! His reflections on the reunion decrees were in part occasioned by the existence of mutual defense pacts between German states; this, together with his fear of an imperial enclave within Alsace, led him to wonder

if Your Majesty would be able to find it agreeable that one secretly [*soubs main*] bring the city of Strasbourg to recognize Your Majesty as its sovereign and its only master and protector and to render him faith and homage as it has hitherto done to the emperors, allowing it to enjoy under his domination the same rights, privileges, exemptions and prerogatives which it has enjoyed till now, above all provided that Your Majesty may have built a good citadel between the Rhine bridge and the city and have the village of DeKellau fortified . . . In my opinion this would be the most important and the most glorious affair which Your Majesty could ever accomplish for himself and for his crown and I am very much mistaken if the imperial court itself would not be disposed to sanction this if in so doing it is allowed to have Freiburg. Finally, all that and several other things would appear to me very possible to effect provided that everyone is relieved of this terrible mistrust in which they are living. Namely, the belief that one wants to enslave them.[19]

As in his reasoning concerning the reunited territories, Wilhelm was gambling on the passive acquiescence of the city if it were assured that its lot would not be materially changed. As far back as January 1671 in a letter to Lionne, Wilhelm revealed his overtures to several members of the Strasbourg magistracy concerning a possible transfer of the cathedral of Strasbourg into Catholic hands. If this happened, he said, he was confident of being elected coadjutor by the cathedral chapter and thus assured of succeeding his brother, "which would be of considerable consequence for a man who isn't better off in his affairs than you know me to be." (The only effect of this transfer which he mentions is his being elected coadjutor!) He believed that the magistrates of the city would be malleable if such a transfer prevented the king from diverting Strasbourg's commerce to other cities in Alsace. Now, ten years later, he proposed that the city itself be brought under French sovereignty and predicted that the burghers would be tractable if given certain assurances. The king, however, declined to accept his proposal: "I do not judge it apropos that you make any attempt to have the city of Strasbourg submit to me. For the security of my states it suffices that the forts which would allow an enemy army to pass into Alsace remain razed and it is not apropos to undertake any innovation respecting this city which may alarm the princes of the Empire." Within a year, Strasbourg would be annexed by Louis XIV. Already its seizure must have been urged in the French council and probably without the propitiatory offer of Freiburg or any other city. For the moment the king bided his time. The Fürstenbergs, however, did not enjoy the luxury of such Olympian detachment. Territorial and financial matters prompted Franz to go to the French court late in 1680 to plead his case in person.[20]

Meanwhile, Max Heinrich continued his jeremiads on the theme of the house of Fürstenberg's being "the cause of all his misery" and once, before the French envoy, wondered whether Wilhelm weren't at his court "on the part of His Majesty." This suspicion is the more interesting since it came after Wilhelm's display of the letters of exchange from Paris. His chances of overcoming this hostility, however, were facilitated by

Franz's absence. Wilhelm courted Max Heinrich assiduously, attempting to convince him that there were no tight bonds between the Egonites. "I think I have remedied this by means of several insinuations which were not disagreeable to the elector, so much so that I hope with the aid of Messieurs Quentel and Widman to be able to inform Your Majesty soon up to what point one will be able to engage this prince and to trust in him." [21] The insinuations of which Wilhelm spoke reveal his distancing himself from Franz, a process which his brother already sensed.

At the end of November, Fürstenberg drew up a balance sheet concerning "the state of Max Heinrich's spirit." The fixed points were a firm resolution never to repose confidence in Franz and to prevent his succeeding him; not to allow a coadjutor for Cologne, unless it be his Bavarian cousin or someone else agreeable to Louis XIV, any exception to result from Franz's misbehavior; to remain on good terms with all his neighbors; and finally, to allow the entire territory and city of Liège to be in a state of upheaval rather than return there before rebuilding the Citadel. [22]

This balance sheet is unexceptionable apart from the section on Liège. Here he transmits quite vividly the desire for revenge which appears to have consumed the elector. Franzen rightly asserts that "Liège had become Max Heinrich's destiny and doom; here lies the key to an understanding of Cologne politics in the seventeenth century." [23] Here, too, is the key to an understanding of Wilhelm von Fürstenberg's return to power in Cologne. By making Wilhelm indispensable to any future settlement of the Liège dispute, Louis XIV hoped to use him and his position as a salient in Rhineland politics.

At the beginning of 1681 the rift between Wilhelm and Franz became more apparent. In February, Wilhelm received the king's permission to talk with his brother in Paris but pressing obligations kept him from arriving there until April 10. Once arrived, he bombarded Louis and Croissy with memorandums. He noted that the campaign of vilification waged by their opposition at Cologne had to be exposed and asked Louis to write a letter to Max Heinrich. (As we shall see, this would produce interesting results.) Regarding the coadjutorship, he claimed that his brother was opposed by many canons in the chapter as well as by the elector. Accordingly, he asked that Louis order Franz to follow his advice on the coadjutorship as well as on family matters. In a separate note to Croissy, he requested these matters be kept secret from Franz, adding that several Cologne canons had begged him to stay near if Franz ever did become elector. While we have no definite proof, the king probably did ask Franz to "cooperate" with Wilhelm. And there is the likelihood that Franz was more amenable than might have been believed in January. Why? The answer probably lies in the discussions which took place concerning the fate of Strasbourg. Clearly, the seizure of the city was envisaged, for when Franz heard about the annexation in September 1681 he wrote to Louvois: "When I had the honor of taking leave of you, you had the goodness to promise to alert me of these affairs so that I might be able to be in Strasbourg with two mules laden with rosaries, as the Dutch have written in their gazettes." [24] Franz thus had hopes of finding solace at Strasbourg for his losses in Alsace and indignities at Cologne.

While in France, the Fürstenbergs followed the emperor's attempt to create an imperial army under his personal control. This soon bogged down amidst refusals to cooperate or demands for power (including the selection of a leading prince, such as Brandenburg or Bavaria, as head of any projected imperial army) which in no way served Vienna's quest for control. In April a new scheme to achieve an Imperial War Constitution was unveiled: the army would be controlled by representatives of the various states of the Empire. A force of 60,000 men was envisioned, but this figure was soon pared down to 40,000 and ultimately would lead to few practical results.[25] Leopold's defeat was viewed as a victory for France; it could not have displeased Wilhelm and Franz.

One of the purposes of Franz's trip had been to secure a greater subsidy from the king; in August 1681 he was granted a four-year pension at 80,000 livres annually. For his part, Wilhelm claimed that of the 63,000 livres income which he received annually, he had only 36,000 after obligatory deductions were made. These included the repayment of loans, repair costs on his benefices, subsidies to his nephews, subsidies to two men injured at the time of his capture in 1674, and a subsidy to a man in Vienna who helped him during his stay in prison and who was treated prejudicially on that account—a total of 27,400 livres. He also had to feed upwards of thirty people in Cologne, outside of his staff, especially at times when Franz was not in the city. Wilhelm made three requests. First, that the king dispense with an envoy at Cologne after the departure of La Vauguyon and instead give the work and money to himself. (He did not indicate if this would entail any change in his position at the electoral court.) Louis did not honor that request; instructions for the next envoy, Tambonneau, were drawn up on May 29, 1681. Wilhelm next urged the king to subsidize two of his nephews and so discharge him from the obligation. Finally, he asked for assistance in acquiring property convenient to Liège and Cologne where he could live at less expense.[26] Already on more than one occasion he had spoken longingly of handling the elector's administration at Liège, of being chosen coadjutor and then bishop there. These desires were doubtless influenced by his friend, the Countess von der Mark, who urged Wilhelm to stay in the Liège area where she felt more at home. Perhaps Fürstenberg was scheming to get money from the king for property near Liège with the expected condition that he remain in Cologne. In any event, in August 1681 Louis accorded him an annual pension of 20,000 livres for the next four years.[27]

Back in Cologne, La Vauguyon confronted Max Heinrich with the "calumny" against the Fürstenbergs. He wanted their accusers to be unmasked and their malice exposed. Gradually, the envoy observed "a great change come over [the elector's] face, followed by a rage so violent that I hardly had time to finish speaking. Since in his emotion he raised the level of his voice high enough to be heard by his domestics, I brought mine to as high a pitch so that nobody would believe that I had allowed myself to be mastered, being sustained by my character and by the good reasons which were furnished by Your Majesty." After the histrionics, the two men resumed their discussions. La Vauguyon stated that both brothers were zealous to serve his interest, indeed that Wilhelm's conduct "was that of disinterested service." The elector agreed "that Prince Wilhelm was wiser, finer than his brother and that his manner of acting had as its end the exclusion of the House of Palatine from ecclesiastical dignities." La Vauguyon replied that "it was not surprising to find that people were ambitious." After a while the elector asked pardon for having exploded and said "it was to be hoped that the maintenance of peace were as easy to assure as his reconciliation with Prince Wilhelm."[28]

The Egonites spent two months in Alsace settling administrative and family affairs and aiding the many canons in the Strasbourg chapter who conjointly were canons at Cologne. The Strasbourg capitularies feared that French sovereign rights over the lands of the bishopric would infringe on privileges hitherto enjoyed under imperial jurisdiction; they petitioned with their bishop to obtain the same rights as were accorded to the nobility of lower Alsace. Wilhelm supported this request, observing that royal benevolence would have a marvelous effect on the ecclesiastical princes in the Germanies who were continually ill at ease for lack of protection and "who would not find the sovereignty of Your Majesty abhorrent if they were assured that under your domination they might keep the same privileges that they possessed under the Empire, that they need not fear that after a short time *tailles* and other impositions would be levied on their subjects, resulting in their being no longer able to draw anything from them themselves." Here was one of the permanent sources of friction between the French crown and the nobility and land-owning bourgeoisie—who would get the peasants' money? What German princes needed was a clear statement of how much tax the king would require in times of peace and war, what kinds of fortifications and winter quarters for his troops he might demand. In exchange for these assurances, he said, German princes would be willing to make the same declarations of homage to the French crown as did Franz Egon and the cathedral chapter of Strasbourg. He was confident that "the city of Strasbourg and several other princes and states would follow the example of the bishopric of Strasbourg, preferring to submit willingly to Your Majesty rather than to await the protection of the emperor and of the Empire and the uncertain outcome of the conferences [at Frankfurt] which will be held on the differences which now exist between Your Majesty and the Empire." [29]

To argue for the rights of the cathedral chapter of Strasbourg was one thing; to speculate on the willingness of the city of Strasbourg to accept French sovereignty was, in the circumstances, somewhat disingenuous. For in May 1681 an imperial diplomat, Baron de Mercy, arrived in Strasbourg, awakening the suspicions of Louvois who ordered close surveillance of his activities. In the same letter in which he pleaded for royal understanding of the chapter's plight, Wilhelm reported the possibility of a 4,000-man imperial garrison being stationed in Strasbourg.[30] Mercy's mission, together with rumblings in the Empire over defensive alliances, may well have decided the king and his ministers on their final plans for the seizure of Strasbourg.

While the Fürstenbergs were preoccupied with the problems of Alsace, a storm was brewing in Liège. The re-establishment of a hated customs duty provided a clear focus for opposition to the elector's rule. Tax offices were invaded, tax officials threatened and government agents who approved of the tax banished. When Max Heinrich sent troops into the territory, the city leaders created an army for themselves. The escalation was rapid and the flash point came when three hundred of the elector's troops seized the little town of Visé, close by Liège, with the aim of blocking navigation on the Meuse. Troops from Liège besieged the town and after twelve hours it capitulated. The German soldiers were freed but partisans of the elector in the town were arrested and brought back to Liège as hostages. These dramatic events divided the mutinous city into factions. The influential cathedral chapter of Liège allied with the local magistrates in opposition to the elector, partly because he suspended justice in the city without consulting the chapter as required by the constitution. In an increasingly radicalized atmosphere, the *bourgmestres* resigned and new ones were elected without permission. The new leaders staunchly opposed the elector: Liège was in open revolt.[31]

Frustrated in his rather feeble attempt to quell the revolt by force, Max Heinrich knew that foreign aid was needed and that the most likely source was France. Small wonder, then, that he even asked Franz Egon for an opinion on the Liège question.[32] Max Heinrich was evidently willing to go to any length to win French aid! The dilemma of Liège would bring Wilhelm von Fürstenberg back into power at Cologne.

VI
RETURN TO POWER
AUGUST 1681 TO NOVEMBER 1682

THE NEED to reconcile Max Heinrich's desires with Louis XIV's convenience taxed Fürstenberg's ingenuity and their patience. Louis knew
that the Liège revolt could not be smothered without outside aid but
postponed action until he nailed down his reunion conquests. His tactic
was to temporize, kindling hopes of future assistance subject to cooperation from the elector. The constants in this game were Louis's determination to prevent the emperor from arbitrating the quarrel and his insistence
that Fürstenberg handle the negotiations for Cologne. The king counted
on natural difficulties and on Wilhelm's good offices in slowing down the
negotiations if they did not suit French plans.

During August and early September Wilhelm consulted with all parties
in the dispute, even managing to combine politics with the mineral waters
at Spa. Preliminary soundings were successful and Liège sent a delegation
to Cologne in mid-September. Max Heinrich's proposals, however, were
judged too harsh; the delegates were recalled.[1] This development improved Wilhelm's position before the elector, who, as usual, needed advice. Indeed, Wilhelm reported the prospect of enjoying more credit at
Max Heinrich's court than ever before "*if* he can be extricated from his
present embarrassment by Your Majesty without being obliged to make
a coadjutor, and in so presenting the things that he would resolve to cede
to Your Majesty that neither the pope nor the chapter of Liège could
reproach him with having dismembered a considerable piece from his
bishopric." To offset the elector's disposition to believe that the French
would assist him against Liège without his offering anything in return,
Wilhelm forwarded the draft of a letter for Louis's consideration, a letter
which Louis might write to Fürstenberg, who, in turn, would show it to
Max Heinrich. After expressing appreciation that the elector no longer
listened to calumny spread about Wilhelm and had entrusted the Liège
negotiations to him, the king would be pleased to see Wilhelm continue
this work but "from the response which this prince has given me on those
things which my zeal and my affection for his interests and those of his
church have led me to propose to him, it is clear that there is still too

much incertitude and irresolution in his spirit to allow Your Majesty to neglect the much more considerable advantages which could accrue to his crown somewhere else." [2]

Before this dispatch reached the king, momentous news arrived from Alsace: Strasbourg was annexed. Some 30,000 troops accompanied by Louvois had surrounded the city and threatened its destruction if it did not surrender forthwith. The magistrates capitulated on September 30, 1681. French sovereignty was acknowledged, the magnificent cathedral was turned over to the Catholics, the French installed a garrison and manned the fortifications. In other respects, the city functioned as before. At the same time, French troops occupied the fortress of Casale in northern Italy with the collusion of the Duke of Mantua and so controlled the main route between the Piedmont and Milan. Still another link in the strategic frontier had been forged; the tentacles were reaching farther and farther. [3]

The seizure of Strasbourg was a meticulously planned and most secretive operation. From the evidence, it appears that the Fürstenbergs did not have advance knowledge of the timing of the action. Louvois's note to Franz Egon was terse: "Just a word to send you my compliments on the submission of this city to the king, which will permanently assure you of enjoying the revenues of your bishopric and will give you the satisfaction of performing your functions in a Church from which the Catholics were chased more than a hundred years ago." In reply Franz said he expected to be forewarned so as to be on hand "with two mules laden with rosaries as the Dutch have written in their gazettes. But I believe, Monsieur, that you were certain that your presence with 30,000 men and forty or fifty cannons would convert this people far better than I could have with my mules and rosaries." He added that couriers had been sent out to fetch Wilhelm back to Cologne. [4] On his arrival there, he witnessed the dramatic effect which the seizure of Strasbourg had produced. As Tambonneau described it, "The thunderclap which Your Majesty has just sent against the city of Strasbourg has thrown the inhabitants of Cologne into such a state of fright that there is no way of reassuring them. Every morning, upon opening the city doors, they expect to find the fields covered with Your Majesty's troops. . . . They look upon you, Sire, as the absolute master of the entire extent of the Rhine and soon of all that he may wish to join to France from Germany." The effect was not lost on Max Heinrich, who probably dreamed of French aid in subduing Cologne as well as Liège. But obviously French troops could find employment in many European theaters, not necessarily in Liège. The elector eagerly drafted a set of requests and promises regarding Liège for Louis XIV's approval.[5]

Wilhelm and Franz wanted to be in Strasbourg as rapidly as possible, the more so since the king and a magnificent entourage were expected there. By October 13 Wilhelm was at Saverne, awaiting the arrival of the royal party. Franz, afflicted by gout, made much slower progress, all the while wondering if Louis would accord him the revenues from the cathedral of Strasbourg and all which had been usurped from it by the city and by the Lutherans. At that moment, Franz's role in the ceremonies at Strasbourg was being debated in the French camp. The initial plan was to have the cathedral "reconciled" to Catholicism during services presided over by Cardinal Bouillon with Abbé Fléchier preaching the sermon in the presence of the king and his entourage. But since this would have been a grievous affront to the bishop, the plan was changed to allow him to perform the official ceremonies before the entrance of Louis XIV into the city. Franz took steps to embellish his day of triumph. He asked Louvois to arrange for the governor of Strasbourg "to receive me with a bit of éclat. . . . And would His Majesty graciously permit me to have the honor of appearing before him . . . at Benfeld and of returning back here [Ehrenstein] in the evening before entering with him into Strasbourg on the following day." Louvois promised "all the éclat which you could desire and His Majesty . . . will see you with pleasure at Benfeld."[6]

The festive entry of Franz Egon into Strasbourg on October 20 was one of the most colorful events in the history of the city. Whether there was joy, or bitterness, or simple curiosity in the eyes of the thousands of spectators is another story—but éclat there was in full measure.[7] The procession included cavalry officers with swords unsheathed, brightly caparisoned horses and mules, exquisitely decorated coaches and carriages, members of the cathedral chapter and vassals of the bishopric, each vying with the other in the splendor of their costumes. Franz and Wilhelm together with their relatives rode in state, surrounded by squadrons of their own body guards and cuirassiers du roi. The sound of music and trumpets and drums filled the air: it was a scene to remember. When the cortege reached the cathedral square, twenty cannon shots reverberated above the din. Without descending from his carriage, Franz Egon proceeded directly to the Hôtel de Bade; the Margrave of Baden was married to Franz's sister and they offered him hospitality during his sojourn in the city. There Franz received homage from deputations including French military officers and representatives from the magistracy of Strasbourg. The Strasbourg contingent had been ordered to attend by the French and their presence amounted to a loss of face, especially when Chamilly arrived and asked Franz for the password for the day, a clear sign that the bishop was at that moment master of the city.

Ceremonies of reconsecration took place on the following day. Because of his gout, Franz was carried on a chair held by four gentlemen. After a brief prayer before the cathedral, his entrance into the superb church was the cue for a flood of organ music and the song of choirs; the transformation back to the Catholic cult had begun. After a ceremony which lasted for two hours, the Bishop of Strasbourg blessed the crowd of people who knelt at his passage. At the Hôtel de Bade, the Strasbourg deputies were again in attendance, this time offering symbolic presents of wine, fish, and grain. On the previous day they arrived with empty hands; in the interim, the French authorities exacted this new obeisance. It was another small triumph for Franz to savor.

The next day he went to Benfeld to see the king. According to the Marquis de Sourches, Louis lauded Franz for "the zeal which he had always had for the interests of France and for the services which he rendered her during the last war." [8] These were suitable words for the occasion, but the fine rhetoric must have been accompanied by a host of *arrière-pensées*! During Franz's absence from Strasbourg, the deputies arrived for a third time and were greeted by Wilhelm, who had a long conversation with them. It was the eve of the greatest of the events in these crowded days: the arrival of Louis XIV into the capital of Alsace.

La Magnifique Entrée of the Sun King into Strasbourg on October 23 was one of the glorious moments of his reign, a scene of almost legendary pageantry. Before the main door of the city more than 200 pieces of cannon were set up, with successive salvos fired as the royal cortege entered the portals. The magistrates greeted him, Chamilly presented the keys of the city, the sovereignty of the King of France over Strasbourg was solemnly proclaimed. The bell-towers of every church throbbed their greeting to the triumphant monarch as companies of cavalry and musketeers, falconers with falcons in hand, the elaborate coaches and carriages of the nobility and members of the royal family paraded through the city— in all a profusion of luxury worthy of a fairy tale.

After spending the night at a sumptuous private home in the city, the king participated in the solemn *Te Deum* at the cathedral on October 24. There preceded him an even greater number of clergy than had taken part in the reconsecration ceremonies three days before. Franz Egon was once again carried in a chair and dressed in his episcopal robes, resplendent with pearls and diamonds. Inside the church, he delivered his famous oration: "It is at this time, Sire, seeing this temple restored to me by your royal hands, a temple from which I and my predecessors have been so long exiled by the violence of heretical ministers, it is now that I can say, with the good man Simeon, that I will from this time forward await the end of my days in peace and when it shall please God to call me to Himself, I will be able to leave this world with much consolation." [9] His words have remained one of the most famous salutations to Louis XIV. They were the heartfelt words of a fervent Catholic whose thoughts and actions in religious matters were those of the Counter-Reformation; they were spoken by an old and embittered man who had been accorded a moment of *gloire* and who was expressing his gratitude. Organ music filled the vast cathedral, the *Te Deum* was sung, and as the cortege filed out the mixture of drums, trumpets, organs and all other instruments was deafening.

Louis XIV remained in Strasbourg for several days, receiving visitors and inspecting the fortifications and the surrounding countryside. A veritable legion of German princes descended on the city to pay their respects to him. Naturally, the Fürstenbergs were in the center of this throng, serving as intermediaries, discussing politics, arranging for introductions. It was a sweet triumph for Franz and Wilhelm before their family and compatriots. Their power and prestige in Alsace was never higher. This was further underlined on October 27 when they played host to the king and his party at the episcopal chateau at Saverne. [10]

The sojourn of the king and his ministers in Alsace afforded a perfect opportunity for political conversation. Franz and Wilhelm worked together on questions pertaining to the bishopric of Strasbourg but Franz was not consulted on Liège. The October 7 memorandum on Liège which Max Heinrich had approved was discussed by Wilhelm and Croissy. From these conferences there emerged the skeleton of a treaty which was communicated to Tambonneau in the form of a second set of instructions. [11]

In the draft treaty Louis XIV pledged to aid the elector to reestablish his authority in Liège, to contribute 200,000 livres for the building of the Citadel, and to ensure Max Heinrich's right to have a garrison in the city. Incursions made by the Metz reunions (which affected the territory of Liège) would not extend beyond those of September 1681, the entire question to be adjudicated at Frankfurt. The king would accept the neutrality of Liège if the emperor, the Spanish, and the Dutch pledged that the neutrality would be observed. A governor well-disposed to French interests was also expected. In return, and before any French aid was given, the elector and the chapter of Liège would allow France to keep the cities and chateaux of Bouillon and Dinant and the city of Thuin for thirty years. Only Wilhelm von Furstenberg would be acceptable as coadjutor at Liège.[12] The remission of the 400,000-livre debt would be reserved until the king was assured of a successor at Cologne agreeable to him. Max Heinrich would receive the same pension as in the past, 20,000 écus annually. Other items included the resolution of Cologne-Dutch territorial squabbles as well as the possible commitment of the elector to vote for a French-backed candidate at the future election of a King of the Romans. All in all, the conditions amounted to a minefield of difficulties; the king counted on Prince Wilhelm to string out the negotiations until the time was ripe.

Tambonneau reviewed these terms with Max Heinrich before the Fürstenbergs arrived on November 24, 1681. Wilhelm received the first audience, assured the elector that Franz would learn nothing pertaining to Liège, and was entrusted with the Liège negotiations. The elector was obviously impatient to achieve a satisfactory settlement and hoped that Wilhelm might travel to Versailles before the end of 1681 "with full power to settle and finish everything with the king."[13] His eagerness was the more understandable in the light of reunion decrees which already violated the territory of Liège and were affecting the Spanish Netherlands.

In the larger picture, these developments, together with the annexation of Strasbourg and Casale, further polarized the politics of Europe. William III of Orange never slackened his efforts to achieve a political and military network against the threat of French arms; he probably hated Louis XIV as much as Hannibal despised Rome. His political activity in the Germanies after the Dutch War was handled by Georg Friedrich von Waldeck, a professional military man with much political and diplomatic experience. In 1679 Waldeck negotiated an alliance with Münster and Hesse-Cassel which was intended to defend the Nijmegen treaty provisions: this humble beginning was the germ of a more far-reaching coalition against the Sun King. At the end of 1681 Waldeck added Fulda, Darmstadt, Würzburg, Bamberg, Gotha, and the Circle of Franconia to his embryonic coalition against France. In June 1682 he succeeded in achieving the so-called Laxenburg Alliance, signed by Austria, the Circle of Franconia, and the Circle of the Upper Rhine. These powers committed themselves to furnish a force of 30,000 men for the defense of the Upper Rhine between Basel and Philippsburg, and another 30,000 between Philippsburg and Coblenz. Efforts to unite Bavaria to this defensive pact were unsuccessful, but the elector would sign a separate defensive treaty with Leopold in January, 1683.[14]

While these treaties may have looked impressive in the dispatch box, their real effectiveness was minimal. French diplomacy countered each move by assiduously courting the party of accommodation, to use Professor Pagès's phrase. The Elector of Mainz was brought into the French alliance system via an outright grant of 40,000 écus and an annual pension of 20,000 écus. The Elector Palatine received a compensation of 600,000 livres for reunion territory plus an annual pension of 200,000 livres. Louis was clearly determined to hold on to his acquisitions at all costs. On January 22, 1682, another treaty was concluded with the Elector of Brandenburg; Louis XIV said he would engage in no more reunions and would only keep the territory in his possession at the time his envoys left for Frankfurt.[15] This, however, was a familiar theme in recent diplomatic correspondence and was not a major concession. Strasbourg was not considered a reunion activity.

Louis XIV next planned to attack the city of Luxembourg but his ambassador to London reported that the Dutch would fulfill their treaty obligations with Spain and send 8,000 men to Luxembourg in case of an attack there. The United Provinces were also attempting to bring England into this venture at a time when Charles II could not easily postpone the convocation of Parliament. In these circumstances, Louis declared that since Vienna would doubtless be besieged by the Turks that very year, he resolved "to prefer the welfare of Christendom to all considerations which might lead him to achieve the cession of Luxembourg and its dependencies for the equivalent of his claims in Flanders." To this high-minded statement we must add the dispatch which he sent to his ambassador in Turkey: "I want to inform you that while I have led people to believe that my recent resolution has no other motive than that of leaving the emperor and his followers free to defend themselves against the Turks, nevertheless, my chief intention has been to be able to use all my forces against the emperor and the German princes who will not accept my propositions."[16]

Before the French relaxed their pressure on Luxembourg, Max Heinrich wanted to conclude a treaty to ensure that his territory was not nibbled away. But the prospect of such a treaty was chimerical at that time. There was no chance of a political settlement, still less chance of territorial cessions being approved in Liège, and no likelihood of French military intervention. There was, of course, another reason for his anxiety: nine years had elapsed since his last French subsidy. To move the wheels a bit he reported that the Neuburgs and the emperor combined promised to give him 600,000 livres if a Neuburg prince were made coadjutor at Cologne. Thus he could settle the French debt with money to spare and also prevent the cathedral chapter from impounding his inheritance after his death if the debt were left unpaid. While this offer may have been a real one, Max Heinrich told Wilhelm that he would

only consider a Bavarian prince as coadjutor at Cologne, with Liège held
in reserve for Fürstenberg. Wilhelm informed the king that plans to give
the coadjutorship to the House of Bavaria could easily be diverted; indeed, were the elector to die, there would be no great difficulty in electing
Franz or himself as Elector of Cologne solely because of the dearth of
money there.[17]

Since neither a treaty nor a subsidy was in the offing, the elector wondered whether the king might nominate him for a cardinal's hat. A new
promotion was expected and since Wilhelm might be elevated to the cardinalate, it would create an embarrassing imbalance in their ecclesiastical
rank.[18] At the end of the dispatch Wilhelm mentioned a development
which soon would overshadow all talk of the college of cardinals: Franz
Egon was very ill. His condition worsened steadily until, after a long and
agonizing nosebleed, he finally died on April 1, 1682.

During the week before his death, activity in Cologne was frenetic.
When Wilhelm informed the king of his brother's critical condition, he
inquired about the succession at Strasbourg. On the same day, Franz dictated a last letter to his royal benefactor. He knew he was near death and
as a last favor asked that the king grant him and his chapter at Strasbourg
the rights and prerogatives which had hitherto been enjoyed when they
were connected with the Empire.[19] By the time these two letters were
answered, Franz had already been dead for twenty-four hours.

The king promised Franz that the Church of Strasbourg would enjoy
all the rights and privileges to which it was accustomed and the chapter
would have all revenues and rights "which are not prejudicial to the
rights of sovereignty acquired by my Crown in the extent of Alsace. Thus
your mind should be at ease and you should have complete confidence
in the esteem and affection which I have for you." To Wilhelm the king
announced: "My intention would not be that he had a successor other
than yourself to so considerable a dignity."[20]

As much as Wilhelm may have mourned his brother's death, it served
as a catapult for the furtherance of his own career. In recent years he
had been hampered by Franz's presence. Now he assumed command of
his family's destiny and set to work. His first instinct was to go to Paris
to iron out strategy for the election since, as he put it in a note to Croissy,
"in one hour's conversation, very often one settles more business and
cuts through more problems than would be accomplished by fifty mémoires and projects." The Paris trip, however, was cancelled due to "a terrible inflammation" of his eyes. All this while Max Heinrich sought
assurance that Wilhelm would handle Cologne affairs even were he
elected Bishop of Strasbourg. To retain him at least part of the year the

elector proposed to make him dean of the Cologne cathedral chapter and took steps to this end.[21]

Before going to Strasbourg, Fürstenberg made a rapid trip to Liège at the end of April. Though his conversations with members of the cathedral chapter were not productive, those with deputies from the city council seemed more promising. (As we shall see in the next chapter, the situation in Liège would soon change dramatically.) His one accomplishment in the city was to officially begin his residency in the Cathedral Church; he thus obtained entry into the chapter and paved the way for a possible election as coadjutor or bishop. Upon returning to Cologne he tried to settle all of his affairs before leaving for Alsace. To Tambonneau, it all seemed like a whirlwind. "Prince Wilhelm is so deluged by affairs that he can scarcely devote several moments to each person who wishes to speak to him. He had resolved to leave for Strasbourg after the ceremony of his brother's burial which will take place tomorrow, but I do not believe that he will be able to before the 23rd or the 24th [of May]. We are in the midst of a great dispute, Sire. He does not want to return here from Strasbourg for the election of the two dignities of *grand prevost* and *grand doyen* which should take place on the 25th of next month." [22] Though there were Neuburg plots to land these positions for themselves, Wilhelm remained confident, claiming that Quentel would do all that was necessary. Tambonneau was not optimistic but, as usual, the king preferred Wilhelm's judgment to that of his envoy.

Fürstenberg arrived in Strasbourg shortly before the election on June 1. Considering his experience, his administrative ability, the influence of his friends in the chapter, and French control of the province, it is understandable that he should have set out for Alsace "not without hope of being elected," as the nuncio reported to Rome. Wilhelm soon informed Visconti that he had been unanimously elected *per viam inspirationis*. After declining the honor three times, he finally acceded to the wish of the chapter.[23] The congratulatory letter which Max Heinrich sent him after the election indicates the extent of Wilhelm's ascendancy at Cologne: "I not only share the great joy in your election but hope that it will serve you to even greater ones. . . . I am inclined to believe that your position at Strasbourg will not bring with it any change in the affection which you have always demonstrated for me and that you will not diminish your interest in the affairs which concern my archbishopric of Cologne and my bishopric of Liège which can concern you some day. That is why I beg you . . . to return here as soon as you will have been able to pass through Paris so that you can inform His Majesty of the bad state of my affairs. . . . I beg you not to abandon me, to return here as soon as possible and to do everything possible so that His Majesty . . . obliges those in Liège to render me the respect and the obeisance which are my due." [24]

One week after receiving this impassioned plea, Wilhelm was unanimously elected dean of the Cologne chapter. Yet despite all entreaties, he remained away from Cologne, working on the affairs of his bishopric and on Alsatian business in general. In addition to the usual round of inspections, conferences and paper work, he applied for papal confirmation of his new office and for permission to retain his other benefices. Wilhelm repeated his brother's tactic when elected bishop: he requested permission to give up the bishopric at any time in the future "if it should be considered useful for his spiritual welfare and for the advantage of the diocese." He further requested that regardless of the reason for the bishop's seat becoming vacant in the future, it could only be filled by an election of the cathedral chapter. Although these outlandish requests were dismissed by the Curia, Wilhelm's petition to retain his other benefices was taken under advisement. The official investigation into his fitness to be bishop was begun on July 17, 1682, with Quentel called as the first witness. [25]

At the end of July 1682 Fürstenberg traveled to Versailles to iron out the details concerning the status of his territory in Alsace. Louis XIV offered the same terms as were given to Franz Egon: all rights which did not infringe on the royal sovereignty. In effect, this nullified most of the *droits régaliens*, including the right to make peace and war, to make laws, to issue money, to pardon criminals, and to contract alliances— in a word, all the real prerogatives of a sovereign power. [26]

Those prerogatives which survived French sovereignty included the exercise of unlimited criminal justice and civil and feudal jurisdiction throughout the entire extent of the bishopric's domain. In the latter case, however, the regency council sitting at Saverne could not hear appeals in cases involving more than 1000 livres; these were reserved for French jurisdiction. The bishop received one-thirtieth of the value on sales of personal property in his territory in recompense for tolls which were suppressed. Twelve annual *corvées* were now at his disposition instead of the unlimited number hitherto in force; these could be transmuted into cash payments by his subjects. No other taxes save those extant in 1600 could be levied. Jews would be received into the territory as before with an annual protection fee set at 12 écus per person. In addition the bishop retained seigneurial rights, including the right of coercion and of enforcing the decrees of the area; hunting and fishing rights as well as fines were likewise reserved to him. He also retained complete control over spiritual jurisdiction: all the former laws, customs, prerogatives and institutions were to remain intact. On September 3 Fürstenberg headed for Strasbourg accompanied by Louvois "so as to adjust that which pertains to the rights of his bishopric." The letters patent confirming these rights reached him in September 1682.[27]

As bishop of Strasbourg, Wilhelm officially pledged faith and homage to Louis XIV in May 1687. But his investiture by the French king concerned only the portion of the bishopric on the left bank of the Rhine. Investiture for the portion in the Holy Roman Empire was, of course, reserved to the emperor. Since there were several inconveniences attached to approaching Leopold on the subject, Wilhelm never did obtain his investiture for the other part of his diocese. By 1684, instead of the one vicar general for the entire diocese, there were two of them, their jurisdictions separated by the Rhine. Much later, while a French exile in 1701, Wilhelm suggested a bold solution to the split diocese in a letter to Leopold: he could alternate his residence on the right and the left banks of the Rhine and, in his capacity as a prince of the Empire, would abstain from voting in the Diet whenever the issue concerned a difference between the emperor and the King of France.[28] That proposal was not favorably received and thus Wilhelm's tenure at Strasbourg came to symbolize not only the assimilation of Alsace by France and the struggle between France and the Empire, but also the perception of Wilhelm as a kind of foreign presence in his homeland. Indeed, the symbolism is so blatant that it would seem forced if it appeared in a work of fiction.

In the summer of 1682, while Fürstenberg conferred in Alsace and at Versailles, Tambonneau was stranded in Cologne, unable to cope with the myriad problems which went unsolved in Wilhelm's absence. The longer Fürstenberg stayed away, the more insistent were the demands that he return, for without him the envoy could get no cooperation from Quentel or Widman. Tambonneau's frustration during Wilhelm's absence was evident in a letter to the French ambassador in England: "I strongly wish to see him here again, more so for the service of the king than for the pleasure I would have in escaping the frightful solitude in which I am placed since his departure. Nobody in the world is as capable as he in dealing with the affairs of all of Germany when he wants to apply himself but these concerns are so numerous and varied that he does not know which ones to attend to [first] and I strongly fear that they will so weaken his health that he will not be able to render to the king those services which his inclination and his gratitude lead him to perform." In his next letter he pursued this theme: "Your Excellency could not possibly imagine the need which all of us have of the mediation of this prince who knows how to join to the suppleness and the capacity of his spirit, reasons of interest which are in my opinion the most efficacious of any which could be used in dealing with the people of this nation." Soon he announced to Fürstenberg: "They wait for you at Cologne and at Liège as one awaits a Messiah." [29]

Such language doubtless pleased and perhaps amused the newly-elected bishop, but it failed to move him. In August Max Heinrich appointed him chief counsellor and prime minister but this did not quicken his steps either. Wilhelm pursued his business in Alsace and Max Heinrich post-poned making any decisions until his prime minister returned. Just when that day would come was anybody's guess. "According to his letters," reported Tambonneau, "we expect him on the 15th of this month, and according to his good custom at the end of the month or perhaps later." Not surprisingly, Wilhelm's "good custom" prevailed. As the weeks melted away, the laments grew louder and more frequent. "Monseigneur de Strasbourg alone can do more at Cologne and at Liège than the most clever ministers which Your Majesty could employ there." Again, "The elector is so determined to do nothing without his advice that on Liège as on all other matters he does not want to take the least resolution unless he has communicated with him." [30] Wilhelm must have enjoyed the flood of letters imploring him to return; perhaps he prolonged his stay in Alsace deliberately so as to dramatize his importance.

Another reason for his delay was the need to calm the resentment of those who were dissatisfied over the new status of the bishop's territories and who viewed Wilhelm as little more than a puppet. Rumors of a pos-sible attack against Fürstenberg prompted him to add more guards to his entourage "to maintain the reputation of my dignity, and to make clear to all Germany that the domination of Your Majesty has neither ob-scured the luster nor annihilated the rights of the bishopric of Strasbourg. Nevertheless, since I have good reason to mistrust my enemies, I hope that in case I find even more positive evidence of their designs Your Maj-esty will approve my leaving Cologne so as to retire in this territory." Louis thought such rumors may have been planted expressly to persuade Wilhelm to leave Cologne and the elector. [31] No more mention was made of these threats in the immediate future. Wilhelm finally left Alsace on October 29, stopped off for conferences with the Electors of Mainz and Trier, and arrived in Cologne on November 9, 1682. Slightly more than three years had passed since his return from an Austrian prison. His strategy had succeeded: he had more than won back his position as the dominant element at the court of Cologne and the elector seemed more dependent on him now than ever before.

VII
DÉNOUEMENT AT LIÈGE

SUMMER 1682 TO DECEMBER 1684

BY THE TIME Wilhelm returned to Cologne in November, Turkish troops had already grouped in Constantinople and plans were being made for an assault on Vienna. While the wider implications of this threat were discussed in Versailles, Vienna, and Rome, the problem of Liège continued to preoccupy the electoral court of Max Heinrich.

During Fürstenberg's visit to the territory in May the main issue was the election of officials in Liège. Though the two *bourgmestres* approved a compromise plan, popular agitation was fomented by the "patriot party" and the thirty-two *métiers* of the city rejected the compromise. The *bourgmestres* subsequently fled and two leaders of the popular party were elected in their places. By November the prospects for renewed negotiations seemed more favorable since the city was beset with a financial crisis. In addition, the French envoy in Liège had impressed upon the city leaders that Louis XIV desired them to give just and reasonable satisfaction to Max Heinrich's demands. (Clearly the provincial autonomy demanded by the Liégeois was viewed in the same way as a regional uprising in France.) With the Turkish invasion imminent, there was no prospect of help from Vienna. Liège officials reluctantly considered some form of compromise even if it entailed intervention in local elections. At the end of November, they sent three delegates to negotiate at Cologne.[1]

In the previous year, political discussions with visiting Liège delegations often spilled over into social gatherings. Tambonneau provided a glimpse of one such evening:

If one says what one thinks under the influence of wine, and still more so in Germany than elsewhere, I should be at ease, for yesterday [Quentel] assured me several times in the midst of a hundred glasses of wine that he is capable of doing everything for the service of Your Majesty and that of Prince Wilhelm. A debauchery lasting seven hours at the home of this canon put everyone in such a state that the two Princes of Fürstenberg and every Domherr in the city would have left the house by the windows instead of by the doors if they had not been taken care of and brought home. Prince Wilhelm assured me that evening that it's in this manner that one penetrates their true sentiment.[2]

Now a totally different atmosphere prevailed, doubtless influenced by the changed character of the Liège government. From the outset Wilhelm was cavalier and peremptory in his dealings with the delegates. He engaged in stalling tactics, perhaps on orders from Versailles, perhaps with the connivance of Max Heinrich, perhaps a combination of both. We have no sure information here. What is clear is that his actions—certainly by design—infuriated his interlocutors.

The first meeting was scheduled at his residence but on their arrival the delegates were informed that Wilhelm was off hunting; the conference was rescheduled for that afternoon at the home of another Cologne representative. At this second rendezvous, they were asked to explain, one by one, a list of offenses committed against the elector's sovereign rights by the leaders and populace of Liège. When they finally did encounter Fürstenberg, the session began with a recital of the questions and answers of the first meeting and then a continued hammering away at abuses committed in Liège. Max Heinrich declared he would involve himself in communal elections and warned the envoys not to be stubborn. If they remained intransigent there would be retribution, though what form it would take was never spelled out: "there is something to fear, but we cannot yet penetrate just what this means although we are doing everything in our power to fathom this secret." A mingling of bitterness, frustration, and pride led to angry exchanges at these meetings. At one point the Liégeois told Wilhelm and his colleagues that they would "sacrifice their blood and their lives rather than consent to see the Republic fall under the servitude of an incensed prince who wanted to take their privileges and liberty away from them."[3] Fürstenberg's propositions were heatedly rejected; the delegates departed at the end of February.

All the while factional disputes in Liège quickened. City councilmen and members of the bourgeoisie in general were disposed to compromise but when the returning delegates described the treatment they had received, the ranks of the opposition became more animated. Soon Wilhelm was characterizing all Liégeois as "stubborn and mutinous." The king refused to intervene before the Frankfurt parleys ended. With fine malice he informed Max Heinrich that the absence of outside aid need not prevent him "from using his own troops to do everything which he believes suitable for his interests." Louis likewise refused subsidies: the elector was merely assured "that if he is attacked by his neighbors he will soon be powerfully aided by my forces."[4] Max Heinrich was back where he started.

Perhaps as a result of the king's goading, the elector finally did take the initiative. Fürstenberg spread the word in Liège that his master would be satisfied with the tax of a sixtieth and the tax on beer, that he would be willing to forget the election issues and would sign an accommodation which included a general amnesty. Since it is virtually impossible to imagine this as a serious proposition, especially the laissez-faire attitude on municipal elections, Huisman is surely correct in describing it as a shrewd maneuver to further divide the city. That, in fact, is what happened: fifteen of the *métiers* were in favor, seventeen opposed. In short order, Liège was covered with barricades and bloody battles took place in the midst of a violent struggle for power. By the summer of 1683 the conservative forces, partisans of reconciliation, triumphed over their radical adversaries in new elections.[5] A divided Liège and a conservative victory there were as much as Max Heinrich could have hoped for at the time. He would still have to rely on negotiations. His options were quite limited without French aid.

In March Fürstenberg learned of the pope's confirmation of his bishopric at Strasbourg and his permission to retain the other benefices. On April 13 he went into retreat to prepare for his entrance into the priesthood. He celebrated his first mass on April 15 in the cathedral of Cologne and was consecrated Bishop of Strasbourg by nuncio Visconti on May 1, 1683. Soon after his consecration Wilhelm began a two-week tour of Westphalia to visit the local estates and oversee work at the fortress of Rheinberg. The union of prelate, military man, and politician had always pleased him and in his new capacity as Bishop of Strasbourg the deference paid him was greater than ever. During this trip he sharply protested the continuing harassment of his abbey at Stavelot by the *procureur général* of the Metz reunion chamber. The abbey and its territory was part of the Holy Roman Empire and Wilhelm did not want it to fall into French hands. His arguments were repeated shortly thereafter in personal conversations with Louvois in Strasbourg prior to an audience with Louis XIV. Wilhelm's reasoning was successful and the administrator at Metz was ordered to desist.[6] This was a crucial negotiation in which Wilhelm fought for the desires of his chapter and proved that he was not a mere puppet at the beck and call of the French ministry. His conversations with Louvois and the king dealt with the implications of the Turkish invasion (Vienna would be invested on July 14), the Liège imbroglio, and Max Heinrich's hopes of being elected Bishop of Münster in September. Louis approved of this latter design and promised aid.

Royal support also made possible one of Wilhelm's cherished projects, the foundation of a seminary in his diocese. Before leaving he arranged for the affairs of the diocese to be placed into the hands of a suffragan bishop. The almost continuous absenteeism of Franz Egon and Wilhelm as well as the Rohans, their successors in the eighteenth century, turned the role of suffragan bishop into a permanent institution at Strasbourg.[7] Naturally, there were objections from Rome; the nuncio in Cologne repeatedly asked Wilhelm to return to his diocese. Wilhelm in turn posed the following question to the papal secretary of state: "Tell me, I beg of you, Monsieur, what you would think of a man who, seeing his son secure and his brother in danger, would neglect to aid the latter by an excess of love which would prevent him from leaving the former? Your Eminence would doubtlessly blame him. Nevertheless, that is the situation in which I presently find myself; between my bishopric and the churches in this region [Cologne] of which I have the honor of being a member."[8] At the end of July 1683 the Bishop of Strasbourg returned to Cologne to help "his brother" in distress.

Max Heinrich was then engaged in a desperate effort to be elected Bishop of Münster. He authorized Dücker to distribute up to 60,000 écus to the chapter; the French agent, Gombauld, had 12,000 écus at his disposal. In the end, Max Heinrich's principal opponent, Friedrich Christian von Plettenberg, was bought off just before Fürstenberg arrived on the scene. The agreement was that upon Wilhelm's arrival, Plettenberg would give over his block of votes to him "out of respect owed to Your Majesty since that is the way you have desired it to be done." In fact, a number of canons wanted Wilhelm himself as their bishop but he declined in favor of Max Heinrich who was duly elected on September 1.[9]

The elector rewarded Dücker by admitting him to the ministry and entrusting him with the affairs of the diocese of Münster.[10] Fürstenberg thus had another of his followers in a position of influence. The one false note in the aftermath of the Münster affair was the pope's refusal to confirm the election. There ensued a veritable cold war between Cologne and the papacy down till the elector's death, a dispute exacerbated by Max Heinrich's success in collecting revenues from Münster.

Before returning to Cologne, Wilhelm and Gombauld discussed the French invasion of the Spanish Netherlands. Fürstenberg preferred to suspend judgment on its outcome until the results of the siege of Vienna were known; in the meantime, he said, the king was free to do as he liked.[11] One week later, on September 12, the imperial forces scored their great victory against the Turks. This event as much as any other in his long reign turned the tide of Louis XIV's fortunes. In a very real sense, the same could be said for Fürstenberg's fortunes, since if the Turks were victorious, Leopold would have been discredited and French troops may well have stepped into the breach. That in turn might have yielded heady political results in the Empire with Louis becoming or appointing the next Holy Roman Emperor. Leopold's triumph, however, paved the way for widespread Austrian gains in eastern Europe and a corresponding rise in the prestige of the Habsburg dynasty throughout the Germanies. While we cannot know what ran through Wilhelm's mind when he received the news from the East, no oracle was needed to inform him that there were clouds in his future.

Even before news of the imperial victory over the Turks had arrived, 35,000 French troops entered the Spanish Netherlands, occupied Chiny, Luxembourg, and Dinant, and lived off the land. Events in the Electorate of Cologne and in Liège during the following year cannot be understood apart from the context of French incursions into the Spanish Netherlands. Louvois ordered one village and county after another to be systematically ravaged. In a gesture worthy of Don Quixote Spain declared war against France on December 11, 1683, partly with the hope of stimulating others to join them. In accordance with treaty obligations, the Dutch sent a contingent of 8,000 troops into the Spanish Netherlands but they were prudently used to defend the barrier fortresses guaranteed by the Nijmegen treaties. William III of Orange pursued his original aim of bringing the Dutch into open warfare with France provided that support could be assured. This threat hastened the conclusion of an offensive-defensive treaty between France and the Electorate of Cologne during Fürstenberg's visit to Versailles at the Christmas season. In exchange for a monthly subsidy of 24,000 écus, the elector guaranteed an army of 20,000 men which would march with France in case of a Dutch offensive. Even if the Dutch did not attack, the treaty could be of use, for if the Austrians made peace with the Turks, the French anticipated that their first move on the western front would be to seize either Cologne or Coblenz or both so as to control the approach to the Netherlands. Max Heinrich ratified the treaty on January 29, 1684.[12]

The imminence of war again raised the possibility of the city of Cologne's opening its gates to Dutch troops or, even worse, to those of the emperor. Max Heinrich believed that if Leopold controlled Cologne, he "would become master of this territory and of the entire Circle of Westphalia and would find here such a quantity of victuals, of munitions and artillery that he would have no need to bring them in from elsewhere."

One solution, he said, would be for French troops to occupy Cologne. Before this latest proposal to storm the city reached Louvois, the minister had inquired about lodging French troops in the electorate. Though he rejected the plan to attack and occupy Cologne, he now requested that 5,000 troops be allowed to enter the electorate.[13] The Cologne ministry refused, believing that only the direct conquest of the city would justify the entrance of French troops. Once this was ruled out, if the troops simply lodged in the territory with the ostensible purpose of blocking Dutch advances, it might very well inspire the burghers of Cologne to open their gates to the enemies of France and Max Heinrich. Fürstenberg dictated an express letter to Versailles:

Today I do not have the time to explain to Your Majesty the thousands of reasons which could be drawn up against this idea. . . . I will take the liberty of telling him that if he gives some thought to the Electorate of Cologne, to my position and still more to the needs of his own service he will drop this design immediately and countermand the order to his troops if they have already been given orders to march into the territory of Cologne. If such an order is carried out, I shall not be responsible for what results. . . . I beseech Your Majesty to have the goodness to act in concert with us on this occasion.[14]

Several days later Wilhelm urged that at the last resort the troops might pitch camp at the frontiers but that in no circumstances should they enter the territory of Cologne unless the Dutch sent troops into the Spanish Netherlands over and above the 8,000 which were already guarding the barriers. In reply, Louis recognized the "inconveniences" of the situation but insisted that the only way to ensure a rapid peace was to present a strong front and thus discourage any opposition. This said, he was willing to agree with Fürstenberg's plan to save Max Heinrich's face before Brandenburg as well as the city of Cologne. The elector was to request that French troops enter his lands if and when the Dutch should increase their contingent in Spanish territory. Louis made it clear that if Max Heinrich did not agree to such a scheme, he would be considered an enemy. "But I am assured," he told Wilhelm, "that you will have prepared the elector so well in this comedy that he will see these declarations as a pretext which I am giving him so that any action which he may take against the Dutch in accordance with treaty obligations will seem reasonable in the eyes of my other allies."[15]

While all those exchanges were hidden from the citizens of Cologne, the recruitment of troops for the electoral army confirmed suspicions in the city that the French had marked it out for conquest in the same manner as Strasbourg. Such mistrust became even more visible when it was learned that the troops would be commanded by a Frenchman, the Count of Choiseul, who arrived in the electorate in the first week of March. Max Heinrich and Fürstenberg were again depicted as hirelings of the Sun King and comparisons with the atmosphere prior to Wilhelm's capture in 1674 were inescapable; the Spanish had little difficulty in recruiting troops in the city.[16]

If the formation of Max Heinrich's army frightened the population of Cologne, it produced no less an effect in Liège. Here the situation was appreciably different since the conservative city officials recently concluded what appeared to be an agreement with the elector. Fürstenberg had traveled to Liège in October and made considerable progress amidst lavish receptions and splendid feasts. One detail, however, stands out: no member of the cathedral chapter was invited to these discussions.[17] Was this exclusion agreed upon by the bourgeoisie and Wilhelm in advance? If so, they may have intended to circumvent endless haggling over the surrender of church land to France and thus present a *fait accompli* to the chapter and the pope. If Fürstenberg were the moving force behind this exclusion, it could be interpreted as a means of inserting a divisive wedge from the outset with the expectation that the city would again be riven by factionalism. But we must not forget the desire of the bourgeoisie to achieve power; for example, they did not secure the approval of the *métiers* of the city before signing a treaty on November 22.

The agreement accorded a full amnesty; the tax of a sixtieth and the impost on beer would be in force; the military guard would be shared by the elector's appointee and the two *bourgmestres* who themselves would pledge fealty to Max Heinrich. Each of the thirty-two *métiers* would submit the names of three men for city magistrate. The elector's deputy in the city would personally select one of the three men in each group, thirty-two in all. Finally, the city pledged a gift of 100,000 écus to its prince, to be paid over a period of two years. A deputation from Liège made a formal submission to Max Heinrich and the treaty was ratified on February 22, 1684.[18] Though it contained many elements of an honorable compromise, the treaty was flawed from the outset: neither the chapter nor the *métiers* had been consulted. Within a few months all hopes for the success of the agreement would be dashed.

The peace terms facilitated rebellion since the amnesty provision enabled radical leaders to reenter the city and rally their followers against the treaty. Members of the cathedral chapter were dissatisfied at having been excluded from the negotiations and listened to voices of dissent. Recruitment for the elector's army was taking place in the territory of Liège, naturally inflaming suspicion that once again Max Heinrich (without consulting his subjects) was bringing them into open conflict with the enemies of France, with the territory of Liège to serve as one of the cockpits of that struggle. When the elector summoned the local estates and asked them for more money, purportedly for contributions to the imperial cause against the Turks, the resentment spilled over into revolt. All circumstantial evidence pointed to the building of a force which might suppress what liberties remained in Liège, and this with the financial aid of the Liégeois themselves! On April 9, 1684, the drapers, one of the more radical *métiers*, began a rebellion which rapidly engulfed the city and divided it into two camps. Despite all efforts of the city magistrates, the radical party triumphed and a civil war once more was imminent. Max Heinrich requested that the 5,000 French troops be used to aid in punishing his seditious subjects, but Louis XIV cautioned the elector to wait until after peace with Spain and the Empire was established before moving into Liège in force.[19]

French hopes for a peace settlement were encouraged by the news that Leopold would continue the war against the Turks; in March the Holy League between Austria, Venice, and Poland was concluded with the blessings of Pope Innocent XI. Moreover, Louvois believed that the Dutch would willingly refrain from aiding Spain, especially if assured of the barrier fortifications accorded them at Nijmegen. He insisted that the Dutch be warned of an attack from Cologne if they went to war.[20]

The formation of the Holy League and the probable lack of Dutch support seemed to seal the fate of Spain, but the French left nothing to chance. Louis XIV decided "to blaze a path to peace by using force," as d'Avaux put it. This "blaze" was literally and tragically true. On April 28, 1684 the siege of Luxembourg began under Vauban's direction; Catalonia was invaded and Genoa bombarded for having outfitted Spanish vessels. The French offensive inspired their opponents to make a last-ditch effort to broaden the conflict. Max Heinrich and Fürstenberg were on tenterhooks. If the elector were drawn into the conflict, all of his territories (except Liège!) had to be united behind him. Wilhelm visited the bishopric of Münster and inspected the fortifications at Rheinberg. A month went by without his writing to Versailles; all correspondence was left to Tambonneau. Meanwhile, Cologne was swarming with Austrian and Bavarian agents. Soon after Fürstenberg's departure, city leaders scattered the troops guarding his home and there was a move afoot to raze it to the ground. There was also talk of seizing Max Heinrich so as to persuade him to change allegiances. (The elector finally fled to Bonn on June 12.) Everything was "in a state of total disorder, in a state of crisis on all fronts."[21]

The ensuing weeks saw a continuance of the crisis and a multiplication of fronts. Wilhelm received reports from Vienna, Brussels, Holland, and elsewhere that he was a marked man, the "object of implacable hate." Only recently, he learned, some Spanish officers at a dinner party in the palace of the Neuburg Duke of Jülich declared that the only thing to do was to put a bullet through Fürstenberg's head and be rid of him. As if this were not enough, the nuncio announced that he had orders from the pope to remind Fürstenberg for the last time to return to his diocese of Strasbourg. If he balked at this request he would be forbidden to exercise any of his religious functions and would be excommunicated. Wilhelm hurriedly drafted a letter resigning his bishopric and submitted it to Louis for approval. He suggested his nephew Felix, Prince of Murbach, as his successor. By the time this dispatch reached the court, news had already arrived of the conquest of Luxembourg. This changed the state of affairs considerably. Louis told Wilhelm to put off sending anything to Rome; he had his ambassador there see Innocent immediately. This action proved successful: Innocent declared that the nuncio had no specific authority to issue such threats. Wilhelm's anxieties were exacerbated by a recurrence of his kidney ailment, gravel, and general physical exhaustion. Tambonneau reported that one of the reasons for this exhaustion was a lack of secretarial help: "M. de Strasbourg allows himself to be buried by affairs. . . . It is true that he does better than anyone else but there is no telling what would happen if he were deprived of M. Dücker. Then he would be left with but one secretary and while he would attempt to assume all the work himself, it is clear that he needs at least two or three men under him so as to have enough time for necessary affairs which are left hanging simply because there are only twenty-four hours in a day." [22]

Once Luxembourg fell on June 3, 1684, the French managed to divide the opposition. Cowed by the prospect of facing the French army, the Estates-General, despite Orangist objections, promised to use their good offices in persuading Spain to accept a truce of twenty years on conditions laid down by France. The Dutch barriers would be secured and France's latest acquisitions from Spain were sufficiently far away. Deprived of her only sure ally, Spain soon accepted the inevitable and gave the emperor full power to treat in its name. [23]

The Truce of Regensburg in August 1684 gave France sovereignty over all territories acquired in reunion proceedings before August 1, 1681, for a period of twenty years. The sovereignty was even more complete than that gained at Westphalia for there was no mention of *immédiateté* of the annexed territory to the Empire nor were fortifications in the acquired land forbidden. The imperial party underlined the provisional nature of the settlement with the implicit assumption that future claims and adjustments, if not a total reversal, were possible. On the French side there was satisfaction since twenty years would give them ample opportunity to solidify their position. Louis did not receive the territories outright in the form of a conclusive peace but he had reason to be gratified with the results obtained: Strasbourg, Casale, and Luxembourg completed the strategic frontier. With Luxembourg in hand, Louvois wrote to Vauban on June 28, 1684 that "from now on the Germans should be considered as our true enemies and the only ones who might be able to harm us if they had an emperor who wanted to mount a horse."[24]

After the truce, Max Heinrich could deal with Liège. The spring riots there had led to reprisals against leaders of the bourgeoisie who were accused of signing the February pact without soliciting the approval of the *métiers*. One *bourgmestre* was deposed, the other intimidated. The vacancy was filled by Macors, a lawyer and member of the nobility, who pursued unity in the city: he distributed weapons to the people, readied the cannons on the walls and entrusted public safety and police powers to the *métiers* themselves. Not even these measures were enough to calm the mounting frustration and hostility in the popular classes. Macors bent with the storm and soon lists of suspects were drawn up. Exile and confiscation of goods were imposed on many who had supported the accommodation with Max Heinrich and who were thus guilty of moderation. On June 26 the houses of several former *bourgmestres* were devastated in popular rioting; prisoners were taken and many more fled for their lives as the rumored approach of the electoral army rent the city to pieces.[25]

The events in those last weeks seem like rituals to canalize frenzy and despair. On July 16 the *métiers* addressed a statement of grievances to Max Heinrich, protesting the manner in which the February settlement had been reached without their approval and denouncing the tendency toward a "despotic domination" which would reduce them to slavery, subject to the tyrannical passions of their overlord. This proclamation was, in effect, a thorough repudiation of the February treaty. On July 25 two leading radicals, Renardi and Giloton, were elected *bourgmestres*: the defiance was complete. That very day the elector's troops entered the principality. The natural instinct of the city's leaders was to seek outside aid. But where? Spain's only concern was to extricate herself from the struggle with France; the emperor was preoccupied with the Turkish war; the Dutch refused to become involved. An urgent supplication was made to Louis XIV, who told them, through La Raudière:

"To promptly end the differences . . . there is no other expedient than to submit to your prince . . . and render him his due."[26] Knowing what we do of the many years of negotiation between Cologne and France on the subject of Liège, these pleas to Versailles impress upon us the terrible isolation of the Liégeois at this bitter moment in their history.

Once the Regensburg truce was arranged, electoral troops accompanied by Fürstenberg moved closer to the city. On August 25 local deputies, including Macors, conferred with Fürstenberg and offered to accept the February accommodation. Though he refused this proposal, Wilhelm left the future settlement sufficiently vague so as to lull the delegation. That very night troops moved into the suburbs. While a council meeting was in session the following morning there came news that soldiers were entering a quarter of the town which had traditionally leaned towards the elector. The hours that followed have a strange, even eerie quality about them. The city was taken and occupied without bloodshed, the populace apparently weary of fighting and hopeful that some reasonable peace terms would be arranged. Leniency was expected, partly because of Fürstenberg's initial noncommittal attitude, but this impression was soon shattered.

When General Choiseul received a supplication from the city leaders, he referred it to Fürstenberg, who was still encamped outside the walls. The keys of the city were given to Wilhelm, who received the *bourgmestres* in audience and then had them escorted to their houses. (Giloton succeeded in escaping.) On the following day, Wilhelm entered the city on horseback at the head of a column of troops and dined at the home of La Raudière. This gesture alone must have made many rue earlier hopes and illusions concerning the prospect of French aid. The army was billeted in the city; the citizens were disarmed, except those in the quarter considered "safe"; a new tax was decreed and provision made for the election of the two new *bourgmestres*. Renardi and Macors were imprisoned; other arrests multiplied as many of the proscribed fled. Fürstenberg presently inspected the site where the new Citadel would be erected. Executions began in the main square with Wilhelm himself in attendance. The victims were sometimes captains of the militia or radical leaders of the *métiers*; afterwards their heads were usually exhibited on the town bridges. All these measures were part of a general plan to "pacify" the city before the arrival of its sovereign lord from Cologne.[27]

The vengeful tactics employed by Fürstenberg in behalf of his master were like lashes of a whip, slashes which cut through all strata of society and spared no group. Heavy taxes and contributions were imposed, merchants and bankers together were assessed a sum of 100,000 florins, various fines were levied, and no requests for mercy were heeded, even those emanating from the cathedral chapter. The capstone of this vengeance came in judging the two former *bourgmestres*, Macors and Renardi. There were, of course, pleas for clemency, even from La Raudière. The French envoy noted rumors that among the captured leaders those who were rich enough to ransom themselves would be spared, the rest killed. Max Heinrich was especially angered by predictions that the richer of the two captured *bourgmestres* (Macors) would not be killed. He declared "that he no longer wanted to hear money spoken of in this connection." La Raudière believed that if any pardons were forthcoming, a share of the credit would go to Countess von der Mark, who was very influential in Liège.[28] But pleas for mercy were of no avail. On the morning of October 9 Macors and Renardi were executed; that afternoon the Elector of Cologne entered the subjugated city.

Max Heinrich made his triumphal entry flanked by Fürstenberg and Choiseul. A splendidly caparisoned entourage took up the train, succeeded by columns of French and German troops. The intended effect was that of conquest. Decorated facades of buildings, the festive ringing of church bells and groups of musicians planted at strategic points throughout the route were perhaps enough to mask temporarily the bitterness and sorrow in the assembled crowds of his subjects. He was received at the cathedral by the chapter members and sat on a throne during the chanting of a *Te Deum*. In the evening bonfires lit up the city and the following morning the bells again rang and cannons sounded. In his episcopal robes, the elector went to the cathedral and assisted at a mass of thanksgiving. Then the political discussions began.[29]

The new constitution drawn up by Fürstenberg and approved by Max Heinrich was designed to suppress systematically the traditional liberties and political privileges of Liège. It took three months to fashion the *Règlement* of 1684, the initial drafting having begun soon after Wilhelm's arrival in the city. In its conception and execution the constitution was a model for the legal annihilation of provincial autonomy. It was in line with the governing principles of Louis XIV and down to the finest details it was Fürstenberg's creation. Practically all of Fürstenberg's writings amount to projects, suggestions, contingency plans. The Liège constitution was the one instance in which he designed a political structure which was put directly into operation. Though his ideas were shaped to suit the autocratic sentiments of Max Heinrich, there is no reason to believe that Wilhelm disagreed with him on essentials. From the outset, his task was greatly facilitated by the presence of troops and the hopelessness of popular revolt. More than at any other moment in his career, he had a carte blanche.

Wilhelm assigned church officials in Liège an important role in the governance of the city. The cathedral chapter, excluded from the February agreement, was given more power than any other body in Liège: the elector agreed never to issue edicts without obtaining the consent of the chapter and accorded it the right to impose its veto on all important acts of sovereignty.[30] In exchange for these concessions, the aristocratic chapter accepted the new political structures which included the extirpation of all popular control over the government. The deference paid to the chapter was also a calculated (and seemingly transparent) maneuver on Fürstenberg's part to remain in the good grace of capitularies who one day might elect him either coadjutor or bishop.

In the preamble the constitution was presented as "the necessary remedy to all past abuses and disorders," the principal source of which lay in the number and variety of people who took part in municipal elections and in the direction of the police. "Although we could keep to ourselves the annual creation of the magistracy of our city, nevertheless we have decided to accord revocably some participation in this process to the generality of the bourgeoisie." This haughty assertion of sovereignty ushered in a political structure devised to keep the generality of the bourgeoisie subservient to their prince. The old system of thirty-two *métiers* was abolished and replaced by sixteen *chambres*. Each of these units contained thirty-six members, including twenty "noble patricians," ten merchants of note, and six artisans. Each of these men had to be legitimate, Catholic, and born in the territory of Liège. The bishop reserved the right to appoint all 576 members on the first round. Afterwards they would be replaced by their peers, but the new member had to be of the same quality and profession as the former and in each instance the selection had to be approved by the sovereign. The city would be administered by two *bourgmestres* and twenty councillors, for a term of one year. Half were nominated by the prince, the other half by the *chambres*. None would be eligible for public office for another four years. Moreover, no artisan was eligible for high office in Liège, permanently screening out members of the lower classes from any influence whatever in the direction of the city's affairs. The former *métiers* were thus transformed in the new organization of *chambres* and most of their autonomies, enjoyed since the Middle Ages, were eliminated. All major resolutions of the city council had to be approved by the sovereign before they were executed and the direction of the police was shared with the cathedral chapter and with the prince. The local militia and judiciary were closely super-vised and the sovereign obtained effective interventionary control over all modalities of levying taxes. This new constitution, inaugurated on November 28, 1684, effectively stripped Liège of its traditional liber-ties.[31] Similar constitutions were drawn up for the other major cities in the principality with all power reserved to a local elite under tight control from above. This system, with some modifications, lasted until 1789. Here, as in Alsace, Fürstenberg's influence was felt until the end of the *ancien régime*.

Max Heinrich left Liège soon after the constitution went into effect but Wilhelm remained behind to supervise its execution and to settle administrative and political matters. Naturally, many citizens cordially despised him as the chief architect of their subservience. He was further detested because of the taxes which he wrung out of the city and which earned him the sobriquet *Ghiame li Stoirdeu*, or the Presser, as if he had put the citizens' change purses into a press. Max Heinrich had already accorded him a *rente* worth 10,000 écus annually and Fürstenberg took advantage of the situation to further increase his fortune. He was often seen in the company of the Countess von der Mark, and her expensive tastes, combined with his own opportunism, left few stones unturned or unpressed. These months of fiscal brigandage did more than anything else to damage his reputation in the city.[32]

Whether Wilhelm cared about his popularity in the city is doubtful. He seems to have grabbed what he could and let the future take care of itself. Considering his European-wide reputation as an opportunist, this attitude could hardly have been out of character. He probably believed that generosity toward the cathedral chapter and local fear of France would assure his succession as ruler of the territory. In the event, he appears to have been quite content with short term gains. Among these was the chateau of Modave and its estate, close by Liège, which he re-ceived from Max Heinrich. Actually, it was more of a sale than a gift, since Wilhelm was not reimbursed for his diplomatic missions over the preceding three years in Max Heinrich's service and he agreed to pay the 18,000 écus which the elector still owed to the former owner of the property.[33]

Modave was a midway point between Versailles and Cologne, a haven where he could try to recuperate from the exhaustion of the past year's activity and from the kidney ailment which had incapacitated him earlier in the year. In September, shortly after the conquest of Liège, Fürsten-berg informed the king of his desire to retire because of ill health as soon as the current business had been dispatched. "A comfortable retreat," he said, "would have no other object than my salvation, my rest, my health, and the payment of my debts, and to have more liberty to render my very humble respects and duties to Your Majesty from time to time." Continuing, he asked the king to disregard the "false reports" being circulated against him, to remember "the twenty-six years of services which I have rendered with an irreproachable fidelity and total abandonment of my health, the fortune of my family in Germany, and my own life." Months later his health was little better; he was weary of the work in Liège and of the intrigues of his enemies in Rome (agents of the Houses of Austria, Bavaria, and Neuburg) to have him ordered back to Strasbourg. Since his chief concern was a cardinal's hat, he wanted to avoid irritating the pope and so once more recommended his nephew Felix as a possible successor at Strasbourg. The king again saw no need to take this step and counselled patience.[34]

Another distressing thought was the fate of his relatives after his death. During Wilhelm's illness in June Tambonneau reported that it was worry over his family that had done most to aggravate his condition. But all these laments over his family, his health, and the need for retirement make us pause to wonder if they were not all part of another carefully orchestrated scheme to solidify his own and his family's fortune. Just at this time Wilhelm reported an offer from Emperor Leopold: if he helped to secure the coadjutorship of Cologne for either the Wittelsbachs or the Neuburgs, Fürstenberg would be guaranteed the coadjutorship of Liège and his nephew Emmanuel given a regiment in the imperial army. The emperor would give 50,000 écus to any member of his family that Wilhelm might care to name and for the sum of 200,000 écus he would have the option to purchase the county of Nellenburg, right in the middle of Fürstenberg family holdings in Swabia. Wilhelm sent a memorandum to Breget, the temporary Cologne envoy at Versailles, requesting him to inform the king of the emperor's offer: "I ask you to make some haste in this affair since Mayersheim [the imperial envoy] is going to return shortly and it would be annoying for me to lose such advantages for my family without knowing what they might expect from the French. You know me well enough to believe that I have never had much trouble in caring for myself since I am able to adjust to circumstances but if I cannot provide for my family during my lifetime they will be the most miserable souls alive after I am gone. Nevertheless, since my preference has always been that they lean towards France . . ."[35] There is no trace of a written reply to this communication but the king must have given Wilhelm assurances concerning himself and the fortunes of his family.

Meanwhile, Fürstenberg continued to reside in the Liège area, principally at Modave, for the next six months. This respite afforded time to reappraise his position. In a few years Alsace had been secured, Liège crushed and a truce established between France and the Germanies. Franz Egon's death had led him into the priesthood, into the succession of his brother's political and church offices, and into a greater degree of influence at the electoral court. Wilhelm's next ambitions were a cardinal's hat and the electoral seat at Cologne. Retirement was tempting but these prizes would soon draw him back into the whirlpool of politics. Now the only survivor among the three Egonites who once conspired to convince the French that they were necessary, Wilhelm would have ample opportunity to ply his trade in the new cold war between Habsburg and Bourbon. The emperor's offer would serve to underline what Tambonneau reported at the height of Fürstenberg's illness earlier in the year: "The more I advance in the knowledge of the internal and external affairs of this territory the more I understand the necessity of his ministry, without which we could do nothing. If God were to carry him off we would not retain our present position more than twenty-four hours." [36]

VIII
POLITICAL SKIRMISHING

THE TRUCE OF REGENSBURG was a lull in the storm; the very word *truce* connoting a state of war, latent though it was. Like other Rhineland states, the Electorate of Cologne sought to placate both great powers; Max Heinrich supported the Imperial Crusade but remained outside alliance systems sponsored by Leopold. The question of Max Heinrich's successor was as delicate as before, especially since Wittelsbach family interests pointed to his nephew, Joseph Clemens. Max Emmanuel of Bavaria, who was then achieving his *gloire* on the eastern front, was Joseph's older brother. Fürstenberg and the French would follow Max Emmanuel's campaign in Bonn as carefully as his more publicized adventures against the Turks.

Early in 1685 Tambonneau was replaced as French envoy before Max Heinrich by Jules de Gravel, Marquis of Marly, the son of the esteemed Robert de Gravel who died in the king's service in Switzerland in July 1684. Jules assumed the Swiss post upon his father's death but remained there only six months before he was nominated as envoy extraordinaire to Cologne and Trier.[1] He was an excellent example of what the French refer to as an *enfant de la balle*, denoting someone in training to take his father's place. Jules served as his father's secretary for four years in Switzerland before succeeding to the post. Possessing a good command of German and well-schooled for the craft of diplomacy, his zeal for the royal service was somewhat marred by a lack of suppleness in his relations with others. As a leading student of French diplomacy in Switzerland has noted, though the younger Gravel "impressed the Swiss with his lively spirit . . . they did not fail to notice the stubbornness, often maladroit and unjustified, of his demands concerning protocol. The result was that they became more and more aware of the reflective, prudent, and benevolent manner with which his father had always treated them."[2] Surely the most difficult feature of his assignment in Bonn would be the need to operate in the shadow of a man who had worked intimately with his father, who had been active across Europe before Jules could walk. Louis expressly ordered him to clear all his moves with Fürstenberg and to do nothing counter to his advice without notice from the court. This subordination and its consequences would grate on the new envoy.

When Gravel arrived in Cologne in April 1685 Wilhelm was still at Modave, receiving reports on developments in the politics of Europe. On February 6, 1685 Charles II of England died. The succession of his brother James to the throne again raised the specter of an England dominated by Rome; the Elector of Brandenburg soon began talks with William III of Orange regarding the fate of the Protestant cause. Of more immediate concern was the serious illness of Elector Karl Ludwig of the Palatine who had no heirs. By pre-arrangement, the succession would fall to Philipp Wilhelm of Neuburg, the father-in-law of the emperor and one of Fürstenberg's bitterest enemies in the Empire. Since the sister of the dying elector was married to Louis's brother, the Duke of Orléans, Croissy had to determine the possibilities of inheritance and the action to be taken at the time of succession.

Actually, the French knew next to nothing about the legal position of La Palatine, as the Duchess of Orléans was called. Croissy asked Foucher, the king's envoy at Mainz, to ferret out information on the subject. The farrago of statutes, precedents, customs, assumptions, and misinformation which attended his inquiry proved Pufendorf right—the Holy Roman Empire was indeed a "political monstrosity." Foucher's discreet investigation at first led him to a dead end; nobody would admit to any certain information. He was told that the pertinent documents were in the imperial archives in Vienna! He tried another approach, an interview with the most renowned legal expert in the region, a Frankfurt lawyer named Junckmann. As a ruse, he declared that a private French citizen was curious about the law in the Empire and had sent him a list of twenty questions for which he desired answers. When he arrived at the home of the lawyer, the old man was bedridden. Foucher suggested that perhaps it might be better to return another time, all the while fingering the list of questions. No sooner did Junckmann spy the paper than he asked to see it. At the sight of the first question, he perked up and "began a long discourse on the laws and customs of the Greeks and Romans since the birth of Christ." In the midst of an interminable flow of erudition, the envoy gleaned bits and pieces of what he was seeking.[3] Such intelligence came none too soon; the elector died on May 20, 1685.

The succession was immediately claimed by Philipp Wilhelm of Neuburg. Louis XIV's special envoy to Heidelberg, Abbé Jean Morel, soon made it clear that the king had no intention of allowing a German court to judge the question of the possible inheritance of the Duchess of Orléans on the basis of German law: there he would be assured of the irreducible minimum. The new elector was naturally reluctant to give up any territory or property to France and stalled for time. On October 10, 1685, Louis offered to let the pope arbitrate. He could thus avoid an imperial tribunal in addition to embroiling Protestants and Catholics in the Empire (Protestants might have accepted mediation but not arbitration) and putting the Neuburgs in a difficult position. Philipp Wilhelm's response was ambiguous. He was willing to let the pope decide but since his succession could one day revert to relatives or to the emperor, he had to have their permission before committing the dispute to arbitration.[4] What most infuriated him was that Louis refused to put any of his claims in writing. The French were obviously trying to keep the feudal rights open to discussion, something which was clearly contrary to German law.

The majority of German princes were partial to Neuburg. Indeed, the attitude which a prince took on the Palatine question was a touchstone for the strength of his ties with France. The Elector of Cologne had his minister at Regensburg make a declaration in support of French claims. Trier was overjoyed at the prospect of arbitration, but he was far too intimidated by French power to think otherwise. Though Mainz favored Neuburg, Louis XIV was confident that the elector would fall in line "after due reflection."[5] He did eventually approve papal arbitration in principle, the same hedging approval which the new Elector Palatine had rendered.

With the arbitration issue in the air, the Edict of Nantes was revoked: Protestant worship was forbidden in France. Max Heinrich unreservedly praised Louis's example, but he would not follow it. Though exhorted by the nuncio to forbid Protestant services in all his territories, the elector refused. He was surrounded by the Elector of Brandenburg, the Landgrave of Hesse-Cassel, and the Prince of Orange.[6] It would have been folly to take steps against Protestants in such a situation.

Fürstenberg returned to Bonn only in August 1685 after a long rest at Modave and treatments at several mineral springs. Before his first interview with Max Heinrich he was apprehensive, since the elector had only recently received Johann Wilhelm of Neuburg, son of the Elector Palatine, a possible rival for coadjutorships at Cologne and elsewhere. All doubts were dispelled when Max Heinrich told him that "there is nobody in whom I can have a greater confidence for everything which concerns my interests than you." Since the elector had promised his Neuburg visitor not to tell Wilhelm what they had talked about, he arranged to tell it to a third party who then passed on the information to Fürstenberg.[7] That such egregious casuistry should have been practiced by two of the leading prelates in Europe—both of them trained by Jesuits, Pascal would have reminded us—must be kept in mind when assessing the political and financial entanglements of these and perhaps other German bishops in the seventeenth century.

At that moment, the elector's main concern was the disposition of the troops which he had contributed to the campaign against the Turks. Since the pope offered him no prospect of succeeding at Münster unless he strongly supported the Crusade, Max Heinrich sent 6,000 troops in time for the spring campaign, funded by a tax whose expected yield would be 400,000 écus.[8] These troops had so impressed Leopold that he wished to buy them. Max Heinrich had only enough money to support the soldiers until the end of October and so would either have to sell them or see them desert. Fürstenberg suggested that Louis XIV foot the bill for the Cologne troops in Hungary but despite his flowery phrases regarding the pope's good will and the collective gratitude of Christendom, there was no prospect of a French subsidy. There was even less hope of further taxes from the Estates in Cologne. A further complication was Fürstenberg's attempt to have his nephew Emmanuel given a regiment in the imperial army. Here he was under considerable pressure from Emmanuel's wife, the former Countess von der Mark.

The final arrangement resulted in the sale of 2,000 infantrymen and 600 cavalry to the emperor. Another 2,000 infantry and two regiments of cavalry returned to the electorate. Leopold received a cavalry regiment in exchange for advancing Emmanuel. Max Heinrich gave Leopold 1,600 infantrymen and 400 cavalry; in exchange, Cologne was not asked for money or men during the next two years. Though no action had been taken in Rome regarding the confirmation at Münster, Leopold released the *Régale* so that Max Heinrich enjoyed the revenues from Münster while waiting to be confirmed. Inevitably, his quarrel with Pope Innocent was sharpened. Innocent said that Max Heinrich would not be confirmed at Münster unless he gave up one of his other bishoprics.[9] However unseemly this traffic in church offices may appear, papal policies regarding multiple sees created a legal and moral situation which was far from being black or white. And it was in this atmosphere that German bishops had to operate. With his desperate need of money to support the Turkish war, Innocent was anxious to multiply his sources of revenue. Max Heinrich was also trying to get as much as he could. A clash was virtually predestined.

These matters and the related issue of a general armament of the Empire were discussed by Wilhelm and the French ministry during his sojourn at Versailles in the first half of 1686, his second prolonged absence from the electorate in a year. This time his departure occasioned serious problems, especially because of the illness and death (in May 1686) of his nephew Felix, Prince of Murbach, who had been serving as interim prime minister. Throughout Murbach's illness, Wilhelm attempted to guide events through his friends and agents as well as through directives to Gravel from the French ministry. The thought of Wilhelm pulling strings at Versailles irritated Gravel. The explosion came at the beginning of February when he complained of a rumor that Fürstenberg's young nephew Ferdinand would soon be sent by Louis to Bonn with money for Max Heinrich. Ferdinand would thus ingratiate himself before the elector and make a first step in succeeding Murbach after his death. Diplomats seldom favor special envoys and Gravel was no exception. He resented the possibility of being passed over in summary fashion and sent off a spirited protest to Croissy: "It seems that I am only here to listen to the complaints and lamentations on all subjects relating to Cologne and Liège . . . without being given anything to say to the elector which may be able to appease his anger or give him some cause for rejoicing." Croissy replied that as yet there was no definite plan to give money to the elector; Gravel's suspicions, or at least the rumors, were not well founded. Continuing with studied coldness, the secretary of state observed that the king made the decisions and Gravel's role was to carry them out. Nothing could be more useful to His Majesty's service than increasing the credit of Fürstenberg and his family before Max Heinrich. Louis XIV told Gravel to act in unison with Fürstenberg on all matters. Gravel naturally replied with profuse apologies and protestations of the esteem which he had for Wilhelm and his family,[10] but there remained a lingering undercurrent of resentment which could not easily be effaced.

Though chastened, Gravel's sense of timing still left something to be desired. In April he proposed a split of Max Heinrich's coadjutories, allotting Liège and Cologne to Fürstenberg and Hildesheim and Münster to the Neuburgs. It was understandable that he wished to initiate some action on his own. But it was equally understandable that his unilateral proposal should have met with a stern rebuke. Louis reminded him that he was to do or say nothing on so important a topic without prior consultation with Fürstenberg or orders from the court.[11] It was in this context and on the eve of Murbach's death that Wilhelm cut short his stay in France and returned to the Rhineland.

On his arrival in Bonn, Max Heinrich upbraided him for not achieving any tangible results at the French court, charging that he had worked more for his own private interests than for those of the Electorate of Cologne, a suspicion which would not appear to be ill-founded. In spite of this shaky start, Fürstenberg felt confident enough to broach the problem of the succession one month later. In view of Max Heinrich's concern for his family as well as for the interests of the electorate, Wilhelm suggested that the security of his territories required that the next elector's policies be consonant with those of France. Accordingly, if Joseph Clemens of Bavaria—then fifteen years old—were to be considered for the succession, he should receive French guidance, perhaps even a French education, during his adolescence. (The incompatibility of Max Emmanuel's allegiance to Austria and a French education for his brother would provide Wilhelm with ample room for maneuver in future discussions.) He emphasized that if Wittelsbach interests were to be protected, Neuburg attempts at the succession had to be thwarted at all costs. Once in control of Cologne, the large Neuburg family could establish itself indefinitely, perhaps for centuries. Since Max Heinrich was not on the best of terms with the Neuburgs, he could nod in agreement with this line of reasoning.[12]

Wilhelm did not venture further during this discussion. It was all that could be safely said at the outset, what with the opposition to the Fürstenbergs at Bonn and Cologne and the increasing tensions over rearmament. After an Austrian-led alliance for the defense of southern Germany was formed—including Austria, Bavaria, and the Circles of Franconia, Swabia, and the Upper Rhine—a more ambitious program was planned. The members of the above Circles were invited to assemble at Augsburg to discuss the extension of their alliance. Though attempts to entice the ecclesiastical electors into this system were not successful, Max Heinrich sought to capitalize on this state of affairs in June of 1686, insinuating that "the torrent of majority opinion in the Empire" might force him to consider joining the cause of armament. As a gesture he sent a dispatch to his delegate at Regensburg to ensure cooperation with France, but obviously he was angling for more subsidies. Louis preferred to let insecurity dictate the prince-archbishops' course of action. Thus when Trier complained that France was infringing on the terms of the Regensburg pact, Gravel simply urged that nothing "trouble the calm which is deemed so necessary by the people and states who are only beginning to breathe after the preceding war."[13] As empty as this rhetoric may have sounded, it was clearly understood in Trier and elsewhere in the Rhineland.

The defensive league formed at Augsburg on July 9, 1686 included Austria, Bavaria, and the Circles of Franconia and the Upper Rhine. The original plan was to allocate 58,000 troops for the defense of southern Germany but in practice this figure was quickly reduced to 41,000. Almost all the contingents, including 16,000 imperial and 10,000 Bavarian troops, were then fighting in Hungary.[14] Spain and Sweden adhered to the League but they contributed little of military value. Neither the Rhineland bishoprics, nor the United Provinces, nor Brandenburg were members. While there were pacts between the latter two powers and between each and the emperor, there was still no cohesive opposition united against France. In any event, the League did not provide protection for northern Germany. It was largely a paper alliance viewed with much more detachment by Louis XIV than by many historians of his reign.

These latest attempts at armament did not overly disturb the French because most of the troops pledged by the respective Circles were then fighting in Hungary. The greatest threat lay in the consequences of a peace with the Turks which would enable Leopold to turn his attention to the Rhineland. Such a peace was far from being mere conjecture. Even before the 1686 campaign began, the Porte requested that Louis mediate a peace between the Ottoman Empire and the Holy Roman Empire. Louis's response was a firm, if diplomatic, "No." "The interests of my crown having always been directly opposed to those of the House of Austria, the offices which I would employ to bring about the peace would be suspected by the German emperor. Any offer of mediation would expose me to a refusal which would of course be to the detriment of my dignity." All the same, Louis knew that the Turkish front could be rolled up in the coming campaign; certainly the imperial forces were likely to make sizable gains. After the League of Augsburg was formed, he ordered his ambassador in Constantinople "to let it be known where you are that next year there is the likelihood of a renewal of disturbances in the Empire. The Turks must not be disabused of the hope which they have conceived of a union between myself and the Kings of England and Denmark against the House of Austria, Sweden and all other states which up till the present have sided with them."[15]

On September 2, 1686, the imperial army triumphed at Budapest. In the midst of *Te Deums*, the booming of cannons, and the explosion of fireworks across the Germanies, the Austrians were eager to follow up their dazzling military success with victories in the political and diplomatic fields. At Versailles the news from Budapest inspired Louvois to achieve not only an adequate defense system but the capability of preventive warfare. A bridge was built north of Basel and fortifications were built there and elsewhere on the territory of the Empire.[16] All this violated the Truce of Regensburg but complaints were brusquely dismissed, the League of Augsburg usually serving as a pretext for the new fortifications. No recourse to laws, treaties, or truces was possible when Louis XIV was, at one and the same time, the accused party and the judge of his own culpability.

As Leopold celebrated his resounding victory against the Turks, he received word of a lesser triumph scored by Louis in Rome. On September 2, the very day on which Budapest fell, Pope Innocent named twenty-seven new cardinals. Wilhelm Egon von Fürstenberg was one of the elect. The pope acceded to Louis's request partly to preserve a balance in his appointments and partly with the hope that the French king might soften his attitudes towards the Holy See.[17] Innocent probably looked upon Fürstenberg as a pawn in an international competition which (from the pope's point of view) had the destruction of the Turks as its ultimate goal. Nevertheless, the news disappointed the emperor. One possible benefit to Vienna would be Wilhelm's estrangement or separation from Max Heinrich but this remained problematical. With increased prestige, there was every prospect of his continuing to play the role in which he had been cast by imperial propagandists: *turbator publicae quietis*.

Fürstenberg learned of his promotion in a dispatch from the French ambassador at Rome. The new cardinal, then vacationing at Aix-la-Chapelle, immediately contacted Louis XIV who arranged to bestow the red hat upon him in a ceremony at Versailles. Wilhelm's next concern was the way in which Max Heinrich would react to the pope's decision. In a conversation with Gravel, the elector said that when he looked at the list of new cardinals, "he had looked in vain for his name on the list . . . and recognized that the emperor had not troubled overmuch on his behalf at Rome." Despite his chagrin—he knew that it was, in all likelihood, the last promotion during his lifetime—he was happy to hear of Fürstenberg's good fortune. Many had predicted a rift from the moment that the elector learned that his prime minister now possessed a higher Church dignity and that his own desire to become a cardinal had been frustrated. But Max Heinrich displayed a surprising magnanimity. He wrote a cordial congratulatory letter to Wilhelm and solved the awkward situation at the court by agreeing to the substitution of the cardinal's twenty-five–year-old nephew, Ferdinand, as prime minister. It was understood that the latter would follow the political advice of his uncle. As for the possibility that his new dignity might necessitate Fürstenberg's permanent absence from Bonn, Max Heinrich said that they would always have pencils with which to keep in touch.[18] He had been dependent on Wilhelm's advice for so long, he never really doubted that it could be otherwise.

The elector's need for advice was soon apparent. Max Emmanuel of Bavaria, in the full flush of his victory at Buda, decided to visit Bonn to present his uncle with a large share of the booty won from the Turks and to introduce him to Joseph Clemens. He wanted his brother to become acquainted with the elector and the canons of the cathedral chapter and to fulfill the necessary six-week residence requirement which would qualify him for election as coadjutor.[19] Here was the first clear test of Max Heinrich's loyalty in the succession struggle. What course of action should he adopt?

The question was posed to Fürstenberg, then at Modave. Wilhelm knew that the visit had been suggested by his enemies, Burman, at Bonn, and Widman, the head of finances in the Munich cabinet and the brother of the deceased (1683) Widman who earlier refused to accept a *gratification*. Both were aware of Max Heinrich's avarice and hit upon the idea of the spoils of war as the best lure for the initial acceptance of Joseph Clemens. But Wilhelm also knew that Max Heinrich disapproved of his nephew's having joined the League of Augsburg and of his inclination to procrastinate on any decision which might displease Louis XIV. He advised the elector that if the visit could not honestly be dispensed with, it could at least be postponed so as to let affairs ripen and to allow more time for preparation. Next, he urged Dücker and Schönheim at Bonn to insinuate that the moment was not propitious and that the Elector of Bavaria should be notified that the international situation was too unsettled for a commitment on the coadjutorship.[20] In effect, he wished Joseph Clemens to be left out of the party; Max Emmanuel would probably not come without his brother and the danger would be skirted.

Fürstenberg's strategy worked like a charm. Even before he arrived in Bonn the entire affair had been resolved, his script literally followed by all concerned. Though Max Heinrich lost out on the presents, he avoided Louis's wrath. In Munich, the young elector was furious. One of his first steps was to have Emmanuel von Fürstenberg removed from his command in the imperial army. He cut his correspondence with Max Heinrich and a year elapsed before a Bavarian envoy went to Bonn.[21] The tourney had begun, the first lances had been crossed, and the stage set for a battle which all hoped could be kept within the political and diplomatic arena.

Soon thereafter, a major diplomatic breakthrough seemed imminent during a conversation at Versailles between Croissy and nuncio Ranuzzi. While discussing the climate of mistrust which enveloped Europe, the secretary of state reiterated the list of grievances against Austria and observed that it was necessary for the French to continue their fortifications due to the threat of imperial aggression. Ranuzzi replied that while the Augsburg alliance could probably not be undone, the existing tensions were no more welcome at Vienna than at Versailles; the emperor wished to convert the truce into a permanent peace. Croissy stated that this was precisely what the French wanted, that here was a project worthy of Pope Innocent's attention.[22]

Ranuzzi based his information on a letter from nuncio Buonvisi who informed him that at Vienna "peace was more desirable than a truce if transacting it did not infallibly bring about clashes between the two parties." In his enthusiasm to see a permanent peace reached, Ranuzzi did not stress the qualifying phrase in his conversation with Croissy. From the evidence at hand, it appears that Croissy asked Fürstenberg to draw up a memorandum on the conversion of the truce into a permanent peace. Wilhelm emphasized the need to act quickly, preferably through the pope.[23] He further suggested that if peace were to be established with any degree of permanency in the Germanies, all French fortifications in imperial territory should be torn down or abandoned and the French should renounce any such expansion in the future. In one sense this amounted to scrapping Richelieu's and Mazarin's policy of "strategic frontiers," enclaves deep into the Holy Roman Empire. Mazarin's League of the Rhine aimed at creating an atmosphere of harmony and confidence between Rhineland princes and France. Louis XIV's subsequent actions had destroyed that atmosphere. Fürstenberg's proposal can be seen as an attempt to revive the amity between France and the Rhineland states, an amity formerly cemented by their common distrust of the Habsburgs. In light of what Louis had done since 1664, nothing short of retrenchment would have convinced the Germans of his good faith. The alternative, from Wilhelm's point of view, was increased distrust of France, increased dependence on Austrian protection.

Louis rejected Fürstenberg's advice on the fortifications. Papal mediation, however, did meet with approval and discussion began via Ranuzzi. But the nuncio's truncated version of opinion at Vienna, together with French refusal to accept the heart of Fürstenberg's proposal, doomed any prospect of success from the outset. All the same, the course of the negotiation affords a revealing insight into Louis XIV's assumptions regarding imperial affairs and the temper of Europe in the face of his demands.

Croissy, despite his gruff, ill-tempered demeanor, was the advocate of a pacific, diplomatic approach in foreign affairs. Louvois led the war party at the king's council table. After reflecting upon the conversation with Ranuzzi, Louis's decision amounted to a compromise between the rival factions: he chose to open peace negotiations in a very peremptory fashion. Cardinal d'Estrées in Rome was instructed to present the French case and to ask for Innocent's support in bringing about a peace settlement. The king cited rumors that the Austrians, abetted by the Spanish, would conclude a peace with the Turks either at the beginning or the end of 1687. Innocent must comprehend that while the French had the welfare of Christendom at heart, there was no assurance that they would not be attacked once the war was concluded. Thus it was necessary that the emperor's intentions be known *before* the beginning of the spring campaign, before April 1687. Cardinal Ranuzzi informed him that Leopold would consider converting the twenty-year truce into a permanent peace, but to prevent confusion or deception such an agreement had to be concluded quickly. The best approach would be to circumvent the usual series of negotiations and to simply transform the Regensburg truce into a Peace: France would keep what she had, including the recently-constructed bridge north of Basel. The Palatine question would be consigned to the arbitration or mediation of the pope. To expedite matters at Rome, Louis held out the possibility of an annual French donation for the continuation of the Turkish war.[24]

When he received the king's instructions, d'Estrées immediately asked for an audience. Innocent was ill so discussions were held with Cardinal Cibo. D'Estrées presented two memoranda (which he himself had drawn up) stipulating Louis's conditions. As they were stripped of the usual diplomatic cushioning, the conditions sounded very much like an ultimatum. Some historians have castigated the Frenchman for the handling of this negotiation, their criticisms ranging from charges of ineptitude to deliberate and malicious destruction of any possibility that the proposition would be accepted. There is reason to believe that Louvois was in secret correspondence with d'Estrées and urged him to make acceptance impossible, but we lack sufficient information to make any final judgment—d'Estrées' dispatches from the first few months of 1687 are missing. What is known, however, makes it transparently clear why the French initiative was rebuffed. When Ranuzzi's reference to the emperor's desire for a general peace was cited, Cibo replied that while such a message had not been transmitted via Rome, it nonetheless was an excellent idea. He went on to explain why Innocent could not act as mediator in securing such a peace. The Palatine affair was not the only impediment to papal intervention; the Treaty of Westphalia was objectionable and therefore the pope could not sanction any pact, such as that of Regensburg, which was organically linked with the Westphalian agreement. Nevertheless, though he demurred on the deadline stipulated by Louis, Innocent said that he would urge Leopold to enter into peace negotiations at the Imperial Diet. The pope then communicated the French proposals to Cardinal Pio, who dealt with imperial affairs at Rome, as well as to the representatives of Spain and Venice. Finally, he turned over the French offer to a group of advisors, asking them to deliberate on the matter and to suggest a future course of action. With all this publicity, it was inevitable that news of Louis's proposals should have spread across Europe, giving rise to speculation regarding France's reaction if her "ultimatum" were turned down.[25]

There really was no question but that it would be turned down. All the objections to the plan were neatly summarized by Cardinal Pio in his letter to the emperor.[26] First, it was imprudent of the pope to go so far so soon merely on the passing comment of a nuncio in Paris who had neither explicit orders from Rome nor certain information from Vienna to justify saying what he did. Moreover, while "peace" was a noble word, what did it really amount to? There was difficulty enough enforcing the truce; who was there to suggest that such problems would disappear simply by changing the name? As for the deadline, similar to those demanded by France at Nijmegen and again at Regensburg, this was hardly a suitable stipulation if the complex problems which beset the Germanies were to be resolved. It was precisely the gravity of the issues involved which made one hesitate to accept a time limit.

Innocent issued a noncommittal statement on January 9, 1687 which was interpreted as a refusal to accept the offer in the terms presented by Louis XIV. A dispatch from Cibo to Ranuzzi sealed this impression: the king must realize that since the peace concerned all German princes, it was hardly feasible that they could deliberate in so short a span of time. Again, while it was true that Leopold desired "peace," it was "peace in a generic sense and not in the particular sense" of the transformation of the Regensburg agreement into a permanent settlement. Indeed, everyone understood that the Regensburg agreement had been a temporary one. For his part, Leopold let it be known through Buonvisi that since the truce affected the interests of many princes in the Empire, it was unthinkable that a peace could be reached through a simple bi-lateral negotiation. Buonvisi wrote letters in all directions in an attempt to explain how it all began. In his letter to the papal secretary of state he minced no words in assessing Ranuzzi: "I do not want to write any more to Cardinal Ranuzzi about negotiations nor do I wish to send him news items. I have told him so myself and he sought to justify himself before me with threadbare excuses. . . . His Holiness will know how prejudicial it is to his service not to have more confidence existing between his distant ministers."[27]

If Louis could not have his way with the peace, he at least wanted to have a declaration from Leopold attesting to his respect for the guarantee of the truce. He asked for a general guarantee on the part of the emperor and the states of the Empire. But was the guarantee to be reciprocal or merely unilateral? The argument swayed back and forth at Versailles. Louvois argued for a unilateral guarantee, a demand which would have been all the more humiliating since France had already violated the truce with her bridgeheads into the Empire. But the war minister determined to proceed at all costs with the fortifications and did not want to engage in any pledges to the contrary. Discussion on these points was also brisk at the Imperial Diet. Leopold wanted to have the electoral princes join him at Regensburg to discuss mutual defense as well as the question of a general guarantee. Such a meeting was viewed with misgivings at Versailles for it might be used to strengthen the League of Augsburg or, worse still, as a pretext to assemble the electors to vote for a King of the Romans. Under these circumstances, the electoral archbishops did not think it politic to accept the imperial overtures.[28]

In the end, Leopold was unwilling to jeopardize the opening of his spring campaign. He agreed to send a memorial to the French court affirming his respect for the Truce of Regensburg, adding that it would be respected even if the Turkish war came to an end before the expiration of the truce.[29] If this innocuous document enabled the French to save face while retreating from an embarrassing diplomatic position, it did not veil the growing mistrust and resentment which the Germans felt towards France in the wake of Louis's abortive peace efforts. With the change of seasons the imperial army prepared for the coming campaign while French troops solidified the bastions on the German frontiers. A great deal was expected to happen before the armies returned to winter quarters. The most one could hope for was that they would not be closer than they were in the spring.

IX

THE COADJUTORSHIP

APRIL 1687 TO JANUARY 1688

LEOPOLD'S GUARANTEE of the Truce of Regensburg produced a sense of deliverance and a somewhat forced gaiety at the courts of many German princes, especially in the Rhineland. But the declaration provided little more than a breathing spell. Gradual consolidation of Austrian power in the Danubian basin provoked a series of meetings at Versailles to devise a counter-strategy that would ensure the French presence in the Empire. The elements in this strategy included continued work on the fortifications, the detachment of Bavaria from the Austrian alliance and the election of Fürstenberg as coadjutor at Cologne and Liège with the assurance of future succession. Since there was more than a slight contradiction in aiming for Bavaria's friendship while intriguing to eliminate the Wittelsbachs from their fief at Cologne, it was imperative that each part of the strategy be isolated from the other. By utmost secrecy the French could at least gamble on the Cologne succession's bearing fruit.

The assignment of handling Max Emmanuel of Bavaria was given to the Marquis de Villars, then thirty-seven years old. He had distinguished himself during the Dutch War and held the rank of colonel, but peace made him restive; time and again he asked for a commission to travel to foreign lands in the king's service. The Bavarian mission provided such an opportunity. To disguise the purpose of his journey he first went to Vienna to offer condolences to Leopold on the death of his mother. After investigating the extent of Austrian military preparation, he stopped off in Munich and began to insinuate himself into the life of the court.[1]

Villars's initial success in Munich surpassed even the most optimistic predictions. His high spirits, keen wit, and zest for military affairs won him the attention and favor of the young Bavarian elector. The Frenchman had a special talent for introducing new mistresses which made him the more welcome. During the course of seemingly endless revelries and carousings the two men became boon companions and Villars stayed on at the court with the prospect of accompanying the elector during the next campaign. Louis and Croissy, elated at their agent's success, underlined the urgent necessity of drawing Max Emmanuel away from his Austrian ties and left it to Villars's resourcefulness to do the rest.

The closer the Bavarian situation was brought into focus, the more did it begin to reveal some possible avenues of approach. Though Max Emmanuel was married to the daughter of Emperor Leopold, the empress, a Neuburg, was determined to secure the coadjutorship of Cologne for her own family. The relationship between Vienna and Munich was further envenomed by the rivalry between Max Emmanuel and Charles of Lorraine. The latter was commander-in-chief of the imperial armies, an honor which was hotly resented by the "Blue Knight," as Max Emmanuel was called. Here, too, was an opening which Villars might exploit. Not to be forgotten was the presence at Versailles of the Bavarian Dauphine, Max Emmanuel's sister, and the nucleus of a French party at Munich, a party which had once been influential during the reign of the elector's father. Yet even though Max Emmanuel exclaimed that his desire to command armies need not mean only the armies of the emperor, his comments flowed more from personal pique against Charles of Lorraine than from any policy differences with Leopold. After all his grumbling he still sallied forth on the next stage of the Hungarian campaign with Villars accompanying him as observer and participant in the freewheeling climate that prevailed on the battlefront. The preparations for this campaign, however, proceeded at a snail's pace. On June 8 Villars informed Croissy that little had been done in spite of huge subsidies provided by the pope.[2] Despite this inauspicious beginning, spectacular successes would be achieved before the winter of 1687.

While the imperial army languished in inactivity, the French made their first move in Cologne. During the course of a May inspection tour in the northeast Louis visited Luxembourg, where, together with Croissy and Louvois, he was joined by Ferdinand von Fürstenberg and Dücker, representing the Elector of Cologne. Wilhelm, inevitably, was present, though in an unofficial capacity. On May 25 they agreed upon the final draft of a new offensive-defensive pact, another version of the one ratified by Max Heinrich in January 1684. In the event of a future war the elector would put his army as well as his fortified places at the disposal of France. There were the usual provisions regarding the passage and recruitment of troops, as well as a yearly pension of 40,000 écus to be paid in quarterly installments. There was no mention in the treaty of Louis's wishes on the issue of the coadjutorship. Once Max Heinrich ratified the treaty (July 9, 1687) the French passed to the next stage of their strategy: direct talks on the succession. Their trump card was the unpaid debt of 400,000 livres which the elector had contracted at the outset of the Dutch War. Perhaps the debt could be cancelled in exchange for Fürstenberg's becoming coadjutor with rights of future succession. Louis told Gravel that whenever the elector mentioned the debt he could stall for time by writing for instructions. Further, Max Heinrich had to be persuaded to keep any discussion of the coadjutorship from Fürstenberg. Wilhelm himself suggested these stage directions, for if he became involved too soon the elector might look upon his participation as still another instance of his notorious opportunism. (To simplify matters, he stayed in his chateau at Modave.) The king reminded Gravel to keep the succession at Cologne linked to the succession at Liège: the two coadjutorships were not to be split.[3]

As the lazy summer days drifted into July, Gravel waited for a suitable opening to broach the succession issue. Providentially, the Neuburg Queen of Portugal helped to smooth the way. After visiting her father at Heidelberg, she passed Bonn[4] en route to Düsseldorf where she would visit her brother, the Duke of Jülich. Afterwards, in the company of another brother, Franz Ludwig, Bishop of Breslau, she planned a trip to England where she was expected to ask for James II's intercession at Rome in favor of the Neuburg claim on Münster. This mission naturally infuriated Max Heinrich, for his claim to Münster had been repeatedly challenged at Rome by the Neuburgs. Gravel reminded him that the Neuburgs would succeed at Cologne and Liège if preventive measures were not taken. In fact, he said, Louis XIV believed that the only way to ensure tranquility after Max Heinrich's death was to have coadjutors already in office to assume command. Thus if the respective chapters were agreeable, what would he think of Fürstenberg's offering himself as coadjutor?

As Gravel told it, the elector paced back and forth in his study, murmuring phrases and half-phrases about the obligation he owed his family. Gravel noted that Max Emmanuel had no heirs and that it was doubtful his wife would bear children. The Blue Knight daily ran the risk of being killed in the war and the only direct heir to his possessions was Joseph Clemens, the Wittelsbach candidate to succeed at Cologne. He was only fifteen years old and had not yet shown any interest in the religious life. This observation struck home, especially since the elector took his religious obligations seriously. If Max Emmanuel were to die without heirs, Gravel continued, Joseph Clemens would become the head of the Wittelsbach clan; any current attempt to set him up as a bishop would be a graver danger to the family than a temporary control of the archdiocese by Fürstenberg. And temporary it would be. Indeed, there was every chance of Max Heinrich's outliving the cardinal. What was most important was a smooth succession, with no civil war. Fürstenberg could be counted on to follow the same wise policies which Max Heinrich himself had pursued and surely there was no one else who had his experience in the affairs of the electorate. Once the Elector of Bavaria was back in the good graces of France, there would be no obstacle to having a Wittelsbach serving as a coadjutor under Wilhelm. Gravel skillfully played variations on these themes. After many hesitations the elector at last agreed to allow Fürstenberg to hold an election, provided that he could be sure of the necessary votes. He did not want to become embroiled in a tangle of controversy and recrimination. He further insisted that nothing be done without his knowledge and permission. Needless to say, the entire affair was to be shrouded in secrecy.[5]

As soon as Fürstenberg learned that his "candidacy" had been accepted, he urged Louis to write a letter in his own hand thanking the elector and encouraging him to remain firm in a resolution which would do much to ensure peace in the Rhineland. The king immediately complied.[6] Wilhelm remained in the Liège area to reconnoiter prospects of support in the cathedral chapter, many of whose members either hated him for his role in suppressing the uprising in 1684 or feared that their personal power would be severely diminished if ever Fürstenberg assumed control. As we shall see, the obstacles in Liège proved to be even more insuperable than those in Cologne.

August came and was almost gone and Wilhelm still gave no sign of returning to Cologne. His measured pace bordered on nonchalance and exasperated Gravel, who endlessly expatiated on the dangers of inaction and delay. Louis, as usual, let Fürstenberg set his own pace. Gravel nevertheless obtained permission to visit Wilhelm at Modave and implored him to leave as soon as possible. Upon returning to Bonn, Gravel had a long conversation with Max Heinrich during which he described the scene which supposedly occurred when Fürstenberg learned "for the first time" that not only had Louis preferred him as coadjutor of Cologne and Liège but that the elector had agreed to this request. The cardinal's first words after "recovering from his astonishment," the elector learned, were to express the pleasure he derived "at the very thought of being able to double his application and zeal in favor of everything which could contribute to the satisfaction and renown of Max Heinrich, and to the well-being and security of his states."[7] Shortly after this comedy had been played out, Wilhelm returned to Bonn and assured Max Heinrich that he would do nothing without his complete knowledge and approval.

Despite all efforts to preserve secrecy, Gravel's dire predictions were fulfilled: news of the intrigue leaked out and reached Philipp Wilhelm of

Neuburg, Fürstenberg's bitterest enemy in the Germanies. The memory of the cannon shot on the Rhine had only inflamed a long-standing hatred toward the cardinal, whom he believed to be the greatest obstacle to Neuburg chances at Cologne, Liège, Münster, or Hildesheim. Moreover, if Wilhelm ever entered the Electoral College he would surely do his utmost to exclude Leopold's son (and Philipp Wilhelm's grandson) from being elected King of the Romans. He sent an urgent dispatch to Munich, urging that Joseph Clemens go to Bonn accompanied by a clever minister; a similar note was sent to the emperor. Max Emmanuel temporized, noting that his brother really had not decided if he would take religious vows. Philipp Wilhelm, however, did not wait for this answer before acting; he thought enough time had been wasted. By adroit maneuvering he enrolled his son, the Bishop of Breslau, in the electoral chapter at Cologne on August 22 with orders to work for Joseph Clemens or, at least, for the postponement of any election.[8] But the Neuburgs always worked on more than one level: enrollment in the chapter not only entitled one to vote in an election but to be a candidate as well. Thus the seeds of confusion, and perhaps division, were sown in the ranks of Wilhelm's enemies.

Max Emmanuel's half-hearted response may well have stemmed from a disbelief that his uncle would have given approval on such a serious matter without consulting him. Besides, his preoccupation with the war precluded any political engagement in the distant Rhineland. The past few weeks had been eventful: on August 12 Charles of Lorraine led the imperial armies to a resounding victory at Mohacs, followed by still another victory at Esseck. Transylvania was secured; the situation in the Turkish camp was desperate. An insurrection in the Janissary corps provoked a palace revolt that would topple the Grand Visir and replace Sultan Mohammed IV with his brother Suleiman II in November 1687. With the elimination of Turkish power in Hungary, the kingdom was ripe for annexation. While most of the nobility would retain power in their domains, their traditional liberties, as well as the constitutional right to resist the king, were abolished. As a finishing touch, "the crown was made hereditary in the Habsburg house and the Golden Bull of 1222 was 'corrected' in such a way as to place all real power in the hands of the king." The stage was set for the crowning of Leopold's eldest son Joseph as King of Hungary on December 8, 1687. These developments were grave omens to the French and to many Germans as well. The Venetian ambassador reported that the rapid progress against the Turks was leading to jealousies and suspicions. Such misgivings were especially acute among Protestant princes who knew that an increase in Habsburg power might reduce their own liberties. This in turn was linked to their fear of Catholic power everywhere in Europe; their co-religionists were oppressed in Hungary and in France and endangered in the England of James II.[9]

The success of the imperial armies made it imperative that Fürstenberg sew up the Cologne election. Neuburg machinations made it easier for him to persuade Max Heinrich that his own activity was directed against them rather than against the Wittelsbachs. This theme was repeated in private talks with individual canons: the Neuburgs were depicted as *arrivistes* with no interest in or knowledge of Cologne affairs. After forty years of service in the electorate, Wilhelm was in a position to make such charges and to drive them home; he worked the chapter ceaselessly, solidifying old ties and bargaining with the fence-sitters.[10] Throughout his career he had rendered hundreds of little favors which he hoped could be converted into a hard core of support when he needed it. Besides, many canons expected him to die in the near future, affording them still another chance to profit from the windfall of bribery and corruption which attended every important election in the Empire.

Despite the support of the great majority of canons, Wilhelm never forgot that while the chapter could postulate him, approval had to come from Rome. Since July there was a new apostolic nuncio at Cologne, Sebastiano Antonio Tanara. Fürstenberg courted him assiduously, going so far as to claim that at the electoral court "he was considered too partial in favor of the interests of Rome." Despite French suspicions, Tanara proved to be one of Wilhelm's best advocates before the Holy See; he tipped off Fürstenberg on all the Neuburg maneuvers at Rome.[11]

Wilhelm mapped out his strategy for the electoral contest at the beginning of October.[12] It was understood that Max Heinrich did not want an election to take place unless Wilhelm was sure of the canons, and further, that Joseph Clemens would be the next coadjutor of Cologne, provided that Bavarian policies were acceptable to France. Finally, since a two-thirds vote was required for postulation in each chapter, he would need sixteen votes in Cologne and thirty-three in Liège. Wilhelm chose to hold the first election in Cologne. Besides being the greater prize, there were fewer canons to win over and a victory there would pave the road for triumph in Liège, or so he thought. A preliminary poll showed that he could be sure of fourteen votes in the Cologne chapter, but since three canons had died within the past two years there might yet be replacements; it was difficult to make any absolute predictions. In any event, the chances for success seemed better now than if they waited until the elector died, since many expected that if Fürstenberg ever did succeed, it would be with one foot in the grave. Rome and Bavaria would be notified three weeks before the election, thus giving them little time in which to act.

Most of the canons had received pensions from Wilhelm since his release from prison and joyfully anticipated the upcoming contest as a source of more money. As Breget put it, "it is hoped that on this occasion the king will have the goodness to grant subsidies in proportion to the importance of the affair, without which it would not be apropos for the cardinal to involve himself at all." Wilhelm asked for an outright grant of 60–80,000 livres plus a 30,000-livre increase in his yearly pension from the time he became coadjutor until he became Elector of Cologne. Louis sent 60,000 livres and agreed to increase the pension when he became coadjutor.[13]

The wheels were in motion none too soon. Since the secret of Wilhelm's designs at Liège was known in the city itself and in the United Provinces, the king urged him to strike while the iron was hot. Gravel heard that many canons at Liège opposed a coadjutor, for that would diminish their own power; they calculated that publicity would force Wilhelm to back down. While Tanara could not confirm such reports, he believed it unlikely that an affair of such magnitude could remain hidden for long with forty canons involved.[14]

The reports from Liège made the rumors concerning Cologne more credible; the pleas of the Elector Palatine were finally heeded. Leopold's Secret Council determined to prevent an election or else to support Joseph Clemens. Regardless of tactics, Fürstenberg had to be stopped; Count Kaunitz was commissioned to represent both Bavaria and Austria at Bonn. Meanwhile, the Bishop of Breslau and the Duke of Jülich sojourned in Max Heinrich's capital from October 18 to 23 to scout the possibilities of electing Joseph Clemens or of preventing the election. They avoided the elector, fearing charges of self-interest or the accusation that if they thought a coadjutor necessary, it implied that Max Heinrich was unfit.[15] Moreover, the elector knew that the Neuburg family was seeking to arrange a marriage with Joseph Clemens and so eliminate him as a candidate at Cologne. The young man's preferences were not known and this added to Max Heinrich's confusion. He feared that if Wilhelm succeeded the electorate might forever pass out of Wittelsbach control. Through an intermediary he asked Fürstenberg what would happen if Joseph Clemens were rejected as unsuitable by the French after Wilhelm's death. Would the electoral crown then be placed on the head of one of the "Messeigneurs les Enfans de France"? Wilhelm said that as far as he knew, "no one in France had dreamt of such a thing," but if Joseph

Clemens were to marry, "no greater blessing could be bestowed upon the churches of Cologne and Liège than to have one of the 'Messeigneurs les Enfans de France' as Prince." The dioceses could thus recover many rights and possessions kept from them by neighbors or through unfortunate circumstances. Max Heinrich accepted this answer for the moment, contenting himself with Wilhelm's promise not to do anything without his participation and consent.[16]

Despite Fürstenberg's confident façade, apprehension could be glimpsed in the ciphered dispatches between Cologne, Rome, and Versailles. Wilhelm asked Tissier (the Cologne agent in Rome) and Cardinal d'Estrées to detail the opposition against him at the papal court. He feared that the Neuburgs and the Austrians could persuade the pope to forbid a vote by the chapter. If so, he planned to maintain his supporters' loyalty and hold the election upon news of the pope's death. Otherwise, he felt free to go ahead since Innocent had the power to confirm or reject the chapter's decision.[17]

Wilhelm especially feared the efforts of his opponents in Rome because he knew that the biggest stumbling block to his ambition was the clash between the pope and Louis XIV. Innocent XI was a strong-willed, fiercely combative zealot who was even more concerned about the dignity of his office than was Louis XIV about his, and who determinedly opposed the French king and his policies across the board in Europe. During a quarrel in 1680 over the *Régale*, Agostino Favoriti, the most influential papal adviser at the time, expressed the belief "that in Paris they now know that in Pope Innocent XI there is the spirit and the conduct of those great pontiffs whom God has used to make the Church great and that we are no longer in the era of womanly popes (*papesses*)." This last gibe referred to recent overly-pliant popes, for two of whom Favoriti had delivered much-applauded funeral orations. Favoriti's choice of words suggests that *machismo* as much as principles and politics played a role in the duel between Rome and Versailles. The papal secretary's intensity was shared by his relative and successor, Lorenzo Casoni, Innocent's most intimate and influential adviser in the last years of his pontificate.[18] The fact that Louis XIV's navy had destroyed so much of Casoni's native city of Genoa in the 1684 bombardment added fuel to his hatred of the French.

The animus of his advisers against France was equally evident in the pope himself. Innocent's chief concern—the key to an understanding of practically every decision he ever took in foreign affairs—was the war against the Turks. Louis refused to support this crusade; indeed, he had preferred a Turkish victory, perhaps so as to emerge as the last Christian champion and thus to displace Leopold as Holy Roman Emperor. Papal rancor against France deepened as a result of the Gallican Articles of 1682 and the dragonnades in connection with the Revocation of the Edict of Nantes. Finally, there was the affair of the French quarter in Rome, the problem of the *franchises*. Foreign embassies and their immediate surroundings had formerly been accorded a diplomatic immunity which prevented Roman police from intruding. Over the years this privilege was abused: the areas in question became sanctuaries for criminals and fugitives of every description who were protected (for a price) by the ambassadors or their favorites. Innocent XI's efforts to correct this practice were largely successful since every major power except France abolished the abuses attendant upon these diplomatic immunities. Louis XIV refused to bend: "He was to give examples to others, but not to receive any from them." When Cardinal d'Estrées's brother (long the French ambassador in Rome) died on January 30, 1687, the pope refused to recognize his successor unless the disputed prerogatives were surrendered. In November Louis sent the Marquis of Lavardin to Rome as his ambassador, accompanied by 100 guards, to force his way into the embassy if necessary.[19] As reports of Lavardin's steady approach reached the city, there began to trickle in rumors of a prospective election of the French-backed Cardinal von Fürstenberg as coadjutor at both Liège and Cologne. To say the least, Lavardin's armed entry into Rome could only lessen Wilhelm's chances of obtaining the pope's approval.

While Lavardin traveled towards Rome, the Neuburgs stepped up their activity in Cologne. The Duke of Jülich sent his stable-master, Velbruck, to inquire at Bonn if it were true that an election was planned; if so, he would work for Joseph Clemens. Fürstenberg, however, had played this game many times before and was not going to be trapped by a stable-master from Düsseldorf. In spite of all the rumors Velbruck could point to nothing official, nothing public concerning an election. He made inquiries, spoke disparagingly of the cardinal on several occasions and set his sights for future activity. On his return, he said that obviously the canons of the Cologne chapter were exceedingly venal.[20]

Velbruck's visit offered Wilhelm a golden opportunity to attack and he took full advantage of it before the chapter on November 7. Most of the canons disliked the Neuburgs anyway and since Wilhelm was a gifted orator with a mordant wit they could enjoy the performance. He began by observing that there was no record of any steps to elect a coadjutor. Under the pretext of working for Joseph Clemens, Velbruck was spinning a web of intrigue in behalf of those who sent him. He protested against the slander and innuendoes directed against his person: since he was dean of the chapter, it was an affront to all present. Wilhelm then attacked Velbruck's basic assumption, that the Electorate of Cologne belonged to the House of Bavaria. If so, then nobody else could aspire to such a dignity. As the nuncio observed, such a statement amounted to a declaration of his candidacy while flattering the hopes of the other canons.[21]

At Versailles the Velbruck affair was viewed as a case of amateur bungling. Kaunitz had yet to arrive and Max Heinrich had yet to expose himself to the pressure and criticism which lay ahead. On this subject, Louis was firm: "It is absolutely necessary that the Elector of Bavaria be prevented from having any credit in the Electorate of Cologne or of having any hope that his brother might succeed there. I can no longer consider the Elector of Cologne to be my friend if he lends an ear to the propositions which will be made to him by Count Kaunitz or if he offers him any hope of success in his negotiation."[22]

Fürstenberg and Gravel decided to handle the pre-election maneuvering in two stages: the chapter would vote on the desirability of having a coadjutor; if it agreed, a date for the election would be set. These votes required a majority and not a two-thirds vote and might lead the imperial party to think that Wilhelm allowed such a test because he was confident of winning the election. In the interim, they hoped that Max Heinrich would influence some of the fence-sitters to support the cardinal. Upon approaching the elector, however, Gravel again witnessed his fear of abandoning family interests. He unrolled the previous arguments concerning Neuburg ambition and the probable sterility of Max Emmanuel's wife, but without much success.[23] Max Heinrich clearly wanted something else before he would give his full support. At Versailles they understood; the debt had to be settled.

The first real test of the elector's loyalty came on November 15 when Johann Wilhelm and Franz Ludwig came to talk with him in person. Fürstenberg saw this visit as the crisis point: "Provided that [Max Heinrich] sustains this assault with firmness, I believe that he will soon find himself out of difficulty." The elector greeted the Neuburgs warmly but his disposition soon changed upon remembering their designs on Münster. When his visitors tried to shift the conversation by discussing Joseph Clemens as a future coadjutor the elector cut them short, noting that their own family was negotiating to have his nephew marry a Neuburg duchess. Besides, he could not be sure about the young man's intentions until he spoke to Count Kaunitz nor could he afford to irritate Louis XIV. The Neuburgs exclaimed that any attempt to elect Fürstenberg was pointless since neither the emperor nor the electoral college could ever accept him. The elector retorted that in the light of Wilhelm's qualifications and the presence of French troops in the nearby area, there were few capitularies who would not vote for the cardinal if an election were held.[24]

Max Heinrich's visitors were tenacious. The Duke of Jülich delivered a long polemic against Fürstenberg, parading the old skeletons from the closet, accusing him of leading a scandalous life and of bribing the canons. After consigning Wilhelm to the lower reaches of the Inferno, he painted an idyllic picture of Joseph Clemens, working upon Max Heinrich's sentiments of affection and loyalty to his family. Worn out by the long interview, beset with his old doubts and hesitations, and anxious to dismiss his guests, the harried elector gave them permission to act in his name for the candidacy of Joseph Clemens.[25] The two brothers departed in a state of euphoria.

Max Heinrich did not have time to compose himself before he was confronted by Gravel and Rotkirch, Fürstenberg's liaison in Cologne. They reminded him that he had reneged on his previous promise, that he could no longer be considered a friend of the king and that they could not answer for the consequences which were sure to follow. In his overwrought state of mind, the confused elector made another about-face. Not only did he retract the permission to use his name in favor of Joseph Clemens, he pledged his full support to Fürstenberg and wrote letters to this effect to two fence-sitters, using the cardinal's name in the letters.[26] In this one melodramatic day a major obstacle had been removed, but disaster had narrowly been averted.

The Neuburgs were stunned; Philipp Wilhelm asked the Elector of Brandenburg to strengthen his military forces and to send an envoy to Bonn immediately. He then attempted to visit Max Heinrich but was rebuffed. After brushing aside Philipp Wilhelm's charges of undue pressure by Fürstenberg, Max Heinrich promised to do everything in good conscience to ensure that his diocese would continue to benefit the Church and the public welfare. "I would be deeply grateful if you would no longer importune me during the course of this affair, an affair which depends upon the Divine will and disposition." Since Wilhelm drafted this letter, he must have relished the bit about the Divine will and disposition. He told Gravel that the letter was couched in such fashion as to represent the Palatine as hot-tempered and inconsiderate and to make it clear that Max Heinrich was of no humor to receive similar requests. He predicted that Kaunitz would try to persuade him to renounce the Cologne post in exchange for concessions.[27] This proved to be true.

In a final effort, Johann Wilhelm told the nuncio that the canons had been bribed, that the stain of simony was everywhere, and that it was

Rome's duty to ban the election. When Tanara brought these charges to Fürstenberg, he was asked for proof: the Duke of Jülich should itemize the supposed acts of corruption and then the facts could be "juridically verified." Tanara begged off, saying that it was "an unlikely case . . . which demanded no present need of justification."[28]

Wilhelm was encouraged by these signs; in spite of Louis's permission to halt the proceedings, he resolved to go forward. At a chapter meeting on November 20 he reviewed the risks to the electorate if Max Heinrich died without a successor. Chaos, possibly civil war, could ensue with no one to profit except the surrounding Protestant powers. Thus, would the canons approve of his asking for the elector's permission to have the chapter vote on the usefulness (*Nützlichkeit*) of having a coadjutor? All but two of the canons approved, with the Bishop of Breslau raising the most violent objections. Such a maneuver was not unknown in cathedral chapters at the time; certainly it suited Fürstenberg's style. Sufficient deference had been paid to the capitularies; he could go before the elector as the humble representative of the chapter. At the same time, he kept his promise to Max Heinrich: the elector was fully informed and left with the final decision. On the other hand, it gave Wilhelm the welcome alibi, in case it be required, that it was the chapter which had cited the need for a coadjutor; he had initiated nothing to the detriment of the elector's family. Max Heinrich agreed to write a letter to the chapter approving of its request.[29]

Fürstenberg informed Tanara of Max Heinrich's decision and requested papal approval of the future election. He and Gravel then met in Cologne to discuss ways of handling Max Emmanuel. At first they decided to ask Max Heinrich to persuade his nephew not to enter the competition, but Wilhelm thought better of such a move for it would needlessly offend the elector. Besides, Joseph Clemens could always obtain an indult from Rome. A small delegation was sent to Munich to inform Max Emmanuel that his uncle had approved the upcoming election.[30]

On November 28 the chapter agreed on the necessity of holding an election for coadjutor. The vote was 18–1, with only the Bishop of Breslau opposed. He abstained on the next vote which fixed the date of the election for January 7, 1688, the day after Epiphany. The election of a coadjutor was to be the first order of business in the New Year. On November 20 Louis XIV promised to remit the 400,000-livre debt as soon as Fürstenberg was approved as coadjutor with the assurance of succession. As in the past, the Austrians tried to woo the cardinal away from France with impressive offers: the coadjutorships of Liège and Hildesheim; the Landgraviat of Dinguen and Neuenburg in Swabia, with a guaranteed annual income of 15,000 écus; and a leading position in the Austrian government for his nephew Emmanuel. All Wilhelm had to do was to renounce his designs on Cologne and work for the election of Joseph Clemens. While he refused these offers, he did not fail to express his doubts as to the final outcome. The major hurdle would be papal confirmation but there were others, including acceptance by the other electors.[31]

Proof that Wilhelm's doubts were legitimate was then en route from Rome in the form of a ciphered letter to Tanara. "With respect to the coadjutorship," it read, "the thinking of His Holiness is that you should refrain from adhering to any of the parties concerned. You should make known to the elector that his age and health are so vigorous that he does not appear to have any need of a coadjutor. In any event, His Holiness does not feel disposed at the present time to allow him one, especially in view of the charges and counter-charges of corruption which have been brought to our attention."[32]

If the pope's decision cast a shadow over Fürstenberg's activity in Cologne, the situation in Rome, had he known the whole of it, would have left him even more pessimistic. On November 18, 1687, Innocent decided to inform Louis and his ministers that they ran the risk of excommunication as a direct consequence of the Lavardin mission. The latter arrived in Rome on November 16 and closed off the streets of the quarter surrounding the Farnese Palace. Flouted in his own city, flagrantly ignored in spite of all his public proclamations, Innocent XI saw no other recourse than to threaten "the censure and the wrath of God" upon the king and instructed his nuncio in Paris to inform Louis as soon as possible.[33]

When Ranuzzi received his orders, he was already a persona non grata: the king refused him an audience until Lavardin had been accredited in Rome. Yet after explaining the difficulties involved, he declared himself ready to fulfill the wishes of his superiors. Before his return dispatch had reached Rome, still another message had been sent to him. Innocent acknowledged Ranuzzi's delicate position and suggested that he give the assignment to a trusted aide, Dr. Amonio, who had served as a liaison in the recent crisis between the nuncio and the French ministry. These instructions did not reach Paris until after the Cologne election. But even had there been time to negotiate, Innocent was not one to engage in compromise: the die had been cast.[34]

All this secret correspondence, of course, was unsuspected on the Rhine. In Bonn and Cologne the major concern was the visit of the Austrian ambassador and the effect that his coming would have on the spirit of the old elector. Already Max Emmanuel had denied the rumors concerning Joseph Clemens's imminent marriage. Such tales, he said, "have been invented by those who wish to carry away this precious jewel [the coadjutorship] from our Electoral House, an injury and a loss which would be irreparable." He decided to send his own emissary since Kaunitz had come down with a fever and might have a relapse. For the Cologne assignment, Max Emmanuel chose his most trusted diplomatic aide, Johann Friedrich Karg.[35]

Karg wanted to leave immediately without waiting for Max Heinrich's representative to arrive in Munich; the latter could be expected to stall so as to leave the Bavarian and Austrian delegates less time for activity in Cologne. As for Kaunitz, after recovering he found that he did not have full power to treat with Max Heinrich and so had to send back to Vienna for additional documents. Karg thus set off for Bonn alone and arrived there on December 13. In an interview with Dücker and Schönheim, he was told of Neuburg inquiries at Rome concerning the possibilities of succeeding at Cologne. He was also informed that the Neuburgs had been told that only when the Bavarian candidate was out of the race would their request be considered. Since this information could not be checked in Rome before the election, it was probably planted so as to stir up dissension in the enemy camp. This camp had not yet assembled. Only after Kaunitz arrived, and with the participation of the Neuburgs, could they begin to coordinate their activity and prepare for the assault. As December wore on the pressure intensified. Cologne magistrates in debt to the Elector Palatine were told to pay or cooperate. There was the threat of bringing more Brandenburg troops into the city and news that the Duke of Jülich had letters of exchange from Dutch bankers worth 100,000 écus.[36] While the figure may have been exaggerated, bribery was rampant.

Kaunitz finally arrived on December 18; he met with Karg and Wachtendonk from Brandenburg and they agreed to speak to Max Heinrich one at a time in an attempt to shake his resolve. Karg was the first to present his case. He began by emphasizing that Max Heinrich was the oldest member of his family and that the entire Wittelsbach clan looked to him for direction. The family had long served as one of the spearpoints of the Counter-Reformation and there was still much work to be done against heresy. This mission was not only an honor, it was a responsibility which had to be met. Only by transmitting the electoral dignity to a Wittelsbach could he truly fulfill the trust which had been placed in him. He avowed that Joseph Clemens had every intention of entering the

Church and added that Max Emmanuel and his wife were young enough to look forward to children. This said, Karg thought it best not to press his point and retired in favor of the envoy from Brandenburg. Wachtendonk had a small role to play, if only because he represented a Protestant power in an affair regarding the Catholic Church.[37] He merely asked that the election be postponed for the sake of ensuring peace in the region and insinuated that this step would surely gratify the pope.

When Kaunitz's turn came, "he entered the elector's chambers with great vigor and soon delivered high-handed protests, if not actual menaces, to Max Heinrich." In an obvious reference to the events of the Dutch War, he warned Max Heinrich of the dangers which might befall him, his states, and the Fürstenberg family if he persisted in his support of the cardinal's election. This harsh language only served to stiffen the elector's resistance. Max Heinrich told him flatly that Fürstenberg was at that time the most worthy and certainly the most capable man to govern the archdiocese after his death. In any case, the decision was no longer his to make: it was up to the chapter to decide.[38]

In contrast to Karg's tactics of persuasion, Kaunitz's asperity had only exasperated the elector and he knew it. To make amends, he asked for and received another audience. Kaunitz changed his approach and lowered his voice. He presented two letters, one from Joseph Clemens and the other from Max Emmanuel. Joseph Clemens said he was convinced that he had a vocation to the religious life; the elector was deeply moved. The other letter, however, produced a totally different effect: Max Emmanuel berated him in rather shrill tones about the loss of honor to the Wittelsbach family and so angered him that Kaunitz could do little else but retire.[39]

The three envoys held another strategy session, this time accompanied by the two Neuburg brothers. They decided to drop Joseph Clemens from contention and to concentrate on stopping or adjourning the election. The French anticipated such a move: on Christmas Day Louis XIV accorded Wilhelm an additional 100,000 livres "to use as he thought best." Meanwhile, Fürstenberg hinted that the French would remember every canon who reneged on his promise of support.[40]

Karg realized that it was too late; the canons excused themselves by saying that it would be necessary to wait for another occasion to demonstrate the respect they had for the House of Bavaria. Kaunitz fared no better. As a last resort he presented Fürstenberg with a personal letter from the emperor, beseeching him to think of the welfare of the Archdiocese of Cologne and the German fatherland and to consider the propositions which Kaunitz was empowered to make. These offers were the same ones that Wilhelm had earlier refused. He again regretted his inability to accept Leopold's terms but claimed that "he could not sacrifice all of his friends for his own interest, nor could he default in the duty which he owed the Church in Cologne. He asked him to consider what he himself would do if he were in his place."[41] The only real hope of preventing the election lay in a prohibition from Rome.

Pope Innocent was in a delicate, even embarrassing position. He did not want to offend Leopold, upon whom he depended for the prosecution of the war against the Turks, and he was trying to avoid any undue provocation of Louis XIV. Finally, he did not wish to irritate the Cologne chapter, which, like all German chapters, was very jealous of its rights and prerogatives. Thus while the pope would not approve of the election at that time, neither would he expressly forbid it. He wanted Fürstenberg to postpone the election in the interests of a general peace. Following instructions, Tanara stated that Innocent looked upon all the contestants with an indifferent eye, that his one concern was public tranquility and that in the last analysis the electorate really had no need of a coadjutor. What with his outstanding qualifications and the extreme youth of Joseph Clemens, the cardinal would undoubtedly succeed after Max Heinrich died. Fürstenberg met this argument head on. He approved highly of the pope's intentions, but unfortunately Innocent built his case upon faulty assumptions, upon reasoning which was hardly relevant. The pope was not aware of the extent to which the atmosphere had been poisoned by all the Neuburg intrigues. If the election took place now, it would be attended by no violence; if they waited until the elector died, serious disturbances were inevitable. Furthermore, the emperor was "trampling upon the liberty of the chapter and arrogating to himself the right to exclude him a priori from consideration for the electoral dignity."[42] He was determined to meet this challenge and hold the election.

In Rome, Cardinal Pio asked that the election be prohibited but Innocent said there were no German precedents for such an action. Pio argued that such statutes were created for the utility of the Church and that if it served the Church's interest to forbid a postulation, then that was the road of reason. The pope declared that France should not be given another reason for disturbing the peace. The only step which Pio was permitted to take was to obtain a writ of inhibition from the *auditore camerae* which the Bishop of Breslau had indicated could be used to great effect before the chapter. As soon as the writ arrived, the Neuburgs had it tacked up on the door of the cathedral in Cologne. Fürstenberg underlined the worthlessness of the document by ordering his secretary to tear it down and rip it up.[43]

On December 26 the eagerly-awaited courier from Rome reached Munich, but the desired prohibition of the Cologne election was not in his dispatch case. The last hope of the imperial camp seemed to have vanished. At the eleventh hour, the Bishop of Breslau sent a memorial to the chapter asking for the suspension of the election and vilifying Fürstenberg. He accused Max Heinrich of naively allowing himself to be trapped by the finesse and the ruses of the cardinal and argued that the entire election proceedings were being foisted upon the chapter. After this statement was read, the canons refused to register it and sent it back to the bishop.[44]

Karg was (or claimed to be) scandalized by the attack, asserting that he had no previous knowledge that such an outburst had been planned and thus had been unable to prevent its reaching the floor. He insisted that his master in no way sanctioned such caustic and shocking accusations; indeed, he could hardly hope to profit from them. Gravel used this declaration to good advantage before the canons; they were heartened by Karg's aloofness from the Neuburg attack and felt justified in the decision they had made.[45] The reputation of the Neuburgs was further blackened, but a reservoir of good will toward the House of Bavaria remained.

Just before the canons voted they were notified of the nuncio's exhortation against the election. Attached to this message was Max Heinrich's response to Tanara: there was no need to defer the election since the pope would always have the final decision. Moreover, he himself was not qualified to take action on the matter since the chapter had initiated the election proceedings. He denied that Louis XIV had interfered in any way and reiterated that the Protestants desired nothing more fervently than the confusion which would ensue once the electoral seat was vacant.[46] Encouraged by Max Heinrich's stand, the canons went ahead with the election on January 7, 1688. With two abstentions, the final vote was unanimous in favor of Cardinal Wilhelm Egon von Fürstenberg.

Soon after his postulation, Wilhelm presented eight Gobelin tapestries to the Cologne chapter in gratitude for its support. The tapestries, based upon sketches by Peter Paul Rubens, were part of a cycle entitled "The Triumph of the Eucharist," a fitting subject for the Counter-Reformation. These superb compositions soon took their place among the treasures of the city. It was a gift worthy of a prince, a cardinal, or an elector.[47]

X

"A COADJUTOR FOR A DEAD MAN?"

JANUARY TO JUNE 1688

THE NEWS of Fürstenberg's victory quickly reverberated across Europe. In communicating the chapter's decision to the pope, Wilhelm declared that a combination of "divine permission and the good opinion which, without vanity, the canons have of me after the continual services which I have tried to render to the Church for almost forty years led them to postulate me unanimously for coadjutor of this archbishopric *cum futura successione* subject to the approval of Your Holiness." Louis suggested that Wilhelm go to Rome to plead his case but Fürstenberg refused, believing that the pope would make it a point of honor to annul the postulation if undue pressure were exerted upon him. The king promised Max Heinrich that he would always remember his firm and generous response to French wishes concerning the coadjutorship.[1] For his part, the elector thought of little else except the quittance, which was to be delivered after the pope ratified the chapter's action.

In Munich the elector was perplexed, unsure if and when the pope would act on Wilhelm's postulation; he took no hard and fast stand against the cardinal or against France. His disenchantment with Austria persisted since the command of the imperial army remained in the hands of his opponent, Charles of Lorraine. Villars told Max Emmanuel that if he supported French interests at Cologne and at the Diet, the French would support him in the next election for the King of the Romans. The Blue Knight responded graciously but was unwilling to commit himself. Such a course would make him a declared enemy of the House of Austria in exchange for French support for a title which the other electors might hesitate to bestow upon him.[2] In sum, he shied away from Villars's overtures.

In Vienna, according to the Venetian ambassador, the court "recognized the error of having accelerated the cardinal's success by sending Kaunitz to act in behalf of Bavaria." Though they could take comfort in the fact that Fürstenberg was fifty-eight years old, with failing health, Max Heinrich was in still worse condition. On January 13 the emperor asked the electors and leading German princes for their help and advice in the face of Fürstenberg's triumph. He assailed Wilhelm for having worked "to pave the way for the enemies of the Empire to enter into our midst," a favorite theme since the League of the Rhine was organized. But the Venetian ambassador observed that the Cologne affair was seen chiefly as a quarrel between France and the House of Austria; if Fürstenberg succeeded, the consequences would be especially prejudicial to the interests of the emperor.[3]

Circumstances turned all eyes toward Rome. Innocent was bedridden with a serious inflammation of the lungs which barely allowed him to breathe; it was reported that "he confided solely in the crucifix, before which it is said that he rises from the ground as if in a state of ecstasy." The preceding month had sorely tested his willpower but he was determined to remain on the course he had previously charted. On Christmas Day Lavardin braved a papal prohibition to receive communion at the French church in Rome; Innocent excommunicated him. As the report of this incident was reaching Versailles, the pope again reminded Ranuzzi of his instructions. He need not have bothered. Shortly before January 12, 1688 (the exact date is not known) Dr. Amonio allegedly approached Louis and told him that he and his leading ministers risked excommunication because of their insistence on the *franchises* and their flouting of papal directives by means of Lavardin's embassy. In Ranuzzi's words, "The king listened attentively and with reflection to all that the doctor told him, and asked him to put down the major points in writing so that he might refresh his memory in the future. ... The king imposed the strictest silence upon him, making it clear that the life of Dr. Amonio depended upon it." Though Louis was concerned about the possible excommunication being made public, he appeared unperturbed. As he noted during his audience with Amonio, "Cardinal Ranuzzi looks upon excommunications in the same way as they are looked upon at Rome, but we consider them otherwise."[4]

While this account of Amonio's conversation with the king seems plausible—and is dramatically most appealing—Ranuzzi sent back contradictory reports to Rome. To Casoni he supplied the above narrative; conversely, he informed Cardinal Cibo that it did not seem opportune for Amonio to undertake such a task. Ranuzzi later told the Venetian ambassador that several times he had received "terrifying commissions from Rome which he modified by delaying execution without following them up." Finally, it must be remembered that we cannot test Amonio's veracity: if Ranuzzi did not dupe Casoni, Amonio could still have beguiled Ranuzzi. It is understood that Louis could have been informed by any spiritual adviser that he ran the risk of excommunication because of his having flouted papal wishes concerning the *franchises*.[5]

Whether or not the king conversed with Amonio, it is a matter of record that in this same month of January 1688 Louis had Advocate-General Talon make a strong speech in which he condemned the excommunication of Lavardin, upheld the *franchises*, and called for a council of the church to rule on the legitimacy of the pope's sanctions in this connection. Although Talon was subsequently excommunicated for this outburst, Innocent did not publicize the warning he gave to Louis XIV. With respect to Cologne, he adopted a dilatory strategy, acting neither for nor against Fürstenberg.[6] In the larger sense, he, too, viewed the affair as one of several clashes between the Bourbon and Habsburg monarchies in which the lines of opposition were clearly marked. The monarchs and princes of Europe had no other recourse than to bide their time—and wait.

The first initiative came from the Rhineland. Fürstenberg sought to move the wheels a bit in Rome and to give the lie to charges that the electorate of Cologne was but a puppet in the hands of Louis XIV. Accordingly he notified Austria that Cologne would raise 2000 men before the spring campaign, provided that the emperor paid their expenses. In addition, Max Heinrich pledged to give 400 troops at his own expense and Fürstenberg volunteered 200, to be paid for out of his personal funds. He trusted that such a move would be viewed benevolently in Rome. Leopold was willing to accept the Cologne contingent but he refused Fürstenberg's personal offer, not wanting to put himself under any obligations to the cardinal. Wilhelm countered this move by offering to put the 200 troops at the disposal of the pope. Whether they fought on the side of the Venetians or in the Hungarian campaign would not in the least affect his proposal.[7]

All this while, tension and worry gnawed at Max Heinrich; his not receiving the quittance produced a state of mental depression. At the beginning of March, though his faculties were unimpaired, he was so emaciated that "he was hardly recognizable, being little more than skin and bones." French troops under Boufflers were alerted and Louvois strengthened the forces in Alsace. Louis gave Fürstenberg 20,000 écus to improve the fortifications at Bonn and Kaiserwerth, which in turn led to a strengthening of Spanish defensives in the Netherlands in preparation for a possible invasion. Fürstenberg persuaded the chapter to send a memorandum to Rome requesting that action be taken on the January 7 postulation. If the confirmation did not arrive soon, he toyed with the idea of holding another election.[8]

Confronted by silence at Rome, Wilhelm turned to the House of Austria. Though many of the details are unclear, the general picture can be pieced together. Already on February 10 the French ambassador in Rome reported signs of a more flexible attitude toward Fürstenberg on the part of the emperor.[9] The intermediary was nuncio Buonvisi in Vienna who was on very good terms with Fürstenberg since his tour of duty at Cologne in the early 1670's. His main objective was to prevent a war in western Europe which would interfere with the campaign against the Turk. This was the intention of the pope as well, but Buonvisi was more disposed to consider compromises.

On February 22 Wilhelm urged Buonvisi to assure the emperor that if he ever gained authority in Cologne he would use it for the advantage of the Church and the welfare of the Empire. Citing Tanara as witness of his chagrin over the affair of the quarters in Rome, he deplored the way in which this and other incidents had disturbed the pope. But he could not say whether or not Louis XIV "would interest himself in my coadjutorship to the point of withdrawing his claims in order to obtain my confirmation." While he realized that there were difficulties over accepting his proposed contribution of troops, he would continue to press the issue so as to support the "pious intentions of His Holiness." As for the emperor, Wilhelm averred that he would be "always zealous to merit the honor of his good graces and wished nothing more than the increase of his glory and the continued prosperity of his armies."[10] These high-sounding phrases amounted to a renewed attempt to dissociate himself from French policies towards the pope, to curry favor with Innocent via Buonvisi's dispatches to Rome, and to inform Vienna that he awaited an offer.

Buonvisi suggested that Wilhelm's confirmation might be exchanged for Lavardin's removal from Rome and the abolition of the *franchises* in the French Quarter. This proposal was surely not cleared with Rome but Wilhelm passed it on to Gravel who relayed it to Versailles. Louis branded the proposition "too unreasonable to require attention." The king's categorical refusal increased Wilhelm's uneasiness, especially since he saw little chance of being accepted by the electoral college without the support of either the pope or the emperor. Mainz and Trier had congratulated him on his victory in January, but they fell back on the rule of plurality decision with respect to support for the electoral dignity. The Elector of Brandenburg never answered the cardinal's notification of his postulation, pleading that he had gout and was not able to write. The other electors were openly hostile.[11]

There still seemed room for maneuver. Buonvisi proposed to the emperor that he favor Fürstenberg after Max Heinrich's death provided that Wilhelm promise in writing to cast his electoral vote for Leopold's son Joseph as King of the Romans, thus ensuring his succession. Wilhelm subsequently rejected this proposal but in the interim he used Buonvisi as an intermediary to continue the negotiation and to "explain" his activity in behalf of France before and after his imprisonment. He drafted a memorandum to the emperor, apologizing to Buonvisi for writing in French "since I'm not too accustomed to writing in Italian and Latin." He asked him to make the presentation in Italian, including what he believed to be suitable, "seeing that the truth does not always lend itself to words." [12]

In this apologia, after protestations of good will and assurances of his laudable intentions for the future, Wilhelm declared: "I am always reproached at Vienna for the great partiality which I have for France and I avow quite frankly that my not having been able to obtain employment at the Imperial Court during the reign of Ferdinand III of glorious memory led me to try to render myself agreeable to the court of France while at the same time serving faithfully the Elector of Cologne." He indeed had strong obligations to Louis XIV for benefits received but maintained that he had always sought peace between the Empire and France as well as between France and Spain. There followed an itemized list of activities which he had undertaken over the years in this connection; all this might have been said in 1674 when he was captured. Wilhelm said it was enough for him to know that Leopold had no knowledge of the threats which had been made to Max Heinrich, the chapter, and himself in connection with the coadjutorship.

I know that there are those who seek to persuade Leopold that as Elector I will sacrifice this archbishopric to France and will blindly carry out whatever the Very Christian King will desire. Besides the fact that His Majesty [Louis] is too just and knows me to be too much a man of honor to demand from me things which would go equally against my honor, my utility, and my conscience, it is easy to judge that if I had designs so pernicious and so removed from the truth I would not want to become master of a considerable state only to see it dismembered or subverted. Rather, as Elector, and in consequence linked by oath and by interest to the emperor and the Empire I would do my duty well and would try to use the esteem, the friendship, and the confidence which the Very Christian King has for me as a means of preserving the repose of the Empire and of establishing a solid union and correspondence between their Majesties.[13]

Gravel reported that while such a statement would be treated lightly in Vienna it could be used to good advantage in Rome. This was true enough, yet the very emptiness of the rhetoric leads one to suspect that an

additional message was attached to the memorandum. Whether it was attached then or sent later, Wilhelm let it be known that he would be
willing to let the Neuburgs have the coadjutorships at Münster and Hildesheim in exchange for imperial support at Cologne and Liège. Speaking for Max Heinrich (probably with no authority to do so), he pledged
that Cologne would give 1500 veteran troops, expenses paid, to the emperor and would raise 1000 more if the emperor cared to pay for them.
Leopold, interestingly enough, was willing to listen to such an offer. His
major condition, however, was that if Fürstenberg became elector he had
to vote for Joseph in any future imperial election. Wilhelm would not
make such a promise. By May the chance of a rapprochement appeared
to have vanished. The same d'Estrées who in February spoke of Leopold's flexibility now reported that "terrible batteries" were being set up
at Vienna against the cardinal. The pope, as ever, preferred to do nothing.[14]

Fürstenberg was once more trapped, caught in wheels much greater
than he could cope with. It was virtually inconceivable that Innocent XI
would have accepted a deal in which Lavardin's removal and the abolition of the *franchises* would be exchanged for the Cologne confirmation.
Innocent was even less likely to agree to such a proposal than was Louis
XIV, who had already ruled it out. Indeed, he warned Innocent that a
refusal to confirm Fürstenberg could provoke a European war.[15] Despite
Leopold's willingness to "discuss" the situation, his major demand revealed his distrust and fear of Fürstenberg. He regarded Wilhelm as a
man with an implacable hatred for him and his dynasty; a man who,
once near the levers of power, would do anything to topple the Habsburgs from the imperial throne. Other trial balloons would be released
from Vienna in the months ahead but with such stringent conditions that
they amounted to fantasy. Fürstenberg sought some form of independence for himself but like all German princes he knew that he had, ultimately, to choose. In spite of his doubts and his maneuvers, Wilhelm
and the rest of Europe knew which side he would be on.

The need for a breakthrough became even more imperative in light of
Max Heinrich's worsening condition and his growing hostility toward
Fürstenberg. Quickening matters still further, Karg returned to Bonn. He
was instructed not to pester the elector with talk about the coadjutorship
but rather to insinuate himself into his good graces so that Max Heinrich's final testament should be favorable to the House of Bavaria. Karg
could not alienate himself from Fürstenberg since the postulation might
be confirmed yet at the same time he cultivated those canons who had

imperial or Bavarian interests at heart. Once arrived in Bonn, the skillful diplomat took up where he left off two months before and presented himself to Max Heinrich not as a representative of Max Emmanuel but as "a servant of the House of Bavaria." In this guise, he was soon on the best of terms with the elector and gradually began to usurp the position which Fürstenberg had maintained for so long. This became obvious on March 23 when Max Heinrich showed his final testament to Karg, giving him (wittingly or not) an opportunity to consider how it might be retouched in Bavaria's favor at a later date. The doctors attending the elector agreed that his condition improved noticeably whenever Fürstenberg was absent, especially since his presence reminded Max Heinrich of the 400,000-livre debt.[16]

A striking example of Max Heinrich's estrangement from Wilhelm came in the first week of April when the elector assured the pope of his willingness to cooperate and indicated that he would do nothing to displease him. In effect he wished to learn if dropping his support of Fürstenberg would ensure his confirmation at Münster; Max Heinrich did not send this letter through his agent, Tissier, who was a friend of the cardinal, but rather through a counselor from Liège, Baron de Husins. Innocent replied that he was not at all content with the elector's conduct, especially since he allowed himself to be governed by a man (Fürstenberg) "who only seeks after his own satisfaction and ambition and whose life does not conform to his character." The news of this little episode reached Versailles in a dispatch from a M. Roberts, who appears to have served as paymaster for the French legation in Rome. Roberts noted that "this step taken by the Elector of Cologne makes clear that he is seeking to accommodate himself with the pope and that to succeed he will willingly abandon the interests of Cardinal Fürstenberg, who would then have even more difficulty in establishing himself as coadjutor at Cologne."[17]

Gravel presently asked Louis if it were not possible to make some sort of a statement so as to remove the elector's doubts and assuage his troubled mind. This request exasperated the king: "I expressly forbid you to give any quittance or to give any promise that you will furnish one and I revoke the power which I have previously sent you to issue such a quittance, reserving to myself the right to satisfy . . . any engagement which you may enter into in my name in this matter after the cardinal's election is confirmed in the prescribed fashion." Only recently, Louis appointed Gravel as ambassador before Friedrich Wilhelm von Brandenburg. Since he would soon leave for his new post Gravel was instructed to make his next visit to Max Heinrich his last one, in anticipation of the "imminent" arrival of the next envoy to Cologne, Du Heron. If the subject of the 400,000-livre debt arose, Gravel was to say that he no longer had power to act.[18]

The increasing possibility of the elector's death provoked activity in all directions. On April 9 Croissy announced a grant of 40,000 écus to support some five to six thousand troops to be ready at the end of the month. Wilhelm inspected the garrisons at Bonn, Rheinberg, and Kaiserwerth which, all told, numbered 4500 men. He sent his secretary to review with Louvois the defense needs of the electorate and reminded the king that "the animosity of the court of Vienna and the House of Neuburg toward me is such that I am sure that if they do not do everything in their power against me, it will not be through lack of will to do so, but rather due to Your Majesty's protection or their own lack of capacity."[19] As those words were written, Wilhelm was still hopeful of bargaining with the Austrians and allotting Münster and Hildesheim to the Neuburgs.

The intensified military preparation provided a dramatic backdrop to the subject of the quittance. On May 1 Gravel informed Louis of the elector's growing repugnance towards Fürstenberg as well as the wrath of the chapter towards France and the cardinal over the debt issue. Spite or despair might lead Max Heinrich to show the king's written promises regarding the debt to nuncio Tanara. If this happened, then the pope "would not only refuse the confirmation with more reason than he has given up till now, but it is very possible that he would exclude the cardinal from the electoral dignity during his entire pontificate even were he to be postulated in a second election." Gravel proposed a simple declaration concerning the debt, dated after the January 7 postulation, which would amount to a provisional quittance, contingent on the installation of Fürstenberg as coadjutor with undisputed rights to the succession. He planned to use such a statement to placate the elector and also as a means of retrieving the original letter which the king had written to Max Heinrich in November 1687, a considerably more compromising document. Louis agreed to this plan. He sent a simple declaration expressing his gratitude for the chapter's wisdom in postulating so worthy a servant as the cardinal and pledged to remit the debt when the succession was assured. He insisted that Gravel obtain a promise from Max Heinrich not to show this statement to anybody: Rome could easily have used it as grounds for refusing the confirmation.[20]

Once in possession of the provisional quittance, Gravel waited for a suitable opportunity to present it to the elector. He dreaded the possibility of Louis's original incriminating, autograph letter falling into the hands of the enemy. Fürstenberg told him that as executor of the elector's will, he intended to "remove" some of his private papers immediately after his death, including treaties and letters from the king. This, however, proved to be unnecessary for as soon as Gravel presented the new statement from the king, Max Heinrich gave over all the letters which Louis had sent in connection with the coadjutorship and the debt.[21]

Wilhelm used this turn of events to reconnoiter his chances at Liège. It proved to be a tactical blunder. After his departure his enemies persuaded Max Heinrich to rip up the old will and to draw up a new one, with Max Emmanuel replacing Fürstenberg as executor. Dücker believed that Max Heinrich would not live beyond the first two weeks in June and reported that "every day there are couriers or gentlemen from Düsseldorf under the pretext of other affairs." At this juncture Tanara began a ciphered dispatch to Rome with the humorous understatement, "There is no doubt that were it not for all the talk about the Coadjutorship, the Archdiocese of Cologne would enjoy complete peace and quiet."[22]

Wilhelm's absence infuriated Gravel and he sent an express letter to Liège, where the cardinal was accompanied by Du Heron, the next envoy to Cologne and Trier. As soon as he heard of Max Heinrich's critical condition and the mounting political crisis in Bonn, Wilhelm asked Louis's permission for Boufflers to march a company of dragoons into the electorate at his command. Max Heinrich died on June 3; Fürstenberg and Du Heron did not arrive in Bonn until the following day at four in the afternoon. The elector's last words had been addressed to Karg: he wanted his testament opened immediately after his death. Out of courtesy, Karg waited until Wilhelm arrived and then proceeded to open the will as the cardinal looked on with visible emotion.[23]

Max Heinrich's revised will did not measure up to the worst of Wilhelm's forebodings. Joseph Clemens inherited the bulk of the elector's personal effects and patrimony but no specific recommendation on the succession was made. Max Heinrich left 20,000 livres to Fürstenberg, on condition that Louis grant the remission of the 400,000-livre debt. The remission of this debt was to be his personal gift to the Archdiocese of Cologne.[24]

In the thick packet of dispatches which arrived at Versailles in the aftermath of Max Heinrich's death certainly the most curious was Gravel's memorandum concerning Fürstenberg's position in the electorate and his chances of becoming elector.[25] The envoy complained that the Countess von der Mark was playing too great a role in the cardinal's life. Though the wife of Wilhelm's nephew Emmanuel, her previous relationship with Fürstenberg was notorious and her conduct prejudicial to French interests. The countess herself, he claimed, had little affection for France; indeed, she was an avid partisan of the imperial cause and was in close contact with Vienna. She had been miffed due to Louis's refusal to give a French regiment to her husband, especially since one of the reasons for the refusal had been the fact that she was his wife. Gravel said that the cardinal told her too much; that she was perfectly placed to betray him. As for her influence over Wilhelm, Fürstenberg himself compared her to Mme de Maintenon and said that if given the right circumstances she would be capable of governing an entire kingdom. (Croissy judiciously crossed out this passage before reading the dispatch to the king.) Furthermore, the protection which the king afforded to the cardinal was becoming *odieuse* in the Rhineland, in large part because of the suspected relationship between the prelate and the countess. As Gravel put it, "However much I may be persuaded that his life is beyond reproach, notwithstanding certain small familiarities which he indulges in even in public, there is scarcely a soul who does not judge otherwise, not only in these parts but also in Italy, in England, in the North, and in almost all parts of Germany." Gravel believed that Fürstenberg, like the countess, much preferred Liège to Cologne and that if given a choice would have picked the Liège bishopric with the aim of living a life of comfort and ease at Modave. In any case, for Wilhelm to succeed at Liège, the countess had to be kept out of sight. He urged that she and Emmanuel be sent on a mission to Vienna, leaving the cardinal free to attend to the important issues undisturbed.

As trenchant and accurate as Gravel's accusations may have been, Louis's only response was to order him to proceed to Berlin as soon as possible so as to prevent Brandenburg from sending troops into the Electorate of Cologne. To guard against all such maneuvers, Baron d'Asfeld was sent to Cologne accompanied by a war commissary named Heiss. D'Asfeld was a warrior-diplomat chosen by Louvois to persuade Fürstenberg to follow defense plans mapped out at Versailles and report on the fighting strength of the Cologne army. Heiss would evaluate each contingent in that army and appraise each fortification in the electorate. He would then join d'Asfeld in making recommendations to Louvois. The two agents arrived in Cologne on June 11 and had a long conversation with the cardinal. Fürstenberg's position was crystal clear: the watchword was to be "circumspection." General Boufflers had provided d'Asfeld with a letter of presentation to the Cologne chapter, certifying that he was there to "protect their liberty." But Wilhelm insisted that no such letter should be presented; the agents acquiesced. Meanwhile Gravel stayed on at Fürstenberg's request until he obtained the chapter's permission to administer the archdiocese. During the interval, Gravel completed Du Heron's initiation[26] and traveled to Coblenz to take leave of the Elector of Trier.

The concern at Versailles was to prevent outside powers (other than France) from interfering in the affairs of Cologne. At Regensburg Verjus announced that if anyone interfered with the liberty of the Cologne chapter to hold a second election, 100,000 French troops would enter Germany. D'Avaux notified the States-General of the United Provinces that if neighboring states "did not interfere with the liberty of the chapter to elect a good and worthy subject to succeed Max Heinrich, the troops of His Majesty will take no steps in any direction." To this haughty declaration, a member of the Dutch assembly replied, "Since when has the King of France troubled himself over the freedom of Germany?"[27]

As Louis issued threats, Fürstenberg solidified his position. The chapter entrusted the administration of the state to him, reserving to themselves the right to withdraw this authority. In his capacity as Dean, Fürstenberg was given the leadership, but as a member of the chapter he was responsible to them. An election was scheduled for July 19 for the purpose of choosing an elector. Concurrently, Louis asked that Fürstenberg press Rome for a confirmation of the January 7 postulation. Wilhelm, however, clearly saw the need for a second election. After lengthy conferences with Tanara regarding the kind of letter which the chapter ought to send to the pope, he decided to ask for the confirmation of his postulation as a matter of form, but at the same time indicated the date of the next election. In this connection he asked Innocent for an indult of eligibility which would have permitted him to be elected by a majority of the canons instead of the two-thirds vote imposed on those who already possessed a bishopric. D'Estrées in Rome actively worked in support of this request but he, too, was surprised to learn that Louis was urging the confirmation of the January election. Soon everyone at the papal court was repeating Innocent's bon mot, "A coadjutor for a dead man?"[28]

X I
THE COLOGNE ELECTION
JUNE TO JULY 1688

FÜRSTENBERG ASSUMED THE ADMINISTRATION of the electorate scarcely one month before the election, the goal which had given purpose and meaning to so much of his life. The years of scheming with his brother Franz, the foiling of his opponents, the waiting and the maneuvering, all were directed at what would be for him the supreme attainment: the position of an elector of the Empire.[1] Cologne was by now the focal point in the struggle between the Habsburg and Bourbon dynasties, with the fortunes of the Wittelsbachs and Neuburgs, the Houses of Orange and Hohenzollern, swept along in a whirl of activity over which each had but little control.

In Munich the usual indecision prevailed. Max Emmanuel doubted that the canons at Cologne would desert Fürstenberg: the chapter would consider Joseph Clemens too young to rule the archdiocese and the cardinal was already too far advanced to shake their resolution. Besides, Fürstenberg was old and would soon be out of the picture; Joseph Clemens would then have an opportunity to succeed. Moreover, the Bavarian elector was embittered upon learning of the May correspondence between Austria and Fürstenberg according to which the Neuburgs and Fürstenberg would split Max Heinrich's inheritance. Villars, to be sure, did his best to muddy the waters while his rival, Count Kaunitz, sought to convince the elector that Fürstenberg would sooner give Cologne over to France after his death rather than return it to the Wittelsbachs. Leopold pledged to back Joseph Clemens's candidacy to the end and confirmed this in letters to each of the electors in the Empire; soon Brandenburg and Saxony urged Max Emmanuel to run his brother against Fürstenberg in the upcoming election.[2]

While Vienna encouraged the struggle against France, Leopold's Secret Council informed Fürstenberg that if he expressed devotion to the imperial sovereignty (*Reichsoberhaupt*), agreed to divide Max Heinrich's inheritance with the Neuburgs, and promised to vote for the King of Hungary in the next imperial election, then no further steps would be taken at Rome against his candidacy. Further, Kaunitz would support him at Cologne and Liège if Fürstenberg initiated the negotiations with him and promised (1) never again to work against the Empire, to give up all his foreign attachments, to respect the neutrality of the city of Cologne, and to drive all French troops out of the electorate, replacing them with German soldiers; (2) to aid Joseph, the emperor's son, to win the imperial crown; (3) that if for any reason Joseph Clemens could not succeed at Cologne and Liège these posts would be given to a prince of the Neuburg family; and (4) that the Bishop of Breslau would succeed at both Münster and Hildesheim. No sooner was this proposal made known, however, than Leopold's prime minister, Stratmann, raised violent objections and succeeded in scuttling the project. Though the imperial offer was dropped, it had been communicated to Fürstenberg. However difficult such an offer may have been to accept, it led him to believe that Leopold's resistance to his candidacy was not so great as the Neuburgs pretended.[3]

For the Neuburgs, Max Emmanuel's procrastination recalled the preceding autumn when Wilhelm sewed up the election without any effective opposition. Philipp Wilhelm decided to enroll his son, Ludwig Anton, in the Cologne chapter and investigated the possibility of a papal brief of eligibility for his son's nomination as Elector of Cologne. He boldly sketched a plan whereby Cologne and Liège were to be reserved for Ludwig Anton and Hildesheim and Münster for his brother, Franz Ludwig. Pope Innocent, however, was hesitant to accord an indult to Ludwig Anton since it would only serve to split the opposition against Fürstenberg.[4]

Meanwhile, after Wilhelm's first sounding of the chapter he claimed that all who had voted for him earlier, with one possible exception, would do so again. Such a claim is suspect, however, since he wished to keep French troops away from the electorate. Although this first estimate inspired some optimism at the court, Louis XIV shared Du Heron's conviction that troops would eventually have to be sent in and noted that the cardinal's opposition was not "practicable." For the time being, however, he permitted Fürstenberg to hold the reins and govern the pace of all steps in Cologne and Liège. Wilhelm soon made use of this authority: he prevented Du Heron from presenting any credentials before the Cologne chapter until the Austrians or the Neuburgs took the initiative, wanting to keep alive among the canons a sense of freedom from outside interference.[5]

The king's willingness to grant such latitude reflects the conflicting advice which he received from his advisers. After the news of Max Heinrich's death he held long meetings to review all aspects of the problem before acting. According to nuncio Ranuzzi, Louvois "exhorted the king to take vigorous action . . . but others [here we can read Croissy] did not want to go so far. Among the diversity of opinions the king was inclined to avoid war." Thirty battalions of infantry and forty squadrons of cavalry were sent towards the borders of the kingdom near Dinant, there to await the news which Fürstenberg would send from Bonn.[6] Fürstenberg persisted in his refusal to let French troops move over the borders. D'Asfeld disputed his reasoning and his strategic sense but Wilhelm was unshaken.

By minimizing French presence in the electorate Fürstenberg was taking a calculated risk. His advantages included the youth of his opponent and the fact that nobody in the chapter could match his experience or ability in administering the archdiocese. Tanara said as much in a dispatch to Rome, yet hastened to add that he spoke "only in regard to electing an Archbishop, not wanting my judgment to extend to the powers of an Elector or to the needs (*convenienze*) of Germany." Despite the nuncio's support, Wilhelm was convinced that he would not receive an indult because of the conflict between France and the pope. All the while, he supervised the recruitment of troops for the Cologne army. He reported on June 21 that two-thirds of the 5000 troops needed had been recruited. On June 27 Louis XIV sent 100,000 livres to defray expenses in the immediate future.[7]

Elections in the Empire were in varying degrees venal; wild rumors circulated concerning the money that changed hands in Cologne. Professor Braubach notes that the money disbursed by Karg alone totaled 48,000 livres, the highest single amount being 12,000 to Croy. Still more money was spread around by Kaunitz in September to keep the supporters of Joseph Clemens in tow. Predictably, Fürstenberg's expenses were greater. There exists an interesting memorandum drawn up by d'Asfeld, most likely at the beginning of August 1688, which includes an itemized list of the *gratifications* disbursed by Wilhelm before the election.[8] It records a total of 131,000 livres distributed, with one canon (Count Salm) receiving 15,000 livres. In addition to money for those possessing a vote, there are entries of between 1500 and 3000 livres for the "favorites" of some canons, or for "gentlemen attached to" a canon, or, in one instance, a beguiling item of 2000 livres for "a gentleman and his mistress." Money to buy a house, the promise of an abbey in France, the acquittal of past debts, the promise of a specific sum after the election, such were the kinds of "gratifications" offered by Fürstenberg in private chats before the election. One canon, Geyr, was accorded 4000 livres. But he was also on Karg's sheet for 3000 livres. He salved his

conscience by voting for a third candidate! He cast the lone vote for Ludwig Anton von Neuburg, but he later joined Fürstenberg's party. As
reported by d'Asfeld, Count Rietberg was the only canon who refused to
accept anything, whether money or benefices. He was finally prevailed
upon at least to accept a portrait of Louis XIV, fitting tribute for "a man
who has done such marvels for his service." A portrait encrusted with
diamonds was subsequently sent. As we shall see, Louis XIV would give
considerably more money to the canons to hold them in Wilhelm's camp
—but never as much as they demanded.

In France, the Duke of Orléans suggested to Ranuzzi a final attempt
to have "all differences composed" and implied that if the king's conditions at Cologne and Liège were met, Louis might make concessions
elsewhere. Ranuzzi explained that Innocent could not admit of the quarters in Rome or any other ecclesiastical matter being open to barter; he
asked to be dispensed from communicating such a request to Rome since
there was no possibility whatever of its receiving any consideration.[9]

Just at that time a courier from Rome was galloping north en route to
Cologne with the pope's answer to Fürstenberg's request for an indult.
The answer, transmitted through the nuncio, was No: "His Holiness is
greatly displeased at not being able to demonstrate his paternal affection
for Cardinal von Fürstenberg in conceding to him the indult of eligibility,
due to considerations which His Eminence, with his great discernment,
can easily enough comprehend. His Holiness is persuaded that the singu-
lar piety of His Eminence will suffice to keep him far from anything
which may cause quarrels, not wanting to have attributed to him any
contretemps (*inconvenienti*) which could come about to the prejudice of
the Church or of public tranquility." In such manner was Tanara tact-
fully though firmly warned not to espouse the cause of Fürstenberg. On
June 29 Innocent issued a brief for Joseph Clemens dispensing him from
the two-thirds requirement in elections at Cologne, Liège and Hildesheim.[10] When Fürstenberg learned of the pope's refusal to grant an indult
to him,

He received the news with the highest respect for His Holiness's judgment . . .
although he could not keep himself from making it known that there would result
a great discredit to his name . . . once it was known that after having been elevated to the purple and having served the Church in Cologne for some forty years
he was denied a grace which had been conceded to a young prince who certainly
had a great deal of promise, but who then was without experience. . . . He assured me that he would never cease to work for the conservation of the public
peace, although he could not be sure as to how efficacious his actions could be
in the future.[11]

The pope's refusal to grant an indult to Wilhelm was not enough to satisfy the Austrians; they wanted direct action against Fürstenberg's candidacy. Leopold urged Cardinal Pio to persuade Innocent to take the administration of the Cologne electorate away from Fürstenberg. He also wanted Innocent to exhort the canons of the cathedral chapter to elect a man acceptable to the emperor and the Empire. This correspondence was carried on behind the back of Buonvisi in Vienna. The Austrians did not trust him and believed that if he had any preferences at all they lay with Fürstenberg.[12]

A lengthy dispatch from Pio to Leopold on July 3, 1688 recapitulated Innocent's reaction to this pressure.[13] In his audience, Pio enumerated all the imperial arguments against Fürstenberg: his remorseless pursuit of power, his rebellion against Germany and the "most clement" emperor, his slavish attachment to French interests, his fine mind dedicated to little else but machinations. "How detestable it is that a cardinal of the Holy Church, for the sake of advancing his own selfish interests, should work to debilitate the power of neighboring princes, with so much detriment to the Catholic religion." He cited Wilhelm's shameless attempt to enter an electoral college whose members, both Catholic and Protestant, were not of a mind to seat him. In the midst of this confusion there stood Leopold, the advocate and defender of the Church, who asked only that the pope support a candidate at Cologne who would not disrupt the inner unity of the Christian world at a time when that world was imperiled by the attacks of the infidel.

Innocent said that he had already taken all appropriate measures. To Pio's request that he stop the election proceedings until an investigation had been made of simony in the January election, Innocent replied that there was no simony since there had been no election, only a simple supplication from the chapter which he had not acknowledged. As for asking the chapter not to support a man who was wholly under the control of an outside power, he observed that in January the nuncio asked the chapter not to proceed with the postulation but they had ignored him. His concern for the prestige and the dignity of the papacy led him to avoid situations where it might be flouted with impudence. Pio argued that nothing need be done publicly: he could as easily work unofficially through nuncio Tanara. The pope appeared disposed to consider this avenue of approach, but he did not commit himself.

Before the audience ended, Innocent asked the cardinal to assure Leopold that he held this affair "very much to heart, that his chief concern was public peace and that he was acting in such a way as to establish tranquility and satisfy the emperor at the same time. If this were to be accomplished, however, it would be necessary to handle the negotiations in Cologne with care and to avoid the errors of the last election." "To do justice to the pontiff," Pio concluded, "I must assure Your Majesty that he is doing everything possible to maintain peace in Germany . . . but since he is very cautious in all his undertakings it is not easy to get him to take steps which are not first well measured; . . . time is necessary, a great deal of time, in order to move this saintly old man." While the substance of Pio's dispatch could not have been wholly pleasing to Leopold, Innocent eventually did adopt much more of Pio's program than was indicated in the memorandum.

Tissier and d'Estrées appeared before the pope in a last effort to have an indult granted to Fürstenberg. During this audience, Tissier declared that "it was a great disgrace for a cardinal with forty years of service in the diocese and with a distinguished record of administration not to receive a grace which had been conceded to an inexperienced youth." Innocent replied that Joseph Clemens had received the brief not because of his personal merits, but because of the merits of the House of Bavaria. A brief was not conceded to other houses "since they are not of the same rank." In a subsequent audience, d'Estrées asserted that pressure from two heretics, William of Orange and the Elector of Brandenburg, was being exerted on the electoral chapter of Cologne. He tried to wean Innocent from the notion that since Wilhelm as Bishop of Strasbourg had sworn allegiance to the King of France he could not be an elector in the German Empire. That argument had been used with repetitive effect by Pio and Innocent had made it his own. Two days later, on July 9, 1688, the pope instructed Tanara to do everything possible within the bounds of "prudence and circumspection" to promote the election of Joseph Clemens of Bavaria.[14]

The Austrian ministry decided that its best hope for stopping Fürstenberg lay in the wholehearted support of the Wittelsbach candidate. To ensure Max Emmanuel's active cooperation, he was informed that due to the ill health of Charles of Lorraine he had been chosen to lead the imperial armies during the upcoming campaign.[15] Leopold attached one notable condition to the offer: Villars was to be kept away from the battlefront. Despite personal reluctance to part company with his French friend, there was no doubt but that Max Emmanuel would seize the opportunity which had been given him. He sent a letter to Louis XIV noting that he had had every intention of remaining on his estates but the combination of the Duke of Lorraine's bad health and the honor of being awarded the coveted post made his acceptance inevitable and unalterable. He closed with a profuse apology for the proviso regarding Villars.[16]

To remove any doubts regarding imperial wishes, Leopold told the Elector Palatine that he was supporting Joseph Clemens. Kaunitz was instructed to work for the Wittelsbach prince in Cologne, Liège and Hildesheim. Even before Kaunitz's arrival, Karg spread the word in Cologne that if Joseph Clemens were elected the canons would enjoy the spiritual and temporal direction of the electorate as well as one-third of the revenue during his minority. There was a further commitment to restore or refurbish all the buildings at the electoral court and a pledge to do everything possible to preserve the peace. D'Asfeld observed that "the scene is beginning to be a bit livelier than it has been."[17]

In these last weeks before the final reckoning Fürstenberg hoped to keep his supporters in line and to prevent defections. With the memory of his seizure in 1674 fresh in mind, he traveled with a guard of some 150 men; at night, fifty guards surrounded his house. His concerns shifted from a desire for some concession to papal demands on the issue of the quarters in Rome to a request that d'Estrées speak more strongly in favor of his candidacy in Rome. He offered to place his Strasbourg bishopric in the hands of that chapter and to surrender his French abbeys to Louis if the king deemed it necessary. Louis was agreeable to this scheme if future circumstances called for it.[18]

The familiar charge that Wilhelm was not truly "German" was now leveled by the Diet of Regensburg in a message to the chapter in Cologne; at issue was the fact that the Bishop of Strasbourg had pledged faith and homage to the King of France. To counter these and similar accusations, Louis XIV discharged Wilhelm from any subjection which he may have incurred when he was accorded letters of naturalization. Such letters permitted foreigners to hold offices and to possess benefices in France under certain conditions, the regulation having been dictated more by political than by ecclesiastical considerations. The king's declaration was dated July 12, 1688, and would presumably serve as a strong answer to those who claimed that the cardinal was irrevocably bound to French interests. In a closing message, Louis expressed the opinion that if Wilhelm were postulated the pope would confirm him.[19]

In the frenetic last days before the final vote, the most spectacular clash came when Kaunitz delivered a scathing attack on Fürstenberg before the Cologne chapter on July 14. Citing the need for an archbishop who would carry on the policies of the beloved Max Heinrich in the spiritual and temporal realms, he argued that a French slave such as

Cardinal von Fürstenberg could never serve the best interests of a German electorate.[20] Indeed, the pope had not ratified his January postulation and would not now approve the cardinal. Nor would the electoral college admit such a man into its presence. On a more personal level, he attacked Fürstenberg's past activities, his private life, his good faith, and his lack of patriotism. What with his French citizenship, declared Kaunitz, he had seen fit to bring Strasbourg into subjection and delivered the Citadel of Liège over to a foreign power. He concluded with a vague threat in the name of the emperor against any canons who might have the temerity to vote for Fürstenberg.

In response to these charges, Wilhelm's tack was to presume that so offensive an assault upon his person could not have been made "at the wish of so clement a sovereign as Emperor Leopold." He began by reminding the chapter that since he and his family had been restored to all honors after Nijmegen, it was not legitimate to bring old skeletons to light. Then he proceeded to rip into Kaunitz's arguments one by one. In reference to the statement that everyone lamented the passing of Max Heinrich he asked, "How could his role have been so beneficent if his prime minister were as treacherous as Kaunitz described him?" As for the chapter's disregarding the pope's wishes in January, or the pope's lack of action, this was another election and had to be treated as such. In response to the charge of being a French slave, Wilhelm derided Kaunitz's knowledge of recent history. He ridiculed the accusation concerning Strasbourg as an "atrocious calumny" and noted that Liège and her citadel fell after he had been arrested and was tucked away in an imperial prison! As for letters of naturalization, "They do not entail any subjection to another prince; they merely bestow the rights of natural citizenship and enable the bearer to possess offices and benefices and to dispose of or to inherit goods in that country. If it were true that such men were slaves of France, then so is Ludwig Anton von Neuburg, Grand Master of the Teutonic Order: he, too, possesses letters of naturalization from Louis XIV!" Finally, the cardinal claimed that any talk of his not being admitted into the electoral college or any intimations that the canons would suffer reprisals if they voted for him were unwarranted intrusions into the liberty of the chapter. While those in attendance savored these displays of verbal pyrotechnics, it is doubtful that they affected anyone's vote.

The cabal opposing Fürstenberg held a final strategy session on July 17 to coordinate efforts in favor of Joseph Clemens and to agree on tactics for any eventuality. On the following day, nuncio Tanara administered minor orders to Ludwig Anton, thus making him eligible to sit in the chapter as a voting member.[21] It was none too soon: the fateful vote would be cast the next morning.

At 10 a.m. on July 19, after assisting at a Mass of the Holy Spirit in the cathedral of Cologne, the canons gathered together in the Chapter house and set about their business. Wilhelm himself presided. Two preliminary skirmishes took place before the roll call. The first was an attempt to nullify the vote of one member who was absent. This was the Margrave of Baden, an enemy of Fürstenberg's, who was with the armies in the East. It was decided that he be given the vote so as to preclude any charge of irregularity in the election proceedings. An attempt was then made to exclude Wilhelm's nephew, Ferdinand, the Prince of Murbach, on charges that he was excommunicated after disobeying papal directives concerning the Abbey of Murbach.[22] After a heated exchange of words this move was defeated, principally because no proof of excommunication was produced. While both of these tests were abortive, the discussions served to indicate the relative strength of each side. No serious obstacles remained: it was time for the vote, by voice.

Fürstenberg received thirteen votes, Joseph Clemens nine, with one vote each going to Ludwig Anton and to Reckheim. (Wilhelm voted for Reckheim so as to preserve an image of detachment.) In the final tally Wilhelm was three short of being postulated, Joseph Clemens four votes shy of being elected. Under canon law, Innocent XI was free to choose either of the two candidates, or a third party. D'Asfeld perfectly summarized the outcome when he exclaimed: "Voilà M. le Cardinal à la Miséricorde du Pape."[23]

Couriers sped from Cologne in all directions to proclaim the news of the deadlock. In Vienna, the result was particularly gratifying. Leopold viewed it as "having contributed to the repose and tranquility of Europe." Express letters were dispatched to leading cardinals in Rome, urging them to work for the confirmation of Joseph Clemens.[24]

On the day of the election, Louvois left Paris to take the waters at Forges in Normandy. Once arrived, he poured out his anxieties in a letter to his good friend Le Peletier, the Controller-General. He wrote late at night on July 21, before any news had arrived from Cologne, but obviously expecting the worst:

It's not very clear to me just what we can ask of the pope. I would be angry to see the troops of His Majesty . . . there, committed to maintain fortresses in a miserable condition against the combined forces of the Empire, all the more so since the cardinal will have no legitimate right to become archbishop. . . . I cannot prevent myself from telling you once again that this thorny affair is very harmful to our interests. For the Prince of Bavaria to become Elector of Cologne and, apparently, Bishop of Liège or of Münster as well, and to be joined by the Duke of Jülich, the Elector Palatine, the emperor and the Dutch, this appears to me to be a dangerous neighbor, particularly if the Spanish make the Elector of Bavaria governor of the Spanish Netherlands.

Louvois's chagrin and frustration were shared by Louis XIV. He informed the pope that if Fürstenberg were not confirmed there was the possibility of a war. "So as to remove the incompatibility which Your Holiness may find in the cardinal holding the bishopric of Strasbourg," Louis continued, "we propose that he be replaced as bishop there by one of the most worthy subjects of your Kingdom, the Bishop of Meaux [Bossuet], whom your Holiness has declared to be the Scourge of Heretics." The following day Louis told Du Heron that "there are so many reasons which should oblige His Holiness to end this affair to my satisfaction that there is room for hoping that he will prefer to accord the bulls [in favor of Fürstenberg] than to ignite a war in the Empire which would be difficult to extinguish." [25]

Louis's seeming confidence in the pope's "listening to reason" was partly linked to his reliance on the success of an extraordinary plan which had been worked out at the beginning of July on the assumption that Fürstenberg would in fact be postulated. This plan, which would have delighted Dumas himself, involved sending a trusted agent to Venice before the Cologne election. Upon receipt of final orders from Versailles, he would hasten to Rome where he would gain entrance to the papal chambers and bear a personal message from Louis XIV to the pope. The man chosen for this delicate assignment was Jules-Louis Bolé, Marquis of Chamlay, Louvois's most valuable assistant. [26] His past experience on secret missions and the confidence which he inspired at the court determined his appointment for this vital task.

Before leaving for Venice, Chamlay received an extensive set of instructions from Croissy under the personal supervision of the king. [27] He was directed to pose as a Flemish nobleman, one Vicomte d'Orchamp. If, by chance, the French legation discovered his presence in Rome, he was to maintain that he was there on a personal religious matter and was trying to avoid publicity. He would address himself to papal aide Casoni and request an audience with the pope. If Casoni proved difficult, Chamlay had to insist on the importance of his mission. Presumably, this approach would gain him entrance into the papal chambers where he would present a personal letter to the pope from Louis XIV introducing him as the king's official spokesman. Louis insisted on absolute secrecy. Before revealing any portion of the French proposal Chamlay would secure Innocent's solemn promise that all information received was to be as inviolable as that received in the confessional. If for any reason the mission were made public, both the envoy and his king would deny everything.

The French proposals proved to be the first instance in which Louis showed any willingness to make concessions, however unbalanced the return was to be in his favor. The king asked that Fürstenberg be confirmed as Archbishop of Cologne so as to insure peace in Europe; that bulls be expedited in favor of those French bishops already nominated ("forty bishoprics lacking their shepherds"); and that the pope ratify the decision made by the French clergy in 1682 on the question of the *Régale*. In exchange for these concessions, Louis was willing to restrict the area of the French Quarter in Rome and to limit the prerogatives and *franchises* of his embassy there. Lavardin would be removed from his residence in Rome though Innocent should not expect or ask for an immediate recall. The envoy was directed to keep all of these provisions together; they were not to be separated. Nor would the king admit of these points being discussed by a committee of papal advisors: it was to be simply a personal agreement between two sovereigns.

These instructions were drawn up on the assumption that Wilhelm would be postulated. When the results of the election arrived, Louvois urged that a final set of instructions be sent off to Chamlay and negotiations with the pope entered into immediately. In a letter to the Controller-General, Louvois observed that any communication to Chamlay would pass through his own hands. If the instructions were unsealed he would read them and, with Louis's permission, would add his own opinions. If, on the other hand, the instructions were sealed, he would simply indicate in a short note that the adjoining packet contained the king's will and leave it at that.[28]

The new set of instructions dated July 22 authorized Chamlay to agree that Joseph Clemens be made Fürstenberg's coadjutor in exchange for the pope's confirmation. If, in spite of all argument, Innocent would not confirm the cardinal, Chamlay was to request that a new election be held with Wilhelm being eligible to run at Cologne and at another see. These instructions were sent unsealed to Louvois; he added a note to Chamlay, enjoining him "to strongly exaggerate to the pope the imminence of the war which he will bring about between the king and the emperor if he gives the bulls of confirmation to Joseph Clemens, and to assure him that His Majesty will support with all his forces the interests of Cardinal Fürstenberg." The pope had to be persuaded that the young prince had no vocation, that there was no prospect of Max Emmanuel's having children, and that he would eventually be succeeded by his brother as prince of Bavaria. As a last resort, he suggested that the pope might agree to Joseph Clemens's being named coadjutor to Fürstenberg with rights of succession. After he sent off the king's instructions and his own note to Chamlay, Louvois ordered Boufflers to move his troops closer to the Luxembourg frontiers so as to put added pressure on the canons in Liège who would soon be judging Fürstenberg's candidacy in that diocese.[29]

While Chamlay awaited his orders in Venice and while Boufflers's troops began the first of many movements in the next few months, what of Fürstenberg? Since the death of Max Heinrich, Wilhelm had administered the archdiocese and electorate as the representative of the canons, subject to their control. After the election, he suggested a new arrangement: he would accept a mandate, under obligation to and in the name of the canons. Naturally, his supporters begged him not to release the reins of government. The prospect of a divided chapter moved Kaunitz to write an eager dispatch to Vienna in which he openly relished the thought of confusion which would ensue. But Wilhelm's language and gestures were calculated to lull the suspicions of his opponents. On July 25 he responded to the urgent requests of the chapter and accepted their appeals out of love of the Fatherland and the devotion which he owed to the Church of Cologne whose welfare, next to God, was what chiefly animated him ("nächst Gott pro unico scopo actionum suarum vorgestellt").[30] Then came the announcement: to properly carry out the work of administering the electorate he would move to the electoral palace in Bonn. It was a coup de théâtre.

Transferring the government to Bonn would result in his being responsive only to those canons who accompanied him. Most of the anticipated friction would be eliminated. In Bonn, Wilhelm could more easily control the levers of power in the electorate, have more control over the troops and fortifications, and be in closer contact with the French. Wilhelm and a majority of the chapter made a festive entrance into the electoral residence on the evening of July 28. With trumpets blaring in the background, he proceeded to establish himself in the palace and began to remove all reminders of the Wittelsbach dynasty as well as to expropriate the goods of the deceased elector. He ordered two new carriages from Paris, to be decorated with the arms and insignia of the Elector of Cologne.[31] On August 2 his supporters pledged to defend their choice of the cardinal and to use the militia and the fortifications of the archdiocese to back up their decision; they of course expected aid from Louis XIV. Yet in this same declaration the canons made clear (article 3) that the cities and fortresses as well as the militia for the defense of the electorate were to obey the chapter.[32] Wilhelm's position was a delicate one, forcing him to be more cautious, more "politic" than Louvois would have liked. His position was further complicated by persistent rumors that the French sought to make of Cologne another Strasbourg.

The relations between Fürstenberg and the French court in the first few weeks after the election are especially interesting because Louis had still not decided what to do. On July 23 Wilhelm suggested that henceforth the affair was more Louis's concern than his own. His analysis of the situation perfectly explained the position of the French in the Empire: "What little ambition I have to gain this electorate is based upon my desire to render service to Your Majesty. . . . It is more to his [Louis's] interest than his prestige not to suffer that attachment to his person automatically may exclude someone from all kinds of dignities in Germany and above all in this region where he will soon see that the reputation which the French crown has acquired will diminish if the very name of the emperor can gain more respect than the consideration of all the might and the proximity of the estates of Your Majesty."[33] Here Wilhelm was placing himself in the best possible light, but the designs of Mazarin and Lionne for the Germanies were clearly beyond repair.

At Versailles, everyone was dazed by the suddenness of the events in Cologne. The prospect of going to war was not a happy one; the king did not view warfare with the same enthusiasm as in the first years of his reign. A sense of deception was in the air, with courtiers murmuring that "never in a hundred years could France do as much harm to the pope as he has done to the French crown on this occasion." One conceded that the pope had played his game well: the ball had rebounded perfectly to him.[34] In sum, there was the grudging admission that Louis had been checkmated.

Croissy was beside himself with rage yet wary of making any flat commitments to Fürstenberg so soon after the event. Wilhelm had his secretary contact Breget in Paris, urging him to warn the ministry that if Rome believed the king were weakening or bluffing "we would be lost." Above all, a show of strength had to be maintained. Breget told Louvois that Croissy would not commit himself to a definite policy until the pope decided. This noncommittal attitude was a concerted policy as can be seen from Louvois's remarks to Le Peletier after receiving Breget's complaints. One can detect a tone of pity, tinged with derision for Fürstenberg in Louvois's acute summation of the dilemma. Nothing that Wilhelm could do via the nuncio in Cologne, nor any intervention on the part of the King of England in his behalf could have any effect, he claimed, if the pope rejected Chamlay's project. Menaces to Rome, to Vienna or to

Regensburg would be parlous if there were no bedrock resolution to use force; and that decision had not yet been taken. If French threats turned out to be a bluff, then respect for the King of France would dip even lower in the Germanies. Fürstenberg would have to be patient while awaiting the papal decision.[35]

In subsequent letters to Breget, Wilhelm replied to charges that his handling of the election had been maladroit. He reviewed what might have been if Louis had given in on the *franchises*; if a deal had been approved by Versailles concerning the division of coadjutorships between himself, the Neuburgs and the Wittelsbachs; if French troops had entered the electorate before the vote was taken. There remained strong doubts that the Diet of Regensburg would ever recognize him under any circumstances.[36] And beyond these problems, there loomed the complicated question of his candidacy at Liège where the election was scheduled to take place on August 18. If July was frenzied, August promised to be even worse.

XII

RESISTANCE AND FLIGHT

AUGUST 1688 TO JUNE 1689

SELDOM SINCE THE RENAISSANCE had the papacy been so important in the high politics of Europe as during the 1680's. The moral force of Innocent XI as much as the events which he influenced conspired to make this so. Statesmen across Europe looked towards Rome in July 1688, searching for portents which might ease their anxiety. None but a tiny few at Versailles had any knowledge of Chamlay's mission. The courier bearing his final instructions reached Venice on July 30; the "Vicomte d'Orchamp" arrived in Rome on the third of August. The following day he met his first impasse in the person of papal secretary Casoni. When he introduced himself as a Flemish nobleman and asked for an interview with the pope, Casoni recommended him to another official who handled such matters. To avoid complications, the vicomte revealed that he was French and had a secret message from his sovereign to the pontiff. Casoni asked him to return later that evening; in the interim he conferred with the pope and Cardinal Cibo. On his return Chamlay was greeted by Cibo who transmitted Innocent's decision: if there was any business to transact, it could be done through subalterns. No interview would be granted.

Frustrated in his attempt even to begin the assignment, Chamlay disregarded part of his orders and revealed his plight to d'Estrées and Lavardin. D'Estrées immediately spoke in his behalf, guaranteeing Innocent's safety during the projected interview. But all his promises and protestations were of no avail; Chamlay realized that he had to leave without accomplishing anything. Before setting out for Florence, he sent a letter to the king in which he severely criticized the pope and his entourage, especially Casoni, and emphasized the dominating role which Austria played at the papal court. Clearly this was what Louvois would have wished to be written in the circumstances. Upon its reception, both Croissy and Louvois sent dispatches to Florence ordering the erstwhile Vicomte d'Orchamp to return home.[1]

Louis's reaction to the failure of Chamlay's mission was reported with theatrical overtones by Ranuzzi: "The king in public and in private has given expression to the greatest griefs which he has uttered to date. He said that never would he have believed that such a thing were possible, for while he was convinced that His Holiness had an aversion toward him, now it was clear that he was his immortal enemy, and that he never wants to have peace with him." The nuncio argued that Louis himself would not receive a secret agent under such circumstances, but he converted nobody. Indeed, there was serious talk of seizing Casoni in Rome until Lavardin and d'Estrées reported that such a plan was too risky.[2] The fact that it was even considered indicated the prevailing mood at court.

Chamlay's account confirmed other reports of Innocent's "partiality" in favor of Joseph Clemens. The papal advisory body did not make its decision until August 26, yet on August 17 Casoni was stressing the need to keep foreigners out of the Empire and telling Ranuzzi that Joseph Clemens would have to give up the two bishoprics that he already possessed (Regensburg and Freising) and that he would not have authority over Münster. Casoni also noted that he was the brother of Elector Maximilian, who at that very moment was engaged in the defense of Christianity.[3] On August 26 the special congregation advised Innocent to confirm Joseph Clemens of Bavaria as Archbishop of Cologne.

All of this had been foreseen in France after Chamlay's report was read. Soon afterwards, Fürstenberg was defeated at Liège under most peculiar circumstances which disclosed the disarray in the French ministry. The essentials of the situation in Liège can be rapidly summarized. For the majority of the canons in the chapter, French control via Fürstenberg was as distasteful as the continuance of Wittelsbach rule in the person of Joseph Clemens. They were spared this choice, at least, since the July 17 pact by which Wilhelm's opponents rallied to the Bavarian prince at Cologne appears to have included a pledge of joint support of the Neuburg Ludwig Anton at Liège. Cardinal Bouillon, the third candidate, owned territory in the area and was certainly more acceptable to the majority than was Fürstenberg. As for Wilhelm, his association with Max Heinrich's "despotism" and his responsibility for initiating and executing the repressive decrees in 1684 had left a legacy of ill-will and, in some instances, hatred toward him. His candidacy seemed foredoomed to failure, for without an indult of eligibility he had to secure two-thirds of the forty-six votes; only twenty votes could be counted on. Louis asked Bouillon to withdraw his candidacy and to persuade his friends in the chapter to vote for Fürstenberg. Bouillon complied but with little enthusiasm and less effect. His friends were unwilling to support Wilhelm and there were clear signs that Bouillon himself had not yet abandoned hope of being elected.[4] Since the chapter could not pick any of the above candidates without offending a major power, the alternative was to choose a local member of the chapter. The man agreed upon was the dean of the chapter, Baron Jean-Louis d'Elderen, who was seventy-two years old and favored by those canons who came to be known as the "parti de la patrie."

While the French initially supported Fürstenberg at Liège, his defeat at Cologne had come as a shock and the prospect of the entire Rhineland controlled by the enemies of France led to rapid and passionate reappraisals. Louvois stood at the center of this ferment. He had not been sanguine about the success of Chamlay's mission and doubted the pope's willingness to reach any accommodation. What he most feared was a combination of votes at Liège which would throw that election as well into the hands of Innocent. His premonition of Fürstenberg's failure at Liège was sharpened by the animosity which he felt toward the cardinal and his anger at Wilhelm's procrastination and unwillingness to allow a show of force. Louvois argued that if Fürstenberg did not control two-thirds of the canons then another candidate should be backed. He preferred Elderen and persuaded the king to adopt a different course of action. Under the new scheme, d'Asfeld would go to Liège to reconnoiter Wilhelm's chances. If he lacked the necessary votes, the envoy would swing the election to Elderen. D'Asfeld had 100,000 livres at his disposal.[5]

D'Asfeld began by informing the canons that no candidate other than Fürstenberg would be acceptable to France. This warning was followed by threats to those with property in French-occupied areas. Louis forbad Liège customs officials to tax goods coming from France and arrested several of them when they resisted; the property of several canons was ravaged by French troops. This only hardened opposition to French demands. Other factions in the city, whether Austrian, Bavarian, Spanish, Neuburg, or Dutch, separately and together, saw their common interest to be best served by stopping Fürstenberg. They rallied to Elderen and the showdown became a contest between the two men.[6]

Wilhelm went to Liège but was unable to effect any change in his support. The evening before the election his faction assembled; still no more than twenty votes could be mustered. They proposed to shift to Bouillon but d'Asfeld stuck with his instructions in favor of Fürstenberg. As other names were proposed and rejected, the discussion became increasingly empty. Two members left the meeting pledging to vote for Elderen. Finally, after interminable bickering, d'Asfeld produced Louis's letter commanding him to swing the election to the dean of the chapter if Fürstenberg could not be assured of victory. Those present were visibly upset but remained determined to vote for the cardinal.[7]

On August 17, between 9 a.m. and noon, the chapter proceeded with the election. Hardly had the members gone into session than a breathless courier arrived with orders from the king to d'Asfeld to work for Cardinal Bouillon! At the last moment Louis decided that if Fürstenberg were unpalatable then a French cardinal would do well enough. Bouillon, in spite of his past record, could be reasonably depended upon to work for the furtherance of French interests. Yet this last-minute decision, like the courier, came too late. Elderen was elected by twenty-five votes, with eighteen going to Fürstenberg.[8] Louvois's original contingency plan was now the reality, but without Wilhelm's faction having switched its vote. The scene of the courier dashing into the city was almost too dramatic to have really occurred. What it pointed to was the irresolution and frustration at Versailles, the frantic search for a reprieve in the face of impending disaster.

For the king and his ministers, the alarm bell had begun to ring. The almost simultaneous reports from Liège and from Chamlay galvanized them into action. A long council meeting was held, most probably on August 20, during which all the political problems of Europe were discussed and assigned priorities. Louis adopted Louvois's proposal to take the initiative by means of preventive warfare. The war minister argued that France had already passed the point of no return. Or, as Ranuzzi phrased it, that it was impossible to withdraw, to abandon the scene "without rendering the enemies of the Crown arrogant and losing the great credit and reputation which was acquired through past action, [leading Europe to think that the French were] superior to all." There was also the possibility of a Turkish defeat in the near future and a rapid conclusion of the war. This would leave the imperial army free to attempt to wrest from the French the territorial gains made since Nijmegen. As so often in the past, the broad lines of French policy were spelled out in the dispatch to Constantinople. Louis informed Girardin that he had decided to fully support Fürstenberg and that he would place troops in Bonn and Kaiserwerth so as to prevent those of the emperor and the Empire from seizing them. A large contingent of troops in the Palatinate and a diversionary force in Italy would presumably keep the imperial forces occupied.[9]

A troublesome piece in the puzzle was the position of England and the plans of William of Orange. Since the spring, d'Avaux had insisted that the Dutch planned to invade England. When James II refused French aid and advice, Louis XIV left him to his fate and drew up contingency plans for himself. He assumed that a Dutch invasion of England, most likely in the fall (as proved to be the case), would immobilize both powers, thus leaving France free to invade the Empire without interference from either the United Provinces or England.[10] A lightning campaign could lead to a more favorable treaty than that of Regensburg before the Austrians could retaliate. Apart from questions of strategy, diplomacy and politics, Louis XIV's decision to begin hostilities was also influenced by his concept of "grandeur," his need to maintain and to pursue his "gloire." "He was determined," the nuncio remarked, "to maintain the commitments which he had made and to remove from the mind of anyone the belief that he was not capable of beginning a new war."[11]

Croissy, who had earlier favored conciliatory policies, was now an apostle of action. As the Danish ambassador reported, "Monsieur de Croissy told me precisely that the Most Christian King was resolved to maintain the rights of Cologne and not to allow Cardinal Fürstenberg to be dispossessed even if the confirmation of the pope should be for Prince Clemens. . . . Croissy continued: 'I assure you, Monsieur, that of all the men of the Kingdom and of all the ministers of the Most Christian King I am the one who has supported most strongly the sentiments of peace; but I must also tell you that I am now persuaded of the necessity of making war above all in the Empire.'"[12] In conversations with Ranuzzi, Croissy expressed his dissatisfaction at the pope's action and angrily denounced Casoni, whom he viewed as the chief enemy of France in Rome. Casoni replied that Croissy spoke "like an African Moor and as the brutal man which he more than ever shows himself to be."[13]

The war preparations threw into even sharper relief the strategic importance of the Electorate of Cologne and almost instantly Louvois clashed with Fürstenberg. He had asked the cardinal via d'Asfeld about the feasibility of the engineer Choisy going to Bonn and Kaiserwerth to survey the sites and make recommendations. From Liège came Wilhelm's reply: Choisy could come, but he must be incognito. Louvois exploded in a letter to d'Asfeld: "I have been scandalized by Cardinal Fürstenberg's response. . . . Can he desire anything else now except that it be known and not doubted that the king has engaged to uphold him? There is no more time to worry about what will be said, and he can only get out of his present predicament by availing himself of the King's protection." In a return dispatch d'Asfeld clarified the situation. Wilhelm had not wanted Choisy to arrive in Bonn while he himself was in Liège. Unless he prepared the members of the chapter they would suspect that it was precisely during his absence that the French planned to master the city. This explanation hardly calmed Louvois's spirit: it was intolerable that work on the Rhineland defenses could be slowed down just to humor a few canons in Bonn. On Wilhelm's end, his actions were tied to approval by the chapter. Only recently had they tasted what sovereignty was like and they feared that all independence would be lost once French troops possessed the fortifications in the electorate. Strasbourg's destiny was not one they wished to share. Diminishing revenues provided another cause for complaint. And since the pope had not yet decided anything officially, they always had something to fall back on.[14]

Wilhelm hoped to plane away many of these difficulties by means of a treaty between France and the cathedral chapter of Cologne as soon as he arrived back in Bonn. (He returned on August 22.) Louvois tartly reminded him that it was high time to take vigorous measures, to make it clear that anyone who crossed him would have to deal with the French army. Six thousand cavalry and 10,000 infantrymen were being readied for service in the electorate, paid for out of the French treasury. As for the local political problems, Louvois urged Wilhelm to tell the canons "that French troop strength was not the strongest element in your fortifications; but that your intention was that it be so and as they arrive you can evacuate the majority of your troops." The French troops would be bound by an oath of loyalty to the cardinal for as long as they remained within the electorate.[15]

If Louvois's stand was in keeping with his past attitudes, Wilhelm in turn kept up his earlier resistance to French entry. On August 27 he requested that Louvois hold back the contingents earmarked for Cologne until he prepared the canons for the occupation. In the last days of August he drafted a proposed treaty which his supporters, "the greater and saner part of the chapter," were asked to accept. While this was being discussed Wilhelm suddenly panicked—he feared the imminent arrival of Brandenburg and Dutch troops into the electorate and their occupation of the fortifications, as well as their entry into the city of Cologne. Three days after refusing French troops, he asked for 8–10,000 men to guard the approach to the city of Cologne. Louvois had anticipated this development and was gathering information on the territories of Jülich and Liège beyond the Meuse with the end of defending Fürstenberg's position in Bonn. As for the Dutch putting troops into the city of Cologne, he believed that 7,000 French troops would be close enough to prevent any such maneuver. Besides, if the Dutch did this they would violate the Treaty of Nijmegen![16]

On August 31 and September 1 Wilhelm informed the king of the chapter's desire to conclude a defensive treaty.[17] This proposal as well as the request for troops arrived just at the time when military promotions were being made, when the strategy of the upcoming campaigns was being mapped out, and while Louis was burning all his bridges behind him with respect to the papacy by addressing a vituperative letter to Innocent XI which would be sent to all the courts of Europe. In this atmosphere of tension and mobilization Louvois learned of Fürstenberg's *volte-face* and dealt with him in the most abrupt manner possible. His first response was given via d'Asfeld: "Cardinal Fürstenberg undoubtedly believes that one assembles a body of some six or seven thousand men in a day. . . . Once and for all he must be persuaded that His Majesty knows better than he what means must be taken to support him in the archbishopric. Nothing is more disagreeable than to negotiate with people who are uncertain. Two days ago the cardinal didn't want the king's troops. Now he is impatient for their arrival." To Wilhelm he declared: "I will say nothing to you concerning your anxiety on the subject of Cologne; I have already written on that subject so amply to M. d'Asfeld that I believe it useless to repeat it to you." [18]

Never had Fürstenberg seemed more inept and floundering, and he knew it. He adopted a markedly defensive posture in his subsequent dealings with Versailles. In 1673 he was convinced that French aggression was ruinous and said as much in his letters to the court, especially to Louvois. Now, in somewhat different circumstances, he was admitting his mistakes and asking for help. Memories of his seizure and imprisonment were renewed with each rumor of similar designs on his person. But Wilhelm's perceptions appear to have been affected not only by his memory of the past but by his age and his scant travel in the past few years. The frenetic activity devoted to the affairs of Cologne and Liège had severely circumscribed his political vision. On the very day that Louvois sent his curt note, d'Asfeld reported that Wilhelm was not well-informed about events in Hungary or in Vienna, that not even his nephews in the imperial service were writing to him.[19] After making due allowance for the usefulness of such a dispatch in Louvois's hands, it was nonetheless substantially true and a telling observation on the limits of Wilhelm's judgment in the face of the crisis.

This sense of isolation was exacerbated when the advice of the special congregation to Innocent urging him to confirm Joseph Clemens became known. D'Asfeld's description of the reception of this news in Bonn must have been relished by Louvois: "Although for some time past the cardinal and the canons of his party should have been prepared for this news, it has not failed to create great consternation and fear. They now see the necessity of throwing themselves into the arms of the king, and the error of having waited so long before asking the troops of His Majesty to enter." Wilhelm hoped that the city of Cologne would declare itself neutral; he and Du Heron opened negotiations with the magistrates. The insignificant defenses of the city plus the widespread disposition of the populace to surrender rather than be destroyed by a French army augured well for the success of this negotiation. But there remained no assurance that the French were not planning to storm the city; on September 6 the magistrates requested the leaders of the circle of Westphalia (Brandenburg, Jülich, and Münster) to send troops into the city. At the time it seemed too late, almost futile, since Marshal Sourdis had already arrived in Bonn. After conferring with Wilhelm and members of the chapter and inspecting the installations, Sourdis declared that the defenses were in disarray and the canons "a bit tumultuous."[20] Events then began to move in bewildering succession.

On September 9 Louis XIV issued a declaration explaining his reasons for sending troops into Cologne; copies were sent to all the courts of Europe. That very day Fürstenberg issued an edict stating that the chapter was empowered to declare when a state of emergency existed; it also asserted the right to confiscate the goods of those who fled. On the following day 6000 French troops entered the Electorate of Cologne under the joint leadership of Sourdis and d'Asfeld. On September 12 Wilhelm declared that the troops were there as guarantors of the treaties of Münster and Nijmegen and in fulfillment of the treaty between France and Cologne signed at Luxembourg in May 1687. Their role was to safeguard the peace and tranquility of the electorate and the electoral rights of the chapter, all purportedly threatened by enemy forces. This rapid series of events led to a decisive split in the chapter when representatives of both factions clashed in a joint session on September 15. Joseph Clemens's partisans bitterly attacked the September 9 edict and opposed the presence of foreign troops. On September 17 another meeting was held without Fürstenberg's party in attendance; the edict of September 12 was assailed and a solemn protest registered. Within a few days 2000 troops from Brandenburg and Jülich marched into the city, strengthening the garrison and giving encouragement to the imperial camp. In numbers the relief was not that great, but symbolically it had the highest significance. Their arrival seemed like a deus ex machina and, as Braubach notes, the magistrates of Cologne may very well have been as surprised as everyone else. Wilhelm's faction asserted that Cologne was no longer safe and requested that the chapter move to Bonn. Joseph Clemens's supporters refused, declared the chapter in Bonn to be illegal and continued to reside in Cologne: there were now two chapters.[21]

As French troops continued their penetration of the Rhineland, Cardinal d'Estrées read a royal declaration to the pope on September 15. Louis XIV was always adept at placing the blame for a situation on somebody else; here was a classic example of this kind of polemic. Innocent silently listened to a long list of accusations, including his refusal to recognize Lavardin, his partisanship in the Cologne affair, his unwillingness to treat with French envoy Chamlay, and his open espousal of the imperial cause. Louis said he would seize the disputed papal territories of Castro and Ronciglione and give them to the Duke of Parma. He further threatened to occupy Avignon, to continue to support Fürstenberg, and to refuse any papal mediation in the Palatine succession issue.[22] Copies were distributed to the cardinals in Rome and circulated widely among all the princes of Europe.

As menacing as these threats may have seemed, the atmosphere in Rome was totally changed in two days. By a wonderful coincidence it was at this very juncture that news arrived from the Turkish front: Max Emmanuel had led the Christian host to victory at Belgrade! The last great bastion on the outer rim of the Ottoman Empire had been taken. Amidst fireworks and *Te Deums*, Innocent issued a brief confirming Joseph Clemens as Archbishop of Cologne with rights to the temporal administration of the archdiocese as well, thus ratifying the verdict of the consistorial congregation given during the preceding month. Immediately upon receiving word of the papal brief, Joseph Clemens took minor orders and a *Te Deum* was sung in the Frauenkirche in Munich.[23] But the celebration could not last too long; the French had begun their invasion of the Empire. Already on September 13 the papal vice-legate had been chased from Avignon and French troops soon moved into the territory. Croissy reportedly said that papal buildings would be turned into powder and Rome itself reduced to such a state that grass would not be seen there for ten years.[24]

On September 24, in a manifesto explaining why he felt compelled to take up arms, Louis XIV offered concessions. For one, he promised to let Joseph Clemens become coadjutor if Fürstenberg were accepted by the emperor. He also pledged to restore·Freiburg as well as Philippsburg (as soon as he could seize it), provided that their fortifications were torn down and that the Truce of Regensburg were converted into a definitive peace with the French keeping what they had at the moment. Significantly, he placed a three-month deadline on the acceptance of these terms. Once more the king was issuing what could justifiably be termed "ultimatums." At the same time, regiments of French troops were pouring into the Palatinate and preparing to invest the fortress of Philipps-

burg. The siege began on September 27 under the personal supervision
of Vauban, with the Dauphin on hand to "command the army."[25]

As the pace quickened and as German princes planned to enter into
combat against the Sun King, the situation in the Electorate of Cologne
took on both tragic and comic proportions. Marshal Sourdis told Louvois that were he the general of an enemy army he would go straight
to Bonn, for it was ripe for the picking, without munitions or a single
cannon capable of firing two shots. An intensive effort was launched to
improve the defenses. Sourdis believed that news of Belgrade's conquest
would enable Fürstenberg to govern his followers "more despotically."
Yet though Wilhelm wished to extricate himself from the grip of the
canons, he was even more apprehensive of French tutelage. He felt that
there was "more dignity for him in acting out his present role, as painful
as it was, than in another role which he might be asked to play in the
future." Despite these misgivings, the yoke of the chapter was finally
lifted on October 4. His faction gave over the entire administration and
temporal government of the archbishopric to Wilhelm on condition that
he do nothing contrary to present treaty provisions and that French
troops be used only for defense. This action followed the report that
Joseph Clemens had already donned the electoral habit in Munich with
ceremonies scheduled to take place in the city of Cologne. Wilhelm now
feared that the pope would strip him of his title of cardinal. To avoid
this disgrace he proposed to Louis that he be permitted to send his hat
back to Rome. He further expected nuncio Tanara to ask that he desist
from his pretensions under threat of excommunication, a threat that
would loosen his control over the canons.[26] The nuncio did not visit him
nor did Louis think it at all necessary to give up the dignity of the cardinal's office, but these incidents reveal how jangled Wilhelm's nerves
had become.

On September 30 the emperor directed all concerned to recognize
Joseph Clemens as the lawful Elector of Cologne and to break their ties
with Fürstenberg. Karg, who had been in Rome seeking to expedite
papal action, returned to Cologne on October 10 with authorization
from the pope and the new elector to oversee the official transition. On
the following day, accompanied by the nuncio and commanders of the
garrison, he watched Prince von Croy together with several other canons
take over the administration of the archbishopric in the absence of the
Bavarian prince. Joseph Clemens was thus officially proclaimed ruler of
Cologne. In his name, his followers, including Karg, took possession of
the bishop's palace and the church grounds.[27] Naturally there were cele-

brations in the city; according to d'Asfeld, however, the citizens of Cologne did not render the customary ceremonial homage to an elector so
as not to attract Louis's ire.[28] In a symbolic reprisal, Wilhelm, on his
own authority, ordered all Bavarian officials and agents in Bonn to leave
the city on October 14. Upon learning of this affront, Munich requested
Innocent to act against the cardinal, but the pope declined to issue a
statement, claiming that he had no immediate power to enforce his will
and did not wish to have papal decrees flouted.[29]

October 1688 saw the intensification of French preparations to ward
off the expected counter-offensive from the Germanies before winter
brought military operations to a virtual standstill. Even more significant
were Dutch preparations for the invasion of England. As the political
and military dimensions of the war expanded, there was a corresponding
decline in Fürstenberg's importance. Louvois informed d'Asfeld that he
need no longer feel obligated to negotiate with Wilhelm but instead
should "speak to him always as a man who has received an order so as
to avoid the ordinary irresolutions and delays." For his part, Wilhelm
promised that "things would move faster in the future." Louvois's riposte
had a sharp sardonic edge: "It is with considerable joy that I see you are
finally resolved to right matters better than in the past. . . . M. Breget can
tell you that I refuse him no audience and that he speaks to me as often
as he wishes. I must acknowledge that in the conversations which I've
had with him the time has not always been employed praising you. If
I had less interest in what concerns you I would have been able to look
on with more *sang froid* at all the time which has been uselessly consumed. . . . Excuse the liberty with which I speak to you. It stems only
from the concern which I have for that which affects your interests."
Wilhelm accepted this reproach, admitted irresolution and delay, and did
not excuse himself from blame.[30] He had always been sensitive to the
charge that he was little more than a puppet manipulated from France;
now his masters were too preoccupied to even pull the strings.

The obloquy which Wilhelm received in the past was marginal in comparison with the hate now directed against the French and their allies.
For the autumn of 1688 was to be the scene of the worst atrocities per-
petrated in all of Louis XIV's reign. The terror tactics of Louvois in the
Palatinate, the scorched earth policies aimed at making entire peoples cry
out and demand that their rulers surrender—these calculated horrors
were to have a catalytic effect on the German-speaking peoples throughout the Empire, affording them a sense of common identity which was
almost nationalistic in its fervor. After overrunning the Palatinate, General Boufflers asked the Electors of Mainz and Trier to hand over their

chief cities. Mainz complied and the capitulation was signed on October 17.[31] Trier, however, was obstinate and refused to give over Coblenz. Since Boufflers needed cannons to do his job well, he waited until Philippsburg was taken on October 29 and then had the weapons transferred before Coblenz. Vauban complained of the unnecessarily harsh measures planned by Boufflers. He maintained that more negotiations were in order, that bombardment was not especially necessary, that inhumane treatment could only bring unfavorable political repercussions throughout the Empire and, as in the past, stiffen German resistance to French demands.[32] Fürstenberg would have concurred in these views, but all of Vauban's warnings were in vain. On November 11 Boufflers reported that the bombardment had been "an extraordinary success. Everything which had not been burned in the city had been broken, toppled, or ripped apart by bombs and bullets. Only twenty homes were habitable; the electoral palace had received special treatment and was in rubble." In reply, Louvois noted that the king was pleased to learn that after having burned Coblenz well and having done all possible damage to the electoral palace he had once again marched toward Mainz.[33]

These frightful policies hardened resistance throughout the Empire: there would be no rapid end to the fighting, no humble prostration before the Sun King as expected. Instead there was the prospect of a long, costly war. Since the garrisons in the Electorate of Cologne were intended to hold the lower Rhine, a renewed effort to shore up the defenses was undertaken. The peasants in the territory were commandeered to help with the fortifications but they did not work with any great zeal. In fact, their lackadaisical attitude seemed to be encouraged by Fürstenberg's leniency. D'Asfeld used French troops to ensure that the cardinal's orders were enforced. In addition to uncooperative workers there was inclement weather. The very storm which delayed William of Orange's departure for England produced snow and rain sufficient to swell the Rhine and threaten the outworks at Bonn, not to mention the delays in construction and transportation. As reports of the slow progress reached him, Louvois became increasingly irritable, asserting that the peasants of the electorate did not earn the bread they received. Little came of all his outrage; the French engineer at Bonn had been promised 1200 workers but no more than 700 were on hand. At the outset men had reported for duty at nine in the morning and "worked languidly" for the remainder of the day. Before long they stayed home and sent their children instead, including girls between eight and ten years of age! Wilhelm himself defended the peasants in a dispatch to Louvois, noting that they had to travel one and one-half hours each way to work. When they arrived there were not enough tools, wheelbarrows were bogged down in the mud, and there was a shortage of planks to smooth the way. One can well imagine Louvois's mood upon learning that the defenses of the lower Rhine were being constructed with the aid of eight-year-old girls. But the work went on through the winter, paid for through contributions exacted from occupied territory (105,000 écus from Cologne). The adjoining Duchy of Jülich was assessed a sum of 200,000 écus. When the local deputies attempted delaying tactics Louvois instructed Sourdis "to burn villages every day until the sum of 200,000 écus which the king requests is reached. His Majesty wishes the territory to pay not only for the current year, but for the coming year as well." [34] Hatred toward France could be likened to the swollen Rhine in the dismal winter of 1688.

Louis's deadline of January 1, 1689 passed without any noticeable willingness among his opponents to submit to his demands. William III of Orange had already succeeded in England and would become the leader of another and more powerful coalition against the threat of French hegemony. War was officially declared by the Empire against France on February 15, 1689, and allegiance to Leopold I was more intensive than at any time during his reign. Officials and officers devoted to Fürstenberg (including Rotkirch) began to slip away, submitting to Karg in Cologne and pledging their loyalty to the emperor and his allies.[35] As Brandenburg and Dutch troops made gains against the French in the electorate itself, Wilhelm's position became desperate and he himself despondent. There seemed nothing else to do except to take refuge in France. He had undoubtedly aired this project many times in conversation with French envoys; in mid-March he openly suggested it. Louis's permission came in the return post with his promise to support the canons of Fürstenberg's party and to speak for them at the peace conference.[36]

Wilhelm's departure from Bonn was the clearest possible sign of his essential failure. Most of his baggage, together with the canons who still stood by him, went on ahead to Metz on April 1, 1689. The cardinal remained behind for several days attending to the most pressing matters and then departed on April 6, guarded by five companies of cavalry and four of dragoons. D'Asfeld reported that he left "with sorrow." After spending two days at Trier he went to Metz where his entry was greeted by regiments of cavalry and cannon salutes on April 14. These were indeed gloomy days for Wilhelm. He was embittered by charges concerning his inept handling of military preparations in the electorate. Military expertise, after all, was inseparably a part of his family tradition. Perhaps Wilhelm felt that in a sense he had betrayed his ancestors. In an attempt to save pride, if nothing else, he told Louvois that he would be indeed sorry if after all the time and effort he spent at Bonn on military matters he came to be thought of as little more than "a negotiator out of season." To compound his misfortunes there came news that Dutch soldiers had destroyed his residence at Modave; his town house in Liège was likewise plundered. The abbeys at Stavelot and Malmédy were ravaged and burned by French troops. The crowning disaster came in Metz where the house in which he lived burned down, killing eight of his servants and destroying much of his belongings.[37]

The sojourn in Metz lasted two months, during which time several of the canons accompanying him deserted to the other side in the hope of preserving their offices and possessions.[38] Wilhelm next proceeded to Verdun, where his troops staged a two-hour military review followed by a harangue from the cardinal. After he bade them adieu they all threw their hats into the air and shouted: "Vive le Roy et Son Eminence!" The troops then swore allegiance to Louis XIV and dispersed to new assignments. Louvois was informed by the commandant of Metz that of all the new regiments of dragoons entering French service those belonging to Fürstenberg had the best men. The journey ended with a warm reception accorded to the refugee on June 30 at Versailles.[39]

Behind him he left the territory of Cologne, a land which was to be crisscrossed by troops and ravaged by battles during the coming year. Enemy armies rolled up the French on several fronts, resulting in a retreat from Neuss, the surrender of Rheinberg and the capture of Kaiserwerth. A ferocious battle raged around Bonn until that city finally capitulated on October 12, 1689. The concluding passage in the official description of the campaign could serve as the epitaph of this doomed adventure: "M. d'Asfeld died of his wounds. This place had truly become useless to us. Its loss was the end of the affairs of Cologne."[40]

XIII

EXILE AND RETIREMENT

SEPTEMBER 1689 TO APRIL 1704

WILHELM'S FLIGHT from the Rhineland ended his active political career. The French policies he both feared and cooperated with destroyed his position and blasted his ambitions; he never again returned to his homeland. But the acrimony of the Cologne drama pursued him to Rome at the conclave which elected a successor to Innocent XI.

The French party which left Toulon on September 10, 1689 included the Duke of Chaulnes, ambassador to Rome, and Cardinals Bonzi, Bouillon, and Fürstenberg. Bouillon joined the party at Ville Franche; despite fears of a row with Fürstenberg, the two apparently agreed to bury the hatchet.[1] On September 23, after travel by ship and coach, they slipped into Rome at 4 a.m. to please Wilhelm, who feared "that in the crowd of people who would be in the street if we arrived in broad daylight, evil designs against him might thereby be executed more easily." Rumors of an intended seizure abounded and Louis XIV ordered special measures to guard Wilhelm's residence and person.[2] His very presence was an event: when the French delegation first filed into the conclave, it was attended "by a huge crowd drawn by curiosity to see Cardinal von Fürstenberg."[3] Not every day could one see a cardinal of the Holy Church who had been in jail for five years and whose personal and public careers were so filled with scandal and adventure.

Throughout the conclave Wilhelm was the object of Austrian hostility. In a routine vote which would have permitted three assistants to accompany him, there were four opposing votes, understood to be cast by Austrians who regarded even this matter as "an affair of state."[4] Despite these petty annoyances he appears to have discharged his functions adequately. After Cardinal Ottoboni was elevated as Alexander VIII, Chaulnes praised the entire French party and remarked Fürstenberg's "solid counsel and his devotion to the will of His Majesty."[5]

Wilhelm hoped to solicit papal intercession in behalf of the expelled canons who supported him at Cologne. First he had to correct, as he put it, the commonly held opinion of him: "that of a man capable of sacrificing the repose and the tranquility of all Christendom to his interests and private passions." He claimed to have insinuated himself well enough into the opinion of the Sacred College and even to have assuaged somewhat the hostility of the powerful Cardinal Leopold Kollonitsch in the Austrian delegation. (He may have dispelled some unfavorable opinion; in the early 1690's Kollonitsch corresponded with Wilhelm in an attempt to bring an end to the war.) With the stage thus set, he asked Louis XIV for 18,000 livres to support his stay in Rome and an additional 5000 livres to bring Quentel to assist him in his lobbying activity. The King sent 20,000 livres but ordered him home after the ceremonies at which he received his cardinal's hat from the pope. On the same day, in a dispatch to Chaulnes, Fürstenberg's position was limned in its true perspective. Louis above all wanted to maintain good relations with the Holy See and did not want an attempt to procure a red hat for the Bishop of Beauvais (Forbin-Janson) nor the litigation over the Cologne canons to result in a rupture between France and Rome: "I desire that you omit nothing to obtain the hat for the first and some adjustment [*temperament*] which may satisfy the other, but without pushing to the breaking point and without saying a word of what I am writing to you to those whom these affairs concern."[6]

Meanwhile, Fürstenberg prepared for audiences with the pope's nephew and with the pontiff himself. Chaulnes predicted "a very favorable reception, the more so since His Holiness has much consideration for him and he has made himself well liked by everyone at the papal court. As a result, his trip will win him a very great reputation." Soon thereafter Wilhelm received his red hat and learned of Louis XIV's promise to give up the disputed franchises.[7] Two years earlier he might have been elated; now the king's decision could only have seemed ironic.

One evening Fürstenberg became quite agitated due to the arrival in Rome of two expelled canons, one of them his nephew. On the following day, however, the pope assured Chaulnes that he had thoroughly investigated the case and that he would ask Joseph Clemens to reinstate the canons. If he refused, Alexander promised to do it on his own authority. This news greatly relieved Fürstenberg,[8] but left him little excuse to stay on in Rome. (The official reinstatement of the canons occurred after the war was over; by 1697 all but three were dead.)

Wilhelm's departure from Rome was a scene out of a comic-opera. He originally planned to take a short excursion outside of Rome, leaving his baggage and retinue behind. Then, incognito, he would head for Turin and be far enough away before his enemies knew he was gone.[9] A different scheme was hatched at Versailles. This entailed borrowing a galley from the Duke of Tuscany without disclosing the purpose for which it would be used and then transporting Wilhelm to Genoa or to France. Foucher (since transferred from Mainz to Florence) handled the negotiation. He dealt with the abbé de Gondi, prime minister of Cosimo III, and met with a solid wall of opposition: Cosimo's daughter-in-law was the sister of Joseph Clemens and with all the speculation in Roman gazettes about Wilhelm's departure, he easily guessed the French plans. Behind the scene Cosimo suggested to Chaulnes that a galley be furnished by the pope or by Genoa. Foucher sent a note to Gondi at midnight on November 24 pleading for an audience with his master but to no avail. Meanwhile, the day before Foucher's dispatch was sent off, Wilhelm left Rome disguised as a chevalier of the Knights of Malta. He was accompanied by the abbé Morel, earlier involved in the Palatinate affair, by an Italian gentleman, and two valets. At Livorno they learned of the Duke of Tuscany's refusal and so pressed on to Genoa. From there Fürstenberg took a ship to Toulon. On December 3 he announced his safe arrival in Cannes and promised to be at Versailles before Christmas.[10]

Back in Rome, the rumor of Wilhelm's departure led to much "movement along the route." Chaulnes kept his courier in Rome until the previous one returned. Fürstenberg's fears were hardly imaginary: the second son of Colbert de Croissy, C. J. Colbert, who accompanied Wilhelm to Rome as an assistant, was captured by Spaniards on his return and kept prisoner for a year in a Milanese chateau.[11]

Wilhelm received a warm welcome upon his arrival at Versailles on December 19. On January 9, 1690, the king named him abbot of Saint-Germain-des-Prés, one of the most lucrative benefices in the kingdom. The appointment included the abbot's palace in Paris, the property of Berny, and 80,000 livres in income per annum. Unfortunately, a fire subsequently destroyed the records of the abbey and we have little solid evidence of Fürstenberg's administration.[12] We do know that he enjoyed presiding over ceremonies, often traveling across Paris to assist at high masses in other churches. He faithfully carried out his episcopal functions: in 1693, for example, he officiated at the ceremony at which the newly-appointed Bishop of Ypres was anointed; in September 1695 he consecrated twelve men as priests and confirmed several persons. Wilhelm took a great interest in the historical research being carried out by the Benedictine fathers of the Congregation of St. Maur and wrote numerous letters of introduction for historians, including Jean Mabillon and Thierry Ruinart, who sought entry into the archives of princely families in the Empire. Perhaps his most notable contribution was the restoration of the abbot's palace and grounds at Saint-Germain-des-Prés. In testimony to his work in repairing and beautifying the residence and the surrounding area, the charming Place de Fürstenberg, close by Saint-Germain, was dedicated to the cardinal.[13]

Socially, Wilhelm's career in these twilight years must have come close to his dreams of retirement. He continued to be well-received at the court and in 1694 the king accorded him the title of Commander in the exclusive Order of the Holy Spirit. At Berny he hosted receptions for distinguished visitors, including the Duke of Bourgogne, the Duke of Orléans, and other members of the royal family.[14] His favorite retreat, however, was at La Bourdaisière, near Tours. Here he stayed in the chateau bought by the Countess von der Mark from the Marquis of Dangeau whose second wife was a niece of Fürstenberg's, Sophie-Marie of Bavaria, Countess of Löwenstein-Rochefort. Wilhelm often spent eight months out of the year at La Bourdaisière in the company of the countess. On July 4, 1696, he became an honorary canon of Saint-Martin de Tours. (Contemporaries claimed that in addition to the charms of the Loire valley, these sojourns enabled him to escape his Parisian creditors.) From all evidence, the countess increasingly came to dominate him; her extravagant life style, her love of clothes and gambling, expenses for paramours—all these required considerable money, and Wilhelm's income was depleted without much difficulty. Saint-Simon estimated that his yearly income amounted to more than 700,000 livres, with more than 500,000 livres coming from Strasbourg and Saint-Germain alone. None of this proved sufficient and his pleas for money as well as benefices for relatives became proverbial; at the court, he was familiarly referred to as "the dear cardinal."[15]

What of politics? Throughout the 1690's the so-called War of the League of Augsburg dragged on. As in the Dutch war, Fürstenberg's rights as a prince of the Empire were suspended. After so close a connection with the outbreak of the war, his role during its course was minimal. In cooperation with Versailles, he sent a letter to Cardinal Kollonitsch on November 30, 1692, in an attempt to establish the ground plans for a peace settlement. Kollonitsch's response on January 9, 1693, outlined general principles for a negotiated peace. The king ordered Croissy to remain in close contact with Fürstenberg in this affair, especially in drafting the reply to Kollonitsch on February 7. But this episode proved to be a brief flurry with no consequences. Wilhelm was occasionally consulted thereafter, but there is no sign that his role was very important.[16]

In 1694, after Louis d'Elderen's death at Liège, Wilhelm insinuated himself into the election from afar. On the surface, he backed a French candidate, but a devoted clique of supporters in the chapter raised his hopes of succeeding there himself. Such hopes were illusory; once again

Joseph Clemens was triumphant.[17] This was Wilhelm's last fling at elective office.

With the end of the war in sight, Fürstenberg followed the peace preparations with an active interest. In August 1697 he thanked Louis XIV for attending to his interests at Ryswick and lamented his inability to serve: "Having become, to my very great regret, entirely useless to the service of Your Majesty, I will not fail to employ a good part of my time in beseeching God very fervently that He second with his celestial benedictions all the designs and enterprises of Your Majesty."[18] During the preliminaries to peace a question was raised concerning Max Heinrich's inheritance. Where had the money and valuables from the electoral treasury gone? Wilhelm submitted a memorandum in this connection, undoubtedly working in collaboration with the faithful Jean Breget, now intendant of the House of Fürstenberg. Originally, he claimed, there were 178,633 écus in the coffers. Some of this was used to pay debts and the salaries of Max Heinrich's servants. Most of the remainder (said to be 98,482 écus) was used for levees and fortifications. On Louvois's orders, the elector's jewels had been sent to Paris. Wilhelm cited Louvois's declaration that by the express wish of His Majesty all of these belongings be taken away by right of war. Following this directive, Wilhelm made use of the money. He also brought 3237 pieces of German silverware with him from Cologne.[19] "The dear cardinal" was no slouch in gaining his "piece of bread."

Once news of the peace between France and the Empire was declared in January 1698, Fürstenberg ordered a solemn *Te Deum* to be sung in Saint-Germain-des-Prés. A church historian records that "the entire choir and sanctuary were illuminated in an extraordinary manner. The cardinal officiated pontifically in the presence of the papal nuncio, several archbishops and bishops, two ambassadors, and numerous persons of quality who had been invited. In the evening the exterior courts of the abbey were illuminated and fireworks went off between the two belltowers of the church, which made a fine effect."[20]

The terms of the Ryswick pact satisfied Fürstenberg. Article 44 of the treaty provided for the complete reinstatement of all rights pertaining to him as a German prince. Although this was a keen personal victory, he severed most of his ties with the Empire, ending his association with the chapter at Cologne and resigning his position at St. Gereon in that city.[21] Regarding those parts of the bishopric of Strasbourg which lay on the right bank of the Rhine and so had immediate ties to the emperor, no satisfactory solution was ever devised whereby he could exercise his regalian rights or vote in the Diet. Though he was officially returned into the emperor's good graces, inevitably the polemics pursued him beyond the pale of the Empire. The news that Wilhelm was refurbishing the abbot's residence at Saint-Germain led one German lampoonist to suggest a little dedication for the library of the abbey to be used for the instruction of posterity: "Here lives the ex-Elector of Cologne, W. E. Fürstenberg, traitor to his country. Having fled before the military might of the German homeland, he has come here amid sighs and tears to deplore the inconstancy of fortune, the temerity of his ambitions, and the impotent power of his French protector."[22] Wilhelm had experience in shrugging off such attacks; he may even have yawned.

With the completion of one war, the issue of the Spanish Succession gave reason to expect another one. Since papal intervention or arbitration could never be ruled out, Louis XIV used Fürstenberg to sound out Cardinal Buonvisi on his opinion of the Spanish affair, especially since he was being considered as the next pope. Wilhelm contacted Buonvisi through a mutual friend, the abbé Atto Melani, a native of Pistoia, who had originally been recruited into French service by Mazarin. One of Melani's first assignments had been a reconnaissance mission to Munich at the time of the Frankfurt Congress in 1657. Now, more than forty years later, he told Buonvisi that Fürstenberg was "the most constant, the most faithful friend that I have known in the world, and Your Excellency is right to like him because such friends are rare."[23] In Fürstenberg's attempt to read Buonvisi's mind concerning the pope's role—what it might be, should be—in the Spanish Succession there was constantly the implication that Buonvisi's stated opinion would commit him if he became pope. Wilhelm assured him that it was not a question of commitments but rather the judgment of an experienced man of affairs. But the Italian cardinal's experience led him to see through this scheme and he refused to play the French game.[24] Buonvisi died later that year and unfortunately never had the chance to prove himself as pope. Despite his clashes with the Fürstenbergs while nuncio at Cologne, he always retained a respect and warmth for Wilhelm which was reciprocated.

The eighteenth century had dawned and most of Wilhelm's old friends and antagonists were gone. Now in his seventies, he must have seemed like a relic from another age. It was during these later years that Saint-Simon traced his famous portrait of Fürstenberg, describing him as "a man of medium height, heavy-set but carrying himself well, with the most handsome face in the world . . . who spoke French very badly, who, to see him and listen to him in an ordinary fashion, seemed to be a foolish person and who, acquainted with and put on to politics and affairs of state, according to what I have been told by ministers and others from many countries, surpassed the ordinary bounds of capacity, finesse and industry."[25] The most often-quoted descriptions of Wilhelm, like the above, are those made after he was seventy years old. Besides, when one considers that Saint-Simon (1675–1755) was born one year after Wilhelm's capture in 1674, we cannot expect him to be overly familiar with his capacity in handling affairs of state.

At the time of the conclave of cardinals in 1700, which he did not attend, Fürstenberg was depicted by an Italian in the following manner: "A seigneur of great spirit and high capacity and a total attention . . . profound, subtle, suspicious and eloquent, but without that charity for his neighbor which is necessary for a good ecclesiastic. . . . All the same, a great supporter of the poor, generous and bizarre but vain in all his proceedings."[26] One is tempted to conclude that such a description was made not by one man but by a committee. What certainly did seize the imagination of contemporaries was the prodigious sums of money which trickled through the cardinal's fingers. At the end of his life he had a greater income than ever before. While the countess doubtless squandered most of it, Wilhelm's entire life, like that of Franz Egon, had been dedicated to lavish living. One of the first comments of Mlle de Montpensier was that he spent money like a profligate. To the end he was supported by the king, who seldom refused his requests for money or favors, who never forgot Wilhelm's service and imprisonment in his behalf.

Though shunted aside from the world of high politics after 1689, Fürstenberg's experience and diplomatic talents were put to good use in the administration of his benefices. The minor ones, including Saint-Arnould, were given over to Ludwig Peter, the countess's son, and perhaps his own.[27] The major offices and their emoluments he retained for himself. As an absentee bishop, he kept in fairly close touch with Strasbourg and used his connections at the court to good advantage. In 1693, to relieve the bishopric of a debt which mounted to more than 1,200,000 livres, he proposed the selling of offices, an expedient which was agreed upon on March 9, 1693. All the money from the sale of places would go to pay the debt on buildings which then mounted to 266,000 livres. A sum of 50,000 livres would be donated to the royal treasury. This scheme was confirmed by a decree of the Conseil d'Etat on March 17, 1693. When the buildings were finally paid for the surplus was to be given over to the church on condition that the financial office of the bishopric contribute 200 livres each year to the vicars of the cathedral to celebrate masses for the repose of Wilhelm's soul and that of his brother Franz. An additional 200 livres would be distributed on these occasions to the poor of the bishopric.[28]

In that same year, a new crisis developed at Strasbourg. War expenses led to royal exactions everywhere in France. In July 1693 the controller-general informed Wilhelm that since prelates and ecclesiastics in the frontier provinces had offered a quarter of their revenues to the king as contributions to the war effort, the clergy of Alsace would be asked to do as much. Fürstenberg took charge of the negotiation from this time forward and reacted sharply when La Grange, acting on his own authority as the royal intendant in Alsace, asked for 50,000 livres from the Alsatian clergy and demanded specifications of all property and revenues of the Church in Alsace so as to tax it. Wilhelm won the king's intervention in the case. The sum would be given as "a free gift" voted by the diocesan general assembly and the principle of ecclesiastical immunity thus maintained. In 1695 La Grange sought to impose the *capitation* on the clergy of Alsace. Once again, Wilhelm defended them from direct government action. A compromise was reached whereby more money was voted but it had to stay in the diocese and be used for the upkeep of the seminary and the payment of royal pensions.[29]

The war also affected another of Wilhelm's benefices, Stavelot-Malmédy. At the outset, the principality had its neutrality recognized by France, the United Provinces, and England. Since it was part of the Empire, Leopold put it under his protection on condition that as a member state it contribute to imperial expenses. Since Fürstenberg was then proscribed, the leaders of the two monasteries were forbidden to correspond with him or to forward any of his revenues. The principality was without fortifications or soldiers and so needed every possible assurance of its neutrality. Tragically, its privileged status was not enough. On October 4, 1689, French troops warned the inhabitants of Stavelot and Malmédy to evacuate their homes and to take their belongings. They then set fire to the towns. As Mme Moisse-Daxhelet has noted, such destruction was not part of the systematic terror campaigns launched by Louvois—warnings were given and no pillaging took place—but rather a means of preventing enemy troops' moving from Bonn and setting up winter quarters in the region.[30] This may have afforded some consolation to the inhabitants, but all the same, their territory was repeatedly criss-crossed by troops of various armies during the war. Fürstenberg persistently sought to minimize impositions on his subjects; in fact, only in 1696, after seven years of warfare, did the French begin to levy contributions there. (The king was annoyed at the money given to the emperor; at least it was a convenient pretext.) Despite imperial prohibitions, the prior of Stavelot continued to correspond with the cardinal and sent him his revenues; during the first five years of the war Fürstenberg received 31,270 écus

from this source alone.[31] The prior of Malmédy was far less accommodating (and Wilhelm reciprocated in kind) but the reason was more due
to the traditional hostility between the two monasteries than any special
devotion to Emperor Leopold.

The long-standing tension between the two chapters led Wilhelm to
propose that they be united. This project was first broached in August
1692, but after repeated attempts and changes of formula the opposition
proved unsurmountable. Similar attempts would founder throughout the
eighteenth century and no deep structural changes could be made until
the era of the French Revolution.[32] Wilhelm made six attempts to solve
the problem of administering the principality during his absence but
these, too, dashed against the obstinate wall of local hostilities.[33] He was
working on these affairs right down to the day of his death. Fürstenberg's
zeal for reform led the historian of his administration at Stavelot-Malmédy to extol "the incontestable clarity of his views, their generosity, the
constancy and sincerity of his action when it was a question of the welfare of his abbey and of his principality."[34]

Wilhelm's last important activities involved the determination of successors in his major benefices. Cardinal d'Estrées was already slated to
succeed him at Saint-Germain. With backing from Versailles, one of Wilhelm's nephews tried to become coadjutor at Stavelot-Malmédy but he
was defeated by Francis of Lorraine who had the support of the emperor.[35] The biggest prize of all, Strasbourg, was transmitted amidst
fierce rivalry. Cardinal Bouillon expected to win it for his family but his
intrigues led to still another disgrace. Fürstenberg acceded to the king's
wishes and supported the candidacy of Armand-Gaston de Rohan who
was unanimously elected as coadjutor on February 28, 1701. Less than
three months after Rohan's election, Wilhelm received a *gratification* of
120,000 livres in recognition of his latest service to the crown.[36] After
his death, Rohan thus became the first French subject to reign as Bishop
of Strasbourg. His family continued to hold the bishopric down to the
Revolution and aided considerably in the assimilation of Alsace into
France.[37]

The episode of the Strasbourg succession proved to be the last act. In
spite of his enormous revenues and the agreeable sojourns in the Tou-
raine, Fürstenberg's last years were saddened by physical ailments and
the crushing burden of his own and the countess's debts. Already in
1700 he had suffered several "attacks of apoplexy" and was severely
injured by a fall when attempting to climb into a carriage.[38] Debts, according to the chroniclers, forced him to sell much of his plate and silverware, to cut back on domestic help, to worry incessantly about bills and

creditors. Two hours after midnight on April 10, 1704, he died at the age of seventy-five after another apoplectic attack, without benefit of the last sacraments.[39] He was buried in the chapel of Ste. Marguerite in the church of Saint-Germain-des-Prés. The burial place was in a family tomb, a striking mausoleum designed and decorated by the famed Coysevox, which stood until the Revolution.[40]

XIV
CONCLUSION

WILHELM'S LAST YEARS and the circumstances of his death provided useful moral lessons for those who wished to see them. The death of Bossuet in the same year led Saint-Simon to draw a parallel between the two prelates. Bossuet, he said, even in old age far surpassed the most robust of bishops and the wisest of scholars. Fürstenberg, on the other hand, "after having for so long agitated and interested the whole of Europe, had for some time become a useless weight upon the earth."[1] This is good rhetoric but it does less than justice to Wilhelm's activity in church administration during the last decade, an activity which was genuinely conciliatory in nature and reformist in spirit. That there were more failures than successes is not the same as saying that he was a useless weight upon the earth. As we have seen, Fürstenberg permanently influenced Liège and, to a lesser degree, the relationship between the French state and the province and churches of Alsace. Still, the activity of politics and negotiation in which he was engaged left fewer visible results than the activity of a Bossuet. How indeed would one evaluate a life which was a ceaseless whirlwind of striving, scheming, and spending, a life seemingly devoted to opportunism? This task was entrusted to the redoubtable abbé Le Prevost who delivered the funeral oration at services for the deceased cardinal in Saint-Germain-des-Prés on June 5, 1704. Before a distinguished congregation he proceeded with superb audacity to compare Wilhelm to Joseph in Egypt!

Take note, Messieurs, with what attention Providence prepares a Joseph and where she leads him in order to give him to a realm upon which designs of mercy are to be executed. Such a soul may be called one day to go into Egypt in order to govern it. Superior to the passions, it must ignore those weaknesses which proceed from them; greater than fortune, such a soul plays with its alterations; tranquil in its innocence, neither calumny nor bondage cause it dismay or unease; mistress of its affections, it is ready to forget house and homeland, reckoning as homeland and house only that country where the most good is to be procured. By means of such a soul, prepared in such a manner, does God wish to do honor to himself in a favored land. Joseph is drawn from his place of birth to become counselor to a king and the mainspring of his kingdom. . . . Thus, by degrees,

Messieurs, I am establishing the character of the prince whom we mourn, by tracing for you the story of Joseph; if Heaven had not the same designs for him, it did endow him with the same wisdom.[2]

What a pity that Lisola, Louvois, and Max Heinrich were not present to hear that explication of Wilhelm's life! Lionne might well have savored the oration more than anyone else, with the possible exception of Wilhelm himself. As for his close association with France, Le Prevost continued,

Here it is not a question of infidelity or of ingratitude. At the outset it was the love of his native land that drew him to France; he went there to prevent the war which menaced his homeland; he was kept there by the bishopric of Metz which he received, and then became naturalized so as to legitimately enjoy the rights to this benefice. What am I saying? He was always on the side of the true interests of his country and when he preferred justice to it, it was done with regret. The emperor was so persuaded of this and so recognized the fidelity of M. de Fürstenberg that after his retreat he entrusted him with establishing the union between France and Germany.[3]

Had Wilhelm really been as worthy as the good father pretended, his life would not have been so interesting. One can only regret that he did not leave behind a set of memoirs.[4] If he himself offered few commentaries on his career, contemporaries were not as hesitant to render a judgment. The assessment of an Italian observer in the 1690's underlines one of the central issues in any consideration of Wilhelm's activity: "The esteem which Monsieur de Lionne had for him was the cause of the great effect which he had on the king, since no other person in the world understood German affairs better than he, but [he understood] nothing in effect outside of his province."[5] In addition to Lionne, of course, Mazarin decisively influenced the king's estimate of Fürstenberg's ability.

Lionne's death in 1671 proved to be the turning point in Wilhelm's relationship with the French crown. Until then he influenced policy decisions at the court; afterwards, with rare exceptions, he functioned as an agent, pure and simple, his advice often disregarded. The invasion and occupation of German states by French troops led to a steady stream of political information sent to Versailles from agents attached to the army and therefore working for Louvois. During times of peace, especially during Lionne's lifetime, Wilhelm was regarded as the foremost expert on German affairs. In wartime he was "a negotiator out of season," more often than not reduced to a cipher.

Louvois's part in diminishing Fürstenberg's influence is undeniable, but other reasons were present as well. One of the chief of these was the increasing strength and aggressiveness of the Austrian monarchy in the latter half of Leopold's reign. His seizure of Fürstenberg in 1674 symbolized the role he wished to play in German politics and his willingness to defy the Sun King. In the 1660's and just prior to the Dutch war the situation in the Empire was much more fluid, the possibility of unseating the Habsburgs much more likely, than after 1679. Leopold's recovery from a near-fatal illness, the birth of an heir to the throne, the repulsion of the Turks from Vienna and the development of an increasingly anti-French consciousness in the Germanies all worked against Fürstenberg as well as against French interests. By this time one glimpses the beginning of a new era in European politics, an era "which was to last until the middle of the eighteenth century, in which French power declined and the power of others began to rise by comparison." [6] Louis XIV's declaration of war in 1688 was a "preventive measure" aimed at winning rapid concessions from the German states before Austria could mobilize the Empire against France. The long, ruinous war which ensued was destructive to all concerned, not least to France.

In addition to the military and diplomatic offensive of the Habsburgs within the Empire, there was the persistent and successful use of papal diplomacy in countering French ambitions in the 1680's. Innocent XI played the major role in thwarting Fürstenberg and the French at Cologne. Despite the accumulation of titles and honors in the 1680's, Wilhelm's tide was running out and his failure at Cologne was very much a part of this process. All the same, for one who "lost," he was very nicely cushioned in his retirement in spite of the pressure of debts.

The Italian commentator cited above refers to Wilhelm's ignorance of everything apart from German affairs. It will be remembered that in 1688 he was accused of totally losing touch with events in Hungary. This can in part be explained by his preoccupation with the political and military scene in Cologne and also by his inability to travel as much as in the past. The record of his political activity, the volumes of his dispatches do indeed reveal an almost exclusive concern with the affairs of the Germanies. This does not of course prove that Wilhelm was ignorant of everything else. It does, however, remind us that the king looked upon him solely as a resource for information on the Empire. There were other people to ask about, say, England. If Louis XIV took so lively an interest in Fürstenberg's dispatches and his personal reports at Versailles, it is because Wilhelm handled matters that totally absorbed the attention of the king, the realm of foreign affairs, the high politics of Europe. Louis XIV was far more interested in this area than in the interior affairs of his kingdom. He paid great attention to the minutiae of foreign courts: who should be persuaded and how should it be done? As Tapié notes, "the secret was to find out in what ways the political and personal interests of foreign sovereigns and their entourages could be coincident with French interests."[7] Here was one of Wilhelm's most valuable functions in the French service, suggesting ways of approaching German princes and then carrying out the assignment. With French financial and military might behind him, he thus acted on a much more important stage than if he were the mere representative of Cologne. He chose this role deliberately and took the consequences, both good and bad.

While we cannot know his secret thoughts, we can safely presume that Wilhelm's earlier dreams of power and influence went far beyond what he achieved. Had events conspired to bring Louis XIV to the imperial throne, then the Fürstenbergs might have come into their own; their political and administrative abilities could further have been tested. Much of the latter part of Wilhelm's active career was spent in cautioning the king and his ministers against pressing the Germans too hard. He ceaselessly urged them to reduce fears in the Empire, to clarify French territorial ambition. After nine years of warfare French concessions at Ryswick included the abandonment of Philippsburg and Luxembourg, the return of several reunion gains, the surrender of most French holdings in northern Italy; for a time it seemed that even Strasbourg would have to be given up to terminate the war. One recalls Wilhelm's memorandum in late 1686, at a time when papal intervention in the disputes between France and the Germanies was being considered. He then urged that France give up her possessions and enclaves in the Empire to dispel the rising fears of French ambition. Despite the ambiguities of Fürstenberg's position and his desire for personal gain, it is fair to say that he desired some form of accommodation, some chance of a lasting peace between France and the Germanies. His action in keeping Stavelot-Malmédy within the Empire and apart from French jurisdiction further underscores his zeal for retaining and nurturing what independence could be had in the midst of larger competing powers.

In a recent book Robert Mandrou states that the study of diplomatic and political history contributes to our knowledge of "the modalities of information in the elaboration of decisions at different levels of execution." An analysis of these modalities, he continues, should enable us "to fix the essential coordinates."[8] Although this work has not been precisely fashioned to meet the above specifications, surveys of the careers of men such as Fürstenberg do offer striking examples of the ways in which policy makers obtained information, the ways in which they reached decisions, and the manner in which those decisions were implemented. We witness the perennial quarrels between the home office and envoys "in the field" and are led to speculate on the ways in which personal friendship, as in the case of Lionne, may influence a minister's political judgment. Inevitably, one is tempted to replay the game, to match dis carded advice against policies that failed. For we are, in the end result, dealing with failure: the personal failure of Wilhelm von Fürstenberg, the failure of French foreign policy, and the larger failure of European states to solve their problems without recourse to war.

Throughout his life, Fürstenberg played the game of politics as he found it. Born into the upper aristocracy in the midst of the Thirty Years' War, he died as a Prince of the Empire and of the Church in the early stages of another of Europe's most destructive wars. Before his death he had the ironic satisfaction of seeing Maximilian of Bavaria and his brother Joseph Clemens, Elector of Cologne, become the sole allies of Louis XIV in the War of the Spanish Succession. Karg, his wily adversary in the Cologne affair, became abbot of Mont St. Michel. As a connoisseur of German politics and diplomacy, Wilhelm could hardly have been surprised.

NOTES

(Citations are in shortened form; for a complete source consult the bibliography, which follows.)

ABBREVIATIONS OF ARCHIVAL SOURCES

AAE   Archives des Affaires Etrangères, Paris
AG   Archives du Ministère de la Guerre, Vincennes
ASL   Archivio di Stato in Lucca
ASV   Archivio Segreto Vaticano, Vatican City
HHSt   Haus,-Hof-und-Staatsarchiv, Vienna

CHAPTER I

1. Dumont, *Mémoires politiques*, pp. 74–75.

2. Moisse-Daxhelet, "François-Egon, Prince de Fürstenberg," p. 322. For a solid account of the earlier Fürstenberg's career, see Wagner, *Graf Wilhelm von Fürstenberg*. On the life of the *condottiere*, see Gauthiez, *Jean des Bandes Noires*, p. 185, cited by Redlich, "The German Military Enterpriser and His Work Force," p. 30. Redlich's monumental and absorbing work, which includes a treasure trove of bibliography, is indispensable for an understanding of the milieu and tradition in which Fürstenberg was raised.

3. Ibid., pp. 163–64; Kuckhoff, *Die Geschichte des Gymnasium Tricoronatum*, pp. 318–19.

4. Steinhuber, *Geschichte des Collegium Germanicum Hungaricum in Rom*, pp. 403–4; Le Prevost, *Oraison Funèbre de Tres-Haut et Tres-Puissant Prince Guillaume-Egon de Fürstemberg*, p. 10.

5. Grimmelshausen, *The Adventurous Simplicissimus*, p. 35; Thoma, *Die Kirchenpolitik der Grafen von Fürstenberg*, p. 134.

6. Engels, "Aus den Anfängen fürstenbergischer Politik in Kurköln," p. 479; and Franzen, "Drei Informativprozesse," p. 368.

7. Braubach, *Kurköln*, pp. 1–18.

8. The term "strategic frontiers" was employed by the French historian Gaston Zeller. See his solid articles, "La monarchie d'Ancien Régime et les frontières naturelles," pp. 305–33; "Histoire d'une idée fausse," pp. 115–31; and "Saluces, Pignerol et Strasbourg," pp. 97–110. The latter two articles have been reprinted in a recent edition of Zeller's essays, *Aspects de la Politique Française*

sous l'Ancien Régime (Paris, 1964). Cf. my paper on "Louis XIV's Strategic Frontier in the Holy Roman Empire," pp. 108–17.

9. Dickmann, "Der Westfälische Friede und die Reichsverfassung," pp. 11, 28.

10. Huisman, *Essai sur le Règne du Prince-Evêque de Liège*, p. 67; Braubach, *Kurköln*, p. 23.

11. Huisman, p. 67; Braubach, *Kurköln*, pp. 26–27.

12. Mazarin's assertion is found in AAE, *Allemagne, Mémoires et Documents* 35, fol. 63, cited by Göhring, "Kaiserwahl und Rheinbund von 1658," p. 78 n. 21. On the distribution of the pamphlets, see Valfrey, *La Diplomatie française au XVIIe Siècle*, pp. 115–18; and Pillorget-Rouanet, "Louis XIV Candidat au Trone Impérial (1658)," pp. 5–17. Concerning Louis XIV as candidate for the imperial throne, see Vast, "Des Tentatives de Louis XIV pour arriver à l'Empire," pp. 1–45; Zeller, "Les Rois de France candidats à l'Empire," pp. 497–534; and Gie, "Die Kandidatur Ludwigs XIV.," pp. 1–108.

13. Mazarin to Servien, July 22, 1657, *Lettres de Mazarin* 8 : 63.

14. For the instructions to the French delegation, see Chéruel, *Histoire de France sous le Ministère de Mazarin*, pp. 98–99. Mazarin to Gramont, July 20, 1657, *Lettres de Mazarin* 8 : 71–74.

15. Göhring, p. 80.

16. Braubach, *Kurköln*, p. 31; Mazarin to Gramont and Lionne, August 18, 1657, *Lettres de Mazarin* 8 : 113–14; Mazarin to Gramont and Lionne, August 21, 1657, *Lettres de Mazarin* 8 : 121–22.

17. Ibid., p. 124.

18. Braubach, *Kurköln*, pp. 34–35; and Valfrey, pp. 99–102. Mazarin to Lionne, January 11, 1658, *Lettres de Mazarin* 8 : 254–55.

19. Joachim, *Die Entwickelung des Rheinbundes vom Jahre 1658*, pp. 354–55.

20. Gramont and Lionne sent two dispatches to Mazarin on April 17, 1658 (AAE, *Allemagne* 140, fols. 424–25; and *Allemagne* 141, fols. 29–36). See Braubach, *Kurköln*, p. 37; and Pagès, "Comment Guillaume de Fürstenberg entra au service de Louis XIV," pp. 730–31. Lionne to Mazarin, April 19, 1658, AAE, *Allemagne* 141, fol. 43. Franz's reply to "l'Amy" cited by Pagès, "Comment Fürstenberg entra au service de Louis XIV," p. 732.

21. *Mémoires du Maréchal de Gramont*, p. 294.

22. Mazarin mentioned the visit of the two German deputies in a letter to Gramont on May 18, 1658 (*Lettres de Mazarin* 8 : 359). Gramont and Lionne to Mazarin, May 23, 1658, AAE, *Allemagne* 141, fols. 127–28; Gramont and Lionne to Mazarin, May 28, 1658, ibid., fol. 133; Lionne to Mazarin, June 13, 1658, ibid., fols. 162–67.

23. Ibid., fols. 190ff. The text of the contract has been published by Pagès, "Comment Fürstenberg entra au service de Louis XIV," pp. 733–35.

24. For a good discussion of the various considerations weighed by the Fürstenbergs, see Braubach, *Kurköln*, pp. 21–22.

25. Mazarin to Lionne, July 21, 1658, AAE, *Allemagne* 140, fols. 481–82.
26. *Mémoires du Maréchal de Gramont*, p. 293.
27. Gramont and Lionne to Brienne, August 19, 1658, AAE, *Allemagne* 141, fol. 313.
28. See Schnur, *Der Rheinbund von 1658*. Livet, "Louis XIV et l'Allemagne," p. 34.
29. Cialdea, *Gli Stati Italiani e la Pace dei Pirenei*, p. 209.
30. Braubach, *Fürstenberg*, pp. 56–59. The German saying is found in Huisman, p. 50 n. 1. Mazarin's appraisal of Wilhelm was in a letter to Robert de Gravel, October 19, 1660 (*Lettres de Mazarin* 9 : 662). Lionne drew up the minutes for this letter.

CHAPTER II

1. Mignet, *Négociations relatives à la Succession d'Espagne sous Louis XIV* 1 : lviii.
2. Braubach, *Fürstenberg*, p. 65; *Mémoires de Mademoiselle de Montpensier*, p. 365.
3. Braubach, *Kurköln*, p. 6. In 1652, during carnival time, Wilhelm spent fourteen days at the court of the Neuburgs in Düsseldorf. During the nights he frequented the ladies' chambers and only at daybreak did the dancing cease. At the end of his sojourn, he distributed 130 thalers so as to escape from "jeering gossip." These events were related by Wilhelm in a letter to his eldest brother, Ferdinand Friedrich, who died in 1662 (cited by Braubach, *Fürstenberg*, p. 24 n. 37). Pagès, *Le Grand Electeur et Louis XIV*, p. 241.
4. Braubach, *Fürstenberg*, pp. 61–62; Lionne to Wilhelm, October 7, 1662, AAE, *Cologne* 3, fol. 160. See Badalo-Dulong, p. 65.
5. Wilhelm to Lionne, November 8, 1662, AAE, *Cologne* 3, fol. 168. The papal nuncio is cited by Franzen, "Drei Informativprozesse," p. 335. Badalo-Dulong, p. 65.
6. The French plenipotentiary is cited by Pagès, *Louis XIV et l'Allemagne*, p. 27. As one historian put it, "The treaty of Münster gave France some territories and some rights in Alsace, but above all it gave her hopes" (Pfister, "La réunion de l'Alsace à la France," p. 363). Volmar's comment is from Livet, *L'Intendance d'Alsace sous Louis XIV*, p. 122. See Batiffol, "Les difficultés de Louis XIV avec les Alsaciens," pp. 578–79.
7. Reuss, *L'Alsace au Dix-Septième Siècle* 1 : 213.
8. For an excellent survey of the relations between the papacy and the German episcopacy, including an account of the guidelines for the election of German bishops as worked out in the fifteenth century, see Raab, *Die Concordata Nationis Germanicae*. On the machinations of the Fürstenbergs, see Braubach, *Fürstenberg*, pp. 70, 357–58; he depicted them as brokers in *Kurköln*, p. 41.
9. Franzen, "Drei Informativprozesse," pp. 353–55.
10. Raab, "Die oberdeutschen Hochstifte," p. 99. See Franzen, "Eine Krise

der Deutschen Kirche im 17. Jahrhundert?," pp. 56–111; as well as his "Französische Politik und Kurkölns Beziehungen zu Frankreich," pp. 169–210. On the union of the churches, see Sonnino, *Louis XIV's View of the Papacy, 1661– 1667*, pp. 44–46; and Mentz, *Johann Philipp von Schönborn*, pp. 184–86.

11. Bittner and Gross, *Repertorium der diplomatischen Vertreter aller Länder seit dem Westfälischen Frieden* 1 : 381; Reuss, *L'Alsace au Dix-Septième Siècle* 1 : 213–14.

12. Chatellier, "Frontière politique et frontière religieuse," p. 155. Chatellier's informative and perceptive essay is one of a number of excellent contributions in this collective tribute to Professor Tapié.

13. Wolf, *Louis XIV*, p. 187; Wilhelm to Lionne, April 25, 1664, AAE, *Allemagne* 191, fols. 352–56.

14. Münch, *Geschichte des Hauses und Landes Fürstenberg*, 3 : 117–24.

15. Franz von Fürstenberg to Lionne, October 20, 1664, AAE, *Cologne* 3, fol. 260.

16. Louis XIV to Gravel, October 17, 1664, cited by Wagner, "Der Wiener Hof," p. 123 n. 77.

17. Wilhelm to Lionne, January, 1664, AAE, *Cologne* 3, fols. 236ff.

18. Lionne to Wilhelm, October 1, 1665, ibid., fols. 371–72; Wilhelm to Lionne, October 14, 1665, ibid., fols. 379–80, 393ff; Lionne to Wilhelm, October 24, 1665, ibid., fols. 404–5.

19. The importance of the year 1665 in Wilhelm's career is discussed by Braubach, *Fürstenberg*, pp. 93–96. The significance of the War of Devolution as a turnpoint in Louis XIV's reign is emphasized by Lossky, "France in the System of Europe in the Seventeenth Century," p. 43.

20. Wilhelm's memorandum (AAE, *Cologne* 3, fols. 456ff.) is published in Pagès, *Contributions*, pp. 12–13.

21. Louis XIV to Wilhelm, February 5, 1666, ibid., fols. 493–94. See Pagès, *Contributions*, pp. 13–14.

22. Max Heinrich's negotiations with the Spanish were reported by the papal nuncio on January 29, 1666, cited by Franzen, "Französische Politik und Kurkölns Beziehungen zu Frankreich," p. 198. Wilhelm to Lionne, February 24, 1666, AAE, *Cologne* 3, fols. 509–10.

23. The report of this conference is in Croissy's dispatch to Louis XIV on March 7, 1666, published in *Urkunden und Actenstücke zur Geschichte des Kurfürsten Friedrich Wilhelm von Brandenburg* 2 : 1, pp. 358–63.

24. For the text of the treaty, see *Lettres, Mémoires et Négociations de Monsieur le Comte d'Estrades*, 3 : 190–98.

25. *Urkunden und Actenstücke* 11 : 7, pp. 722–27. On Wilhelm's journey to Rome, see Kohl, *Christoph Bernhard von Galen*, pp. 242–43. I have seen no other reference to this trip. Braubach does not mention Wilhelm's sojourn in Rome in his biography of Fürstenberg.

26. Badalo-Dulong, p. 100.

27. Wilhelm to the Elector of Mainz, January 30, 1667, AAE, *Cologne* 4, fol. 8.

28. Wilhelm to Lionne, January 24, 1667, AAE, *Autriche* 23, fols. 170–86. Wenzel Eusebius von Lobkowitz, the *Obersthofmeister*, was much the most powerful minister in Vienna at that time. He was generally partial to an alliance and friendship with France. See Henry Frederick Schwarz, *The Imperial Privy Council in the Seventeenth Century*, originally issued as vol. 53 in the "Harvard Historical Studies" series (Cambridge, Mass., 1943). I have used the reprinted edition issued by the Greenwood Press (Westport, Conn., 1972). On Lobkowitz, see especially pp. 146–90 and 289–90. Fürstenberg's mission to Vienna is reviewed in pp. 159–62.

29. Ibid., fol. 207. Cf. Spiegel, *Fürstenbergs Gefangenschaft*, p. 175.

30. Cited by Tapié, *Monarchie et Peuples du Danube*, p. 455 n. 1. Tapié here cites Bérenger's article "Les relations franco-hongroises pendant la conjuration du Palatin Wesselenyi 1664–1668," *Revue de l'Académie des sciences de Hongrie* (no date given). I have not read this article. For a useful overview of French ties with Hungary see Bérenger, "Les relations franco-hongroises pendant le règne personnel de Louis XIV," pp. 101–7.

31. Wilhelm to Lionne, February 7, 1667, AAE, *Autriche* 23, fol. 233; Louis XIV, *Mémoires for the Instruction of the Dauphin*, p. 133.

32. Wilhelm to Lionne, February 10, 1667, AAE, *Autriche* 23, fols. 240–41.

33. Wilhelm to Lionne, March 6, 1667, ibid., fols. 272, 274–75.

34. Wilhelm to Lionne, March 8, 17, 1667, ibid., fols. 279–82, 307.

35. Ibid., fol. 314.

36. Braubach, *Fürstenberg*, p. 128.

37. See Bérenger, "Une Tentative de Rapprochement entre la France et l'Empereur," pp. 298–300. Pribram, *Franz Paul Freiherr von Lisola und die Politik seiner Zeit*, p. 406.

38. Bérenger, "Une Tentative de Rapprochement," pp. 308, 310–11.

39. Wolf, *Louis XIV*, p. 206; Wilhelm to Lionne, January 18, 1668, AAE, *Cologne* 6, fols. 27–38; De Witt's appraisal of Wilhelm cited by Münch, *Geschichte des Hauses und Landes Fürstenberg*, 3:115–16.

40. Franken, *Coenraad Van Beuningen's Politieke*, p. 263. See Rowen, "John de Witt and the Triple Alliance," pp. 1–14.

41. For a discussion of the boundary adjustments after the War of Devolution and other wars during Louis XIV's reign and throughout the eighteenth century, see the fine study by Girard d'Albissin, *Genèse de la Frontière Franco-Belge*.

CHAPTER III

1. Böhmer, "Forschungen zur französischen Bündnispolitik im 17. Jahrhundert," p. 229; Wilhelm to Lionne, December 8, 1668, AAE, *Cologne* 6, fols. 269–70.

2. Badalo-Dulong, p. 141; Böhmer, p. 231. There is no evidence to support the widely-held belief that Wilhelm was the colonel of a French regiment earlier in his career, at the end of the Thirty Years' War (see Braubach, *Fürstenberg*, p. 21 n. 25). His regiment achieved great distinction during the Dutch War

(see Fieffé, *Histoire des Troupes Etrangères au Service de France*, p. 223).

3. Breget to Arnauld (Cologne resident in Paris), April 5, 1669, cited by Braubach, *Fürstenberg*, p. 156.

4. Döberl, *Bayern und Frankreich*, 2 : 86.

5. Munich State Archives, schw. K378/48, published in ibid., p. 90. Cf. Döberl's commentary in ibid., 1 : 429–36.

6. Max Heinrich to Wilhelm, July 10, 1669, copy in AAE, *Cologne* 6, fol. 306.

7. Wilhelm to Lionne, August 1, 1669, ibid., fols. 308–313.

8. Wilhelm to Lionne, September 24, 1669, ibid., fols. 311ff. Extracts are published in Pagès, *Contributions*, pp. 14–15. See Pagès, *Le Grand Electeur*, pp. 212ff.; and Böhmer, pp. 233–34.

9. Lionne to Louis XIV, October 1, 1669, AAE, *Mémoires et Documents: France* 416, fol. 158.

10. Pagès, "L'Alliance bavaroise de 1670 et la politique de Louis XIV en Allemagne, d'après un ouvrage récent," p. 686.

11. Lionne to Louis XIV, October 4, 1669, published in ibid., pp. 686–88.

12. Braubach, *Fürstenberg*, pp. 163–65.

13. Wilhelm to Lionne, December 20, 1669, AAE, *Cologne* 6, fols. 323ff. Cf. Böhmer, p. 235.

14. Ibid., pp. 238–39; Wilhelm to Lionne, February 6, 1670, AAE, *Cologne* 6, fol. 353, published in Pagès, *Contributions*, pp. 27–28.

15. The following account of Wilhelm's negotiation is based upon his correspondence with Lionne and pertinent archival documents in Berlin; large extracts from each are published in ibid., pp. 14–33. The original material has been used extensively by Böhmer, pp. 237–43; and by Pagès, *Le Grand Electeur*, pp. 228–35.

16. This maneuver reported by Wilhelm is not mentioned in the Berlin minutes. I agree with Pagès that there is no overriding reason to doubt Fürstenberg's testimony here (ibid., p. 232 n. 1).

17. Vaubrun (French envoy extraordinary in Berlin) to Louis XIV, January 22, 1670, AAE, *Brandenburg* 6, cited by Pagès, *Contributions*, p. 33 n. 1. Cf. Spiegel, *Fürstenbergs Gefangenschaft*, pp. 67–68.

18. Wilhelm to Lionne, February 6, 1670, AAE, *Cologne* 6, fol. 353, published in Pagès, *Contributions*, pp. 27–28.

19. In April 1672, the Elector of Bavaria gave an auxiliary regiment of 1200 men to Max Heinrich; in January 1673, in exchange for a French subsidy, he posted an observation corps to prevent any passage of troops across his territory. A new military convention was agreed upon between France and Bavaria in June 1674, several months after Wilhelm's arrest (cf. Pagès, "L'Alliance bavaroise de 1670," p. 689).

20. Wilhelm to Lionne, May 30, 1670, AAE, *Cologne* 6, fols. 375–76.

21. Cf. Braubach, "Geheime Friedenshandlungen am Niederrhein 1711–12," p. 190; and his *Kurköln*, pp. 271–76.

22. Pagès, *Le Grand Electeur*, p. 241. Mignet, *Négociations relatives à la*

Succession d'Espagne 3 : 292–93. Louis XIV to Colbert de Croissy, October 7, 1670; and the latter's response on November 17, 1670, published in ibid., pp. 233, 242.

23. The memorandum to Brandenburg is published in Pagès, *Contributions*, pp. 35–41; a similar memorandum with some alterations was sent to Münster and Hanover. The latter is published in Köcher, *Geschichte von Hannover und Braunschweig* 2 : 485–90. Pagès, *Le Grand Electeur*, p. 242.

24. Verjus's instruction is dated February 2, 1671 and is published in *Recueil des Instructions* 16 : 163–69. Pagès, *Le Grand Electeur*, p. 245 n. 2.

25. Letter to Hanover published in Köcher, *Geschichte von Hannover und Braunschweig* 2 : 508–9. Verjus to Lionne, April 15, 1671, ibid., pp. 509–11.

26. See Junkers, *Der Streit zwischen Kurstaat und Stadt Köln*, pp. 28, 35.

27. Wilhelm to Lionne, April 29, 1671, AAE, *Cologne* 7, fols. 63–64.

28. Cited by Rowen, *The Ambassador Prepares for War*, p. 173.

29. Lionne to Wilhelm, February 17, 1671, AAE, *Cologne* 7, cited by Pagès, *Le Grand Electeur*, p. 259 n. 1. Louvois had not yet been admitted to the royal council but his influence was quite apparent; his scathing assessment of German armies usually put him at odds with Fürstenberg. Lionne may not have supported the offensive alliance as warmly as Fürstenberg but he was more accommodating than Louvois.

30. Lionne to Wilhelm, July 17, 1671, cited in ibid., p. 260.

31. Wilhelm to Lionne, June 6, 16, 1671, AAE, *Cologne* 7, fols. 84, 94.

32. On neutrality, see Huisman, p. 13; Mignet, *Négociations relatives à la Succession d'Espagne* 3 : 292–94.

33. Wilhelm to Lionne, July 20, 1671, cited by Pagès, *Le Grand Electeur*, pp. 262–63. On the reversal of policy, see ibid., pp. 263–64 and Braubach, *Fürstenberg*, pp. 200–206.

34. Exchange of letters between Wilhelm and Lionne cited by Pagès, *Le Grand Electeur*, pp. 264, 271 n. 2.

35. Wilhelm to Lionne, September 7, 1671, AAE, *Cologne* 7, fol. 243.

36. Cited by Köcher, *Geschichte von Hannover und Braunschweig* 2 : 209.

37. Wilhelm's plea for a restricted offensive alliance is cited by Pagès, *Le Grand Electeur*, p. 266; Wilhelm to Louis XIV, November 14, 1671, AAE, *Cologne* 7, fol. 517.

38. Wilhelm to Louvois, November 30, 1671, ibid., fols. 616–17; Franz's belligerence is recounted in Wilhelm to Verjus, November 25, 1671, AAE, *Cologne* 7, cited by Braubach, *Fürstenberg*, pp. 213–14.

39. Letters from Louvois to Louis XIV, January 1, 1672 and Louvois to Le Tellier, January 4, 1672, cited by Rousset, *Histoire de Louvois* 1 : 342–44.

40. See Mignet, *Négociations relatives à la Succession d'Espagne* 3 : 705–7; Lavisse, *Histoire de France depuis les Origines jusqu'à la Révolution française*, pp. 307–8.

41. Louvois to Le Tellier, January 4, 1672, cited by Rousset, *Histoire de Louvois* 1 : 343–44.

42. Wolf, *Louis XIV*, p. 223. Wolf gives a good succinct account of the invasion, pp. 219–27.

43. Immich, *Geschichte des europäischen Staatensystems*, p. 76; *Works of Sir William Temple*, p. 225.

44. Wilhelm to Louvois, November 6, 1672, AG, A¹280, no. 64.

45. Wilhelm to Louis XIV, January 14, 1673, AAE, *Cologne* 11, fols. 99–101.

46. For the terms of the pact, ibid., vol. 10, fols. 430–40.

CHAPTER IV

1. Pagès, *Le Grand Electeur*, pp. 304–5.

2. Verjus's instructions were dated March 19, 1673, AAE, *Brunswick* 2, fols. 408–9. Published in *Recueil des Instructions* 16: *Prusse*, pp. 192–96. Pomponne to Wilhelm, March 19, 1673, AAE, *Cologne* 10, cited by Pagès, *Le Grand Electeur*, p. 312 n. 2.

3. Ibid., pp. 316–17.

4. The memory of the king's surprise was noted in Wilhelm's letter to Pomponne on September 20, 1673, AAE, *Cologne* 11, fols. 234–35.

5. Cf. Wolf, *Louis XIV*, pp. 230–34.

6. See Braubach, *Kurköln*, pp. 56–57.

7. Spiegel, p. 50. It is important to establish their official representative role at the congress since it would later be brought into question by imperial propagandists.

8. Far and away the best treatment of the Cologne Congress is Braubach's *Kurköln*, pp. 43–80.

9. Ibid., pp. 50–51, 55.

10. Cited by Badalo-Dulong, p. 202.

11. Wilhelm to Pomponne, August 5, 1673, AAE, *Cologne* 11, fols. 193–97.

12. Franz von Fürstenberg to Pomponne, February 22, 1674, AAE, *Cologne* 12, fol. 99; Valkenier, *Das verwirrte Europa*, p. 507.

13. See Pillorget, "La France et l'Electorat de Trêves," pp. 138–41; and Rousset, *Histoire de Louvois* 1 : 471–73. Gravel's report cited by Pagès, *Louis XIV et l'Allemagne*, p. 86. Wilhelm to Pomponne, September 20, 1673, AAE, *Cologne* 11, fols. 234–41.

14. On the maneuvering of the two armies see Rousset, *Histoire de Louvois* 1 : 497–503; and Badalo-Dulong, pp. 208–9.

15. Pribram, *Lisola*, pp. 651–52.

16. Cf. Braubach, *Kurköln*, pp. 59–60. Wilhelm to Pomponne, November 1, 1673, AAE, *Cologne* 11, fols. 271–75.

17. Pribram, *Lisola*, pp. 650–51; Wilhelm to Pomponne, November 7, 1673, AAE, *Cologne* 11, fols. 277–78. Wilhelm to Louvois, November 7, 1673, published in Rousset, *Histoire de Louvois* 1:505–7. Louvois received criticism from several generals and diplomats during 1673 (see Ekberg, "From Dutch to European War," pp. 393–408).

19. Courtin to Louvois, November 23, 1673, cited by Rousset, *Histoire de Louvois* 1 : 507 n. 1.

20. Wilhelm to Pomponne, November 14, 1673, AAE, *Cologne* 11, fols. 300–302; the "*coup d'ésclat*" was urged in a letter from the Abbé de Gravel (envoy in Mainz) to Pomponne, November 19, 1673, AAE, *Mayence* 14, fols. 123–24. Courtin's characterization of Franz is cited by Braubach, *Kurköln*, p. 61.

21. Picavet, *Les Dernières Années de Turenne*, pp. 374–83; Pribram, *Lisola*, pp. 647–48, 652–53.

22. Wilhelm to Pomponne, January 2, 1674, AAE, *Cologne* 12, fols. 8, 14.

23. Cf. Braubach, *Kurköln*, pp. 63–65.

24. Max Heinrich to Louis XIV, January 23, 1674, AAE, *Cologne* 3, fol. 61.

25. Braubach, *Kurköln*, pp. 67–68.

26. Louis XIV to Wilhelm, February 20, 1674, AAE, *Cologne* 12, fols. 76–78.

27. Braubach, *Kurköln*, p. 68.

28. Ibid., pp. 68–70; and Spiegel, pp. 5–8.

29. Copy of a letter from Grana to an unknown correspondent, February 15, 1674, ASL, *Archivio Arnolfini* 110, no. 21.

30. See letter from Hocher [Austrian Court Chancellor] to Lisola, February 28, 1674, cited by Pribram, *Lisola*, pp. 665–66. Franz von Fürstenberg to Pomponne, February 23, 1674, AAE, *Cologne* 12, fol. 101; Rousset, *Histoire de Louvois* 2 : 3–4.

31. Louis XIV to the ambassadors, February 24, 27, 1674, AAE, *Allemagne* 270 bis, fols. 338–40, 357–59. Under pressure from parliament, Charles II had come to terms with the Dutch earlier in the month.

32. Louis XIV to the ambassadors, March 24, 1674, ibid., fols. 398–401. French protest over Wilhelm's abduction and the king's reasoning in withdrawing his ambassadors were explained in a widely-disseminated pamphlet, *Lettre du Roy à ses Ambassadeurs et à ses Ministres chez les Princes Etrangers, sur l'Enlèvement du Sérénissime Prince Guillaume de Fürstenberg* (Paris, 1674). The copy I consulted is in the Bibliothèque de l'Arsenal, MS. 6038, no. 710.

33. Franz von Fürstenberg to Pomponne, April 1, June 11, 1674, AAE, *Cologne* 12, fols. 180, 263.

34. Cf. Spiegel, pp. 34–38; and Pribram, *Lisola*, pp. 672–74.

35. Lisola, *Détention de Guillaume Prince de Fürstenberg*, pp. 38–39.

36. Cf. Pribram, *Lisola*, pp. 663–64; and Spiegel, pp. 45–52, 58.

37. Spiegel, pp. 62–63; also pp. 161–69 for the minutes of the first two interrogations. On Hocher, see Schwarz, *Imperial Privy Council*, pp. 174–75, 184–87, 247–49.

38. Cf. Boizet, *Les Lettres de Naturalité*, pp. 145–51.

39. Cf. Spiegel, pp. 66–67.

40. Ibid., p. 85. See pp. 170–75 for the minutes of the third session.

41. Ibid., pp. 63, 140–41. The jail terms for Burmann and Breget lasted less than one and one-half years.

42. Wilhelm to Countess von Löwenstein, undated; copy received in Paris in

September, 1674, AAE, *Cologne* 12, fols. 284–86. The quotations in the text immediately following are drawn from this letter. Wilhelm's choice of Hermann Conring as a prospective defender was most appropriate. Conring, a Protestant, was one of the most distinguished legal historians in the Empire and the recipient of a yearly pension from Louis XIV. He was especially hostile to the role played by the Austrian Habsburgs in the history of the Germanies and was not reluctant to see Louis XIV elected as emperor. In many respects, his writings can be viewed as a theoretical justification for Fürstenberg's career (see the chapter on Conring in Wolf, *Grosse Rechtsdenker der deutschen Geistesgeschichte*, pp. 220–52; as well as the fine analysis of Conring's publications by Gross, *Empire and Sovereignty*, pp. 255–92).

43. Greenidge, "The Conception of Treason in Roman Law," p. 229.

44. Spiegel, pp. 137–38.

45. Ibid., pp. 138–39.

46. Ibid., pp. 136–37.

47. Ibid., p. 100.

48. Ibid., pp. 108–9, 121.

49. Ibid., pp. 122, 124–25.

50. Ibid., p. 125; Ascanio Giustiniani to the Doge, May 21, 1679, copy in HHSt: *Dispacci dell'Ambasciator Veneto in Germania*, vol. 108–9, fol. 152. Cf. Spiegel, p. 151.

51. Wilhelm to Louvois, May 9, 1679, AG, A¹628, fols. 305–6.

CHAPTER V

1. Pomponne to Wilhelm, May 30, 1679, AAE, *Cologne* 14, fol. 72; Wilhelm to Pomponne, July 18, 1679, ibid., fol. 182; Barker, *Double Eagle and Crescent*, p. 103.

2. Huisman, p. 130. See my article, "Guillaume Egon de Fürstenberg reprend le pouvoir à Cologne," pp. 1–15. Franz Egon von Fürstenberg to Louis XIV, June 4, 1679, AAE, *Cologne* 14, fol. 91.

3. Philipp Wilhelm of Neuburg concluded a special treaty with the emperor on July 16, 1674. Two years later his daughter married Leopold I (cf. Rall, "Pfalz-Neuburg und seine Fürsten," p. 13; and Reinhardt, "Zur Reichskirchenpolitik der Pfalz-Neuburger Dynastie," pp. 119–20). For a survey of Neuburg dynastic interests, cf. Ludwig Petry, "Das Haus Neuburg," pp. 87–102.

4. Wilhelm to Pomponne, July 8, 1679, AAE, *Cologne* 14, fol. 161. During Wilhelm's captivity Louis XIV had requested that the pope make the prisoner a cardinal (see Spiegel, pp. 134–36).

5. Cf. Feine, *Die Besetzung der Reichsbistümer vom Westfälischen Frieden*, p. 124; also, by the same author, "Zur Verfassungsentwicklung des Heil. Röm. Reiches," p. 98. The French backed Christoph Rudolf von Stadion, a minister at the court of Mainz (Wilhelm to Louis XIV, October 3, 1679, AAE, *Cologne* 14, cited by Wysocki, *Kurmainz und die Reunionen*, p. 12).

6. Wilhelm to Louis XIV, November 22, 1679, AAE, *Cologne* 14, fols. 341–42, 354.

7. Louis XIV to Dupré des Marets, November 29, 1679, ibid., fol. 359. The instructions to La Vauguyon, dated December 15 and 29, 1679, have been published in the *Recueil des Instructions* 28: *Etats Allemands: 2, Electorat de Cologne*, pp. 45–53. For a survey of the new envoy's career, see Aude, *Vie publique et privée d'André de Béthoulat*. Louis XIV to La Vauguyon, January 22, 1680, AAE, *Cologne* 15, fol. 31.

8. For a succinct overview of Croissy's career, see Bérenger, "Charles Colbert, Marquis de Croissy," pp. 153–74.

9. The memorandum, submitted on March 1, 1680, is in AAE, *Cologne* 15, fols. 201–2.

10. La Vauguyon to Louis XIV, June 25, 1680, ibid., vol. 15, fol. 283.

11. La Vauguyon to Louis XIV, May 7, 1680, ibid., fol. 238; Wilhelm to Louis XIV, June 29, 1680, ibid., fols. 288–91.

12. Girard d'Albissin, *Genèse de la Frontière Franco-Belge*, p. 26; Zeller, "Louvois, Colbert de Croissy et les Réunions de Metz," p. 275.

13. Wilhelm's request was dated July 13, 1680, AAE, *Cologne* 16, fol. 43. Louis XIV to Wilhelm, July 24, 1680, ibid., vol. 17, fol. 71. Much work remains to be done on the influence of *gratifications* on politics and diplomacy. See the interesting article by Hatton, "Gratifications and Foreign Policy," pp. 68–94; also Pagès, "Note sur le rôle de l'argent dans la politique française en Allemagne sous Louis XIV" in his *Contributions*, pp. 66–96.

14. Wilhelm to Louis XIV, October 1, 1680, ibid., vol. 16, fols. 150–51.

15. Wilhelm to Louis XIV, July 13, 1680, ibid., fols. 43–44.

16. Wilhelm to Louis XIV, October 29, 1680, ibid., fols. 205–6.

17. Wilhelm to Louis XIV, October 4, 1680, AAE, *Allemagne* 286, fols. 473–81.

18. Fischer, "Soumission de l'Evêque de Strasbourg," pp. 513–14.

19. Wilhelm to Louis XIV, October 5, 1680, AAE, *Cologne* 16, fol. 170.

20. Wilhelm to Lionne, January 8, 1671, AAE, *Alsace* 21, fol. 239, cited by Livet, *L'Intendance d'Alsace sous Louis XIV*, pp. 437–38; Louis XIV to Wilhelm, October 24, 1680, AAE, *Cologne* 17, fols. 104–5. See the memorandum presented by Franz, probably in November or December 1680, in *Ecclesiasticum Argentinese* (1891), supplement, pp. 53–59.

21. La Vauguyon to Louis XIV, September 24, 1680, AAE, *Cologne* 16, fol. 131; Wilhelm to Louis XIV, November 12, 1680, ibid., fol. 223.

22. Wilhelm to Louis XIV, November 26, 1680, ibid., fols. 237–38.

23. Franzen, "Französische Politik und Kurkölns Beziehungen zu Frankreich," p. 181.

24. "Certain letters which my brother has written . . . make me fear that the unfounded suspicion and mistrust which he has always had against me are increasing rather than diminishing" (Wilhelm to Louis XIV, January 11, 1681, AAE, *Cologne* 18, fol. 22). Wilhelm to Louis XIV, April 21, 1681, ibid., fols.

137–39; Wilhelm to Croissy, April 21, 1681, ibid., fol. 142; Franz Egon von Fürstenberg to Louvois, October 1, 1681, AG, A¹668, no. 155. This last is published in Coste, *Réunion de Strasbourg à la France*, p. 120.

25. Wysocki, p. 23; and Angermeier, "Die Reichskriegsverfassung in der Politik der Jahre 1679–1681," p. 194. For useful surveys of the struggle for an imperial war constitution, see Fester, *Die Armirten Stände;* and Dirr, *Zur Geschichte der Reichskriegsverfassung.*

26. Details of Franz's pension are in AAE, *Mémoires et Documents: France* 1440, fol. 397, cited by Legrelle, *Louis XIV et Strasbourg*, p. 475; Wilhelm's statement on his finances was probably submitted to the king in the first half of April 1681 (AAE, *Cologne* 18, fols. 134–36). This statement is published in Aude, *Vie de la Vauguyon*, pp. 99–101.

27. AAE, *Petites Principautés* 22: *Fürstenberg*, fol. 67.

28. La Vauguyon to Louis XIV, May 2, 1681, AAE, *Cologne* 18, fols. 144–47. Extracts from this dispatch were sent to Wilhelm in Alsace. He replied that from the news *he* was receiving from Cologne, the calumnies against him and his family were worse than ever (dispatch to Louis XIV, May 30, 1681, ibid., fols. 167–68).

29. Wilhelm to Louis XIV, June 6, 1681, ibid., fols. 177–78. Extracts from this dispatch were published by Legrelle, *Louis XIV et Strasbourg*, pp. 476–78. Legrelle summarizes the spirit of Wilhelm's suggestions as follows: "Suppleness and mildness, transitions and concessions; in a word, a respect as extensive as possible for local autonomy, such was the politics which Prince Wilhelm ... urged Louis XIV to adopt in his new province, contrary to the suggestions of violence and rapine which Frischmann set forth to Louvois. ... One could say that [the letter] in some fashion morally served first as a basis for the capitulation of Strasbourg and next as a watchword for the entire French administration beyond the Vosges up till 1789."

30. Wilhelm to Louis XIV, June 6, 1681, AAE, *Cologne* 18, fol. 178.

31. Huisman, p. 143; Visconti to Cibo (papal secretary of state), June 1, 1681, ASV, *Nunz. di Colonia* 57, fol. 265, published in the *Inventaire Analytique*, p. 46, no. 64. This most useful collection of documents is part of the general series *Analecta Vaticano-Belgica: Documents Relatifs aux Anciens Diocèses de Cambrai, Liège, Thérouanne et Tournai publiés par l'Institut Historique Belge de Rome*, deuxième série, section B, nonciature de Cologne, 5. Visconti to Cibo, July 27, 1681, ASV, *Nunz. di Colonia* 57, fols. 375–76 in *Inventaire Analytique*, p. 53, no. 79.

32. La Vauguyon to Louis XIV, July 19, 1681, AAE, *Cologne* 18, fol. 212.

CHAPTER VI

1. In addition to its mineral waters and its proximity to Liège, the spa suited Wilhelm's convenience, since he had been empowered by Franz Egon to negotiate the election of a coadjutor for the abbeys of Stavelot and Malmédy. Not surprisingly, the capitularies chose Wilhelm after he agreed to aid them in their dif-

ferences with the bishopric of Liège (cf. Daxhelet, "La postulation du prince Guillaume-Egon de Fürstenberg," pp. 3–5). Wilhelm's subsequent role at Stavelot-Malmédy bore out the wisdom of the chapter members' decision (cf. Moisse-Daxhelet, *La Principauté de Stavelot-Malmédy*). A copy of the proposed treaty is published in *Inventaire Analytique*, pp. 68–69, no. 108.

2. Wilhelm to Louis XIV, September 16, 26, 1681, AAE, *Cologne* 18, fols. 332, 350–55.

3. For accounts of the annexation of Strasbourg, see Legrelle, *Louis XIV et Strasbourg*, chapter 7; and Franklin L. Ford, *Strasbourg in Transition*, chapter 2. On the acquisition of Casale, see Contessa, *Per la storia di un episodio della politica italiana di Luigi XIV*.

4. Louvois to Franz von Fürstenberg, n. d., AG, A¹633, fols. 79–80; Franz von Fürstenberg to Louvois, October 1, 1681, AG, A¹688, no. 155. Wilhelm was visiting "a person of quality" near Cologne, participating in the settlement of a dispute between two important houses in the area (Wilhelm to Croissy, September 30, 1681, AAE, *Cologne* 18, fol. 358).

5. Tambonneau to Louis XIV, October 7, 1681, ibid., fol. 368; cf. Hölscher, *Die öffentliche Meinung*. The memorandum of October 7, 1681 on Liège is in AAE, *Cologne* 18, fols. 362–65.

6. Franz von Fürstenberg to Louvois, October 14, 1681, AG, A¹663, no. 40, fol. 162. Fabre, *De la Correspondance de Fléchier*, pp. 231–32; Franz von Fürstenberg to Louvois, October 18, 1681, AG, A¹663, no. 43; Louvois to Franz von Fürstenberg, October 18, 1681, ibid., no. 59.

7. For a good account of the Strasbourg festivities, based largely on eyewitness reports, see Pfister, "Le Second Voyage de Louis XIV en Alsace," pp. 24–46. Most of my narrative is based on Pfister's article.

8. Cited by Pfister, ibid., p. 32.

9. The text of Franz's speech is published by Legrelle, *Louis XIV et Strasbourg*, p. 577 n. 2.

10. Pfister, "Le Second Voyage de Louis XIV en Alsace," p. 44.

11. These instructions were sent to Tambonneau on November 4, 1681 (AAE, *Cologne*, Supplement no. 1, fol. 132). They are published in the *Recueil des Instructions* 28: *Cologne*, pp. 64–70.

12. Louis XIV wanted him to assume the office immediately but Wilhelm refused. Perhaps he sought to remove the issue of the coadjutorship so as to make the other terms more palatable.

13. Tambonneau to Louis XIV, November 25, 1681, AAE, *Cologne* 18, fol. 398; Wilhelm to Croissy, December 23, 1681, ibid., fol. 434.

14. The comparison of Wilhelm and Hannibal was made by Müller, *Wilhelm III von Oranien und Georg Friedrich von Waldeck* 1 : 1. Waldeck became a Prince of the Empire in 1682 and served as a field marshal in the war against the Turks from 1683–1685. William of Orange made him Captain-General of the Dutch army before embarking for England in 1688. For details of his earlier career, ibid., pp. 13–47. For his subsequent activities, see vol. 2 (1890) of Müller's work, pp. 3–10. Professor William Jannen, Jr. (Brooklyn College) has kindly

allowed me to read in advance his solid and well-documented article, "'Das Liebe Teutschland' in the Seventeenth Century—Count George Frederick von Waldeck," pp. 165–95. See also Immich, *Geschichte des europäischen Staatensystems*, pp. 107, 110; and Fester, *Die Armirten Stände und die Reichskriegsverfassung*, p. 51.

15. The king outlined his terms for Mainz in a letter to Foucher on October 14, 1681. See Wysocki, pp. 174–75. The payments to the Elector Palatine are noted in ibid., pp. 65–66; on the Brandenburg treaty, see Pagès, *Le Grande Electeur*, pp. 473–74.

16. Tapié, "Europe et Chrétienté," pp. 284–85; and by the same author, "Aspects de la Méthode de Louis XIV en politique étrangère," p. 27; Louis XIV to Guilleragues, April 8, 1682, AAE, *Turquie* 16, fol. 337ff., cited by Gérin, "Le Pape Innocent XI et le Siège de Vienne en 1683," p. 115. For the surprise which this decision provoked in Europe, see Rousset, *Histoire de Louvois* 3 : 223–27.

17. Wilhelm to Louis XIV, January 18, 1682, AAE, *Cologne* 22, fols. 15–16, 21, 33.

18. Wilhelm to Louis XIV, February 21, 1682, ibid., fol. 88.

19. Wilhelm to Louis XIV, March 24, 1682, ibid., fol. 131; Franz von Fürstenberg to Louis XIV, March 24, 1682, AAE, *Alsace* 24, fols. 390–91. Cf. Chatellier, "Frontière politique et frontière religieuse," p. 158.

20. Louis XIV to Franz von Fürstenberg, April 2, 1682, AAE, *Cologne* 22, fol. 140; Louis XIV to Wilhelm, April 2, 1682, ibid., fol. 141.

21. Wilhelm to Croissy, April 14, 1682, ibid., fol. 155; Wilhelm to Louis XIV, April 26, 1682, ibid., fol. 159.

22. Wilhelm to Louis XIV, May 5, 1682, AAE, *Liège*, supplement no. 3, fols. 126–28; Tambonneau to Louis XIV, May 19, 1682, AAE, *Cologne* 20, fols. 186–87.

23. Visconti dispatch of June 7, 1682, ASV, *Nunz. di Colonia* 58, fol. 285, cited by August Franzen, "Drei Informativprozesse," p. 357.

24. Max Heinrich to Wilhelm, June 19, 1682, copy in AAE, *Cologne*, supplement no. 1, fol. 161.

25. Wilhelm to Louis XIV, June 29, 1682, ibid., fol. 166. One of his friends, Count von Manderscheyt, became grand provost (Wilhelm to Louis XIV, July 4, 1682, ibid., fol. 168). Franzen, "Drei Informativprozesse," pp. 356–72.

26. Cf. Marion, *Dictionnaire des Institutions de la France*, p. 476; and Fischer, "Soumission de l'Evêque de Strasbourg," p. 517.

27. Ibid., pp. 517–18; Tambonneau to Sebeville (French envoy in Vienna), September 3, 1682, AAE, *Cologne* 21, fol. 187; Fischer, *Le Conseil de la Régence de l'Evêché de Strasbourg*, p. 10.

28. Chatellier, "Frontière politique et frontière religieuse," pp. 159, 163–64, especially notes 67 and 75.

29. Tambonneau to Croissy, July 11, 1682, AAE, *Cologne* 21, fol. 27; Tambonneau to Barillon, July 14, 1682, ibid., fol. 38; Tambonneau to Barillon,

August 4, 1682, ibid., fol. 90; Tambonneau to Wilhelm, August 7, 1682, ibid., fol. 100.

30. Braubach, "Minister und Kanzler," p. 153; Tambonneau to Sebeville, September 3, 1682, AAE, *Cologne* 21, fol. 187; Tambonneau to Louis XIV, September 18, 1682, ibid., vol. 20, fol. 341; Tambonneau to Louis XIV, September 25, 1682, ibid., fol. 350.

31. Wilhelm to Louis XIV, October 10, 1682, AAE, *Cologne*, Supplement no. 1, fol. 173; Louis XIV to Wilhelm, October 13, 1682, ibid., fol. 176.

CHAPTER VII

1. Croissy to La Raudière, August 20, 1682, AAE, *Liège* 14, fol. 23. See Huisman, pp. 148–53.

2. Tambonneau to Louis XIV, December 2, 1681, AAE, *Cologne* 18, fol. 407.

3. The deputies' uncertainty over the form of retribution is drawn from their report to the city council of Liège on December 6, 1682 in the *Inventaire Analytique*, pp. 116–19, no. 218. On their anger in meetings with Wilhelm, see Huisman, p. 153.

4. Memorandum from Fürstenberg on Liège, March 5, 1683, AAE, *Liège*, Supplement no. 3, fol. 152; Louis XIV to Wilhelm, March 8, 1683, AAE, *Cologne* 22, fol. 237.

5. Huisman, pp. 154–56. The *soixantième* would have brought in 50,000 écus annually.

6. Wilhelm to Louis XIV, March 2, 1683, AAE, *Cologne* 22, fol. 228; Franzen, "Drei Informativprozesse," p. 372; Wilhelm to Louis XIV, May 18, 1683, AAE, *Cologne* 22, fol. 275. For the full story of the negotiations concerning the abbey at Stavelot, see Moisse-Daxhelet, *La Principauté de Stavelot-Malmédy*, pp. 43–77; and Pauls, "Die Beziehungen der Reunionskammer in Metz," pp. 173–219. For an account of the king's progress through Alsace, see Pfister, "Le Troisième Voyage de Louis XIV en Alsace (1683)," pp. 354–79.

7. See Metz, "Les Fürstenberg et les Rohan Princes-Evêques de Strasbourg," p. 70; and his *La Monarchie française et la provision des bénéfices ecclésiastiques en Alsace*, p. 409. The suffragan bishop during much of Wilhelm's tenure at Strasbourg was Gabriel Haug. For details concerning his administration, see Reibel, "Der Strassburger Weihbischof Gabriel Haug," pp. 159–83.

8. Wilhelm to Cibo, January 20, 1685, copy in AAE, *Alsace* 27, fols. 85–88. This letter is one of the best specimens of justificatory rhetoric that Wilhelm ever produced.

9. Gombauld to Louis XIV, August 15, 1683, AAE, *Münster* 6, fols. 440, 445. Though I have found no evidence, Plettenberg may have been promised full support for the Münster bishopric after Max Heinrich's death. He was elected with Fürstenberg's support on August 5, 1688. For an account of the Münster elections of 1683 and 1688, including details on the factional strife within the chapter and the pressures exerted by outside powers, see Keinemann, *Das*

Domkapitel zu Münster im 18. Jahrhundert, pp. 116–25. Wilhelm to Louis XIV, September 11, 1683, AAE, *Cologne* 22, fol. 302.

10. Wilhelm to Louis XIV, September 18, 1683, ibid., fol. 317.

11. Gombauld to Louis XIV, September 5, 1683, AAE, *Münster* 6, fol. 462.

12. Rousset, *Histoire de Louvois* 3 : 234–35; Lonchay, *La Rivalité de la France et de l'Espagne aux Pays-Bas*, p. 301; Wilhelm to Louis XIV, January 29, 1684, AAE, *Cologne* 28, fols. 17–18.

13. Wilhelm to Louvois, March 14, 1684, AG, $A^1$724; Louvois to Wilhelm, March 24, 1684, ibid.

14. Wilhelm to Louis XIV, March 29, 1684, AAE, *Cologne* 28, fol. 79.

15. Wilhelm to Louis XIV, April 4, 1684, ibid., fols. 89–94; Louis XIV to Wilhelm, April 13, 1684, ibid., fol. 95.

16. Wilhelm to Louis XIV, March 18, 1684, ibid., fol. 62.

17. Huisman, p. 158.

18. For the text of the accommodation, see the *Inventaire Analytique*, pp. 142–44; also see Huisman, pp. 159–61. In the final treaty there was a clause pertaining to the rights of the Church of Liège (*Inventaire Analytique*, pp. 146–50).

19. Huisman, pp. 162–64; Max Heinrich to Louis XIV, April 14, 1684, AAE, *Liège*, supplement no. 3, fol. 176. Wilhelm probably drafted the elector's request for aid but independently he promised to do all possible to keep the elector from sending troops into Liège without French approval (Wilhelm to Louvois, April 15, 1684, AG, $A^1$729, no. 112). Louis XIV to Wilhelm, April 20, 1684, AAE, *Cologne* 28, fols. 107–8.

20. The pope was more influential than anyone else in persuading Leopold to continue the war against the Turks (see Contessa, p. 99; and Fraknoi, *Innocenzo XI e la Liberazione dell' Ungheria*). Innocent actually gave more money to Sobieski of Poland than he gave to Leopold. During the war he gave 1,545,000 florins to the emperor and 3,000,000 florins to Poland (ibid., p. 282). Louvois to Wilhelm, April 28, 1684, AG, $A^1$724, no. 12.

21. D'Avaux's statement cited by St. Léger and Sagnac, *La Prépondérance Française*, p. 239. Wilhelm to Louis XIV, May 25, 1684, AAE, *Cologne* 28, fol. 132.

22. Wilhelm to Louis XIV, June 5, 1684, ibid., fols. 147–50; Louis XIV to Wilhelm, August 24, 1684, ibid., fols. 186–87; Tambonneau to Louis XIV, May 20, 1684, ibid., vol. 27, fol. 141.

23. Lonchay, *La Rivalité de la France et de l'Espagne*, pp. 303–5.

24. In the original Austrian proposals as reported by Verjus on July 17, 1684, there was a clause prohibiting any new fortifications in the land in question. But Verjus was under strict orders to avoid precisely such a commitment and he succeeded (AAE, *Allemagne* 307, cited by Wysocki, p. 133). Louvois to Vauban, AG, $A^1$714, fol. 800, cited by Rousset, *Histoire de Louvois* 3 : 342. Cf. Zeller, *Organisation défensive des Frontières*, p. 84.

25. Huisman, pp. 164–66.

26. Ibid., pp. 166–67; and *Inventaire Analytique*, pp. 165–70, 174–75.

27. A succinct summation of these events is provided in Visconti's dispatches to Cibo on September 8 and 10, 1684. ASV, *Nunz. di Colonia* 61, fols. 288–89, 295 in *Inventaire Analytique*, pp. 180–82, no. 298 and no. 300. Cf. Huisman, pp. 167–68.

28. Huisman, pp. 168–69; La Raudière to Croissy, October 5, 1684, AAE, *Liège* 14, fols. 157–58.

29. Visconti to Cibo, October 15, 1684, ASV, *Nunz. di Colonia* 61, fols. 324–25 in *Inventaire Analytique*, p. 184, no. 304; also Huisman, pp. 169–70.

30. Huisman, pp. 171–72.

31. Excerpts from preamble drawn from Huisman, pp. 172–73. The succeeding résumé of the *Règlement* comes from pp. 173–82 of the same work.

32. Ibid., pp. 149, 184. The French envoy in Liège reported that discontent was especially virulent "because no distinction has been made between those who remained faithful to their bishop and prince and those who did not. One hears the most reputable people openly declaring that if they had believed they would have been treated as they are, they would not have submitted as blindly as they did" (La Raudière to Croissy, November 26, 1684, AAE, *Liège* 14, fols. 164–65).

33. Cf. Balan, "Le Cardinal de Fürstenberg et ses Héritiers," pp. 108–14.

34. Wilhelm to Louis XIV, September 14, 1684, AAE, *Liège*, Supplement no. 3, fol. 184; Wilhelm to Louis XIV, November 30, 1684, AAE, *Cologne* 28, fol. 223; Louis XIV to Wilhelm, December 14, 1684, ibid., fol. 231.

35. Wilhelm to Breget, November 18, 1684, ibid., fols. 223–24.

36. Tambonneau to Louis XIV, June 27, 1684, ibid., fol. 192.

CHAPTER VIII

1. His instructions, dated February 4, 1685, are published in the *Recueil des Instructions* 28: *Electorat de Cologne*, pp. 72–79. Gravel's birthdate appears to be unknown but he should have been at least thirty upon assuming the Cologne post; he died in 1726.

2. Rott, *Histoire de la Représentation Diplomatique de la France*, pp. 294–95.

3. Wysocki, pp. 141–42; Foucher to Croissy, February 9, 1685, AAE, *Mayence* 24, fols. 40–45.

4. Morel's instructions, dated June 22, 1685, are in the *Recueil des Instructions* 7: *Bavière, Palatinat, Deux-Ponts*, pp. 402–5. Letter from papal nuncio Ranuzzi in Paris to Cibo, October 15, 1685, ASV, *Nunz. di Germania* 174. Cited by Immich, *Vorgeschichte des Orleans'schen Krieges*, pp. 20–21. Angelo Maria Ranuzzi (1626–1689) previously served in Turin and Warsaw and was nuncio in France from 1683 to 1689. The best discussion of Ranuzzi's career is contained in Bruno Neveu's long introduction (180 pages) to his *Correspondance du Nonce en France Angelo Ranuzzi (1683–1689)*, vol. 1. The correspondence comprises volumes 10 and 11 in the series "Acta Nuntiaturae Gallicae." Since my research on the Ranuzzi correspondence in the Vatican Archives was accom-

plished years before this edition was published, I shall not cite it as often as otherwise might have been the case. Philipp Wilhelm to Cibo, December 11, 1685, Munich State Archives, K. bl. 44/13 Conc., cited in Immich, *Vorgeschichte des Orleans'schen Krieges*, pp. 30–31.

5. Gravel to Louis XIV, November 27, 1685, AAE, *Cologne* 35, fol. 79; Louis XIV to Gravel, December 13, 1685, ibid., fol. 93.

6. Brandenburg and the United Provinces renewed a defensive alliance on August 23, 1685 (see the political memoirs of the Comte d'Avaux, *Négociations en Hollande*, p. 109; and Pagès, *Le Grande Electeur*, p. 548).

7. Wilhelm to Louis XIV, August 18, 1685, AAE, *Cologne* 31, fols. 50–52.

8. Wilhelm to Louis XIV, April 4, 1684, ibid., vol. 28, fols. 87–88; also memorandum on troops, submitted in early December, 1684, ibid., fols. 258–61.

9. Letters of Wilhelm to Louis XIV, October 4, November 8, and December 19, 1685, ibid., vol. 31, fols. 72, 93, 97.

10. Gravel to Croissy, February 12, 1686, AAE, *Cologne* 35, fol. 104; Croissy to Gravel, February 21, 1686, ibid., vol. 29, fols. 125, 151; Gravel to Croissy, March 5, 1686, ibid., vol. 35, fol. 112.

11. Gravel to Louis XIV, April 23, 1686, ibid., fols. 139–40; Louis XIV to Gravel, May 2, 1686, ibid., vol. 29, fol. 194.

12. Wilhelm to Louis XIV, May 5, 1686, ibid., vol. 31, fol. 106. Gravel to Louis XIV, June 11, 1686, ibid., vol. 32, fol. 361.

13. Opposition to the Fürstenbergs was led by special counsellors Burman and Schönheim (see Braubach, "Minister und Kanzler," pp. 155–56). Gravel to Louis XIV, June 25, 1686, AAE, *Cologne* 32, fol. 377; Gravel to the Elector of Trier, June 23, 1686, AAE, *Trèves* 4, fol. 353.

14. Fester, *Die Augsburger Allianz*, p. 68.

15. Louis XIV to Girardin, June 6, July 19, 1686, AAE, *Turquie* 18, fols. 208, 246–47.

16. Pagès, *Le Grand Electeur*, p. 578.

17. For an illuminating discussion of the pressures exerted upon successive popes to maintain a "national balance" in the college of cardinals and the precedents which ensued, see Biaudet, "Les Nonciatures apostoliques jusqu'en 1648," pp. 50–52.

18. Cf. Louis XIV's letter of September 12, 1686 congratulating Wilhelm on his promotion (AAE, *Cologne* 31, fol. 172). Gravel to Louis XIV, September 17, 1686, ibid., vol. 33, fols. 88–89. Max Heinrich's letter to Wilhelm is dated September 14, 1686 (ibid., fols. 102–3). Ferdinand was accorded an annual pension of 10,000 livres (AAE, *Mémoires et Documents: France* 302, fol. 87; and *Petites Principautés: Principauté de Fürstenberg* 22, fol. 72).

19. Max Heinrich first learned of his nephew's intentions by way of the Cologne agent in Vienna (cf. Gravel to Louis XIV, October 15, 1686, ibid., vol. 35, fol. 210; and Fürstenberg's dispatch from Modave on October 20, ibid., vol. 31, fols. 186–88).

20. A detailed account of this strategy is included in Wilhelm's dispatch to Louis XIV on November 3, 1686 (ibid., fols. 193–94).

21. Böhmländer, "Die Wahl des Herzogs Josef Klemens von Bayern zum Erzbischof von Cöln, 1688," p. 220.

22. Ranuzzi to Cibo, December 16, 1686, ASV, *Nunz. di Francia* 175, cited by Immich, *Vorgeschichte des Orleans'schen Krieges*, pp. 161–62. Ranuzzi was also elevated to the cardinalate in the promotion of September 2, 1686 (see von Pastor, *The History of the Popes*, p. 419).

23. The misunderstanding created by Ranuzzi was explained by Buonvisi in a letter to Cardinal Pio on February 2, 1687, cited by Trivellini, *Il Cardinale Francesco Buonvisi*, p. 90. Francesco Buonvisi (1626–1700), one of the most experienced and cosmopolitan diplomats in the latter half of the seventeenth century, previously held posts at Cologne and Warsaw. He tried to channel all military and political activity in the Empire toward the prosecution of the war against the Turks. For Wilhelm's memorandum, see AAE, *Cologne*, supplement no. 1, fols. 367–80. Though undated and filed in the archives with material from the spring of 1687, the memorandum clearly deals with the problems of December 1686. It was first cited by Pagès in his lectures at the Sorbonne: *Louis XIV et l'Allemagne*, pp. 144–45, 174.

24. Louis's memorandum to d'Estrées is dated December 20, 1686 (AAE, *Rome* 302, fols. 114–24). Excerpts have been published by Immich, *Vorgeschichte des Orleans'schen Krieges*, p. 173 n. 3.

25. See Pagès, *Le Grand Electeur*, pp. 565–86. For Cibo's reply, see d'Estrées's report to the king in AAE, *Rome: Mémoires et Documents* 31, fol. 275ff, published by Immich, *Vorgeschichte des Orleans'schen Krieges*, p. 343. On the role of Cardinal Pio as an intermediary between Vienna and Rome, see Dubruel, "La correspondance confidentielle du cardinal Carlo Pio avec l'empereur Léopold Ier," pp. 602–8. D'Estrées justly complained to Cibo about such consultation and publicity since Louis had insisted on secrecy (cf. Immich, *Vorgeschichte des Orleans'schen Krieges*, p. 345 and Pagès, *Le Grand Electeur*, p. 586).

26. Letter of January 4, 1687, HHSt, *Friedensakten* 150, published by Immich, *Vorgeschichte des Orleans'schen Krieges*, pp. 173–76.

27. D'Estrées's report, ibid., p. 346; Cibo to Ranuzzi, January 10, 1687, ASV, *Nunz. di Francia* 382, ibid., pp. 177–81; Buonvisi to Cibo, January 26, 1687, ASV, *Nunz. di Germania* 213, ibid., p. 192. Louis maintained that Leopold's refusal to settle for a quick bilateral arrangement was proof that he opposed a settlement (Ranuzzi to Cibo, February 3, 1687, ASV, *Nunz. di Francia* 176, ibid., pp. 196–200). Significantly, the tone of Louis's dispatches in the Turkish correspondence had stiffened. On January 19, 1687, he informed Girardin that he had stationed additional troops in Alsace close to the German borders so as to be prepared "to bring the terror of my arms into the states of Austria and her allies; . . . the bridges (*passages*) which I have on the Rhine afford free entry into the heart of Germany and close off to the Empire the entry which it previously had into the territories belonging to my crown" (AAE, *Turquie* 18, fols. 375–76). Again, "The attitude of the House of Austria toward me instills the resolution not to wait until she is able to rally together enough force in the Empire to attack me with fewer losses than she sustained in the last war. It may well happen that

I shall be obliged to do what prudence counsels . . . " (letter of January 30, 1687, ibid., fol. 392). Buonvisi's letter to the papal secretary was dated April 20, 1687 (cited by Trivellini, pp. 117–18).

28. Pagès, *Le Grand Electeur*, pp. 588–89. Louis requested a general guarantee in his letter to Verjus, January 19, 1687, AAE, *Allemagne* 316. Max Heinrich's reply was drafted by Fürstenberg, then residing at Versailles (cf. Gravel to Louis XIV, February 16, 1687, AAE, *Cologne* 33, fol. 253). Wilhelm had arrived at the court on December 28 and received his cardinal's hat from Louis on January 2. The king treated him like a French cardinal and was hatless when he received his German agent in a private audience (see Dangeau, *Journal* 2 : 8). On the day of Wilhelm's departure for Cologne (February 24, 1687), Louis granted him an annual pension of 10,000 écus for the next ten years. Even if he were to die in the interim the payments would continue so as to satisfy his creditors and spare his relations (ibid., p. 29).

29. Cf. Cibo to Ranuzzi, February 26, 1687, ASV, *Nunz. di Francia* 382, cited by Immich, *Vorgeschichte des Orleans'schen Krieges*, pp. 222–23; also Ranuzzi to Cibo, March 10, 1687, ASV, *Nunz. di Francia* 176. Ibid., pp. 238–39, plus n. 1 on p. 239 of same. See Pagès, *Le Grand Electeur*, p. 589.

CHAPTER IX

1. Claude Hector, Marquis de Villars (1653–1734), the son of a former ambassador to Spain, became one of the most renowned marshals in French history. For an account of his earlier career, see the *Mémoires du Maréchal de Villars*. Villars's instructions were dated January 14, 1687 (AAE, *Autriche*, supplement 42). The instructions pertaining to the Austrian mission are in the *Recueil des Instructions* 1: *Autriche*, pp. 114–15; those for Munich are in vol. 7 of the same series: *Bavière, Palatinat, Deux-Ponts*, pp. 82–86.

2. Villars to Croissy, April 30, 1687, AAE, *Bavière* 39, fol. 48; Villars to Croissy, June 8, 1687, ibid., fols. 100–101.

3. The treaty is in supplement no. 1 of the *Cologne* correspondence, fols. 404–25. Cf. Ennen, *Frankreich und der Niederrhein* 1 : 467. Louis XIV to Gravel, June 26, 1687, AAE, *Cologne* 36, fols. 117–25; Louis XIV to Gravel, July 3, 1687, ibid., fol. 127.

4. As the queen's ship was passing Bonn on the journey down the Rhine, a cannon ball went whizzing past the bow. Though it could never be proved, her father was convinced that Fürstenberg had ordered the shot (see Böhmländer, p. 187).

5. Gravel to Wilhelm, July 25, 1687, AAE, *Cologne*, supplement no. 1, fol. 439.

6. Wilhelm to Louis XIV, July 29, 1687, ibid., fol. 437; in his letter to Max Heinrich, dated August 1, 1687, the king signed off with the words, "Vre bon frère, Louis" (ibid., fol. 450).

7. Cf. Gravel to Louis XIV, August 24, 1687, ibid., vol. 34, fols. 94ff; Gravel to Croissy, August 28, 1687, ibid., fols. 112–13. His anxiety over Wilhelm's

behavior is manifest in the dispatch to Croissy: "I hope with all my heart that as clever a man as he may be, he is not deceiving himself in the measures he has taken. . . . He must act with more ardor in an affair where diligence and secrecy appear to be equally necessary. Nevertheless, it will be a kind of miracle if the secret is kept. As of today, there are thirty people among his relatives and friends who know what is going on, not to speak of those whom I do not know." The king's patience with Wilhelm is evident in Louis XIV to Gravel, September 4, 1687, ibid., vol. 36, fol. 159. In this dispatch the king warned Gravel not to write of such matters without using a cipher; this, in the midst of all Gravel's concern over secrecy! Gravel to Wilhelm, September 2, 1687, ibid., vol. 34, fol. 122.

8. Böhmländer, pp. 186, 190; and Prutz, "Die Kölner Wahl und Frankreichs Friedensbruch," p. 168.

9. On the Turkish situation see Immich, *Geschichte des europäischen Staatensystems*, p. 130. On the "correction" of the Golden Bull, see Wolf, *Emergence of the Great Powers*, p. 132; Fedrigo Cornaro to the Doge, November 29, 1687, copy in HHSt, *Dispacci dell' Ambasciator Veneto in Germania* 163, fols. 563–64.

10. For the individual chapter members, their backgrounds and their allegiances, see Braubach, "Das Kölner Domkapitel und die Wahl von 1688," pp. 51–117.

11. Tanara (1650–1724) had previously served in Brussels. After Cologne he was sent to Portugal in 1690 and then to Vienna, during which time he became a cardinal. At his death he was Dean of the Sacred College (see Govaerts, "La Nonciature de Mgr. Tanara à Cologne," pp. 73–80, 85–91; also Just, "Die Quellen zur Geschichte des Kölner Nuntiatur," pp. 271–72). Tanara to Cibo, September 21, 1687, ASV, *Nunz. di Colonia* 64, fol. 480; Wilhelm to Gravel, November 13, 1687, AAE, *Cologne*, Supplement no. 1, fol. 455.

12. His assistant Breget submitted a memorandum to Versailles outlining the cardinal's proposals and asking for French aid in achieving them: "Mémoire touchant l'affaire des coadjutories de Cologne et de Liège que le chevalier Breget a ordre de présenter pour informer S. Mté. et Messieurs les Ministres et apprendre les Intentions du Roi" (AAE, *Cologne* 31, fols. 268–71).

13. The cost of Wilhelm's generosity came to 5,000 écus a year, of which Louis had contributed about 2,000 écus annually since 1679. At the end of 1684 Tambonneau noted that the average canon derived a yearly income of about 1,000 écus as a member of a major cathedral chapter. Many belonged to several at a time, such as Strasbourg, Liège, and Salzburg (ibid., vol. 27, fol. 262). Breget memorandum cited above, note 12; Louis XIV to Wilhelm, October 9, 1687, AAE, *Cologne* 36, fol. 272.

14. Louis XIV to Gravel, October 9, 1687, ibid., fols. 176–77; Gravel to Louis XIV, October 4, 1687, ibid., vol. 34, fol. 176; Tanara to Cibo, October 9, 1687, ASV, *Nunz. di Colonia* 64, fol. 508.

15. On the deliberation of the Secret Council, see Böhmländer, p. 189. Although the minutes of this meeting were undated, Böhmländer places it before October 28, 1687. Dominick Andreas Kaunitz (1655–1705) was later to become

Reichsvizekanzler. He was the grandfather of the famous minister who served Maria Teresa in the eighteenth century. The very argument Breslau and Jülich hoped to avoid was used by the pope against Max Heinrich. If it were necessary to have a coadjutor for Cologne, why was he asking to assume the responsibility of Münster at the same time? The reply from Bonn was that it was not that the elector was overloaded with work so much as the desire for tranquility in the archdiocese after his death (cf. Prutz, p. 178; and Böhmländer, pp. 209–10).

16. Wilhelm to Louis XIV, November 1, 1687, AAE, *Cologne* 31, fols. 278–79.

17. Ibid.

18. The king of France traditionally exercised the right to collect revenues in vacant bishoprics (the money was often given to the next bishop) and to make appointments to certain benefices in those bishoprics. But this right of the *Régale* did not extend to bishoprics in the south of France. In 1673, partly due to the financial pressures of the Dutch War, Louis declared that the powers inherent in his kingship enabled him to exercise the right everywhere in France. He viewed this as primarily a temporal power; but since it contravened earlier agreements with the Holy See, Innocent was willing to listen to the complaints of two pro-Jansenist bishops in the south against the king's action. (Louis's position was supported by the Paris Parlement and essentially was accepted by the great majority of the upper clergy of France.) Due to Innocent's opposition, the affair of the *Régale* became elevated, in the words of Pierre Blet, into a cause worthy of a Saint Ambrose or a Thomas Becket (see my paper, "Louis XIV's 'Cold War' with the Papacy," pp. 127–136). Favoriti to Lauri (inter-nuncio in Paris), July 12, 1680, ASV, *Nunz. di Francia* 339, fol. 244, cited by Blet, "Innocent XI et l'Assemblée du Clergé de France de 1682," 347. The term *papesses* is taken from Blet's translation. For accounts of Innocent XI and his principal advisers, see Neveu, *Sebastien Joseph Du Cambout de Ponchâteau*, pp. 80–96 and Dubruel, *En Plein Conflit*, pp. 24–31; also Morey and Landor, "Lorenzo Casoni and Papal Policy for the Church in France," pp. 77–84.

19. On the *franchises* see de Bojani, "L'Affaire du 'Quartier' à Rome à la Fin du Dix-Septième Siècle," pp. 350–378. Louis's retort is cited by Hanotaux, editor of *Recueil des Instructions* 6: *Rome*, p. 285. A proclamation of the papal non-recognition was affixed to the walls of public buildings and several churches on May 12, 1687 (see Dubruel, "L'Excommunication de Louis XIV," p. 615). Henri-Charles, Marquis de Lavardin (1644–1701) had been a lieutenant-general in command of the army in Bretagne. His long set of instructions, dated July 14, 1687, are included in the *Recueil des Instructions* 6: *Rome*, pp. 287–363.

20. Böhmländer, p. 192.

21. Tanara to Cibo, November 7, 1687, ASV, *Nunz. di Colonia* 64, fol. 606.

22. Louis XIV to Wilhelm, November 12, 1687, AAE, *Cologne* 31, fols. 289–290.

23. Gravel to Louis XIV, November 11, 1687, ibid., vol. 34, fols. 226–27.

24. Wilhelm to Gravel, November 14, 1687, AAE, *Cologne*, supplement no. 1, fol. 456; Böhmländer, p. 195.

25. Gravel to Louis XIV, November 16, 1687, AAE, *Cologne* 34, fols. 238–46.

26. Although Rotkirch was working for Fürstenberg and Gravel, his position was especially delicate since he owned property valued at 60,000 écus in the Duchy of Jülich (Gravel to Louis XIV, November 29, 1687, ibid., fol. 287). A copy of Max Heinrich's letter, dated November 16, 1687, is included with Gravel's dispatch of the same date (ibid., fol. 248).

27. Friedrich Wilhelm approved of the Elector Palatine's suggestion and drafted instructions for his special envoy, Wachtendonk (see Böhmländer, p. 196). Gravel to Louis XIV, November 20, 1687, AAE, *Cologne* 34, fols. 268ff; Wilhelm to Gravel, November 19, 1687, ibid., supplement no. 1, fols. 463–64.

28. Tanara to Cibo, November 16, 1687, ASV, *Nunz. di Colonia* 60, fols. 153–54.

29. On the approval of the canons, see Böhmländer, p. 198. A copy of Max Heinrich's letter to the chapter was included with Gravel's dispatch to the king, November 22, 1687, AAE, *Cologne* 34, fols. 266–67. Louis personally thanked the elector for having taken this step in a letter dated November 28, 1687 (ibid., fol. 274).

30. Tanara to Cibo, November 23, 1687, ASV, *Nunz. di Colonia* 64, fols. 640–41. Wilhelm to Gravel, November 27, 1687, AAE, *Cologne*, supplement no. 1, fol. 479. In Munich, Kaunitz and Villars were awaiting Cologne's representative to Max Emmanuel. Both men often dined together with the elector in a lively and congenial atmosphere. One evening the conversation touched on letters which Max Emmanuel had received from his agent in Rome. He learned that despite all his fighting in the Crusade the pope saw fit to reprimand his *galanteries* and to criticize the expensive pleasures he indulged in, such as gambling, the opera, and lavish banquets. At the same time there were reports that his rival, Charles of Lorraine, would be permitted to nominate a cardinal in gratitude for his aid in the campaign. In the face of the elector's growing wrath, Kaunitz said that the Holy Father would surely have offered him a cardinal's hat for Joseph Clemens but did not want to grant him so high a dignity before he became Elector of Cologne. At this point, Villars exclaimed that "it was not quite fair to the elector to think that he could only have desired this dignity for Prince Clemens. After all, he had many friends and deserving aides." Kaunitz interrupted: "Who then do you suggest that his Electoral Highness give this hat to?" "To me!" replied Villars. "I would serve him very well in the Sacred College. . . . Begin by making me a cardinal and everything will take care of itself." This anecdote first appeared in Villars's dispatch to Croissy on November 26, 1687, AAE, *Bavière* 99, fol. 281, and was later embellished in his *Mémoires du Maréchal Villars* 1 : 84–85.

31. Gravel to Louis XIV, November 29, 1687, AAE, *Cologne* 34, fol. 487. After the vote on November 28, Fürstenberg told the canons that they were not needed in the near future and urged them to take advantage of the good weather to go hunting. Each canon away on the hunt would be another one whom Kaunitz could not reach. Cf. Böhmländer, p. 201. Louis XIV's letter of Novem-

ber 20 is in AAE, *Cologne* 34, fol. 255. On December 3, 1687 the king renewed his assurances to the elector that if the terms were met the debt would be forgotten. Copy in AAE, *Cologne*, supplement no. 1, fol. 490. Gravel to Louis XIV, December 6, 1687, ibid., vol. 35, fol. 461.

32. Cibo to Tanara, December 6, 1687, ASV, *Nunz. di Colonia* 60, fol. 24.

33. Cibo to Ranuzzi, November 18, 1687, ASV, *Nunz. di Francia* 177, fol. 28.

34. Ranuzzi to Cibo, December 15, 1687, ASV, *Nunz. di Francia* 177, fols. 293–95. Cf. Gérin, "L'Ambassade de Lavardin et la Séquestration du Nonce Ranuzzi," pp. 382–432. Amonio was well-liked at Versailles and his professional competence was highly regarded. Although he was a doctor, he was also a cleric possessing benefices in several Italian dioceses (see Dubruel, "L'Excommunication de Louis XIV," p. 620). Perhaps the most difficult aspect of Ranuzzi's mission was that as a diplomat he had very little with which to bargain; Innocent lifted the issues into the realm of principles, to be defended or opposed (see Latreille, "Innocent XI: Pape 'Janséniste,'" p. 31).

35. Max Emmanuel's letter was dated December 7, 1687 (AAE, *Cologne* 35, fol. 499). Karg's instructions were dated December 2, 1687. See Böhmländer, p. 203. Karg (1648–1719) was dean of the cathedral chapter in Munich. He earlier served as an aide to the Bishop of Bamberg who entrusted him with numerous diplomatic missions. When his superior died in 1683, Karg transferred his services to Munich. He later became Joseph Clemens's leading counselor at Cologne. For an interesting account of his career, see Braubach, *Kurköln*, pp. 181–99.

36. Max Heinrich's delegate to Munich, Crane, a friend of the Fürstenbergs, was curtly informed that Max Heinrich's intentions could be learned from the dispatches of Kaunitz and Karg (cf. Böhmländer, p. 204). Villars's influence was by now almost completely defunct. On the planting of the information see ibid.; the pressure on Cologne is documented in Wilhelm to Louis XIV, December 15, 1687, AAE, *Cologne* 31, fol. 322.

37. The most incisive account of the conferences with Max Heinrich which I have found is the long, unciphered dispatch of Tanara to Cibo, December 28, 1687 (ASV, *Nunz. di Colonia* 64, fols. 796ff.). The succeeding narrative is largely based upon this report. The United Provinces were in roughly the same position as Brandenburg. They by no means desired Fürstenberg as elector but decided "not to meddle in an ecclesiastical affair," especially since it might be necessary to deal with the cardinal in the near future and it would not be wise to burn their bridges behind them (ibid., fol. 799).

38. Ibid.

39. Gravel noted that while Kaunitz easily lost his temper, "Karg was much more adroit and supple (*insinuant*) than his colleague. His language is always amiable . . . and he has assured me that he will conduct himself in such a way that the Elector of Cologne and Cardinal von Fürstenberg will have no reason to complain. But this is the last thing one can count upon. This minister is more dangerous than anyone else" (Gravel to Louis XIV, December 27, 1687, AAE,

Cologne 35, fol. 496). Tanara to Cibo, December 28, 1687, ASV, *Nunz. di Colonia* 64, fol. 797.

40. Böhmländer, pp. 206–7; Louis XIV to Wilhelm, December 25, 1687, AAE, *Cologne* 31, fol. 327.

41. For the canons' excuse see Gravel to Louis XIV, December 30, 1687, AAE, *Cologne* 34, fol. 354. Kaunitz made promises to some canons and threatened others, particularly those who had relatives employed in the imperial service (Gravel to Louis XIV, January 3, 1688, ibid., vol. 35, fol. 507). The emperor's letter was dated December 12, 1687, ibid., vol. 31, fol. 338. Gravel to Louis XIV, December 30, 1687, ibid., vol. 35, fols. 502–3.

42. The pope's wishes for postponement are in Cibo to Tanara, December 6, 1687 (ASV, *Nunz. di Colonia* 60, fol. 24). Wilhelm's response was conveyed in Tanara to Cibo, December 28, 1687, ibid., fols. 162–63.

43. Pio to the emperor, December 23, 1687, HHSt, *Geistliche Wahlakten*, 17a. On the writ of inhibition see Böhmländer, pp. 211–12; also Gravel to Louis XIV, January 3, 1688, AAE, *Cologne* 37, fol. 16.

44. The courier's arrival is reported in Breget to Croissy, January 1, 1688 (ibid., vol. 31, fols. 341–42). Breslau's memorial is discussed in Gravel to Louis XIV, January 3, 1688, ibid., vol. 37, fols. 13–14.

45. Ibid. On January 5, 1688, Kaunitz made a speech before the chapter in which he warned of Cologne becoming another Metz, Toul, or Verdun (Böhmländer, p. 213).

46. The notification and Max Heinrich's response to the nuncio are to be found in AAE, *Cologne* 37, fols. 21–24.

47. For an interesting account of the tapestries and their subsequent history, see Elbern, "Die Rubensteppiche des Kölner Domes," pp. 43–88.

CHAPTER X

1. Wilhelm to Innocent XI, January 8, 1688, AAE, *Cologne* 37, fol. 40; Louis XIV to Wilhelm, January 15, 1688; and Wilhelm's reply on January 25, ibid., vol. 40, fols. 25, 31; Louis XIV to Max Heinrich, January 15, 1688, ibid., vol. 42, fols. 14–15.

2. Villars to Louis XIV, January 15, 1688, *Mémoires du Maréchal Villars* 1 : 405–9.

3. Cornaro to the Doge, January 17, 1688, copy in HHSt, *Dispacci dell'Ambasciator Veneto in Germania* 163, fols. 631–33. The emperor's attack on Wilhelm is cited by Böhmländer, p. 215. Cornaro to the Doge, January 23, 1688, copy in HHSt, *Dispacci dell'Ambasciator Veneto in Germania* 163, fol. 639.

4. Innocent's state of health is reported in Casoni to Ranuzzi, January 13, 1688 (ASV, *Avvisi* 50, fols. 463–64). Cibo to Ranuzzi, January 6, 1688, ASV, *Nunz. di Francia* 177, fol. 33. For commentary on Lavardin's excommunication and the threat to excommunicate the king, see Neveu (ed.), *Correspondance du nonce Ranuzzi* 2 : 217 n. 1; and Blet, *Les Assemblées du Clergé et Louis XIV de*

1670 à 1693, p. 487. Ranuzzi to Casoni, January 19, 1688, ibid., vol. 179a, fol. 90; Ranuzzi to Casoni, January 12, 1688, ibid., fol. 88. The traditional viewpoint in France was that "an excommunication pronounced against the king and the bulls to this effect were regarded as null" (Marion, *Dictionnaire des Institutions de la France*, p. 227).

5. For a review of the evidence and the possible conjecture on this subject, see Blet, "Louis XIV et le Saint Siège," pp. 309–37, especially pp. 320–28.

6. On Talon's speech cf. Orcibal, *Louis XIV contre Innocent XI*. Prof. Latreille notes that unlike Gregory VII, Pope Innocent did not speak out in public; despite his phenomenal will-power, he gave concessions here and there without ever remaining firm everywhere (see his article, "Innocent XI: Pape 'Janséniste,'" p. 23). While this may be so, a public condemnation would have inflamed an already dangerous situation and certainly would have jeopardized the next campaign. For a discussion of Innocent's delaying action, see Feine, *Die Besetzung der Reichsbistümer vom Westfälischen Frieden bis zur Säkularisation*, pp. 386–87.

7. Gravel to Louis XIV, January 30, March 6, 1688, AAE, *Cologne* 37, fols. 66, 113–14. On February 10, 1688, the king accorded Fürstenberg an annual pension of 30,000 livres until he became Elector of Cologne in accordance with the pre-election agreement (AAE, *Petites Principautés* 22: *Principauté de Fürstenberg*, fol. 79).

8. On Max Heinrich's appearance, see Gravel to Louis XIV, March 14, 1688, AAE, *Cologne* 37, fol. 134; Louis XIV to Gravel, March 4, 1688, ibid., fol. 97. A *gratification extraordinaire* for the defense of the electorate was sent to Fürstenberg on March 10, 1688 (AAE, *Petites Principautés* 22: *Principauté de Fürstenberg*, fol. 82). Wilhelm tried to blunt the image of his being totally supported by France; he borrowed money from friends and even sold some chinaware (Gravel to Louis XIV, March 6, 1688, AAE, *Cologne* 37, fol. 115). Gravel to Louis XIV, March 6, 1688, ibid., fol. 110. Though Tanara objected to Wilhelm's maneuvers concerning the coadjutorship, Gravel said that he was well-disposed toward Fürstenberg, partly because he hoped to become nuncio at Versailles and wanted to stay in Louis's good graces (ibid., fols. 111–12).

9. D'Estrées to Louis XIV, February 10, 1688, AAE, *Rome* 313, cited by Gérin, "Le Pape Innocent XI et l'Election de Cologne," 92 n. 2.

10. Wilhelm to Buonvisi, February 22, 1688, ASL, *Arch. Buonvisi* 57, no. 58.

11. Gravel to Louis XIV, March 3, 1688, AAE, *Cologne* 37, fols. 104–5; Louis XIV to Gravel, March 11, 1688, ibid., fol. 120; Wilhelm to Louis XIV, March 23, 1688, ibid., vol. 40, fol. 48.

12. Buonvisi to Tanara, March 18, 1688, ASL, *Arch. Buonvisi* 24, no. 65. Cf. Trivellini, p. 91. Wilhelm to Buonvisi, March 25, 1688, ASL, *Arch. Buonvisi* 57, no. 57.

13. Ibid., no. 59.

14. On the usefulness of Wilhelm's statement in Roman circles, see Gravel to Louis XIV, March 27, 1688, AAE, *Cologne* 35, cited by Gérin, "Le Pape Innocent XI et l'Election de Cologne," p. 92 n. 2. On the pledge of troops, see Böhm-

länder, p. 219. Wilhelm's response to Leopold is found in Buonvisi to Cibo, May 2, 1688, ASL, *Arch. Buonvisi* 24, no. 109. D'Estrées to Louis XIV, May 4, 1688, AAE, *Rome* 313, cited by Gérin, "Le Pape Innocent XI et la Révolution Anglaise," p. 446.

15. Louis XIV to d'Estrées, April 24, 1688, AAE, *Rome* 313, cited by Gérin, "Le Pape Innocent XI et l'Election de Cologne," p. 91.

16. The maneuvers surrounding Max Heinrich's will are reported in Böhm-länder, pp. 221–23. The effect of Fürstenberg's presence on Max Heinrich was noted in Gravel to Louis XIV, April 17, 1688, AAE, *Cologne* 35, cited by Gérin, "Le Pape Innocent XI et l'Election de Cologne," p. 93.

17. Roberts to Croissy, April 18, 1688, Archives Nationales, *Correspondance Consulaire*, AE, B¹955, *Rome* (1685–90).

18. Gravel to Louis XIV, April 3, 1688, AAE, *Cologne* 37, fol. 179; Louis XIV to Gravel, April 8, 1688, ibid., vol. 36, fol. 316. Du Heron was a competent military aide and diplomatic agent with a sound knowledge of German affairs. Although he did not arrive in Bonn until the beginning of June, his instructions are dated March 18, 1688 (AAE, *Cologne* 38, fols. 14–21). They are printed in the *Recueil des Instructions* 28: *Cologne*, pp. 82–88. Louis XIV to Gravel, April 15, 1688, AAE, *Cologne* 37, fol. 322.

19. Croissy to Gravel, April 19, 1688, ibid., fol. 204; Wilhelm to Louis XIV, April 28, 1688, ibid., vol. 40, fol. 76; Wilhelm to Louis XIV, May 1, 1688, ibid., fol. 83.

20. Gravel to Louis XIV, May 1, 1688, ibid., vol. 37, fols. 235–36. A copy of the proposed declaration accompanied Fürstenberg's dispatch to the king on May 8, 1688 (ibid., vol. 40, fol. 91). Louis XIV to Gravel, May 13, 1688, ibid., vol. 37, fol. 250.

21. Gravel to Louis XIV, May 22, 29, 1688, ibid., fols. 268–86. Although the full story of the debt was known to but a few persons, portions of it inevitably leaked out. Thus nuncio Tanara had been aware of Louis's having recalled Gravel's power to effect a cancellation of the debt; the source of his information is not provided (Tanara to Cibo, May 2, 1688, ASV, *Nunz. di Colonia* 65, quoted from a copy at the Fürstl. Fürstenberg. Archiv, Donaueschingen. OB. 19 vol. 21–3, no. 69). He cited the widespread fear within the chapter that upon the elector's death the French would demand at least the sixteen years of accumu-lated interest on the debt. In such a case, the capitularies were resolved to seize all the personal property of the elector and to use it to settle the account with the French. Max Heinrich was well aware of this resolution (Tanara to Cibo, May 23, 1688, ASV, *Nunz. di Colonia* 60, fol. 184).

22. Wilhelm's enemies included: Max Heinrich's confessor; counsellor John Peter Burman, who had formerly been one of the cardinal's creatures and who owed all his advancement to him; and secretary of state Schönheim, who had been elevated to the nobility by imperial decree on November 19, 1687 (see Brau-bach, "Minister und Kanzler," pp. 147, 156). Gravel to Louis XIV, June 4, 1688, AAE, *Cologne* 37, fols. 291–92. In the absence of Max Emmanuel, it was agreed that Karg would serve as proxy for his master. Dücker to Gravel, May 30, 1688,

ibid., vol. 42, fols. 88–89; Tanara to Cibo, May 30, 1688, ASV, *Nunz. di Colonia* 60, fol. 185.

23. Gravel to Louis XIV, June 4, 1688, AAE, *Cologne* 37, fol. 291. Wilhelm to Louis XIV, June 3, 1688, ibid., vol. 40, fol. 106. He did not write another letter to Versailles until June 21, leaving all correspondence to the French envoys and agents in Bonn and Cologne. Gravel to Louis XIV, June 4, 1688, ibid., vol. 37, fol. 298. See Böhmländer, p. 228. Du Heron to Louis XIV, June 5, 1688, AAE, *Cologne* 38, fols. 36–37.

24. Ibid., fol. 37. Burman and Schönheim, Wilhelm's enemies, were allotted more money than any of the other members of Max Heinrich's council. Burman received 1000 écus and Schönheim 800 (copy of the will signed by the elector, AAE, *Cologne* 42, fols. 95ff.). The text of the will has been published by Ennen, *Der Spanische Erbfolgekrieg*, Appendix no. 1.

25. Gravel to Croissy, June 4, 1688, ibid., vol. 37, fols. 302–6. In an accompanying note Gravel advised Croissy to be on his guard against the cardinal, especially since he had recently made some indiscreet remarks about the minister and his handling of affairs (ibid., fols. 300–301). Cf. Gérin, "Le Pape Innocent XI et l'Election de Cologne," pp. 96–98.

26. Louis XIV to Gravel, June 6, 1688, ibid., vol. 37, fols. 309–11. The Elector of Brandenburg had died in May; Louis did not display mourning for him even though it was customary to pay at least token respect for the dignity of the electorship (cf. Ranuzzi to Cibo, May 24, 1688, ASV, *Nunz. di Francia* 177, fol. 377). The new elector remained firmly attached to Austria and the United Provinces. D'Asfeld soon reported that the fortifications were inadequate and indicated his suspicions of Tanara, in whom, he believed, Fürstenberg placed too great a trust (D'Asfeld to Louvois, June 12, 1688, AG, A^{1}819). Gravel thought that his successor had come at a good time to get a feel for the affairs of the electorate. He described the scene as "a chaos which changes face almost every minute." (Gravel to Croissy, June 8, 1688, AAE, *Cologne* 37, fols. 330–31).

27. Verjus's threat is found in Prutz, "Die Kölner Wahl und Frankreichs Friedensbruch," p. 190. A copy of d'Avaux's declaration is in HHSt, *Geistliche Wahlakten* 17a; it is dated June 10, 1688. Böhmländer, p. 230.

28. Du Heron to Louis XIV, June 12, 1688, AAE, *Cologne* 38, fol. 61. Louis XIV pressed for the confirmation in Rome in his letter to Du Heron of June 10, 1688, cited by Gérin, "Le Pape Innocent XI et l'Election de Cologne," p. 100. A copy of the chapter's letter to the pope, written by Fürstenberg, is in AAE, *Cologne* 38, fol. 72. For Wilhelm's instructions to Tissier regarding the indult, see ibid., fols. 70–71. Both documents are dated June 12, 1688. The pope's bon mot is cited by Gérin, "Le Pape Innocent XI et l'Election de Cologne," p. 100.

CHAPTER XI

1. One pamphleteer speculated that Louis XIV might have had higher ambitions for Fürstenberg but in that he would be disappointed—the college of car-

dinals would not elect another Borgia! (Cited by Gillot, *Le Règne de Louis XIV et l'Opinion Publique en Allemagne*, p. 112 n. 2.)

2. Böhmländer, pp. 233–35.

3. Ibid., pp. 235–36.

4. Ibid., p. 237.

5. For Fürstenberg's remarks and activity, see Du Heron to Louis XIV, June 12, 1688, AAE, *Cologne* 38, fol. 60. Louis XIV to Du Heron, June 17, 1688, ibid., fols. 77–78; Du Heron to Louis XIV, June 12, 1688, ibid., fol. 61.

6. Ranuzzi to Cibo, June 14, 1688, ASV, *Nunz. di Francia* 177, fol. 387. Fürstenberg sent letters to the United Provinces and to neighboring princes, urging them to respect the liberty of the electoral chapter. He pointedly reminded them of his access to French protection but claimed that all he really wanted was to preserve the dignity of the chapter and to keep the peace. For strategic reasons, the Dutch were more apprehensive of Fürstenberg controlling Münster than Cologne (D'Asfeld to Louvois, June 19, 1688, AG, A¹819).

7. Tanara to Cibo, June 13, 1688, ASV, *Nunz. di Colonia* 60, fol. 199; Tanara to Cibo, June 12, 1688, copy in the Fürstl. Fürstenberg. Archiv, Donaueschingen, OB. 19, vol. 21/3, no. 81; Wilhelm to Louvois, June 21, 1688, AG, A¹819; Louis XIV to Du Heron, June 27, 1688, AAE, *Cologne* 38, fols. 113–14.

8. Braubach, "Das Kölner Domkapitel und die Wahl von 1688," p. 90 n. 169; AG, A¹819, no. 53.

9. Ranuzzi to Cibo, June 28, 1688, ASV, *Nunz. di Francia* 177, fol. 396.

10. Cibo to Tanara, June 26, 1688, ASV, *Nunz. di Colonia* 60, fol. 31. Casoni informed Fürstenberg of the pope's decision in a letter dated July 1, 1688 (AAE, *Cologne* 38, fol. 199). Wilhelm learned of Innocent's partiality towards Joseph Clemens in Tissier's letter of July 2, 1688, ibid., fol. 197. Tissier believed that this was the only step which Innocent was going to take against the cardinal. He regarded it as a means of placating the Austrians and believed that if Fürstenberg were postulated the pope would then confirm the chapter's decision. As we shall see, Tissier was not wholly *au courant*. But his reports were sent to Versailles, giving further grounds for French optimism and more substance to their future sense of deception.

11. Tanara to Cibo, July 11, 1688, copy in the Fürstl. Fürstenberg. Archiv, Donaueschingen, OB. 19, vol. 21/3, no. 97.

12. Leopold's letter to Pio is dated June 20, 1688. See Böhmländer, p. 231. Cornaro to the Doge, June 27, 1688, copy in HHSt, *Dispacci dell'Ambasciator Veneto in Germania* 164, fol. 112. For the distrust of Buonvisi at the Viennese court, specifically on the Cologne question, see Papa, "Innocenzo XI tra Francia ed Impero durante il 1688–89," p. 611.

13. Cardinal Pio to Leopold, July 3, 1688, HHSt, *Geistliche Wahlakten*: Cöln, 17a. The following account of Pio's audience with the pope is entirely drawn from this dispatch. Several of the phrases used by Pio in his arguments against Fürstenberg are identical to those used by Leopold in his letter of June 20, to Pio.

14. D'Estrées's argument is found in Roberts to Croissy, July 6, 1688 (Ar-

chives Nationales, Correspondance Consulaire: *Rome*, AE, B¹955). The heart of Innocent's instruction is as follows: "N. Sr. vuole ch'ella [nuncio Tanara] con la necessaria prudenza e circospezione prendi tutte le congionture che se Le presentarano di aiutare le pratiche che si faranno a favore del Sig. Principe Clemente de Baviera per le vicina elezione di contesta Chiesa" (Cibo to Tanara, July 9, 1688, ASV, *Nunz. di Colonia* 60, fol. 32). The Venetian ambassador glimpsed the openly partisan role of the pope in support of Austria against Fürstenberg and reported it to the Doge in his dispatch of July 18, 1688 (copy in HHSt, *Dispacci dell'Ambasciator Veneto in Germania* 164, fol. 137). In his biography of Innocent XI, Immich claimed that the pope did not try to influence the election (*Papst Innocenz XI*, p. 84). His evidence for this assertion, however, is based upon Gérin's discussion of the question, which in turns rests exclusively upon Tissier's July 2 letter to Fürstenberg cited above, and on a conversation between Cibo and d'Estrées on June 22. In the course of this conversation Cibo referred to the correspondence which Innocent had been keeping up with Tanara through Casoni and assured the French cardinal that the pope was indifferent to the outcome of the election, caring only for the maintenance of the peace and the security of Christendom (Gérin, "Le Pape Innocent XI et l'Election de Cologne en 1688," pp. 101–2). Yet this conversation took place before Innocent had officially refused the indult to Fürstenberg or granted the dispensation to Joseph Clemens, before his conversation with Cardinal Pio. Von Pastor cites Innocent's orders to work against Fürstenberg but gives the wrong date. He goes on to say that the brief to Prince Clement of Bavaria was forwarded on July 17, which is not only the wrong date but such as would have made its reception in the Rhineland before the election impossible. His footnote citation of Böhmländer's work refers to the second part, which deals exclusively with the events *after* the election. There is no evidence in von Pastor that either he or his assistants read Böhmländer very closely, if at all (*History of the Popes* 32 : 379).

15. Böhmländer, p. 238.

16. Max Emmanuel to Louis XIV, July 5, 1688. The text of the letter is in *Mémoires du Maréchal Villars* 1 : 419–20.

17. On Leopold's support of Joseph Clemens see Böhmländer, p. 238. The Venetian ambassador noted that "the intense rivalry between the Houses of Bavaria and Neuburg make it necessary for the Court [of Vienna] to proceed with circumspection and dexterity" (Cornaro to the Doge, June 27, 1688, HHSt, *Dispacci dell'Ambasciator Veneto* 164, fol. 115). For Karg's promises, see D'Asfeld to Louvois, July 6, 1688, AG, A¹819; as well as Böhmländer, p. 240.

18. Wilhelm's bodyguard is described in Heiss to Louvois, July 10, 1688 (AG, A¹819). Letters from Wilhelm to Louis XIV on July 7 and 12, 1688, AAE, *Cologne* 40, fols. 152, 162–63; Louis XIV to Wilhelm, July 13, 1688, ibid., fol. 158.

19. Ranuzzi to Rome, July 5, 1688 reports the accusations against Wilhelm (ASV, *Nunz. di Francia* 177, fol. 404). On the letters of naturalization cf. Boizet, *Les Lettres de Naturalité sous l'Ancien Régime*, especially pp. 145–51. The cancellation of the subjection attached to naturalization proceedings is recorded

in AAE, *Petites Principautés* 22: *Principauté de Fürstenberg*, fol. 88. A copy of this nullification may be found in HHSt, *Geistliche Wahlakten*: Cöln, 17a. Louis XIV to Wilhelm, July 14, 1688, AAE, *Cologne* 40, fol. 165.

20. Kaunitz's speech and Fürstenberg's counter-arguments are summarized by Münch in *Geschichte des Hauses und Landes Fürstenberg* 3 : 320–30. The author comments on the farcical aspect of this pious regard for Max Heinrich, especially in light of his relations with the emperor and the notes exchanged between the two in the past (ibid., p. 321). A copy of the major points made by Kaunitz together with Fürstenberg's replies, arranged in parallel columns, was published in Paris shortly after the election: "Response sommaire de S. A. Emme. Mons. le Cardinal Landgrave de Fürstenberg a la proposition que M. le Comte de Kaunitz, Ambassadeur de Sa Majeste Imperiale a faitte a l'Illustrissime et Reverendissime Chapitre de l'Eglise Metropolitaine de Cologne, le 14 de Juillet, 1688" (AAE, *Cologne* 42, fols. 186–92).

21. Böhmländer, p. 243.

22. Braubach, "Das Kölner Domkapitel," pp. 56–58.

23. D'Asfeld to Louvois, July 19, 1688, AG, A^1819, no. 30.

24. Cornaro to the Doge, July 25, 1688, HHSt, *Dispacci dell'Ambasciator Veneto* 164, fol. 155. Böhmländer, "Die Wahl des Herzogs Josef Klemens," *Oberbayerisches Archiv für Vaterländische Geschichte* 57 (1913) : 227. This and subsequent references to Böhmländer's work refer to the second half of his two-part study.

25. Louvois to Le Peletier, July 21, 1688, AG, A^1818, no. 40. Louis XIV to Innocent XI, July 22, 1688, copy in the Fürstl. Fürstenberg. Archiv, Donaueschingen, OB. 19, vol. 21, Fasc. 1, no. 11. Nothing came of this proposal. Louis XIV to Du Heron, July 23, 1688, AAE, *Cologne* 38, fol. 215.

26. Born in 1650, Chamlay rose rapidly in the king's service. He possessed an extensive knowledge of the various theaters of war on the continent and held the office of *Maréchal général des logis des camps et armées du Roi*. For further details, see *Recueil des Instructions* 17: *Rome*, part 2, p. 6 n. 3.

27. The instructions, dated July 6, 1688, are published in the *recueil* cited above, pp. 6–20.

28. Louvois to Louis XIV, July 22, 1688, AG, A^1818. Cf. Rousset, *Histoire de Louvois* 4 : 76–77. Louvois to Le Peletier, July 21, 1688, AG, A^1818.

29. The additional instructions are in the *Recueil des Instructions* 17: *Rome*, pp. 20–24. Louvois to Chamlay, July 23, 1688, AG, A^1806. Louvois's letter is published by Hanoteau in the aforementioned *recueil*, p. 20 n. 2. Cf. Rousset, *Histoire de Louvois* 4 : 78–80. On the same day Louvois predicted that Fürstenberg would last five or six years in office, during which time it was very probable that Joseph Clemens would renounce the religious life and resign from his post at Cologne (Louvois to Le Peletier, July 23, 1688, AG, A^1806, cited by Rousset, *Histoire de Louvois* 4 : 78). Louvois to Louis XIV, July 23, 1688, AG, A^1819.

30. Wilhelm's response to the chapter is in Braubach, "Das Kölner Domkapitel," pp. 91–92.

31. On his entry into Bonn, see Böhmländer, p. 232. The order for the carriages was noted in Ranuzzi to Casoni, August 16, 1688, ASV, *Avvisi* 179, fol. 190.

32. "Copie de l'Union faite entre les Prelats et Chanoines Capitularies de la Metropolitaine de Cologne, qui ont postulé son Emce M. le Cardinal de Fürstenberg pour Archevesque et Electeur de Cologne." This French translation from the German original is in AAE, *Cologne* 42, fols. 456–58. See Böhmländer, p. 233.

33. Wilhelm to Louis XIV, July 23, 1688, AAE, *Cologne* 40, fols. 187–88.

34. "Un altro ha detto che non poteva venir meglio al balzo la palla a Sua Santa et che l'ha giocata egregiamente." Remarks at Versailles cited in Ranuzzi to Casoni, July 26, 1688, ASV, *Nunz. di Francia* 179a, fol. 175.

35. Du Buat to Breget, July 24, 1688, AG, A¹819, no. 43 bis bis; Breget to Louvois, July 27, 1688, AG, A¹819; Louvois to Le Peletier, July 27, 1688, cited by Rousset, *Histoire de Louvois* 4 : 81–82.

36. See Wilhelm's letters to Breget on July 31, 1688 (AAE, *Liège*, supplement no. 3, fol. 337); and August 3, 1688 (AAE, *Cologne* 40, fols. 244–49). Wilhelm to Louis XIV, July 29, 1688, AAE, *Cologne* 40, fols. 235–36. Leibniz doubted that Wilhelm would ever be recognized "in the Empire or in the Electoral College without a great revolution . . . " (cited by Böhmländer, p. 228 n. 1).

CHAPTER XII

1. Rousset, *Histoire de Louvois* 4 : 84–87. Cf. *Recueil des Instructions*: 17, *Rome*, p. 5.

2. Ranuzzi to Innocent XI, September 13, 1688, ASV, *Nunz. di Francia* 177, fol. 444. Cf. Gérin, "Le Pape Innocent XI et La Révolution Anglaise de 1688," pp. 467–68.

3. D'Estrées to Louis XIV, August 10, 1688, AAE, *Rome* 313, fols. 4–33, cited by Michaud, *Louis XIV et Innocent XI* 3 : 174; ASV, *Avvisi* 122, fol. 189; Casoni to Ranuzzi, August 24, 1688, ASV, *Nunz. di Francia* 177, fol. 54.

4. On the political maneuvers prior to the Liège election, see Harsin, *Relations Extérieures de Liège*, pp. 38–39, 41. Meanwhile, at Münster, the French candidate and Fürstenberg's friend, Plettenberg, won the election on August 5. His candidacy was also supported by the Elector of Brandenburg who did not want the Neuburgs as neighbors (Gravel to Du Heron, July 13, 1688, AAE, *Prusse* 35, fols. 164–165).

5. D'Asfeld's mission is found in Louis XIV to d'Asfeld, July 26, 1688, AAE, *Cologne* 40, fols. 230–31. Harsin, *Relations Extérieures de Liège*, p. 44.

6. Ibid., pp. 42, 48–49.

7. Ibid., pp. 51–52.

8. Ibid., pp. 52–53.

9. Ranuzzi to Cibo, August 23, 1688, ASV, *Nunz. di Francia* 177, fols. 428–29. Cf. Wolf, *Emergence of the Great Powers*, pp. 39ff, for the possibility of the Turkish defeat. Louis XIV to Girardin, August 22, 1688, AAE, *Turquie* 20,

cited by Gérin, "Le Pape Innocent XI et l'Election de Cologne," p. 121. The decisions which led to this preventive warfare as well as French miscalculations concerning the effectiveness of the imperial armies are reviewed in an interesting article by Place, "The Self-Deception of the Strong," pp. 459–73.

10. See Durant, "Louis XIV et Jacques II à la veille de la Révolution anglaise de 1688," pp. 192–204. Wolf, *Emergence of the Great Powers*, pp. 41–42.

11. Ranuzzi to Cibo, August 30, 1688, ASV, *Nunz. di Francia* 177, fol. 431.

12. Meyercrone to Christian V, August 20, 1688, cited by Joseph A. Klaits in his master's thesis, "The Idea of a Diplomat in the Age of Louis XIV," pp. 48–49.

13. Ranuzzi to Casoni, August 23, 1688, ASV, *Nunz. di Francia* 177, fol. 427. Croissy's view was shared by many at the court including the king's confessor, Père de la Chaize, who saw Casoni as a member of the most partisan of all "sects," in favor of imperial preponderance in Europe and completely hostile to Louis XIV (Dubruel, "L'Excommunication de Louis XIV," p. 613). Casoni to Ranuzzi, September 14, 1688, ASV, *Nunz. di Francia* 177, fol. 55.

14. Louvois to d'Asfeld, August 19, 1688, AG, A¹819. no. 69 bis; d'Asfeld to Louvois, August 25, 1688, ibid., no. 72 bis bis; d'Asfeld to Louvois, August 26, 1688, ibid., no. 74.

15. Wilhelm to Louvois, August 19, 1688, AG, A¹818; Louvois to Wilhelm, August 21, 1688, AG, A¹819, no. 70 bis.

16. Wilhelm to Louvois, August 27, 1688, AG, A¹818. In deference to Fürstenberg's wishes the king ordered Boufflers to hold back eight to ten days before entering the electorate (Louvois to Boufflers, August 30, 1688, AG, A¹830, no. 17). This order was soon countermanded. Wilhelm to Louvois, August 30, 1688, AG, A¹819, no. 78. For Louvois's defense arrangements, see Louvois to Catinat, August 24, 1688 (AG, A¹830, no. 6). Louvois to d'Asfeld, September 1, 1688, AG, A¹818.

17. AAE, *Cologne* 40, fols. 264–65, 267. The treaty which Wilhelm drafted is dated September 3, 1688, AAE, *Cologne* 42, fols. 290–96. The major points included (1) a renewal of the May 25, 1687 pact "in all points and articles"; (2) as guarantor of the Münster and Nijmegen treaties Louis would protect the chapter and support its postulation of Fürstenberg as elector; (3) at the request of the Dean and the Chapter Louis would send into the electorate 3000 infantrymen and 3000 cavalrymen, to be kept up at French expense; (4) if the pope should die another election would be held; (5) in withdrawing troops no town or fortification would be destroyed; (6) if Fürstenberg should die before his peaceful possession of the archdiocese, the chapter would elect a candidate which met with French approval; (7) the 400,000 livre debt would be remitted in case Fürstenberg or a French-sponsored candidate were elected; (8) the king would promise to protect the thirteen canons loyal to the cardinal. This latter clause, of course, entailed subsidies. Louis did, in fact, give a total of 20,000 écus in pensions to these canons on September 13. (The list is in AAE, *Cologne* 40, fols. 281–82.) But he balked at the idea of indefinitely subsidizing them. On September 28, the king sent the treaty back after having rejected the provision for permanent sub-

sidies (ibid., fols. 332–35). After occupying the electorate, Louis was in a position on November 5 to call off further negotiations on the treaty. He simply asked for their "good will" (ibid., fol. 393).

18. In the promotion of September 2 d'Asfeld was made *maréchal de camp* (Rousset, *Histoire de Louvois* 4 : 88). On September 1 Boufflers reported the Elector of Trier's willingness to let troops cross his territory. (Boufflers to Louvois, September 1, 1688, AG A¹830, no. 20.) The letter to Innocent was dated September 6 and was read to the pope on September 15. See below. Louvois to d'Asfeld, September 5, 1688, AG, A¹819, no. 93 bis; Louvois to Wilhelm, September 6, 1688, AG, A¹818.

19. D'Asfeld to Louvois, September 6, 1688, AG, A¹819, no. 95.

20. Ibid. On the request of the magistrates for troops, see Braubach, "Der Kampf um Kurstaat und Stadt Köln," p. 38. Sourdis to Louvois, September 9, 1688, AG, A¹819, no. 97.

21. Louis's declaration is in AAE, *Cologne* 42, fols. 306–7. For Wilhelm's edict, see Braubach, "Das Kölner Domkapitel und die Wahl von 1688," p. 97. The entry of the troops was in accordance with the above treaty arrangement. The 6000 men were divided into six regiments of cavalry, three of dragoons and fourteen battalions of infantry (Rousset, *Histoire de Louvois* 4 : 89). Another 1000 troops were stationed outside the frontiers of the electorate awaiting further orders. See Böhmländer, p. 245. On the edict of September 12 and subsequent developments, see Braubach, "Das Kölner Domkapitel und die Wahl von 1688," pp. 97–99 and his "Der Kampf um Kurstaat und Stadt Köln," p. 40.

22. The letter to the pope, dated September 6, 1688 (AAE, *Rome* 319, fols. 34ff.), has been published by Mention, *Documents relatifs aux Rapports du Clergé avec la Royauté*, 104. A covering letter of the same date from Louis to d'Estrées is in Gérin, "Le Pape Innocent XI et la Révolution anglaise," p. 451. Gérin has printed d'Estrées's account of this papal audience, ibid., pp. 452–53. His dispatch is dated September 18, 1688 (AAE, *Rome* 315). On the same day, in an audience with the ambassador from Savoy, Innocent was clearly irritated over the clash with France and resolved never to cede the smallest point to France which was not in accord with justice. He told the ambassador that the French sought to intimidate him so that he would confirm Fürstenberg but he declared that he would put up with that and other indignities down to the day of his death. Becoming excited, he exclaimed that the recent imprisonment of domestics attached to the household of Cardinal Ranuzzi in Paris was an action worthy of Turks and barbarians, and whatever the king might do, Christ would defend him from the force at Louis's disposal. (Cited by Barberis, "Il contrasto tra la S. Sede e la Francia nelle relazioni dell'ambasciatore piemontese Marcello Degubernatis (1686–1693)," p. 95.

23. A draft of the brief was in Innocent's possession on September 10, before d'Estrées made his dramatic appearance (Böhmländer, pp. 252–54).

24. Bartoccetti, "Alla corte del Re Sole," p. 109. Cf. Rousset, *Histoire de Louvois* 4 : 91; and Michaud, *Louis XIV et Innocent XI* 3 : 195–200. The king restricted Ranuzzi's freedom of movement and refused to allow him to leave the

kingdom, as requested by the pope. See Gérin, "L'Ambassade de Lavardin et la Séquestration du Nonce Ranuzzi, 1687–1689," pp. 382–432.

25. The text of Louis's declaration may be found in the series of documents edited by Dumont, *Corps Universel diplomatique*, pp. 170–73. Cf. Rousset, *Histoire de Louvois* 4 : 111–14.

26. Sourdis to Louvois, September 14, 1688, AG, A¹819, no. 100; Sourdis to Louvois, September 17, 1688, ibid., no. 105. Wilhelm's anxieties are recorded in d'Asfeld to Louvois, September 21, 1688 (ibid., no. 120). Wilhelm to Louis XIV, October 5, 1688, AAE, *Cologne* 40, fol. 294. The report on Joseph Clemens and on Wilhelm's reaction is in d'Asfeld to Louvois, October 4, 1688 (AG, A¹819, no. 154). D'Asfeld to Louvois, October 9, 1688, ibid., no. 170.

27. Wilhelm to Louis XIV, October 13, 1688, AAE, *Cologne* 40, fol. 318.

28. D'Asfeld to Louvois, October 14, 1688, AG, A¹819, no. 182.

29. Böhmländer, pp. 258–59.

30. The war minister's directive concerning Fürstenberg was referred to in d'Asfeld's letter to Louvois, October 13, 1688 (AG, A¹819, no. 179). Wilhelm to Louvois, October 15, 1688, ibid., no. 187; Louvois to Wilhelm, October 20, 1688, AG, A¹885, no. 58; Wilhelm to Louvois, October 26, 1688, AG, A¹819, no. 196.

31. For a discussion of the terrorist tactics and their effects, see van Houtte, *Les Occupations Etrangères en Belgique sous l'Ancien Régime*, pp. 111–12; as well as Gillot, *Le Règne de Louis XIV et l'Opinion publique en Allemagne*. Wysocki (p. 154) deals with the capitulation of Mainz.

32. Rousset, *Histoire de Louvois* 4 : 141–42.

33. Ibid., pp. 142–43; Boufflers to Louvois, November 11, 1688, AG, A¹827; Louvois to Boufflers, November 14, 1688, AG, A¹812.

34. D'Asfeld to Louvois, November 5, 1688, AG, A¹820, no. 17. The bad weather is described in Heiss to Louvois, November 8, 1688 (ibid., no. 26). Louvois to Wilhelm, December 11, 1688, AG, A¹833, no. 160. On the laborers' work-habits, see Dupas to Louvois, December 20, 1688 (AG, A¹820, no. 140). Wilhelm to Louvois, December 23, 1688, AG, A¹820, no. 157. Louvois to Sourdis, December 23, 1688, AG, A¹833, no. 170.

35. Braubach, "Das Kölner Domkapitel und die Wahl von 1688," pp. 105–6.

36. Wilhelm to Louvois, March 14, 1689, AG, A¹890, no. 191. Louis XIV to Wilhelm, March 24, 1689, AAE, *Cologne* 43, fol. 182. The king also ordered Du Heron to return to Versailles in a letter of the same date (ibid., fol. 190). Fürstenberg was not happy with this, but the king confirmed his decision in a letter to the envoy on March 31, 1689 (ibid., fol. 203).

37. Details of Wilhelm's entourage are included in his letter to Louvois on April 1, 1689 (AG, A¹889, no. 3). D'Asfeld to Louvois, April 6, 1689, ibid., no. 15; the phrase "negotiator out of season" occurs in Wilhelm's dispatch to Louvois on May 18, 1689 (ibid., no. 107) when he says that he would not want "pour ainsi dire passer dans vostre esprit pour un négotiateur hors de saison." On the burning of the house in Metz, see Braubach, "Das Kölner Domkapitel und die Wahl von 1688," pp. 113–14.

38. Ibid., pp. 110–11.

39. Givry to Louvois, June 24, 1689, AG, A¹886, no. 147; Braubach, "Das Kölner Domkapitel und die Wahl von 1688," p. 114.

40. AG, A¹832. *Mémoires historiques*: Allemagne, 1688–1697, Mss. 57³.

CHAPTER XIII

1. Chaulnes to Louis XIV, September 9, 1689, AAE, *Rome* 323, fol. 50.

2. Chaulnes to Louis XIV, September 28, 1689, ibid., fol. 98; Louis XIV to Chaulnes, October 3, 1689, ibid., fol. 63.

3. "Abrégé de la Vie de M. le Marquis de Torcy écrite par Mme la marquise d'Ancezune, sa fille," p. 194.

4. Ibid., p. 197.

5. Chaulnes to Louis XIV, October 7, 1689, AAE, *Rome* 323, fol. 170.

6. The request for the money is in Wilhelm to Louis XIV, October 7, 1689 (ibid., fols. 178–81). Louis XIV to Wilhelm, October 20, 1689, ibid., fols. 182–83. Wilhelm had already received a hat from Louis XIV at the beginning of 1687. This was a special privilege extended to monarchs; it did not eliminate the official papal ceremony except where grave illness or inconvenience prohibited it. Louis XIV to Chaulnes, October 20, 1689, ibid., fol. 205.

7. Chaulnes to Louis XIV, November 5, 1689, ibid., fols. 286–87; Chaulnes to Louis XIV, November 10, 1689, ibid., fol. 330.

8. Chaulnes to Louis XIV, November 16, 1689, ibid., fol. 341.

9. Chaulnes to Louis XIV, November 5, 1689, ibid., fol. 287.

10. Foucher to Louis XIV, November 25, 1689, AAE, *Toscane* 15, fols. 328–35; Chaulnes to Louis XIV, November 26, 1689, AAE, *Rome* 323, fols. 360–61; Wilhelm to Louis XIV, December 3, 1689, ibid., fol. 372.

11. See *Recueil des Instructions* 20: *Rome*, part 3, p. 165 n. 2.

12. For the perquisites to Wilhelm's appointment see Moisse-Daxhelet, "Guillaume-Egon, Prince de Fürstenberg," p. 371. Reference to the fire is in Ennen, "Franz Egon und Wilhelm Egon von Fürstenberg," p. 306.

13. Bouillart, *Histoire de l'Abbaye Royale de Saint Germain des Prez*, pp. 286, 292, gives the account of his activities. Among many examples of the letters he wrote one can cite Wilhelm's letter in behalf of Mabillon on August 16, 1696 (Bibliothèque Nationale, Mss. Francais 19652, fols. 378–80). Characteristically, the work of restoring the palace was done at small cost to himself. He sold some land to private parties who in addition had to pay a collective sum of 25,000 livres which was earmarked for the repair cost (cf. Bouillart, pp. 294–95). For a sympathetic, though brief, account of these later years, see de Broglie, *Mabillon et la Société de l'Abbaye de Saint-Germain-des-Prés*, pp. 205ff.

14. Moisse-Daxhelet, "Guillaume-Egon, Prince de Fürstenberg," p. 372.

15. Saint-Simon, *Mémoires* 7 : 88. Typical letters from Fürstenberg to the controller-general in which he asked for money are published in ibid., appendix

7, pp. 470–76. For the ties with Dangeau, cf. Mathorez, *Les Etrangers en France sous l'Ancien Régime* 2 : 110.

16. On Wilhelm's contacts with Kollonitsch, see Braubach, *Versailles und Wien*, p. 15. As an example of his counsel, Wilhelm submitted two memorandums to the king in September 1696, dealing with the peace negotiations in progress. A covering letter for these is in AAE, *Alsace* 27, fol. 148.

17. Huisman, p. 189.

18. Wilhelm to Louis XIV, August 5, 1697, AAE, *Alsace* 27, fol. 174.

19. This memorandum, simply dated 1697, is in AAE, *Cologne* 45, fol. 273.

20. Bouillart, p. 293.

21. For Article 44 see Vast, *Les Grands Traités du Règne de Louis XIV* 2 : 246–47. Moisse-Daxhelet, "Guillaume-Egon, Prince de Fürstenberg," p. 372.

22. Concerning the Strasbourg bishopric, see Chapter 6, pp. 100–101. The lampoonist is cited in Gillot, *Le Règne de Louis XIV et l'Opinion publique en Allemagne*, p. 112.

23. Melani to Buonvisi, February 22, 1700, cited in Trenta, *Memorie per servire alla Storia politica del Cardinale Francesco Buonvisi Patrizio Lucchese*, 2: 266.

24. Ibid., pp. 148–55, 263–68.

25. Saint-Simon, *Mémoires* 7 : 86–87.

26. Bibliothèque Nationale, Mss. Clairambault 287, fol. 458.

27. Moisse-Daxhelet, "Guillaume-Egon, Prince de Fürstenberg," p. 352.

28. Fischer, *Le Conseil de la Régence de l'Evêché de Strasbourg*, pp. 14–15.

29. Reuss, *L'Alsace au Dix-Septième Siècle* 2 : 414; and Moisse-Daxhelet, "Guillaume-Egon, Prince de Fürstenberg," pp. 356–57.

30. Moisse-Daxhelet, *La Principauté de Stavelot-Malmédy*, pp. 80–84, 86–93, and 121–22.

31. Ibid., p. 99.

32. Ibid., pp. 155–76.

33. Ibid., pp. 177–205.

34. Ibid., p. 212.

35. Moisse-Daxhelet, "Guillaume-Egon, Prince de Fürstenberg," p. 360.

36. Ibid., p. 353. For details on the transference of the Strasbourg bishopric, see Metz, "L'Accession du Premier Rohan à l'Evêché de Strasbourg," pp. 227–40.

37. Cf. Metz, "Les Fürstenberg et les Rohan Princes-Evêques de Strasbourg au Service de la Cause française en Alsace," pp. 73–76.

38. Bibliothèque Nationale, Fond Italien 368, fol. 152.

39. Saint-Simon, *Mémoires* 7 : 88.

40. For an illustration of the tomb, see Bouillart, plate no. 23, facing p. 292. After Wilhelm's death, the countess occupied herself with paying his and her own debts. "God touched her," said Saint-Simon. She retired to La Bourdaisière where she practiced good works and austere penitence and gave a great deal to the poor. She died there on April 5, 1726. (Saint-Simon, *Mémoires* 7: appendix 7, p. 469.)

CHAPTER XIV

1. Saint-Simon, *Mémoires* 12 : 52–53.

2. Le Prevost, *Oraison Funèbre de Tres-Haut et Tres-Puissant Prince Guillaume-Egon de Fürstemberg*, pp. 5–6.

3. Ibid., pp. 14–15. The latter allusion refers to the Kollonitsch-Fürstenberg correspondence in 1692–93.

4. There were many rumors that Wilhelm had ghost-written the *Political Testament of Charles V of Lorraine*. Charles's biographer makes clear that the real author was a Lorraine priest born in England, Abbé Jean Baptiste Chèvremont. (See Wentzcke, *Feldherr des Kaisers*, p. 355.)

5. Bibliothèque Nationale, Mss. Clairambault 287, fol. 457.

6. Immich, *Papst Innocenz XI*, p. 2.

7. Tapié, "Aspects de la méthode de Louis XIV en politique étrangère," p. 24. The king's special interest in the kind of reports which Wilhelm submitted is implied in the following commentary by Hatton: "Foreign policy problems of a weighty kind . . . loomed large throughout Louis' reign. They were, in any event, those with which, because of the secrecy necessary in negotiations, rulers in all countries were particularly concerned; and in Louis' case they especially suited his temperament and gifts. He was prudent by nature, liked to speculate on the 'interests' of the European states and had a special affinity for negotiations built on meticulous and lengthy reports from a diplomatic corps which was better organized than most." (*Louis XIV and His World*, p. 87.)

8. Mandrou, *La France aux XVIIe et XVIIIe Siècles*, p. 297.

BIBLIOGRAPHY

ARCHIVAL SOURCES

1. Archives des Affaires Etrangères, Paris (AAE):

Correspondance Politique

Allemagne	141	1658
	270 bis	1674
	286	1680 (Suppl.)
Autriche	23	1665–1667
	26	1667 (Jan.–June)
Bavière	39	1687–1688 (Feb.–Jan.)
	40	1688 (Jan.–July)
	41	1688
	Supplement 1	1156–1686
	Supplement 2	1687–1714
Cologne	2	1647–1659
	3	1660–1666
	4	1667
	5	1667–1668
	6	1668–1670
	7	1671
	8	1672 (Jan.–May)
	9	1672 (June–Dec.)
	10	1673 (Jan.–April)
	11	1673 (May–Dec.)
	12	1674–1675
	13	1676–1678
	14	1679
	15	1680 (Jan.–June)
	16	1680 (July–Dec.)
	17	1679–1682
	18	1681
	19	1681 (July–Dec.)
	20	1682
	21	1682 (July–Dec.)
	22	1682–1683

	23	1683 (March–July)
	24	1683 (July–Dec.)
	25	1683–1684
	26	1684 (March–Sept.)
	27	1684 (Jan.–Sept.)
	28	1684
	29	1685
	30	1685–1688
	31	1685–1688
	32	1685–1686 (Feb.–June)
	33	1686–1687 (July–June)
	34	1687 (June–Dec.)
	35	1685–1688
	36	1687–1688 (June)
	37	1688 (Jan.–June)
	38	1688 (March–July)
	39	1688 (Aug.–Dec.)
	40	1688
	41	1688
	42	1688 (Suppl.)
	43	1688–1689
	44	1689 (Suppl.)
	45	1690–1697
	Supplement 1	1611–1687
	Supplement 2	1688–1736
Liège	14	1681–1689
	15	1688–1689
	Supplement 1	1154–1688
	Supplement 2	1542–1777
	Supplement 3	1680–1689
	Supplement 4	1689–1729
Mayence	24	1685
	25	1686
	26	1687
	27	1688
Münster	6	1683
Rome	302	1686–1687
	323	1689 (Sept.–Dec.)
Toscane	15	1689–1690
Trèves	4	1660–1686
	5	1687–1700
Turquie	18	1686–1687

	19	1687
	20	1688
Mémoires et Documents		
France	301	1684–1685
	302	1686–1687
	303	1687–1691
	415	1657
	416	1667
	1440	1681
Alsace	24	1680–1681
	27	1681–1697
Petites Principautés	22	Principauté de Fürstenberg

2. Archives du Ministère de la Guerre, Vincennes (AG):

Series A[1]		
	280	1672
	633	1679–1681
	649	1680
	663	1681
	668	1681
	714	1683–1684
	724	1683–1684
	729	1684
	793	1685–1687
	799	1687–1688
	806	1688 (July)
	818	1688
	819	1688 (June–Oct.)
	820	1688
	827	1688
	830	1688
	832	1688–1697
	833	1688
	885	1688–1689
	886	1689
	889	1689
	890	1689

3. Bibliothèque Nationale, Paris:

Manuscrits	
Mss Clairambault	287
Mss Français	19652
Fond Italien	368

4. Archives Nationales, Paris:

Correspondance Consulaire
AE B¹   955   Rome 1685–1690

5. Bibliothèque de l'Arsenal, Paris:

Pièce 710, Ms. 6038 "Lettre du Roy a ses Ambassadeurs et a ses Ministres chez les Princes Etrangers, sur l'Enlevement du Serenissime Prince Guillaume de Furstenberg." Paris, 1674.

6. Archivio Segreto Vaticano, Vatican City (ASV):

Avvisi	50	1686–1687
	122	1688
	124	1688
Nunziatura di Colonia	60	1685–1688 (ciphered correspondence)
	64	1687
	223	1687–1692
	301	1656–1747
Nunziatura di Francia	176	1687
	177	1687–1689 (ciphered correspondence)
	179a	1683–1689
Nunziatura di Germania	39	1687–1692
	209	1687–1688
	213	1687
	214	1688
Memoriali e Biglietti diversi	19	1686–1690
Lettere de Cardinale	50	1686
	51	1687
	52	1688

7. Haus,-Hof-und-Staatsarchiv, Vienna (HHSt):

Geistliche Wahlakten
17a   Cöln   1547–1688

Dispacci dell'Ambasciator Veneto in Germania (Copies from originals in Venice):

	152	1679–1680 (March–Feb.)
	160	1684–1685 (Aug.–May)
	161	1685–1686 (March–Feb.)
	162	1686 (March–Dec.)
	163	1686–1688 (Dec.–April)
	164	1688 (April–July)

8. Fürstl. Fürstenb. Archiv, Donaueschingen:

OB. 19. V. XXI.

9. Archivio di Stato in Lucca (ASL):

Archivio Arnolfini	110	16th through 18th centuries
Archivio Buonvisi	24	1688
	57	1681–1689
	58	1682–1689
	59	1685–1689
	66	1659–1700

PRIMARY SOURCES

"Abrégé de la Vie de M. le Marquis de Torcy écrite par Mme la marquise d'Ancezune, sa fille." *Revue d'Histoire Diplomatique* 47 (1933) : 51–76, 189–214.

Avaux, Jean Antoine, Comte de. *Négociations en Hollande, 1679–1688*, vol. 5. Paris, 1752.

Bittner, Ludwig and Lothar Gross. *Repertorium der diplomatischen Vertreter aller Länder seit der Westfälischen Frieden*, vol. 1 (1648–1715). Berlin, 1936.

Dangeau, Philippe, Marquis de. *Journal de la Cour de Louis XIV*, vol. 2. Edited by Soulié, Dussieux, and Feuillet de Conches. Paris, 1854.

Dumont, Jean. *Corps Universel diplomatique du Droit des Gens contenant un Recueil des Traitez d'Alliances de Paix, de Trêve etc.*, vol. 3. Amsterdam, 1731.

———. *Mémoires politiques pour servir à la parfaite intelligence de l'Histoire de la Paix de Ryswick*, vol. 3. The Hague, 1699.

Estrades, Comte de. *Lettres, Mémoires et Négociations de Monsieur le Comte d'Estrades, 1663–1668*, vol. 3. Brussels, 1709.

Gramont, Maréchal de. *Mémoires du Maréchal de Gramont, 2e Partie*. In *Mémoires pour servir à l'Histoire de France*, vol. 7. Edited by Michaud and Poujoulat. Paris, 1839.

Immich, Max. *Zur Vorgeschichte des Orleans'schen Krieges, Nuntiaturberichte aus Wien und Paris, 1685–1688*. Heidelberg, 1898.

Inventaire Analytique de Documents Relatifs à l'Histoire du Diocèse de Liège sous le Régime des Nonces de Cologne (1679–1687), part 2. Edited by Jean Hoyoux. Brussels and Rome, 1965.

Le Prevost, Pierre-Robert, abbé. *Oraison Funèbre de Tres-Haut et Tres-Puissant Prince Guillaume-Egon de Furstemberg, Cardinal de la Sainte Eglise Romaine, Evesque et Prince de Strasbourg, Landgrave d'Alsace, Administrateur et Prince de Stavelot & Malmédy, Abbé de l'Abbaye Royalle de S. Germain des Pres, Commandeur des Ordres du Roy. Prononcée dans l'Eglise de l'Abbaye Royalle de S. Germain des Pres le 5e jour de Juin 1704 par M. l'Abbé Le Prevost*. Paris, 1705.

Lisola, Baron Franz Paul von. *Détention de Guillaume Prince de Fürstenberg.* Amsterdam, 1674.

Londorp, Michael Caspar. *Der Römischen Kayserlichen Majestät und des Heiligen Römischen Reiches. . . . Acta Publica,* vol. 11. Frankfurt, 1710.

Louis XIV. *Mémoires for the Instruction of the Dauphin.* Translated by Paul Sonnino. New York, 1970.

Mazarin, Cardinal de. *Lettres du Cardinal Mazarin pendant son Ministère,* vols. 7–9. Edited by G. d'Avenel. Paris, 1906.

Mention, Léon, ed. *Documents relatifs aux Rapports du Clergé avec la Royauté,* vol. 1. Paris, 1893.

Mignet, M. *Négociations relatives à la Succession d'Espagne sous Louis XIV,* vols. 1–4. Paris, 1842.

Montpensier, Mademoiselle de. *Mémoires de Mademoiselle de Montpensier* in *Nouvelle Collection des Mémoires relatifs à l'Histoire de France,* vol. 28. Edited by Michaud and Poujoulat. Paris, 1857.

Pomponne, Simon Arnauld, Marquis de. *Mémoires du Marquis de Pomponne,* vol. 1. Paris, 1868.

Ranuzzi, Angelo. *Correspondance du Nonce en France Angelo Ranuzzi (1683–1689).* Edited by Bruno Neveu. 2 vols. Rome, 1973.

Recueil des Instructions données aux Ambassadeurs et Ministres de France depuis les Traités de Westphalie jusqu'à la Révolution française:
Vol. 1, *Autriche.* Edited by A. Sorel. Paris, 1884.
Vol. 2, *Rome* (Part I). Edited by G. Hanotaux. Paris, 1888.
Vol. 7, *Bavière, Palatinat, Deux-Ponts.* Edited by A. Lebon. Paris, 1889.
Vol. 16, *Prusse.* Edited by A. Waddington. Paris, 1901.
Vol. 17, *Rome* (Part II). Edited by J. Hanoteau. Paris, 1911.
Vol. 18, *Diète germanique.* Edited by B. Auerbach. Paris, 1912.
Vol. 28, *Etats Allemands, I: Electorat de Mayence.* Edited by G. Livet. Paris, 1962.
Vol. 28, *Etats Allemands, II: Electorat de Cologne.* Edited by G. Livet. Paris, 1963.

Saint-Simon. *Mémoires,* vols. 3, 7 and 12. Edited by A. de Boislisle. Paris, 1890.

Sourches, Marquis de. *Mémoires secrets et inédits de la Cour de France sur la Fin du Règne de Louis XIV,* vol. 1. Edited by Cosnac, Bertrand, and Pontal. Paris, 1882.

Temple, Sir William. *Works of Sir William Temple,* vol. 2. London, 1757.

Urkunden und Actenstücke zur Geschichte des Kürfursten Friedrich Wilhelm von Brandenburg:
2 : 1 *(Frankreich).* Edited by B. Simson. Berlin, 1865.
11 : 7 *(Politische Verhandlungen).* Edited by Ferdinand Hirsch. Berlin, 1887.

Valkenier, Petrus. *Das verwirrte Europa,* vol. 1. Amsterdam, 1677.

Vast, Henri. *Les Grands Traités du Règne de Louis XIV,* vols. 1 and 2. Paris, 1898.

Villars, Claude, Maréchal de. *Mémoires du Maréchal de Villars,* vol. 1. Published by the Marquis de Vogüé. Paris, 1884.

SECONDARY WORKS

André, Louis. *Louis XIV et l'Europe*. Paris, 1950.

Angermeier, Heinz. "Die Reichskriegsverfassung in der Politik der Jahre 1679–1681." *Zeitschrift der Savigny-Stiftung für Rechtsgeschichte* 82, Germanistische Abteilung (1965) : 190–222.

Aude, A. F. *Vie publique et privée d'André de Béthoulat Comte de La Vauguyon, 1630–1693*. Paris, 1921.

Auerbach, Bertrand. *La France et le Saint Empire Romain Germanique*. Paris, 1912.

Badalo-Dulong, Claude. *Trente Ans de la Diplomatie française en Allemagne, 1648–1678*. Paris, 1956.

Balan, S. "Le Cardinal de Fürstenberg et ses Héritiers; Seigneurs de Modave, 1684–1706." *Bulletin de la Société d'Art et d'Histoire du Diocèse de Liège* 8 (1894) : 108–14.

Barberis, L. "Il contrasto tra la S. Sede e la Francia nelle relazioni dell'ambasciatore piemontese Marcello Degubernatis (1686–1693)." *Bollettino storico-bibliografico subalpino* 33 (1931) : 77–106.

Barker, Thomas M. *Double Eagle and Crescent: Vienna's Second Turkish Siege and its Historical Setting*. Albany, N.Y., 1967.

Bartoccetti, Vittorio. "Alla corte del Re Sole. La vicende del card. Angelo Ranuzzi, vescovo di Fano, nuncio a Parigi negli anni 1687–89." *Studia Picena* 8 (1932) : 103–41.

Batiffol, Louis. "Les Difficultés de Louis XIV avec les Alsaciens." *La Revue de Paris* 37, part 2 (1930) : 564–93, 843–71.

Bérenger, Jean. "Charles Colbert, Marquis de Croissy" in Roland Mousnier et al., *Le Conseil du Roi de Louis XII à la Révolution* (Paris, 1970), pp. 152–74.

———. "Les relations franco-hongroises pendant le règne personnel de Louis XIV." *Information Historique*, no. 3 (1967), pp. 101–7.

———. "Une Tentative de Rapprochement entre la France et l'Empereur: Le Traité de Partage secret de la Succession d'Espagne du 19 Janvier 1668." *Revue d'Histoire Diplomatique* 79 (1965) : 291–314.

Biaudet, Henry. "Les Nonciatures apostoliques permanentes jusqu'en 1648." *Annales Academiae scientarum Fennicae* (Helsinki, 1910), series B, vol. 2, no. 1, pp. 1–92.

Blet, Pierre. *Les Assemblées du Clergé et Louis XIV de 1670 à 1693*. Rome, 1972.

———. "Innocent XI et l'Assemblée du Clergé de France de 1682. La Rédaction du Bref 'Paternae Charitati.'" *Archivum Historiae Pontificiae* 7 (1969) : 327–377.

———. "Louis XIV et le Saint Siège à la lumière de deux publications récentes." *Archivum Historiae Pontificiae* 12 (1974) : 309–37.

Böhmer, Hans. "Forschungen zur französischen Bundnispolitik im 17. Jahrhundert: Wilhelm Egon von Fürstenberg und die französische Diplomatie in Deutschland, 1668–1672." *Rhein. Vierteljahrsblätter* 4 (1934) : 225–59.

Böhmländer, Ernst. "Die Wahl des Herzogs Joseph Klemens von Bayern zum Erzbischof von Cöln 1688." *Oberbayerisches Archiv für Vaterländische Geschichte* 56 (1912) : 185–249 and 57 (1913) : 244–84.

Boizet, Jacques. *Les Lettres de Naturalité sous l'Ancien Régime.* Paris, 1943.

Bojani, Ferdinando de. "L'Affaire du 'Quartier' à Rome à la Fin du Dix-Septième Siècle: Louis XIV et le Saint-Siège." *Revue d'Histoire Diplomatique* 22 (1908) : 350–78.

Bouillart, Jacques. *Histoire de l'Abbaye Royale de Saint Germain des Prez.* Paris, 1724.

Braubach, Max. "Geheime Friedenshandlungen am Niederrhein 1711–12." *Düsseldorfer Jahrbuch* 44 (1947) : 189–209.

———. "Der Kampf um Kurstaat und Stadt Köln in den Jahren 1688–89." *Annalen des Historischen Vereins für den Niederrhein* 124 (1934) : 25–94.

———. "Das Kölner Domkapitel und die Wahl von 1688." *Annalen des Historischen Vereins für den Niederrhein* 122 (1933) : 51–117.

———. *Kurköln: Gestalten und Ereignisse aus zwei Jahrhunderten rheinischer Geschichte.* Münster, 1949.

———. "Minister und Kanzler, Konferenz und Kabinett in Kurköln im 17. und 18. Jahrhundert." *Annalen des Historischen Vereins für den Niederrhein* 144–145 (1946–47) : 141–209.

———. *Versailles und Wien von Ludwig XIV. bis Kaunitz, Die Vorstadien der diplomatischen Revolution im 18. Jahrhundert.* Bonn, 1952.

———. *Wilhelm von Fürstenberg (1629–1704) und die französische Politik im Zeitalter Ludwigs XIV.* Bonn, 1972.

Broglie, Emmanuel de. *Mabillon et la Société de l'Abbaye de Saint-Germain-des-Prés*, vol. 2. Paris, 1888.

Carsten, F. L. *Princes and Parliaments in Germany.* Oxford, 1959.

Chatellier, Louis. "Frontière politique et frontière religieuse. L'exemple du diocèse de Strasbourg, 1648–1790." *Etudes Européennes. Mélanges offerts à Victor-Lucien Tapié*, Etudes, vol. 6, Publications de la Sorbonne (Paris, 1973), pp. 149–70.

Chéruel, A. *Histoire de France sous le Ministère de Mazarin, 1651–1661*, vol. 3. Paris, 1882.

Cialdea, Basilio. *Gli Stati Italiani e la Pace dei Pirenei. Saggio sulla Diplomazia Seicentesca.* Milan, 1961.

Contessa, Carlo. *Per la Storia di un episodio della Politica Italiana di Luigi XIV al tempo dalla Pace di Nimega: Le Negoziationi diplomatiche per l'Occupazione di Casale, 1677–1682.* Alessandria, 1897.

Coste, A. *Réunion de Strasbourg à la France.* Strasbourg, 1841.

Daxhelet, Geneviève. "La postulation du prince Guillaume-Egon de Fürstenberg à l'administration de Stavelot-Malmédy." *Académie Royale de Belgique: Bulletin de la Commission Royale d'Histoire* 129 (1963) : 1–50. See Moisse-Daxhelet, Geneviève.

Dickmann, Fritz. "Der Westfälische Friede und die Reichsverfassung." *For-*

schungen und Studien zur Geschichte des Westfälischer Friedens (Münster, 1965), pp. 5–32.

———. *Der Westfälische Frieden*. Münster, 1959.

Dirr, Pius. *Zur Geschichte der Reichskriegsverfassung und der Laxenburger Allianz*. Munich, 1901.

Döberl, M. *Bayern und Frankreich, vornehmlich unter Kurfürst Ferdinand Maria*. 2 vols. Munich, 1900.

Dubruel, Marc. "La correspondance confidentielle du cardinal Carlo Pio avec l'empereur Léopold Ier. Le pontificat d'Innocent XI et le rôle politique du cardinal Pio (1676–1689)." *Revue des Questions Historiques* 75 (1904) : 602–8.

———. *En plein Conflit. La Nonciature de France, la Secrétairerie d'Etat du Vatican, les Congrégations des Affaires de France pendant la Querelle de la Régale (1674–1694). Etude des Archives Romaines*. Paris, 1927.

———. "L'Excommunication de Louis XIV." *Les Etudes* 137 (1913) ; 608–35.

Durant, R. "Louis XIV et Jacques II à la veille de a Révolution anglaise de 1688: Les trois missions de Bonrepaus en Angleterre." *Revue d'Histoire moderne et contemporaine* 10 (1908) : 28–44, 111–26, 192–204.

Ekberg, Carl J. "From Dutch to European War: Louis XIV and Louvois Are Tested." *French Historical Studies* 8 (Spring, 1974) : 393–408.

Elbern, Victor H. "Die Rubensteppiche des Kölner Domes. Ihre Geschichte und ihre Stellung im Zyklus 'Triumph des Eucharistie.'" *Kölner Domblatt* 10 (1955) : 43–88.

Engels, Wilhelm. "Aus den Anfängen fürstenbergischer Politik in Kurköln." *Spiegel der Geschichte: Festgabe für Max Braubach*. Edited by Konrad Repgen and Stephan Skalweit (Münster, 1964), pp. 478–500.

Ennen, L. *Frankreich und der Niederrhein oder Geschichte von Stadt und Kurstaat Köln seit dem 30 jahrigen Kriege bis zur französischen Occupation*, vol. 1. Cologne and Neuss, 1855.

———. "Franz Egon und Wilhelm Egon von Fürstenberg." *Allgemeine Deutsche Biographie*, vol. 7. Leipzig, 1878.

———. *Der Spanische Erbfolgekrieg*. Jena, 1851.

Fabre, Antonin. *De la Correspondance de Fléchier avec Madame des Houlières et sa Fille*. Paris, 1871.

Feine, Hans Erich. *Die Besetzung der Reichsbistumer vom Westfälischen Frieden bis zur Säkularisation, 1648–1803*. Stuttgart, 1921.

———. "Zur Verfassungsentwicklung des Heil. Röm. Reiches seit dem Westfälischen Frieden." *Zeitschrift des Savigny-Stiftung für Rechtsgeschichte*, Germanistische Abteilung 52 (1932) : 65–123.

Fester, Richard, *Die Armirten Stände und die Reichskriegsverfassung, 1681–1697*. Frankfurt, 1886.

———. *Die Augsburger Allianz von 1686*. Munich, 1893.

Fieffé, Eugène. *Histoire des Troupes Etrangères au Service de France*. Paris, 1854.

Fischer, Dagobert. *Le Conseil de la Régence de l'Evêché de Strasbourg.* Colmar, 1865.

———. "Soumission de l'Evêque de Strasbourg François-Egon de Fürstenberg à la Couronne de France." *Revue d'Alsace-Lorraine* 18 (1867) : 512–18.

Ford, Franklin L. *Strasbourg in Transition, 1648–1789.* Cambridge, Mass., 1958.

Fraknoi, M. *Innocenzo XI e la Liberazione dell'Ungheria.* Florence, 1903.

Franken, M.A.M. *Coenraad Van Beuningen's Politieke en Diplomatieke Aktiviteiten in de Jaren 1667–1684.* Groningen, 1966.

Franzen, August. "Drei Informativprozesse anlässlich der Bischofsweihen des Kölner Weihbischofs Georg Paul Stravius und der Strassburger Bischöfe Franz Egon und Wilhelm Egon von Fürstenberg. Ein Beitrag zur rheinischer Kirchengeschichte des 17. Jahrhunderts." *Annalen des Historischen Vereins für den Niederrhein* 155/156 (1954) : 320–72.

———. "Französische Politik und Kurkölns Beziehungen zu Frankreich unter Erzbischof Max Heinrich (1650–1688) in römischer Sicht." *Römische Quartalschrift für Christliche Altertumskunde und Kirchengeschichte* 52 (1957) : 169–210.

———. "Eine Krise der Deutschen Kirche im 17. Jahrhundert?" *Römische Quartalschrift für Christliche Altertumskunde und Kirchengeschichte* 49 (1954) : 56–111.

Gauthiez, Pierre. *Jean des Bandes Noires, 1498–1526.* Paris, 1901.

Gérin, Charles. "L'Ambassade de Lavardin et la Séquestration du Nonce Ranuzzi." *Revue des Questions Historiques* 16 (1874) : 382–432.

———. "Le Pape Innocent XI et l'Election de Cologne en 1688." *Revue des Questions Historiques* 33 (1883) : 76–127.

———. "Le Pape Innocent XI et la Révolution Anglaise de 1688." *Revue des Questions Historiques* 20 (1876) : 427–81.

———. "Le Pape Innocent XI et le Siège de Vienne en 1683." *Revue des Questions Historiques* 39 (1886) : 95–147.

Gie, S.F.N. "Die Kandidatur Ludwigs XIV. bei der Kaiserwahl vom Jahre 1658 mit besonderer Berücksichtigung der Vorgeschichte." *Abhandlungen zur mittleren und neueren Geschichte* 61 (1916) : 1–108.

Gillot, Hubert. *Le Règne de Louis XIV et l'Opinion publique en Allemagne.* Paris, 1914.

Girard d'Albissin, Nelly. *Genèse de la Frontière Franco-Belge: Les variations des limites septentrionales de la France de 1659 à 1789.* Bibliothèque de la Société d'Histoire du Droit des Pays Flamands, Picards et Wallons, vol. 26. Paris, 1970.

Göhring, Martin. "Kaiserwahl und Rheinbund von 1658. Ein Hohepunkt des Kampfes zwischen Habsburg und Bourbon um die Beherrschung des Reiches in geschichtlichen Kräften und Entscheidungen." *Festschrift zum 65. Geburtstag von Otto Becker* (Wiesbaden, 1954), pp. 65–83.

Govaerts, J. "La Nonciature de Mgr. Tanara à Cologne (1687–1690)." *Léodi-*

um: Chronique Mensuelle de la Société d'Art et d'Histoire du Diocèse de Liège 17 (1924) : 73–80; 85–91.

Greenidge, A.H.J. "The Conception of Treason in Roman Law." *Juridicial Review* 7 (1895) : 228–40.

Grimmelshausen, H.J.C. von. *The Adventurous Simplicissimus*, book 1. Translated by A.T.S. Goodrich. Lincoln, Nebraska, 1965.

Gross, Hans. *Empire and Sovereignty: A History of the Public Law Literature in the Holy Roman Empire, 1599–1804.* Chicago, 1973; Midway Reprint, 1975.

Guitton, Georges, "Le Père de La Chaize et la 'Feuille des Bénéfices.'" *Revue d'Histoire de l'Eglise de France* 42 (1956) : 29–47.

Harsin, Paul. "Esquisse de la Politique de la France à l'égard de la Principauté de Liège, particulièrement au XVIIe Siècle." *Revue d'Histoire Moderne* 2 (1927) : 99–128.

———. *Les Relations extérieures de la Principauté de Liège sous Jean-Louis d'Elderen et Joseph-Clement de Bavière, 1688–1718.* Liège and Paris, 1927.

Hatton, Ragnhild M. "Gratifications and Foreign Policy: Anglo-French Rivalry in Sweden during the Nine Years War." *William III and Louis XIV: Essays by and for Mark A. Thomson, 1688–1728.* Edited by R. Hatton and J. S. Bromley (Liverpool, 1968), pp. 68–94.

———. *Louis XIV and His World.* New York, 1972.

Hölscher, Karl. *Die öffentliche Meinung in Deutschland über den Fall Strassburgs während der Jahre 1681 bis 1684.* Munich, 1896.

Houtte, Hubert van. *Les Occupations Etrangères en Belgique sous l'Ancien Régime*, vol. 1. Ghent and Paris, 1930.

Höynck, Paul O. *Frankreich und seine Gegner auf dem Nymwegener Friedenskongress.* Bonn, 1960.

Huisman, M. *Essai sur le Régne du Prince-Evêque de Liège, Maximilien-Henri de Bavière.* Brussels, 1899.

Immich, Max. *Geschichte des europäischen Staatensystems von 1660 bis 1789.* Munich, Berlin, 1905.

———. *Papst Innocenz XI.* Berlin, 1900.

Jannen, William, Jr. "'Das liebe Teutschland' in the Seventeenth Century—Count George Frederick von Waldeck." *European Studies Review* 6, no. 2 (April 1976) : 165–95.

Joachim, Erich. *Die Entwickelung des Rheinbundes vom Jahre 1658.* Leipzig, 1886.

Junkers, Karl. *Der Streit zwischen Kurstaat und Staat Köln am Vorabend des Holländischen Krieges, 1667–1672.* Düsseldorf, 1935.

Just, Leo. "Die Quellen zur Geschichte des Kölner Nuntiatur in Archiv und Bibliothek des Vatikans." *Quellen und Forschungen aus italienischen Archiven und Bibliotheken* 29 (1938–39) : 249–96.

Keinemann, Friedrich. *Das Domkapitel zu Münster im 18. Jahrhundert.* Geschichtliche Arbeiten zur westfälischen Landesforschung, vol. 2. Münster, 1967.

Klaits, Joseph A. "The Idea of a Diplomat in the Age of Louis XIV: The Danish Envoy Extraordinary to France, 1688." Master's thesis, University of Minnesota, 1966.

Köcher, Adolf. *Geschichte von Hannover und Braunschweig, 1648 bis 1714.* 2 vols. Leipzig, 1895.

Kohl, Wilhelm. *Christoph Bernhard von Galen. Politische Geschichte des Fürstbistums Münster, 1650–1678.* Münster, 1964.

Kuckhoff, Josef. *Die Geschichte des Gymnasium Tricoronatum.* Cologne, 1931.

Latreille, André. "Innocent XI: Pape 'Janséniste.'" *Cahiers d'Histoire* 1 (1956) : 15–40.

Lavisse, Ernest. *Histoire de France depuis les Origines jusqu'à la Révolution française,* vol. 7, 2. Paris, 1911.

Lefevre, Joseph. *La Secrétairerie d'Etat et de Guerre sous le régime espagnol, 1594–1711.* Brussels, 1934.

Legrelle, Arsène. *La Diplomatie française et la Succession d'Espagne,* vol. 1. Paris, 1895.

———. *Louis XIV et Strasbourg.* 4th ed. Paris, 1884.

Livet, Georges. *L'Intendance d'Alsace sous Louis XIV: 1648–1715.* Paris, 1956.

———. "Louis XIV et l'Allemagne." *XVIIe Siècle,* nos. 46–47 (1960) : 29–53.

Lonchay, Henri. *La Rivalité de la France et de l'Espagne aux Pays-Bas, 1635–1700.* Brussels, 1894.

Lossky, Andrew. "France in the System of Europe in the Seventeenth Century." *Proceedings of the Western Society for French History* 1 (1974) : 32–48.

Mandrou, Robert. *La France aux XVIIe et XVIIIe Siècles.* Paris, 1967.

Marion, M. *Dictionnaire des Institutions de la France.* Paris, 1927.

Mathorez, J. *Les Etrangers en France sous l'Ancien Régime,* vols. 1 and 2. Paris, 1921.

Mentz, Georg. *Johann Philipp von Schönborn, Kurfürst von Mainz, Bischof von Wurzburg und Worms, 1605–1673.* 2 vols. Jena, 1896.

Metz, René. "L'Accession du Premier Rohan à l'Evêché de Strasbourg. Le jeu de la diplomatie royale." *Cahiers alsaciens d'archéologie, d'art et d'histoire* 11 (1967) : 227–240.

———. "Les Fürstenberg et les Rohan Princes-Evêques de Strasbourg au Service de la Cause française en Alsace." *Deux Siècles d'Alsace française,* foreword by Marcel Simon. Strasbourg and Paris, 1948.

———. *La Monarchie Française et la Provision des Bénéfices Ecclésiastiques en Alsace de la Paix de Westphalie à la Fin de l'Ancien Régime.* Strasbourg and Paris, 1947.

Meyer, Rudolf. *Die Flugschriften der Epoche Ludwigs XIV.* Basel and Stuttgart, 1955.

Michaud, Eugène. *Louis XIV et Innocent XI,* vol. 3. Paris, 1883.

Moisse-Daxhelet, Geneviève. "François-Egon, Prince de Fürstenberg." *Biographie Nationale publiée par l'Académie Royale des Sciences, des Lettres et des Beaux-Arts de Belgique* 34 (Brussels, 1967) : 322–46.

————. "Guillaume-Egon, Prince de Fürstenberg." *Biographie Nationale publiée par l'Académie Royale des Sciences, des Lettres et des Beaux-Arts de Belgique* 34 (Brussels, 1967) : 346–76.

————. *La Principauté de Stavelot-Malmédy sous le règne du Cardinal Guillaume-Egon de Fürstenberg: Problèmes politiques et institutionnels 1682–1704.* Anciens Pays et Assemblées d'Etats, vol. 29. Namur, 1963. See Daxhelet, Geneviève.

Morey, Adrian, and Anthony Landor. "Lorenzo Casoni and Papal Policy for the Church in France, 1682–1689." *Journal of Ecclesiastical History* 4 (1953) : 77–84.

Müller, P. L. *Wilhelm III von Oranien und Georg Friedrich von Waldeck: Ein Beitrag zur Geschichte des Kämpfes um das europäische Gleichgewicht.* 2 vols. The Hague, 1873–1890.

Münch, Ernst. *Geschichte des Hauses und Landes Fürstenberg*, vol. 3. Aachen and Leipzig, 1832.

Neveu, Bruno. *Sebastien Joseph Du Cambout de Pontchâteau (1634–1690) et ses Missions à Rome d'après sa Correspondance et des Documents Inédits.* Paris, 1969.

O'Connor, John T. "Guillaume Egon de Fürstenberg Reprend le Pouvoir à Cologne, 1679–1682." *Revue d'Histoire Diplomatique* 83 (1969) : 1–15.

————. "Louis XIV's 'Cold War' with the Papacy: French Diplomats and Papal Nuncios." *Proceedings of the Western Society for French History* 2 (1975) : 127–36.

————. "Louis XIV's Strategic Frontier in the Holy Roman Empire." *Proceedings of the Western Society for French History* 3 (1976) : 108–17.

————. "William Egon von Fürstenberg, German Agent in the Service of Louis XIV." *French Historical Studies* 5 (Fall, 1967) : 119–45.

Orcibal, Jean. *Louis XIV contre Innocent XI: Les Appels au futur Concile de 1688 et l'Opinion française.* Paris, 1949.

Pagès, Georges. "L'Alliance bavaroise de 1670 et la politique de Louis XIV en Allemagne, d'après un ouvrage récent." *Revue d'Histoire moderne et contemporaine*, vol. 5, no. 10 (July 15, 1904), pp. 677–90.

————. "Comment Guillaume de Fürstenberg entra au service de Louis XIV." *Mélanges offerts à Nicolas Jorga* (Paris, 1933), pp. 727–37.

————. *Contributions à l'Histoire de la Politique française en Allemagne sous Louis XIV.* Paris, 1905.

————. *Le Grand Electeur et Louis XIV, 1660–1688.* Paris, 1905.

————. "L'Histoire Diplomatique du Règne de Louis XIV: Sources et Etat des Travaux." *Revue d'Histoire moderne* 7 (1905–6) : 653–80.

————. *Louis XIV et l'Allemagne, 1661–1715* (Les Cours de la Sorbonne). Paris, 1937.

Papa, Egidio. "Innocenzo XI tra Francia ed Impero durante il 1688–89." *La Civiltà Cattolica* 99 (1948) : 608–24.

Pastor, Ludwig von. *History of the Popes*, vol. 32. London, 1940.

Pauls, Emil. "Die Beziehungen der Reunionskammer in Metz zur Abtei Stablo-Malmedy und zur Aachener Gegend." *Zeitschrift des Aachener Geschichtsvereins* 27 (1905) : 173–219.

Petry, Ludwig. "Das Haus Neuburg und die Ausläufer der Gegenreformation in Schlesien und der Pfalz." *Festschrift für Georg Biundo* (1952), pp. 87–102.

Pfister, Christian. "La rénunion de l'Alsace à la France." *La Revue de Paris* 7 (1900) : 361–77.

———. "Le Second Voyage de Louis XIV en Alsace (Octobre, 1681)." *Séances et Travaux de l'Académie des Sciences Morales et Politiques, Compte Rendu* (2e semestre, 1921), pp. 24–46.

———. "Le Troisième Voyage de Louis XIV en Alsace (1683)." *Séances et Travaux de l'Académie des Sciences Morales et Politiques, Compte Rendu* (2e semestre, 1922), pp. 354–79.

Picavet, C.-G. *Les Dernières Années de Turenne, 1660–1675.* Paris, 1918.

———. *La Diplomatie française au Temps de Louis XIV, 1661–1715.* Paris, 1930.

Pillorget, René. "Jean-Hugues d'Orsbeck Electeur de Trèves et la Politique des Réunions, 1678–1688." *Revue d'Histoire Diplomatique* 79 (1965) : 315–37.

Pillorget-Rouanet, Suzanne. "Louis XIV Candidat au Trône Impérial (1658): Un Document Inédit." *Revue d'Histoire Diplomatique* 81 (1967) : 5–17.

Place, Richard. "The Self-Deception of the Strong: France on the Eve of the War of the League of Augsburg." *French Historical Studies* 6 (Fall, 1970) : 459–73.

Préclin, Edmond and Victor-Lucien Tapié. *Le XVIIe Siècle; Monarchies Centralisées, 1610–1715.* Paris, 1949.

Pribram, A. F. *Beitrag zur Geschichte des Rheinbundes vom Jahre 1658.* Leipzig, 1888.

———. *Franz Paul Freiherr von Lisola und die Politik seiner Zeit.* Leipzig, 1894.

———. "Zur Wahl Leopold I, 1654–1658." *Archiv für österreichische Geschichte* 73 (1888) : 81–222.

Prutz, Hans. "Die Kölner Wahl und Frankreichs Friedensbruch 1688." *Historisches Taschenbuch*, 8th series, no. 9 (1890), pp. 165–204.

Raab, Heribert. *Die Concordata Nationis Germanicae in der kanonistischen Diskussion des 17. bis 19. Jahrhunderts. Ein Beitrag zur Geschichte der episkopalischen Theorie in Deutschland.* Wiesbaden, 1956.

———. "Die oberdeutschen Hochstifte zwischen Habsburg und Wittelsbach in der frühen Neuzeit." *Blätter für deutsche Landesgeschichte* 109 (1973) : 69–101.

Rall, Hans. "Pfalz-Neuburg und seine Fürsten." *Neuburger Kollektaneenblatt* 109 (1955) : 5–52.

Redlich, Fritz. "The German Military Enterpriser and His Work Force." *Vierteljahrschrift für Sozial-und Wirtschaftsgeschichte, Beihefte* 47 (1964) : 1–532 and 48 (1965) : 1–322.

Reibel, Ferdinand. "Der Strassburger Weihbischof Gabriel Haug, 1602–1691." *Archiv für elsässische Kirchengeschichte* 12 (1937) : 159–83.

Reinhardt, Rudolf. "Zur Reichskirchenpolitik der Pfalz-Neuburger Dynastie." *Historisches Jahrbuch* 84 (1964) : 118–28.

Reuss, Rodolphe. *L'Alsace au Dix-Septième Siècle.* 2 vols. Paris, 1897–98. Included in the series Bibliothèque de l'Ecole des Hautes Etudes, vol. 116 and vol. 120.

Rott, Edouard. *Histoire de la Représentation Diplomatique de la France auprès des Cantons suisses, de leurs alliés, et de leurs Confédérés,* vol. 8. Berne and Paris, 1921.

Rousset, Camille. *Histoire de Louvois et de son Administration militaire.* 4 vols. 2nd ed. Paris, 1862.

Rowen, Herbert H. *The Ambassador Prepares for War: The Dutch Embassy of Arnauld de Pomponne, 1669–1671.* The Hague, 1957.

———. "John de Witt and the Triple Alliance." *Journal of Modern History* 26 (March, 1954) : 1–14.

Saint-Léger, A. de, and Philippe Sagnac. *La Prépondérance française: Louis XIV, 1661–1715.* Paris, 1935.

Schnur, Roman. *Der Rheinbund von 1658 in der deutschen Verfassungsgeschichte.* Bonn, 1955.

Schwarz, Henry Frederick. *The Imperial Privy Council in the Seventeenth Century.* Cambridge, Mass., 1943; Greenwood Press reprint, 1972.

Sonnino, Paul. *Louis XIV's View of the Papacy, 1661–1667.* Berkeley and Los Angeles, 1966.

Spiegel, Käthe. *Wilhelm Egon von Fürstenbergs Gefangenschaft und ihre Bedeutung für die Friedensfrage, 1674–1679.* Bonn, 1934.

Steinhuber, Andreas. *Geschichte des Collegium Germanicum Hungaricum in Rom,* vol. 1. Freiburg-im-Breisgau, 1895.

Strich, M. *Das Kurhaus Bayern im Zeitalter Ludwigs XIV und die europäischen Mächte.* 2 vols. Munich, 1933.

Tapié, Victor-Lucien. "Aspects de la méthode de Louis XIV en politique étrangère." *Revue politique et parlementaire,* no. 768 (June, 1966), pp. 22–32.

———. "Europe et Chrétienté: Idée chrétienne et gloire dynastique dans la politique européenne au moment du siège de Vienne (1683)." *Gregorianum* 42 (1961) : 268–89.

———. *Monarchie et Peuples du Danube.* Paris, 1969.

———. "Quelques aspects généraux de la politique étrangère de Louis XIV." *XVIIe Siècle,* nos. 46–47 (1960), pp. 1–28.

Thoma, Werner. *Die Kirchenpolitik der Grafen von Fürstenberg im Zeitalter der Glaubenskämpfe (1520–1660): Ein Beitrag zur Geschichte der Kirchenreform und Konfessionsbildung.* Reformationsgeschichtliche Studien und Texte, vol. 87 (1963).

Trenta, Tommaso. *Memorie per servire alla Storia politica del Cardinale Francesco Buonvisi Patrizio Lucchese.* 2 vols. Lucca, 1818.

Trivellini, Anna Maria. *Il Cardinale Francesco Buonvisi, Nunzio a Vienna (1675–1689).* Biblioteca dell' Archivio Storico Italiano, vol. 7. Florence, 1958.

Vast, Henri. "Des Tentatives de Louis XIV pour Arriver à l'Empire." *Revue Historique* 65 (1897) : 1–45.

Wagner, Georg. "Der Wiener Hof, Ludwig XIV, und die Anfänge der Magnatenverschwörung." *Mitteilungen des österreichischen Staatsarchivs* 16 (1963) : 87–150.

Wagner, Johannes Volker. *Graf Wilhelm von Fürstenberg (1491–1549) und die politisch-geistigen Mächte seiner Zeit.* Stuttgart, 1966.

Wentzcke, Paul. *Feldherr des Kaisers: Leben und Taten Herzog Karls V. von Lothringen.* Leipzig, 1943.

Wolf, Erik. *Grosse Rechtsdenker der deutschen Geistesgeschichte.* 4th ed. Tübingen, 1963.

Wolf, John B. *The Emergence of the Great Powers, 1685–1715.* New York, 1951.

————. *Louis XIV.* New York, 1969.

Wysocki, Josef. *Kurmainz und die Reunionen: Die Beziehungen zwischen Frankreich und Kurmainz von 1679 bis 1688.* Mainz, 1961.

Zeller, Gaston. *La France et l'Allemagne depuis Dix Siècles.* Paris, 1932.

————. "Histoire d'une Idée fausse." *Revue de Synthèse* 11 (1936) : 115–31.

————. "Louvois, Colbert de Croissy et les Réunions de Metz." *Revue Historique* 131 (1919) : 267–75.

————. "La Monarchie d'Ancien Régime et les Frontières naturelles." *Revue d'Histoire moderne* 6 (1933) : 305–33.

————. *L'Organisation défensive des Frontières du Nord et de l'Est au XVIIe Siècle.* Paris, 1928.

————. "Politique Extérieure et Diplomatie sous Louis XIV." *Revue d'Histoire moderne* 6 (1931) : 124–43.

————. "Les Rois de France Candidats à l'Empire: Essai sur l'idéologie impériale en France." *Revue Historique* 173 (1934) : 273–311, 497–534.

————. "Saluces, Pignerol, et Strasbourg: La Politique des Frontières au Temps de la Prépondérance Espagnole." *Revue Historique* 193 (1942) : 97–110.

INDEX